MathWorks 10

MathWorks 10

Pacific Educational Press
Vancouver, Canada

Copyright Pacific Educational Press 2010

ISBN 978-1-89576-651-6

All rights reserved. No part of this publication may be reproduced, stored in a retrieval system, or transmitted in any form or by any means, electronic, mechanical, photocopying, recording, or otherwise without the prior written permission of the publisher.

Printed and bound in Canada.

Writers
Katharine Borgen, Vancouver School Board and University of British Columbia
Catherine Edwards, Pacific Educational Press
Sheeva Harrysingh-Klassen, J.H. Bruns Collegiate, Winnipeg
Mark Healy, West Vancouver Secondary School, West Vancouver
Craig Yuill, Prince of Wales Secondary School, Vancouver

Pilot Teacher
Don Chandler, Salisbury High School

Consultants
Katharine Borgen, PhD, Vancouver School Board and University of British Columbia
John Willinsky, PhD, Public Knowledge Project
Jordie Yow, Mathematics Reviewer

Design, Illustration, and Layout
Warren Clark
Laraine Coates
Sharlene Eugenio
Five Seventeen
Craig Yuill

Cover photo courtesy Colin Pickell

Editing
Christa Bedwin
Theresa Best
Diana Breti
Laraine Coates
Barbara Dominik
Catherine Edwards
Leah Giesbrecht
Deborah Hutton
Barbara Kuhne

Contents

How to Use this Book — 8

1. Unit Pricing and Currency Exchange — 10
- **1.1** Proportional Reasoning — 12
  - Puzzle It Out: Magic Proportions — 22
- **1.2** Unit Price — 23
- **1.3** Setting a Price — 28
- **1.4** On Sale! — 34
  - The Roots of Math: Canadian Currency — 40
- **1.5** Currency Exchange Rates — 41

2. Earning an Income — 52
- **2.1** Wages and Salaries — 54
  - The Roots of Math: The Minimum Wage in Canada — 63
- **2.2** Alternative Ways to Earn Money — 64
  - Puzzle It Out: A Weird Will — 71
- **2.3** Additional Earnings — 72
- **2.4** Deductions and Net Pay — 79

3. Length, Area, and Volume — 92
- **3.1** Systems of Measurement — 94
  - The Roots of Math: The Origins of Standard Measurement — 104
- **3.2** Converting Measurements — 106
- **3.3** Surface Area — 115
- **3.4** Volume — 124
  - Puzzle It Out: The Decanting Puzzle — 131

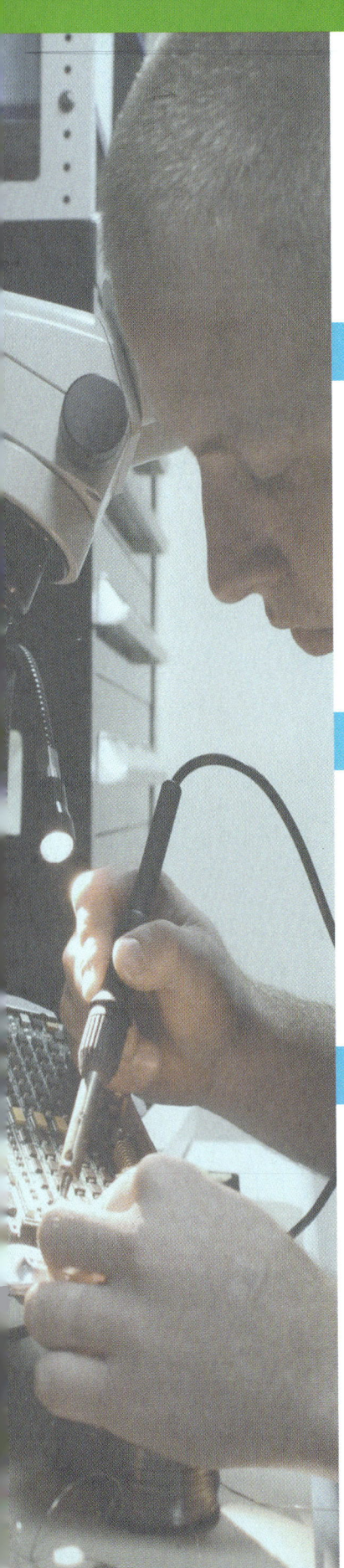

4 Mass, Temperature, and Volume — 136

- **4.1** Temperature Conversions — 138
- The Roots of Math: Measuring Temperature — 145
- **4.2** Mass in the Imperial System — 146
- **4.3** Mass in the Système International — 154
- Puzzle It Out: The Counterfeit Coin — 160
- **4.4** Making Conversions — 162

5 Angles and Parallel Lines — 172

- **5.1** Measuring, Drawing, and Estimating Angles — 174
- **5.2** Angle Bisectors and Perpendicular Lines — 187
- The Roots of Math: Geometric Perspective in Art — 197
- **5.3** Non-Parallel Lines and Transversals — 198
- **5.4** Parallel Lines and Transversals — 209
- Puzzle It Out: The Impossible Staircase — 218

6 Similarity of Figures — 224

- **6.1** Similar Polygons — 226
- **6.2** Determining if Two Polygons are Similar — 236
- The Roots of Math: Euclidean Geometry — 246
- **6.3** Drawing Similar Polygons — 247
- Puzzle It Out: Rationing Chocolate Bars — 255
- **6.4** Similar Triangles — 257

7 Trigonometry of Right Triangles 270

7.1	The Pythagorean Theorem	272
7.2	The Sine Ratio	283
	The Roots of Math: Trigonometry in History	292
7.3	The Cosine Ratio	293
7.4	The Tangent Ratio	301
7.5	Finding Angles and Solving Right Triangles	307
	Puzzle it Out: 16 Squares	314

Glossary	320
Answer Key	324
Index	355
Credits	363

How to Use this Book

MathWorks 10 focusses on mathematics that you will use in the workplace, especially if you are planning to apprentice for a trade, take a college course, or enter the workplace directly after graduation from secondary school. Several of the chapters include a focus on consumer and business mathematics. Others concentrate on mathematics that will be essential knowledge for specific trades and occupations.

This textbook contains seven chapters, each focussed on a particular topic. Topics include unit pricing and currency exchange; earning an income; linear and area measurements; temperature, mass, and volume measurements; angles and parallel lines; similar figures; and trigonometry.

Each chapter contains the following features that will aid in your learning.

CHAPTER INTRODUCTION Each chapter begins with an introduction that describes the overall themes of the chapter and lists the specific mathematical tasks you will learn as you work through it. A list of key concepts will help focus your learning.

CHAPTER PROJECT Each chapter contains a project related to the mathematical theme of the chapter. You will be introduced to the project as you begin the chapter and will revisit it periodically to complete activities, sometimes with a partner or in a small group. You will add these new materials to a chapter file or portfolio. When you have completed the chapter, you will use these materials to create a presentation to share with your peers. The project gives you an opportunity to practise your mathematics skills in a real-life context.

MATH ON THE JOB Each section of the chapter begins with a profile of an individual. The profile will give you a sense of the scope of the person's job and the type of mathematics that someone with a similar job will need to know. Each profile ends with a typical mathematics problem that a person with this job would need to solve.

EXPLORE THE MATH This section of the chapter contains a brief lesson that outlines the main mathematical concepts of that section and links these to real-life examples. A series of examples and solutions shows you various strategies you can use to solve problems.

DISCUSS THE IDEAS These discussions focus on one aspect of the section you are working on. They will give you an opportunity to learn some details about the topic and investigate related issues.

ACTIVITIES   Each chapter contains several hands-on activities for you to complete. They provide an opportunity for you to collaborate with your fellow students and apply your learning in a realistic setting.

BUILD YOUR SKILLS   This is a set of problems for you to solve. It will give you practice applying the mathematical concepts you have learned.

PUZZLE IT OUT   Each chapter also contains a game or puzzle that uses the mathematical concepts in that chapter. The puzzles and games challenge you to develop a personal strategy. Some of these puzzles and games are linked to workplace applications of mathematics; others challenge you to analyze mathematical thinking. All of them are fun!

THE ROOTS OF MATH   Mathematics has a history. It has changed and grown through time. In The Roots of Math, a math history topic related to the chapter content is provided, along with a few questions for you to consider.

REFLECT ON YOUR LEARNING/PRACTISE YOUR NEW SKILLS   The chapter concludes with a point-form summary of your main accomplishments to reflect on. A series of problems will allow you to practise the new skills you acquired while working on this chapter.

HINTS   Hints suggest strategies you can use to solve problems.

DEFINITIONS   Mathematical terms that may be new or unfamiliar are defined or explained in the sidebar columns. They are also included alphabetically in a glossary at the back of the book.

MENTAL MATH AND ESTIMATION   Mental Math and Estimation problems invite you to practise using mathematics in your head to solve problems or arrive at estimates.

This symbol is used to alert you to opportunities to use technology tools to assist you or enhance your work.

ANSWER KEY   An answer key to the problems in this textbook is contained at the back of the book.

Chapter 1

Unit Pricing and Currency Exchange

GOALS

Both in the workplace and in your daily life, you will need to make decisions about what to buy and how to pay the best price for what you need. In this chapter, you will use some familiar mathematics concepts—including fractions, percent, rate, and ratio—in a new context. You will apply these mathematical ideas to

- learn how to determine which purchase is the best buy, considering quality and quantity as well as unit price;
- investigate sales promotions and compare their effects; and
- convert Canadian dollars into a foreign currency and foreign currencies into Canadian dollars.

KEY TERMS

- buying rate
- exchange rate
- markup
- promotion
- proportion
- rate
- ratio
- selling rate
- unit price
- unit rate

PROJECT—THE PARTY PLANNER

START TO PLAN

PROJECT OVERVIEW

Have you ever planned a party? In this chapter, your project will be to plan a wind-up party for the end of the school year for a team, club, or committee at your school.

You will plan the party for 15 guests plus yourself. It will be held on a Saturday evening between 6:00 pm and 11:00 pm.

Each guest will contribute $15.00, and your club, team, or committee will contribute $10.00 per member as well. The total budget for the party will therefore be $400.00. This amount must cover all the expenses of the party.

GET STARTED

To begin your project, start planning your party. First, make a list of all the things you will need to consider and buy. Keep these questions in mind:

- Where will the party be held?
- What decorations will you choose?
- What activities or entertainment will you plan for the guests?
- What kind of music will you choose?
- What food and drinks will you need?
- Where will you purchase supplies?

Students from a North Vancouver high school golf team are practising at a driving range.

FINAL PRESENTATION CHECKLIST

You will make a final presentation to your fellow team, club, or committee members when you have completed this project. Your presentation will include these items:

- a description of the party, its location, and any decorations you plan to use;
- a sample invitation;
- a list of activities and entertainment for the guests;
- a table or spreadsheet itemizing the expenses, suppliers, and the total cost and unit cost of each item; and
- a calculation of the cost per guest and the total cost of the party.

Chapter 1 Unit Pricing and Currency Exchange

1.1 Proportional Reasoning

MATH *ON THE JOB*

Sandra Tuccaro is an Inuvialuit nurse originally from Hay River, Northwest Territories. She now works in the Home Care department of Yellowknife Health and Social Services Authority. She has a diploma in nursing and her job encompasses many tasks. As a home care nurse, Sandra provides short- and long-term care to people in their homes. She helps patients with nursing and rehabilitation needs and assists with their nutrition and daily living.

Sandra has to administer 300 mg of a drug that comes in a vial that has 120 mg of the drug dissolved in 2 mL of fluid. How many mL of fluid will she need to give her patient? How can Sandra use proportional reasoning to solve this problem?

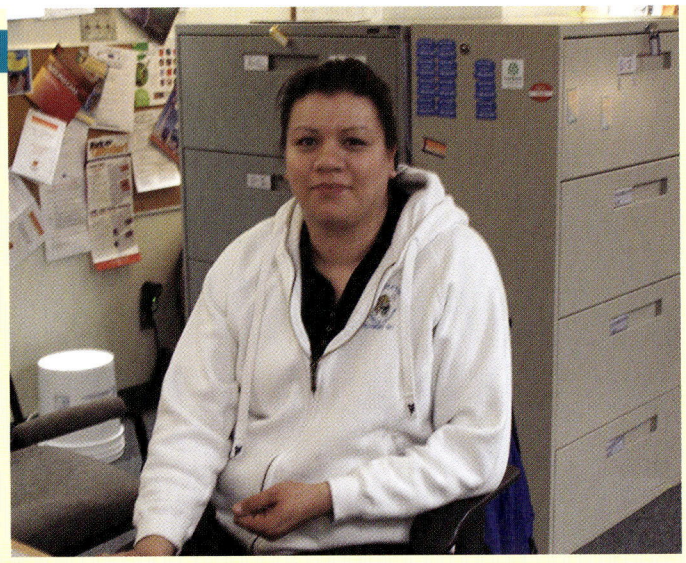

Sandra is shown here in her Yellowknife office.

PRACTISE YOUR PRIOR SKILLS

RATIO

ratio: a comparison between two numbers with the same units

proportion: a fractional statement of equality between two ratios or rates

In this chapter, you will learn to apply your knowledge of **ratios** in new areas.

Remember that a ratio compares two numbers that are measured in the same units. A ratio can be written in several ways. For example, the ratio 20 to 50 can be written as 20:50 or as $\frac{20}{50}$. The notation $\frac{20}{50}$ is often the most useful notation because your knowledge of fractions can be used in calculations.

When working with ratios, simplify them first. For example, the ratio 20:50 can be simplified by dividing each term by 10. To solve calculations using this ratio, you can use 2:5 instead of 20:50.

The two ratios 20:50 and 2:5 are equivalent statements and the fractional equation $\frac{20}{50} = \frac{2}{5}$ is referred to as a **proportion**.

Ratios are often expressed in real-life situations as proportions. For example, you may need to mix a certain shade of paint. The proportion needed is 3 parts blue to 1 part green, or 3:1. You can use this ratio to mix the amount of paint you need in the correct proportions. Mixing 3 parts and 1 part means there are 4 parts in all.

In a ratio, since the units are the same, they essentially cancel each other out. In your calculations, you can omit the units but remember to include them in your solution.

DISCUSS THE IDEAS

ADAPTING A RECIPE

You have invited five friends over to your house and decide to serve them homemade fudge brownies. You found a great recipe that makes 20 large brownies, but you only need 12, two per person. How would you change the recipe to make only 12 brownies and have them taste exactly the same as they do when made from the original recipe?

Example 1

Engines that require you to mix oil with fuel to provide lubrication are called 2-stroke engines. A faller at a logging site needs to refill a chainsaw's fuel can. The ratio of gasoline to oil that is needed is 40 parts of gasoline to 1 part of oil. The chainsaw's fuel can holds 8 litres of gasoline. How much oil should be added to the gasoline to obtain the correct ratio?

SOLUTION METHOD 1

The ratio of litres of gasoline to oil can be written as $\frac{40}{1}$.

Let x represent the amount of oil needed.

The problem can be expressed as a proportion.

$$\frac{40}{1} = \frac{8}{x}$$

The proportion forms an equation involving fractions. To solve this equation, one strategy is to simplify the equation by eliminating the denominators. This can be done by multiplying both sides of the equation by the common denominator.

$$\frac{40}{1}(x) = \frac{8}{x}(x)$$

Multiply both sides of the equation by the common denominator.

The common denominator for $\frac{40}{1}$ and $\frac{8}{x}$ is x.

$$\frac{40(x)}{1} = \frac{8(x)}{x}$$

This logger is using a chainsaw at a logging site in BC.

$$40x = 8$$

$$\frac{40x}{40} = \frac{8}{40}$$

$$x = \frac{8}{40}$$

The ratio $\frac{8(x)}{x}$ can be simplified to 8 since $\frac{x}{x} = 1$.

To isolate the variable, divide by its coefficient. Since the coefficient of x is 40, divide both sides of the equation by 40.

The ratio $\frac{40x}{40}$ equals x since $\frac{40}{40} = 1$.

The answer can be simplified to $\frac{1}{5}$ by dividing both the numerator and the denominator by 8.

The answer could be expressed as a decimal by dividing 8 by 40 to obtain 0.2.

The faller needs to add 0.2 litres of oil to the fuel can.

SOLUTION METHOD 2

$$\frac{40}{1} = \frac{8}{x}$$

The faller reasons that the numerator, 40, has been divided by 5 to equal 8. To keep the fractions equivalent, he must also divide the denominator, 1, by 5 to equal x.

The faller needs to add $\frac{1}{5}$ of a litre of oil to the fuel can.

Example 2

Jean-Luc, a builder, has found that he can arrange the work cubicles of his employees best if the ratio between the length and the width of a room is 3:2. If a room is 6 m long, how wide should the room be?

SOLUTION

The ratio of length to width in metres is $\frac{3}{2}$.

Let w represent the width of the room.

The two ratios can be expressed as the following proportion.

$\frac{3}{2} = \frac{6}{w}$ This proportion forms an equation involving fractions. To solve this equation, one strategy is to simplify the equation by eliminating the denominators. This can be done by multiplying both sides of the equation by the common denominator.

$2w\left(\frac{3}{2}\right) = \left(\frac{6}{w}\right)2w$ Multiply both sides of the equation by the common denominator. The common denominator for $\frac{3}{2}$ and $\frac{6}{w}$ is $2w$.

$\frac{6w}{2} = \frac{12w}{w}$ Simplify both sides of the equation.

$3w = 12$

$\frac{3w}{3} = \frac{12}{3}$ To isolate the variable, divide by its coefficient. Since the coefficient of w is 3, divide both sides of the equation by 3.

$w = 4$

The width of the room should be 4 metres.

ALTERNATIVE SOLUTION

The builder might also reason that since the numerator, 6, is twice 3, that w will be twice 2, or 4 metres.

ACTIVITY 1.1
VISUALIZE A PROPORTION

A right triangle is created by joining the ends of two line segments drawn at 90° to each other, as shown below.

1. Copy the triangle below onto a sheet of 0.5 cm graph paper.

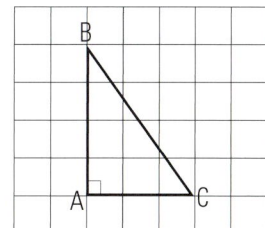

Chapter 1   Unit Pricing and Currency Exchange   **15**

2. For each item, draw the new figure and determine whether the new figure is proportional to the original figure or whether it is distorted.

   a) Double the length of line segments AB and AC.

   b) Add three squares on the graph to the length of each of these segments.

   c) Subtract 2 squares from the length of each of these segments.

   d) Divide the length of each of these segments by 2.

3. What conclusions can you draw from your results?

ACTIVITY 1.2
FRUIT DRINK TASTE TESTER

You are part of a taste tester team for a healthy lifestyle company. Your team is developing some new drinks to put on the market. The company has produced orange concentrate that is packaged in 1-cup portions. Buyers will mix the concentrate with water, and the best proportions of concentrate to water need to be identified.

The company is considering two different recipes. It is your team's job to compare the recipes and produce a taste tester report.

Recipe #1
3 cups of concentrate
7 cups of water

Recipe #2
2 cups of concentrate
5 cups of water

Complete a table like the one below for the company. A batch is one recipe.

MIXING THE CONCENTRATES

Batches	Recipe #1 Orange concentrate (cups)	Water (cups)	Recipe #2 Orange concentrate (cups)	Water (cups)
1				
2				
3				
5				
10				

16 MathWorks 10

1. Using the patterns in the table above, how many cups of orange concentrate would be needed to make 100 batches of the orange drink following Recipe #1?

2. Using the raw data in the table, can you tell which of the two recipes has a stronger taste of orange? Explain mathematically how you know.

3. Suppose you had only 1 cup of concentrate. How many cups of water would you need to make Recipe #2? Set up a proportion and solve this question.

4. You only want to make 8 cups of Recipe #1. How many cups of concentrate and how many cups of water will you need? Explain your solution.

5. You have been given a recipe for a completely new fruit drink. The recipe has 3 ingredients as listed below:

   Fruit Drink Recipe
   2 cups pineapple juice
   3 cups cranberry juice
   5 cups lemon juice

HINT

In question 5, add up all the cups used in the recipe. Then each kind of juice can be expressed as a fraction of the total recipe.

You need to make 4 cups of juice for the taste test. How much of each ingredient will you need? Explain your solution.

PRACTISE YOUR PRIOR SKILLS
RATE

This carpenter is taking a measurement.

A **rate** is similar to a ratio, but it compares two numbers with different units. Here are some examples of rates:

- the number of words you can type per minute
- the number of hamburgers a concession stand sells each day
- the price of lumber per linear foot
- the price of stone per kilogram

rate: a comparison between two numbers with different units

Chapter 1 Unit Pricing and Currency Exchange 17

A rate can be expressed using the same notation as a ratio. Because the units are different in the two terms, they must be used. For example, if you see salmon for sale at $1.89 for 100 grams, you can write the rate in these ways:

$1.89:100$ g

$1.89/100$ g

$$\frac{\$1.89}{100 \text{ g}}$$

A proportion is an equivalent statement between two ratios. You can also think of a proportion as an equivalent statement between two rates.

DISCUSS THE IDEAS
CINDY KLASSEN, SPEED SKATER

Cindy Klassen

At the 2006 Olympic Winter Games in Torino, Cindy Klassen of Winnipeg became the first Canadian athlete to win five medals at a single Winter Olympics. She won gold in the 1500 m speed skating event, silver in the 1000 m, silver in the Team Pursuit, bronze in the 5000 m, and bronze in the 3000 m. Combined with her bronze medal at the 2002 Winter Games, Cindy became the first Canadian to win six Olympic medals.

Cindy finished the 1500 m race in 1:55.27 (115.27 seconds). How would you calculate Cindy's average speed?

Example 1

If salmon costs $1.89 for 100 g, how much will it cost to buy 250 g of salmon?

SOLUTION

Let c represent the cost of 250 g of salmon.

The problem can be expressed as a proportion.

$$\frac{1.89}{100} = \frac{c}{250}$$

The proportion forms an equation involving fractions. To solve this equation, one strategy is to simplify the equation by eliminating the denominators. This can be done by multiplying both sides of the equation by the common denominator.

$$\frac{1.89}{100}(25\,000) = \frac{c}{250}(25\,000)$$ Multiply both sides of the equation by the common denominator. A common denominator for 100 and 250 is 25 000.

$$\frac{(1.89)(25\,000)}{100} = \frac{25\,000c}{250}$$ Simplify both sides of the equation.

$$472.5 = 100c$$ The coefficient of the variable is 100 because 25 000 divided by 250 equals 100.

$$\frac{472.5}{100} = \frac{100c}{100}$$ To isolate the variable, divide by its coefficient. Since the coefficient of c is 100, divide both sides of the equation by 100.

$$4.725 = c$$ Since c represents a value in dollars, it must be rounded off to 2 decimal places.

It will cost $4.73 to buy 250 g of salmon.

ALTERNATIVE SOLUTION 1

Since 250 g is 2.5 times 100 g, the cost of 250 g of salmon would be 2.5 times the cost of 100 grams of salmon.

$$(1.89)(2.5) = 4.725$$ Round the answer to 2 decimal places since it is the cost in dollars.

It will cost $4.73 to buy 250 g of salmon.

ALTERNATIVE SOLUTION 2

Cost of 250 g of salmon.

| 100 g | + | 100 g | + | 50 g | = | 250 g |

 +  +

$1.89 + $1.89 + $\frac{\$1.89}{2}$ = $4.73

It will cost $4.73 for 250 g of salmon.

HINTS

1. Make sure you are comparing the same unit or units when you set up a proportion.

2. To find a common denominator, you can multiply the given denominators. In the example, 25 000 is obtained by multiplying 100 and 250.

- Are there other common denominators that could have been used?
- How would the choice of 500 as a common denominator affect your calculations?
- The lowest common denominator is the smallest number that all given denominators will divide into evenly.

HINT

To simplify an equation containing fractions, multiply both sides of the equation by a common denominator. This will create an equivalent equation that will not contain fractions.

Example 2

A local plumbing store sells 100 copper-plated pipe straps for $4.97. You have estimated that you require 75 straps. How much will you pay for 75 straps?

SOLUTION

$$\frac{4.97}{100} = \frac{x}{75}$$

Let x represent the cost of 75 straps and create a proportion. The proportion forms an equation involving fractions. To solve this equation, one strategy is to simplify the equation by eliminating the denominators. This can be done by multiplying both sides of the equation by the common denominator.

$$\frac{4.97}{100}(7500) = \frac{x}{75}(7500)$$

Multiply both sides of the equation by a common denominator. One common denominator for 100 and 75 is 7500.

$$\frac{(4.97)(7500)}{100} = \frac{7500x}{75}$$

$$372.75 = 100x$$

The coefficient of the variable is 100 because 7500 divided by 75 equals 100.

$$\frac{372.75}{100} = \frac{100x}{100}$$

To isolate the variable, divide by its coefficient. Since the coefficient of x is 100, divide both sides of the equation by 100.

$$3.7275 = x$$

Since x represents a value in dollars, it must be rounded to 2 decimal places.

It will cost $3.73 to buy 75 pipe straps.

ALTERNATIVE SOLUTION

Since 75 is $\frac{3}{4}$ of 100, you can find the cost of 75 straps by multiplying the cost of 100 straps by $\frac{3}{4}$.

$$(4.97)\left(\frac{3}{4}\right) = 3.73$$

It will cost $3.73 to buy 75 pipe straps.

Mental Math and Estimation

The pipe straps in the example above each cost $0.0497. About how much will 50 pipe straps cost?

PRACTISE YOUR NEW SKILLS

1. A computer repair technician fixes 8 printers for every 2 computers she repairs. What is the simplest form of this ratio? What are two ways you can write this ratio?

2. If a secretary types 55 words per minute, how long will it take her or him to type a 2000-word director's report?

3. An apprentice mechanic rotates the 4 tires on a pick-up truck in 15 minutes. How long would it take him to rotate the tires on 5 trucks? How long does rotating 2 tires take?

4. An Edmonton car salesperson sells 4 cars on Thursday, 6 on Friday, and an equal number each on Saturday and Sunday, for a total of 36 cars sold over the four days. How many cars were sold each day on Saturday and Sunday? What proportion of the total sales took place on Saturday?

This vehicle is a hybrid that is powered by either gasoline or electricity.

5. The ratio between Siu's height and the height of her brother Tai is 5:6. If Tai is 145 cm tall, how tall is Siu, to the nearest centimetre?

6. If the Sound Source music store makes a profit of $2550.00 on the sale of 200 DVDs, how much profit would the store make on the sale of 50? On the sale of 900?

7. If a 5-kg jar of olives costs a restaurant $15.00 through a wholesaler, how many kilograms would it get for $75.00? How much would it cost the restaurant to buy 20 kilograms?

8. A carpenter wants to mix a shade of stain for a set of kitchen cabinets he is building. The ratio for the shade he wants is 3 parts of Spanish oak to 4 parts of red mahogany. If he needs 12 litres in all, how many litres of each stain does he need?

Chapter 1   Unit Pricing and Currency Exchange   **21**

The high speed Japanese Bullet Trains run on a network that joins the major cities on the island of Honshu.

Extend your thinking

9. Keiko says that the Japanese Bullet Train (Shinkansen) takes about 6 minutes to travel 30 km. Yuki says that at this rate, he could travel around the world at the equator in less than 8 days. Keiko disagrees; she thinks it will take longer. Who is correct? Justify your response. The circumference of the earth at the equator is approximately 40 074 km.

PUZZLE IT OUT

MAGIC PROPORTIONS

In this puzzle, the object is to fill a 3 × 3 square with the nine numbers from 0 through 8 (using each of them exactly once) in such a way that the numbers in the first, second, and third rows will add up to three numbers in the proportion 1:2:3. Simultaneously, the same proportion has to be achieved for the first, second, and third columns.

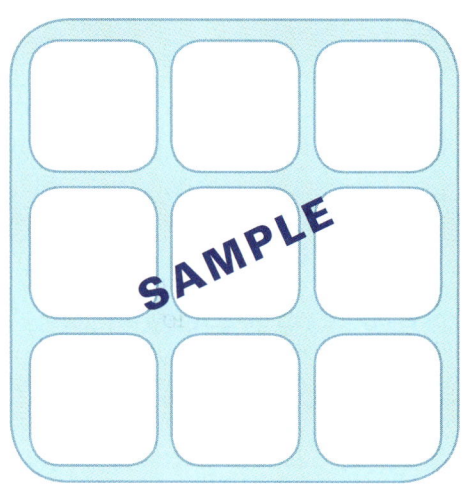

One possible solution is shown here.

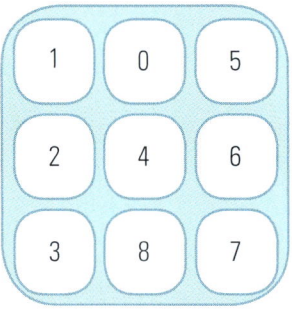

Can you find other solutions? What strategy did you use?

22   MathWorks 10

Unit Price 1.2

MATH ON THE JOB

Linda sells her produce at a seasonal farm stand and at farmers' markets.

Linda Fogarty is self-employed as an organic farmer and greenhouse grower. She completed a horticulture technology diploma at Kwantlen Polytechnic University in Langley, BC.

Linda operates The Green Room, a 3.5-hectare farm in Upper Gibsons, BC. She grows tomatoes, peppers, cucumbers, carrots, and many other crops throughout the year. She uses math on the job in many ways: to calculate plant density, to determine production statistics, to calculate sales revenue and expenses, and to handle sales transactions.

Linda wants to buy a species of heritage tomato seedlings from a wholesaler. Company A sells 20 plants for $45.95. Company B sells 24 plants for $48.50. What is the unit price at each wholesaler? What is the unit price difference between the two companies? What factors apart from price might Linda want to consider?

EXPLORE THE MATH

Products are packaged and sold in various sizes, such as a 1-litre, 2-litre, or 4-litre jug of milk. How do you determine the least expensive choice? Different brands may package their products in different sizes of packages. Brand A may sell a 250 g package of meat, while Brand B may sell a 375 g package. Which is the better buy? Finding the **unit price** will allow you to compare prices, and help you determine the best buy.

Consumer goods, such as pens or rolls of toilet paper, are often bundled together and sold in bulk. To compare the price when the quantity in the package is not the same, it is often useful to look at the unit cost of one item. If you have a business, you may buy items in a bulk purchase that you later want to charge to your customers one item at a time. To do this, you also need to calculate the cost of one item.

A unit price is the cost of one unit. It is sometimes referred to as a **unit rate**. To calculate a unit price, you can use a proportion where the second rate has a denominator of 1. For example, if you buy a package of 4 rolls of Eco-Friendly toilet paper for $2.68, you can calculate the cost of 1 roll by using this proportion:

$$\frac{\$2.68}{4 \text{ rolls}} = \frac{x}{1 \text{ roll}}$$

unit price: the cost of one unit; a rate expressed as a fraction in which the denominator is 1

unit rate: the rate or cost for one item or unit

HINT

To determine the product or brand that is the best value, or the size of purchase that is the best value, shoppers often compare the unit cost of different brands of the same product or different sizes of the same product.

The 1 in the denominator of the second rate is obtained by dividing the denominator of the first rate by 4. Therefore, to find x, you will also divide the numerator by 4.

$$\$2.68 \div 4 = \$0.67$$

One roll of toilet paper costs $0.67 or 67¢. Thus, cost per unit or unit price can be determined by dividing the price of a product by the number of units contained in a purchase.

Comparing unit prices can save you money at home and in the workplace. Unit price is not the only factor to consider, however. You may prefer the quality of one product over another. You may also find that there are more items in a large package than you can use. In this case, it may be a better choice to spend more on a per unit basis, and buy only what you need.

Example 1

Rosa buys supplies for the hamlet office in Arviat, Nunavut where she works as a clerk. She wants to buy pens. The supplier sells a box of 12 pens for $6.25. Calculate the unit price of 1 pen.

SOLUTION

In this case, the unit is 1 pen. The cost for 12 pens is $6.25. What is the cost of 1 pen?

$6.25 ÷ 12 pens = $0.52/pen, rounded to the nearest cent

Note that $0.52 can also be written as 52¢.

Example 2

It can save you money to pick your own fruit.

Claire picks fresh strawberries at a U-pick farm in Portage la Prairie, Manitoba. If she fills a pint basket (0.5506 litres), it will cost her $1.50. If she fills a 4-litre ice cream pail, it will cost $9.00. Which size of container will give her a better buy?

SOLUTION

Make sure you compare the same units. The pint basket can also be measured as 0.5506 litres.

Find the price per litre if Claire uses the pint basket by dividing the price by the volume.

$1.50 ÷ 0.5506 L = $2.724/L or $2.72, rounded to the nearest cent.

Then find the price per litre if she uses the ice cream pail.

$9.00 \div 4 \text{ L} = \$2.25/\text{L}$

Since the unit price if Claire fills the ice cream pail is lower, it is a better buy. However, Claire will also need to consider whether she can use 4 litres of strawberries.

ACTIVITY 1.3
WHICH PRICE IS RIGHT?

You and a partner own a janitorial service. Your janitorial service buys cleaning products for the office buildings that you clean. Before making your purchases, you research prices from local stores or online stores to calculate and compare the unit price of each item. You could record your research on tables similar to the following samples.

Shopping List
- Light bulbs
- Paper towels
- Garbage bags
- Cleaning sponges
- Paper hand towels
- Tissues
- Toilet paper
- Cleaning cloths
- Rubber gloves
- Other?

Part A

You may need to compare the unit price charged by different companies for the same size of package. For each item shown in the table, calculate the cost per unit and record it in your notebook.

COMPARING DIFFERENT BRANDS—SAME SIZE

Item	Items per pkg.	Brand A	Unit price	Brand B	Unit price
Light bulbs	4	$2.29		$2.99	
Paper towels	6	$6.49		$9.29	
Garbage bags	20	$8.79		$7.48	
Sponges	5	$7.95		$7.69	

SAMPLE

Part B

Sometimes you may need to compare the unit cost of different sizes of packages. For each item shown in the table, compare the cost per unit of two different package sizes. Record in your notebook which size has the lower cost per unit.

COMPARING DIFFERENT SIZES—SAME BRAND

Item	Smaller size	Price	Unit price	Larger size	Price	Unit price
Light bulbs	3	$2.49		6	$4.49	
Paper towels	3	$3.69		6	$6.49	
Garbage bags	20	$8.79		30	$9.99	
Sponges	5	$7.95		8	$11.99	

SAMPLE

Discuss the following questions with your partner.

1. For each item, which brand and which size of package is the best buy for your janitorial business? Why?

2. Why might a package of 20 garbage bags have a lower cost per unit than a package of 30 in the same brand? Which is the better buy?

3. Why might a person choose to buy the product that does not have the lowest unit price?

BUILD YOUR SKILLS

This horticulture technician mows the lawn prior to fertilizing it.

1. Vikram purchases 12 sinks for his plumbing business at a wholesale price of $1053.00. He wants to sell each sink to a different customer. What is the unit price of one sink?

2. A horticulture technician buys lawn fertilizer for several customers. She finds the following prices: 7 kg for $19.99; 14 kg for $35.95; 21 kg for $50.99. Which package has the lowest unit cost?

3. A locksmith in Winkler, Manitoba is buying locks for a new apartment building. One supplier sells locks at $120.00 for four. Another supplier sells six for $192.00. Which supplier has the lower cost for one lock? What other factors might you consider when selecting a lock?

26 MathWorks 10

4. Joel is a salesperson in a department store that sells T-shirts individually and in packages of two or three. One T-shirt sells for $9.98, a package of two sells for $15.49, and a package of three sells for $22.99.

   a) Find the unit price when T-shirts are sold in a package of two. How much is the unit price in a package of three?

   b) Suppose a customer wants to buy seven T-shirts. Which combination of packages will be the least expensive?

5. The meat department at a large supermarket sells boneless steaks at the following prices: $7.50 for 500 g; $12.50 for 1 kg; and $19.50 for 1.5 kg. Which of these packages has the lowest unit price? If a customer needs 2.5 kg, which combination of packages should he or she buy to get the best price but not have leftover meat?

6. A different store sells boneless steaks for the following prices: $4.25 for 250 g; $7.95 for 500 g; and $29.50 for 2 kg. Which of these packages has the lowest unit price? How do these prices compare to those in question 5?

Extend your thinking

7. A uranium mining company in northern Saskatchewan is buying industrial first-aid kits in bulk. First-aid kits are available in three sizes. A small kit costs $42.50 and contains enough supplies to meet the needs of 1–9 workers. A medium-sized kit costs $58.25 and will serve 10–40 workers. A large kit costs $70.50 and will serve 41–75 workers. Jason, the buyer, needs to buy kits for 250 workers. Which combination of kits will be the least expensive? What will the total cost be before taxes?

1.3 Setting a Price

MATH ON THE JOB

Maurice is a cost estimator for a construction company in Gravelbourg, Saskatchewan. He develops the cost information that the company manager needs to make bids for contracts. First he gathers information about the site and the project; then he prepares a cost summary for the entire project. He includes the costs associated with labour, equipment, architectural plans, materials, and subcontractors as well as the overhead, taxes, insurance, and a markup, as well as any other costs that may affect the project. He presents the final cost in various ways, for example, the cost per square foot or the cost per labour hour.

Maurice is estimating the cost of stuccoing a home. After calculating that the exterior walls are 3600 square feet, he determines the cost of the wire, paper, concrete, and labour. His total cost for the job is $30 600.00. What is the cost per square foot for stuccoing?

Estimating the costs of construction requires research into the prices of many materials.

EXPLORE THE MATH

markup: the difference between the amount a dealer sells a product for and the amount he or she paid for it

percent: percent means "out of 100"; a percentage is a ratio in which the denominator is 100

The price at which goods and services are sold has an impact on you whether you are a consumer or working in a business.

Prices rise and fall due to consumer demand and supply. If demand rises, suppliers are able to charge more. If demand falls, or if there is a large supply of a product, prices may fall.

Prices also rise and fall according to the cost of the materials and labour that go into the creation of a product or service. An additional amount, called **markup**, is added to these costs so that a profit can be made. For example, when the owner of a retail store buys items to re-sell, he or she buys them at a wholesale price. This price is then marked up and the item is sold at a higher retail price. The markup is usually a **percent** of the wholesale price.

When setting the prices for goods and services, companies consider psychological factors that have an impact on buyers as well as the cost of their products. Have you ever wondered why something costs $39.95 instead of $40.00? If you sell something in your store for $39.95 rather than $40.00, the difference in price, though small, can have a big impact on sales because the item seems less expensive. If you are a butcher, you may advertise a price of $2.39/100 g of meat, because that seems less expensive to consumers than $23.90/kg, even though these prices are equivalent.

28 MathWorks 10

Remember that in many cases taxes are added to arrive at the total price. Taxes are calculated as a percentage of the price paid. All Canadians pay the federal Goods and Services Tax (GST), which was 5% at the time of publication (2010). Most of the provinces also charge Provincial Sales Tax (PST), shown in the table below. The northern territories do not charge a Territorial Sales Tax. Copy this table into your notebook to use when solving problems that include taxes. What are the rates today?

FIGURE 1.1
Provincial Sales Tax Rates

	PST
Alberta	0%
British Columbia	7%
Manitoba	7%
Saskatchewan	5%

DISCUSS THE IDEAS
CONCERT PROMOTER

This francophone concert is an annual event.

Imagine that you are a concert promoter. You are responsible for promoting concerts for up-and-coming bands and selling tickets to these concerts. For your next concert, you have set a ticket price based on the amount it will cost you to put on the concert, plus a 30% profit.

Consider the following situations.

1. If ticket sales are high and you realize you are going to sell out quickly, what could you do?

2. If ticket sales are low and you realize you will not be able to sell them all, what could you do?

3. Under what circumstances might you consider selling tickets for a price that would not cover the cost of the concert?

HINTS

1. To change a number written as a percent to a fraction, write the number over 100.

2. To change a fraction to a decimal, divide the denominator into the numerator.

3. Since a percentage is a fraction over 100, you can convert it to a decimal by dividing the percentage by 100.

Example 1

Arlene purchases fabric at a wholesale price for her custom sewing business in Dawson City, YT. She pays $46.00/m. She charges a markup of 20% on the fabric. What will Arlene charge her clients per metre?

SOLUTION

When working with percents, it is often simplest to use them in their decimal form. To calculate a 20% markup, convert 20% to 0.2 and multiply.

$46.00/m × 0.2 = $9.20

Add the markup amount to the price.

$46.00/m + $9.20 = $55.20/m

The price Arlene will charge her clients will be $55.20/m.

ALTERNATIVE SOLUTION

You could also find the marked-up price by multiplying $46.00/m by 1.20. You may notice that the new price, $55.20/m, includes both 100% of the original price and the 20% markup, or 120%. To calculate the price, convert the percentage to a decimal, 1.20, and multiply to find the marked-up price.

Example 2

A furniture store in Saskatoon is selling a bedroom suite. The list price for the suite is $1599.00. What will the total cost be, including GST and PST?

SOLUTION

To arrive at the total cost, consider both GST and PST, and use percents to calculate them.

PST in Saskatchewan is 5%.

$1599.00 × 0.05 = $79.95

GST is also 5%.

$1599.00 × 0.05 = $79.95

Find the total cost.

$1599.00 + $79.95 + $79.95 = $1758.90

ALTERNATIVE SOLUTION

Another way to calculate the total cost is to add the two taxes together to get 10% and add this to 100% of the price before taxes. Convert this percentage to a decimal and multiply to find the total cost including taxes.

$1599.00 × 1.10 = $1758.90

Although there are several ways to calculate the final price, a store needs to keep track of the PST and GST amounts.

DISCUSS THE IDEAS

SEASONS AND HOLIDAYS

The demand for many goods and services varies with the seasons and, as a result, so does the price of these goods and services. Consider summer and winter in different parts of the country. Can you name some goods or services that have higher prices in summer or winter?

Demand for many items also increases around holidays, which may cause an increase in the price. In small groups, discuss the following questions.

1. Consider the price of roses. What time of year are roses most expensive? Why?

2. Consider the price of a litre of gasoline. What time of year is gasoline most expensive? Why?

3. Name two or three other goods or services that have a higher price at certain times. Why do their prices fluctuate?

4. Name two or three products that command higher prices because they are rare or unique.

5. Find two examples where prices are advertised in a way that makes an item seem less expensive. Share your examples with your classmates.

In many cultures, flowers are a common gift for special occasions.

Mental Math and Estimation

If you set the price of a bike helmet at $49.95 and sell 25, how much less income will your store generate than if you sold the same number at $54.95?

BUILD YOUR SKILLS

This dragline is located in the Alberta oil sands.

1. Max owns a clothing store. He buys an order of shirts for $22.75 per shirt. In order to make a profit, he wants to mark them up 60%. What will the list price of the shirts be for customers?

2. An outfitter in Fort McMurray, Alberta sells full-brim aluminum hard hats for $49.95 and steel-toed work boots for $129.95. If you purchase a hard hat and two pairs of boots, what will your total cost be, including tax? How much GST will you pay on these three items?

3. If the outfitter in question 2 opens a store in Axe Lake, Saskatchewan where exploration for oil is taking place, it may sell hard hats and work boots for 10% more than it charges in Fort McMurray. What would you pay for a hard hat and a pair of steel-toed boots in Saskatchewan, taking into account that PST of 5% applies?

4. Roberta works for a retail hardware store in Dauphin, Manitoba. She buys 3 sinks for $89.95 each, 2 bathtubs at $639.95 each, and 2 faucets for $74.95 each. She sells one sink, one bathtub, and 2 faucets to a customer at a 25% markup. How much does she charge her customer?

5. Parminder runs an organic blueberry farm in the Fraser Valley, BC. She sells her crop in three ways: direct to customers who come to the farm, at $3.50 a quart; at the local farmers' market at $3.99 a quart; and wholesale to organic food stores for $2.00 a quart.

   a) If she sells 50 quarts at $3.50, 175 quarts at $3.99, and 250 quarts at $2.00, what is her total income?

   b) Compare her income from 100 quarts sold directly at the farm to 100 quarts sold to a wholesaler. What is the difference in income? Why would she sell to a wholesaler?

6. When Julie completed the baker apprenticeship program and started her own cake business, her first order was to provide cakes for 100 people at a business luncheon. After calculating the cost of all her supplies and ingredients, her time, and the cost of gas for delivering the cakes, she found that her price of $2.50 per portion did not cover her costs.

   a) If she increased her price by 15%, what would the new unit price be?

   b) How much more would she make on 100 servings at the higher price?

   c) If she thought customers would reject a 15% price increase, how might she lower her costs?

7. At the end of the summer season, Marie has a lot of unsold $29.99 tank tops left in her Grande Prairie shop. She decides to put the remaining tank tops on sale. What might the sale price be? How will this sale affect her total profits? What reasons might Marie have for doing this?

This woman is an apprentice in a baking program.

Extend your thinking

8. You plan to sell imported cheese in your butcher shop and need to set a price. If the wholesale price you pay for a 10 kg wheel of medium Dutch Gouda is $175.00, what is the price for 250 grams if you sell it at cost?

   a) What factors will you consider in setting the retail price?

   b) If you decide on a markup of 40%, what would 250 g of cheese cost?

   c) If you found that your supply of Gouda exceeded the demand for it, you might decide to offer a 15% discount off the regular price. What would a customer now pay for 250 g?

   d) At the discounted price (15% off), would you still be making a profit? Explain your thinking.

1.4 On Sale!

MATH *ON THE JOB*

Daniel is the owner of a company in Brandon, Manitoba, that installs ceramic tile, marble, slate, terrazzo, and granite for exterior and interior walls, floors, and other surfaces. Early spring is a slow time for this type of business, so Daniel's company is offering discounts on materials left in stock from last year. To get the most from this **promotion**, Daniel needs to calculate what percentage discount to offer on each type of material, taking into account what his costs were and how much stock remains. He may also offer a variety of discounts based on quantities bought.

The company has in stock 12" × 12" slate in sandstone colour that sold for $6.99 per square foot last year. If Daniel offers it at a 15% discount, what will the sale price be for 50 square feet of slate, before taxes?

This floor in an apartment building foyer is made of ceramic tiles.

EXPLORE THE MATH

promotion: an activity that increases awareness of a product or attracts customers

When you go shopping, you often see that something is on sale for a discounted price. Frequently, the discount is expressed as a percent. For example, a clothing store may be selling certain items at 20% or 50% off. This may be because the clothes are out of season, out of fashion, or the store buyer may have ordered more than he or she could sell.

Businesses may use other sales promotions to attract buyers. Coupons usually give you a certain amount off the retail price, 25¢ or $1.00 for example. Companies often use coupon offers to attract consumers so they will try out a new product. More and more, businesses use points systems or customer cards to encourage customer loyalty by offering lower prices or prizes. Do you participate in any rewards programs?

As a consumer, remember to consider the amount of taxes as well as the listed price when making a decision to buy.

Example 1

Jonas needs to buy a new winter jacket. He has waited for a sale, and a jacket that originally cost $249.95 is now discounted 20%. How much will the jacket cost if Jonas lives in Nunavut, where there is no PST?

34 MathWorks 10

SOLUTION

Note that GST (and PST, if applicable) is charged on the sale price, not the initial price. Thus, you must first find the discounted price.

Find the amount of the discount.

$249.95 × 0.20 = $49.99

Find the sale price by subtracting the discount from the list price.

$249.95 − $49.99 = $199.96

Another way you could calculate this discount is to reason that if there is a 20% discount, then Jonas will have to pay 80% of the original price.

$249.95 × 0.80 = $199.96

However, the store needs to know the dollar value of the discount.

Determine the GST on $199.96.

$199.96 × 0.05 = $10.00, rounded to the nearest cent

Add the GST to the discounted price to find the total.

$199.96 + $10.00 = $209.96

Jonas will pay $209.96 for the jacket.

Example 2

A fisher sells fresh salmon, live crabs, and prawns at the dock in Steveston, BC directly to customers on Saturdays and Sundays. As the weekend winds down, he needs to sell off his stock, otherwise it will spoil. He has a sale! He offers 20% off all his prices.

Salmon is regularly $18.50/kg and prawns are $34.50/kg. At a 20% discount, what is the price of a salmon that weighs 3 kg? How much would 500 g of prawns cost?

SOLUTION

Calculate the discount per kg of salmon.

$18.50 × 0.20 = $3.70 discount

Then calculate the price per kg at the discounted price.

$18.50 − $3.70 = $14.80

The discounted price is $14.80/kg.

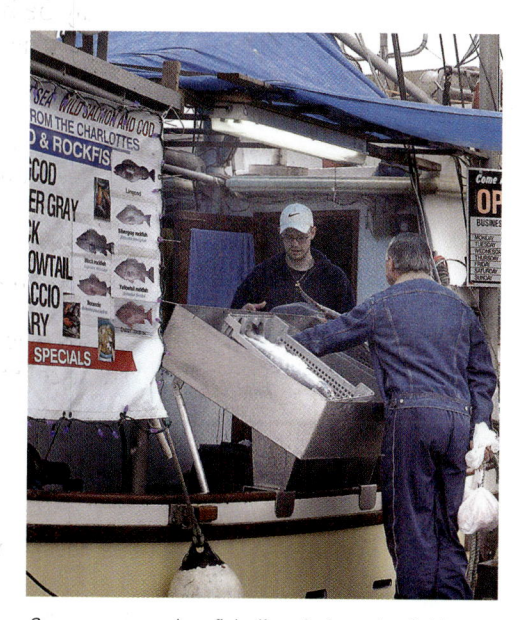

Consumers can buy fish directly from the fishing boats in Steveston, BC.

Next, calculate the price for 3 kg of salmon.

$14.80 × 3 = $44.40

To calculate the price of prawns, use another way to calculate a discounted price.

100% − 20% = 80%

Then calculate the discounted price per kg.

$34.50 × 0.80 = $27.60

Convert 500 g to kg.

500 g = 0.5 kg

Find the cost of 0.5 kg.

$27.60 × 0.5 = $13.80

At a 20% discount, a 3 kg salmon would cost $44.40 and 500 g of prawns would cost $13.80.

Mental Math and Estimation

You are shopping at a sale and see a $995.00 barbeque marked down 20%. Approximately what price do you estimate the sale price is before taxes?

ACTIVITY 1.4
TAKING ADVANTAGE OF SALES PROMOTIONS

You have just moved into your first apartment and you are planning a housewarming party. You need to buy a stereo to play music, a couch and two chairs for your guests to sit on, and some drinks for your guests. You decide to see what stores have promotions on these products.

1. Using your local newspaper, flyers, or the internet, find promotional sales advertisements for each of the items you need.

2. Record the store's name, the product, the promotional pitch or slogan, the regular price, and the sale price or percent discount in a table such as the following sample.

Setting up your first apartment will require you to research the best prices on furnishings.

ASSESSING PROMOTIONS

Item	Store name	Product	Promotional pitch	Regular price	Sale price	Percent discount
Stereo						
Couch						

SAMPLE

3. Did the company advertise the promotion as a percent decrease or as a full-value discount? Calculate either the percent decrease in price or the full value discount for each item, whichever is *not* given.

4. Were any of the promotions misleading? If so, explain.

5. Compare the information you found with a partner's information. Who found the better deal?

BUILD YOUR SKILLS

1. A supermarket regularly charges $5.89 for a package of Pizza Pockets. During a sale, the supermarket offers this promotion: "Buy one at the regular price, get a second one for half price."

   a) If Marylyn buys two packages, what will she pay?

   b) Approximately what percent does Marylyn save during this sale? Explain your reasoning.

2. Ross works at a sports store in St. Albert, Alberta where the price of a best-selling tennis racquet is $49.95. His friend Al works at a competitor's store where the regular price of a similar tennis racquet is $55.95, but it is on sale at 15% off. Al says his store offers the best price.

   a) Calculate the total price of the tennis racquet at each store, including GST.

   b) Is Al right? Explain why or why not.

3. A hairstylist at Top Cuts is preparing a discount offer. The regular cost of highlighting is $55.00. To attract more customers early in the day, he offers 15% off for appointments before 10:00 am. Mid-afternoon is also a slow time on Wednesdays and Thursdays, so he offers $5.00 off coupons for appointments made during those times.

   a) Which appointment time will get you the lowest price?

   b) Which promotion do you think will appeal to more people, coupons or percent off? Explain your thinking.

This apprentice hairstylist is learning to cut and style hair at a community college.

4. A roofer in Mission, BC buys metal roofing at a builder's discount of 20% off the retail price of $27.50 per square metre. If the roof of your house is 74 square metres and the roofer passes on 50% of the discount he receives to you, how much will you pay for the materials? If his usual hourly rate for labour is $36.00 and he gives you a 5% discount, how much will you save in labour costs if the job takes 16 hours? Omit the taxes in your calculations.

5. Pole mount industrial fans are on sale at two wholesalers in Cochrane, Alberta. An electrician needs 20 fans for installation in an office building. The sale price at the first store is 5% off the regular price of $157.00. The price at the second store is $165.00 each, but $149.00 for 10 or more. GST applies.

    a) Calculate the total cost of 20 fans at each store.

    b) Which wholesaler offers a better buy?

6. A storewide sale in Yellowknife advertises the following sales items:

    A shirt that was $31.99 is marked down to $19.99.

    Shorts that were $24.95 are marked down to $16.95.

    A jacket that was priced at $49.99 is marked down to $24.99.

    a) Calculate what percentage of markdown each item has been given.

    b) If a customer bought all 3 items, how much would he or she save in total? On which item would the customer save the most?

Extend your thinking

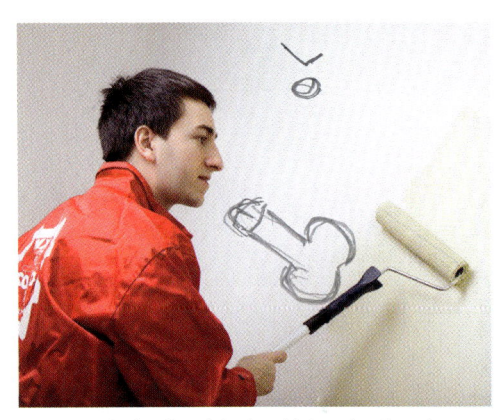

House painting is a job that high school and college students may do over the summer months.

7. An exterior house painter in Swift Current, Saskatchewan is offering a sales promotion. If you sign a contract to have your house painted and get a neighbour or friend to sign a contract at the same time, you each get a discount of 5% on the labour rate of $26.00/hr. Both GST and PST apply.

    a) If your house takes 55 hours to paint, how much would you pay at the regular price and how much would you pay with the discount? How much did you save?

    b) If the second person's house takes 60 hours to paint, how much more would that person save than you would save?

PROJECT—THE PARTY PLANNER

RESEARCH YOUR IDEAS

Earlier, you started making plans for a party. It is time now to put your plans on paper and calculate your costs.

- Write a description of your party and explain why it would be enjoyable for you and your friends.

- Explain how you will find out about and handle any allergies or other restrictions the guests may have.

- Design a sample invitation that will be sent to the guests. Include all the needed details, such as the time, date, location, and any other important information.

These members of a drama club are rehearsing for their school play.

- **T** Make a chart like the sample below or use a spreadsheet to list all of the items you will need to purchase. Include all unit costs, the number of items needed, GST and PST (if applicable), and totals. Add columns/rows as needed for your particular party.

- Once you have worked out a total cost for your party, make sure that it falls within your budget. If it does not fall within the budget amount, you may need to revise your original plans and recalculate your costs. If this happens, keep a record of both plans and include a summary explaining your reasons for changing your original plan.

PARTY SUPPLIES

Purchases	Name of store (if online, include the URL)	Unit cost	Number of items needed	Taxes (GST and PST)	Total cost
Invitations					
Activities					
Decorations					
Snacks					
Drinks					
				Total cost	$
				Cost/guest	$

SAMPLE

Chapter 1 Unit Pricing and Currency Exchange

THE ROOTS OF MATH

CANADIAN CURRENCY

Haida symbols adorn the Canadian 2004 $20.00 bill. Today, this $20.00 bill can be exchanged for something, such as groceries or a haircut. Traditionally, the Haida and other aboriginal groups also had currency exchange systems—between and within groups and with European traders.

In British Columbia, archaeological evidence indicates that there was extensive trade in obsidian (volcanic glass that could be made into sharp blades or arrowheads) as early as 9500 years ago. Researchers have also found evidence that 4000–3500 years ago, coastal peoples had exchange systems more complex than simple bartering or sharing. Researchers have inferred from archaeological evidence that there was a social ranking system for members of the coastal First Nations (some members and nations were more "wealthy" in goods) and that exchange and distribution of elaborate wood, antler, and soapstone carvings and other ornamental goods occurred at potlatch ceremonies. Beads made from shells were also exchanged and were indicators of wealth.

When the Europeans arrived, the Haida traded fur pelts for clothing, tools, and ornamental goods such as glass beads, abalone shells, and metals that were used to make items like iron bracelets and copper shields. These shields were a symbol of wealth and were exchanged at potlatch ceremonies. High-ranking chiefs could own many shields.

In eastern Canada, among the Iroquois and Huron peoples, wampum came to be used as a kind of money. Wampum is a European word derived from the Algonquin word *wampumpeague*. Wampum were often small beads made from white or purple shells, but other media such as porcupine quills and coarse animal hair were also used to create wampum.

Traditionally, wampum had complex uses. It was a system of record-keeping and was used to record important historical events such as peace treaties and trade agreements made between aboriginal peoples. It was also used for personal decoration. After Europeans arrived, wampum came to be used as a currency in the fur trade between aboriginal peoples and Europeans. In New England, for example, wampum was considered legal tender with a value of eight white beads or four purple beads to a penny.

This copper shield was a symbol of wealth within the Haida Nation.

1. Do you know of other items that were traditionally used by aboriginal peoples for trading or exchange?

2. Have you ever traded either a good, like a CD you no longer wanted, or a service, like mowing the lawn, with another person for something you wanted without exchanging money? How did you determine the value of your good or service?

3. Why do you think $5.00 is worth $5.00? What gives money its value?

Currency Exchange Rates

1.5

MATH ON THE JOB

Naomi Coates works for a potato grower in Sherwood Park, Alberta that sells a number of varieties of seed potatoes to the United States and table potatoes to Mexico. The prices are negotiated based on the Potato Growers of Alberta price list. Naomi negotiates for multi-year contracts in foreign currencies with buyers who want large shipments of potatoes. She must also ask for and compare quotes from shipping companies in the currency of the destination country.

Naomi has to pay the monthly shipping invoice to a firm in Idaho. She has 30 days in which to make the payment. As the exchange rate changes every day, how much she pays (in Canadian dollars, which are converted to US dollars) will depend on the day she converts the money to US dollars. What strategies can Naomi use to ensure she gets the best rate?

Potatoes are just one of the many agricultural products that Canada exports to other countries.

EXPLORE THE MATH

People travel to different countries on business and for pleasure. Goods and services are also bought and sold between countries. Since different countries use different systems of **currency**, international trade requires an organized system for exchanging money.

Currency is exchanged by banks, currency exchange companies, and businesses such as travel agencies. Not all currencies are available at every exchange. If the currency you need is not requested very often, you may have to order it in advance. It may take some time to obtain a currency, so it is best to plan ahead. Since banks and other exchange agents charge a fee for this service, it can be a good idea to shop around for the best price.

If a Canadian company wants to buy goods made in Japan, it must exchange Canadian dollars for yen to complete the purchase. The **exchange rate** between the two currencies is used to calculate how many dollars the company must convert to yen.

The exchange rate fluctuates from day to day, and from one currency exchange to another. Exchanges set a **selling rate** and a **buying rate** for currency exchange, and these rates are different from each other. If you plan to travel to Italy and need to obtain euros from your bank, you will pay the selling rate (the bank is selling the euros to you). If you have euros left

buying rate: the rate at which a currency exchange buys money from customers

currency: the system of money a country uses

exchange rate: the price of one country's currency in terms of another nation's currency

selling rate: the rate at which a currency exchange sells money to its customers

HINT

When working with foreign currency, it is often useful to begin with an estimate.

over when you return to Canada, you will receive the buying rate when you convert them back into Canadian dollars (the bank is buying them from you). You pay more for the foreign currency than the banking institution will pay you in return.

When travelling in a foreign country, it is often helpful to estimate what something costs in your own currency. Estimating can help you compare prices.

Mental Math and Estimation

If the exchange rate for the euro is $1.644814 CAD and your hotel in Paris costs €95.00, about how much is your hotel in Canadian dollars?

ACTIVITY 1.5
WHAT'S YOUR RIDE? SURVEY

The current issue of *What's Your Ride?* magazine includes a feature article about the international automotive scene. Vehicles from five countries are profiled. The chart below lists the vehicles, their country of origin, and their list prices in the local currency. Your task is to research the price of each vehicle in Canadian dollars at today's exchange rate.

This Peugeot 308 SW costs about €220 000.00 in France.

1. Use the internet to research information for currency conversion. Try using the Bank of Canada website (www.bank-banque-canada.ca) and select "currency converter." Then create a chart like the sample below to record the exchange rate and the price in Canadian dollars for each vehicle.

COMPARING CARS

Name of country	Make and model of vehicle	Name of currency	Exchange rate	Foreign amount	Canadian amount
France	Fiat 500	euro		€10 900.00	
India	Maruti Gypsy King	rupee		Rs 537 921.07	
England	Mini Cooper S	pound		£16 245.00	
United States	Dodge Ram 3500	US dollar		US$30 420.00	
Japan	Daihatsu Move Latte L	yen		¥1 073 380.00	

SAMPLE

42 MathWorks 10

2. If you have high-speed access to the internet, research each vehicle in the chart and decide which one you would most like to purchase. If you don't have internet access, choose any vehicle from the list to purchase.

3. You will need to purchase a money order to send to the seller (for now, ignore international shipping charges, import taxes, and duty).

   a) Using the foreign exchange calculator on the Royal Bank website (www.rbcroyalbank.com), find the selling exchange rate and work out the total amount of the money order you will need to purchase your vehicle.

   b) You may notice that the exchange rate does not match the rate you found on the Bank of Canada website (www.bank-banque-canada.ca). Why is this?

4. On your way home from the bank, you see the same vehicle for sale at a local automotive dealer. When you consider the international shipping costs, import taxes, and duty you will have to pay, you realize that you should buy the vehicle locally. You decide to exchange your money order back into Canadian dollars.

   a) At your bank's website, you find a different exchange rate than when you purchased the money order. Why?

   b) Using the foreign exchange converter on the Royal Bank website (www.rbcroyalbank.com), find the buying exchange rate and the total Canadian value of your money order. What is the difference between the buying and selling rate of the currency you converted?

Example 1

On a specific date, the selling rate for the Danish krone compared to the Canadian dollar is 0.221778. How many kroner will you receive for $500.00 CAD?

SOLUTION

One Danish krone is worth $0.221778 CAD. This exchange rate can be written in the form of a fraction where the numerator represents Danish kroner and the denominator represents Canadian dollars.

$$\frac{1.00}{0.221778}$$

Let x represent the number of kroner you will receive for $500.00 CAD.

HINT

The unit of Danish currency is the krone, which is the Danish word for crown. The plural of krone is kroner.

HINT

Since an exchange rate tells you the price of one nation's money in terms of another, you can use proportions to determine the value of the amount exchanged.

$$\frac{1.00}{0.221778} = \frac{x}{500.00}$$

The proportion forms a fractional equation. To simplify the equation, multiply both sides of the equation by the common denominator.

$$\frac{1.00}{0.221778}(110.889) = \frac{x}{500.00}(110.889)$$

The common denominator is (0.221778)(500.00) which equals 110.889.

$$\frac{110.889}{0.221778} = \frac{110.889x}{500.00}$$

Simplify both sides of the equation.

$$500.00 = 0.221778x$$

To isolate the variable, divide by its coefficient. Since the coefficient of x is 0.221778, divide both sides of the equation by 0.221778.

$$\frac{500.00}{0.221778} = \frac{0.221778x}{0.221778}$$

Simplify both sides of the equation.

$$2254.506759 = x$$

The value must be rounded since it represents the number of kroner received.

You will receive 2255.00 kroner for 500.00 Canadian dollars.

ALTERNATIVE SOLUTION

The exchange rate given states that 1.00 krone equals $0.221778 CAD.

1.00 krone = $0.221778 CAD

$$\frac{1.00}{0.221778} \text{ kroner} = \frac{\$0.221778 \text{ CAD}}{\$0.221778 \text{ CAD}}$$

Dividing both sides of the equation by 0.221778 will give the number of kroner that would equal $1.00 CAD.

4.50901 kroner = $1.00 CAD

Since $1.00 CAD is worth 4.50901 kroner, $500.00 CAD is worth (500.00)(4.50901) or 2255.00 kroner.

You will receive 2255.00 kroner for 500.00 Canadian dollars.

FIGURE 1.2
Exchange Rates Compared to the Canadian Dollar

Bank buying rate	Country	Currency units	Bank selling rate
0.950964	Australia	dollar	1.006964
1.580814	Austria	euro	1.644814
1.580814	Belgium	euro	1.644814
0.534900	Brazil	real	0.697000
0.127100	China	yuan	0.162600
0.210778	Denmark	krone	0.221778
1.996146	England	pound	2.060146
0.159300	Egypt	pound	0.217300
1.580814	European Community	euro	1.644814
1.580814	Finland	euro	1.644814
1.580814	France	euro	1.644814
1.580814	Germany	euro	1.644814
1.580814	Greece	euro	1.644814
0.128451	Hong Kong	dollar	0.133451
1.580814	Italy	euro	1.644814
0.009295	Japan	yen	0.009855
0.012510	Kenya	shilling	0.017300
0.083443	Mexico	peso	0.108443
1.580814	Netherlands	euro	1.644814
0.748264	New Zealand	dollar	0.798264
1.996146	N. Ireland	pound	2.060146
0.194863	Norway	krone	0.205863
0.012360	Pakistan	rupee	0.019360
1.580814	Portugal	euro	1.644814
1.580814	Republic of Ireland	euro	1.644814
1.996146	Scotland	pound	2.060146
0.737280	Singapore	dollar	0.762280
1.580814	Spain	euro	1.644814
0.165558	Sweden	krona	0.175558
0.982007	Switzerland	franc	1.017007
0.026550	Thailand	baht	0.035120
1.004350	United States	dollar	1.038650

Example 2

On the same day as example 1 occurs, the buying rate for kroner was 0.210778. If, after purchasing your kroner, you decided not to go to Denmark and sold the kroner back to the bank, how much would you lose?

SOLUTION

You now have 2255.00 kroner. The rate is 1 krone: $0.210778 CAD.

Let y represent the number of Canadian dollars you will receive in return.

$y = 2255.00 \times 0.210778$

$y = 475.30$

You would receive $475.30 CAD from the bank.

$500.00 − $475.30 = $24.70

Therefore, you would lose $24.70 in this transaction.

ACTIVITY 1.6
CALCULATE FOREIGN EXCHANGE

You need to upgrade some equipment. In this activity, you will investigate and compare Canadian and foreign prices for the same item.

1. Choose two items you'd like to upgrade. Items could be game systems, cameras, sports equipment, or other items of your choice.

2. Use the internet to research the cost of these items in a foreign currency. Calculate what each item would cost in Canadian dollars. Record this information in your notebook or on a spreadsheet.

3. Find a Canadian supplier and record the prices, including taxes.

4. Which is a better buy, buying these items locally or from a foreign supplier?

5. What factors apart from price might you consider when deciding which supplier to choose?

Manufacturers of snowboards exist in several countries, including Canada.

BUILD YOUR SKILLS

Use the table on p. 45 to answer the following questions.

1. What would the cost be, in Canadian dollars, to buy the following currencies from a bank?

    a) euro

    b) Hong Kong dollar

    c) Pakistan rupee

2. If you had the following foreign currencies, what rate would you use when a bank is buying the currency from you?

    a) Japanese yen

    b) Australian dollar

    c) United States dollar

Switzerland still uses francs rather than euros.

3. Calculate the amount of money you would receive in Canadian dollars if you sold the following currencies to a bank.

    a) 4500.00 pesos

    b) 25 000.00 Hong Kong dollars

    c) 2200.00 euros

    d) 8545.00 Scottish pounds

4. Megan is attending a three-day trade fair in Germany. Her travel allowance is $1200.00 CAD. How much money will she have in the local currency for her expenses in Germany?

5. Opal is planning a trip to Europe. She wishes to buy $650.00 Canadian dollars' worth of each of the following currencies. How much of each currency will she have?

    a) euro

    b) Swiss francs

    c) Swedish kronor

    d) If Opal cancels her trip to Sweden and changes the kronor back into Canadian dollars, how much will she receive? Why does she receive a lower amount back in Canadian dollars than she initially paid?

Chapter 1 Unit Pricing and Currency Exchange 47

6. Chris is planning a golfing trip. He plans to golf at five highly rated international golf courses. He estimates how much money he will need in each of the different currencies. For each of the countries that he will visit, calculate how much he will need in Canadian dollars (CAD). What is the total amount of Canadian money he needs?

GOLF VACATION

Country	Golf course	Estimated funds needed	Estimated funds needed in $CAD
United States	Pebble Beach	US$5000.00	
Scotland	St. Andrew's	£8500.00	
China	Spring City Golf & Lake Resort	¥26 600.00	*SAMPLE*
Singapore	SAFRA Resort & Country Club	S$15 000.00	
Austria	Leopoldsdorf	€4000.00	

Extend your thinking

7. Your company produces a line of herbal vinegars. In Canada, you sell each bottle of vinegar for $8.95 before taxes. Your company is planning to expand and sell its products in the United States and Australia.

   a) What would the equivalent price be for the bottle of vinegar in US and Australian dollars? Use www.rbcroyalbank.com or a similar site to calculate your conversion.

   b) The costs of shipping and exporting are $1.00/bottle to the United States and $2.00/bottle to Australia. How much will the retail price be in the US and Australia if you incorporate shipping costs and set the price so that the income per bottle is equal to the Canadian income of $8.95 per bottle before taxes?

PROJECT—THE PARTY PLANNER

MAKE A PRESENTATION

You are now ready to present your party plan to your fellow team, club, or committee members to get their approval. Use all the information you have gathered to complete this project.

Presentations are often made using posters and handouts accompanied by oral explanations. Presentation software could also be used. Prepare your presentation with these items:

- a poster showing your location and decorations. Be creative—include some pictures! List any activities that you have planned and the entertainment;
- the sample invitation; and
- the detailed itemized list, chart, or spreadsheet of all supplies and final costs.

Be prepared to explain to your friends why your party plans will make the wind-up party the best one ever!

- Finally, reflect on how well you completed your project.

These students are planning a wind-up party for their debating club.

REFLECT ON YOUR LEARNING
UNIT PRICING AND CURRENCY EXCHANGE

Now that you have finished this chapter, you should be able to

☐ apply your prior knowledge of ratios and rates in new contexts;

☐ appreciate how proportional reasoning is used in several jobs;

☐ calculate unit price and use your knowledge to determine the best buy;

☐ understand some of the factors that influence how prices are set;

☐ predict the impact of promotions on prices;

☐ consider other factors, such as quality and your needs, when making purchasing decisions, at home or in the workplace;

☐ comprehend how foreign currencies are bought and sold.

In addition, you have completed a project that applied your new skills in a practical context.

PRACTISE YOUR NEW SKILLS

1. Use mental math to solve these problems.

    a) If the posted speed limit is 80 km/h, how far will you travel in half an hour? In two-and-a-half hours?

    b) If the exchange rate for 1 euro is $1.59 CAD, how many Canadian dollars could you buy with 10 euros?

2. If the ratio of loaves of white bread sold compared to loaves of whole wheat bread sold is 3:1 and a bakery sells 100 loaves of whole wheat bread in a day, how many loaves of white bread would it sell in a day?

3. Calculate the unit rate for each of the following. Include correct units in all your answers.

    a) 30 metres in 4 seconds

    b) $2.80 for a dozen eggs

4. The standard sizes for photographs are 4″ × 6″, 5″ × 7″, and 8″ × 10″. Can you use a photocopier to enlarge a 4″ × 6″ photo to one of the other standard sizes? Explain. If you reduce an 8″ × 10″ photograph, what sizes could you make?

5. At the St. Norbert Farmers' Market in Winnipeg, a 5 lb bag of potatoes sells for $1.89 and a 20 lb bag sells for $5.99.

    a) Find the unit price for each size. Which is a better deal?

    b) Name two things other than price that you should consider when buying potatoes.

    c) You meet a vendor at the farmers' market who is from Altona. He tells you that he can sell you a 75 lb bag of potatoes for $15.00. Do you buy them? Why or why not?

6. During a Boxing Day promotion in Edmonton, Alberta, Krazy Krazy Televisions advertises a 42″ flat-screen television for $300.00 off and they will "pay the GST" while Too Good To Be True Electronics is discounting the same television by 30%. If the original price of the television at both stores was $1299.99, which store offers a better deal?

7. A recipe for calls for $2\frac{1}{2}$ cups of flour to $\frac{1}{2}$ cup of sugar.

    a) How many cups of flour would you use with 1 cup of sugar?

    b) This recipe makes 12 scones but you only want 8. How much flour and sugar do you use?

At St. Norbert Farmers' Market, vendors offer a variety of products such as produce, baking, and crafts.

8. Glynis wishes to purchase 500.00 euros for her business trip to Austria. The rate of exchange is 1.00 euro equals $1.59 CAD.

    a) How much will it cost her in Canadian dollars to purchase the euros?

    b) Her financial institution charges a 0.5% handling fee on the currency exchange. The handling fee is charged on the Canadian amount. What is her final cost?

9. Karisha travelled to Milan for a weekend to purchase fabric for her children's clothing business. She bought 15 metres of hand-painted designer cotton for €28.92/m and 40 metres of reversible fleece for €9.95/m. How much did her fabric cost in Canadian dollars if $1.00 CAD equals 0.6478 euros?

10. Natalia earns $28.50 caring for a child for 3 hours.

    a) Using mental math, calculate how much she would earn in one hour.

    b) Copy the following table or use a spreadsheet to make a table showing the number of hours versus dollars earned.

    CALCULATING EARNINGS

Hours	Dollars earned
0	
1	
2	
3	
4	
5	

    c) Use a spreadsheet tool or pen and paper to graph what Natalia earns. Graph up to 15 hours worked.

    d) Using your graph, estimate how much Natalia would earn for 3.5 hours of work. For 12.5 hours?

This childcare worker at the St. Mary's Indian Reserve in Cranbrook, BC wants to calculate her earnings.

Chapter 2

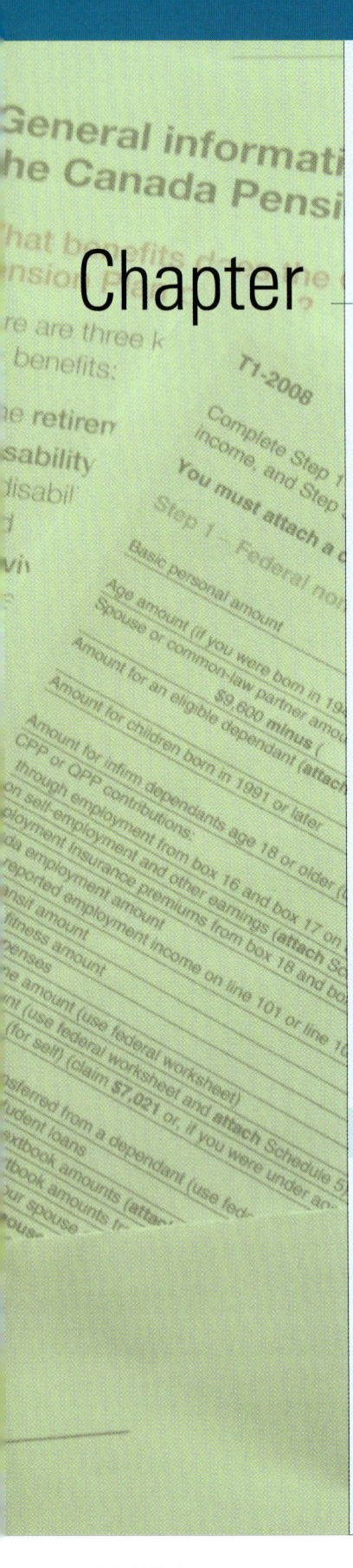

Earning an Income

GOALS

Once you enter the workforce, you will earn an income. In this chapter, you will learn about some of the different ways that income is calculated and paid by employers—or by yourself, if you are self-employed. You will be introduced to some of the deductions that may reduce your pay, including taxes and government and industry benefit programs. You will use some mathematics you are familiar with, such as fractions, percents, and rates, to make calculations in the context of earning an income. You will use these mathematical ideas to

- calculate how much you will earn, given the rate of pay and amount of time worked;
- learn about a range of payment types that vary from employer to employer and industry to industry; and
- calculate deductions and find net pay.

KEY TERMS

- benefits
- bonus
- commission
- contract
- deductions
- gross pay
- minimum wage
- net pay
- overtime
- pay statement
- piecework
- salary
- self-employment
- shift premium
- taxable income
- tip
- wage

PROJECT—A PAYROLL PLAN FOR A SUMMER BUSINESS

START TO PLAN

PROJECT OVERVIEW

Have you considered becoming a business owner? The project for this chapter will be to imagine that you have started a small business that employs students in the summer months to do yardwork, such as lawn mowing and gardening, in your community. As part of the business, you will need to plan the payroll (a list of employees and the amount they will earn) and make decisions about payroll policies.

GET STARTED

To begin your project, you will need to make some decisions, consider your options, and find some information. When you have considered the questions below, record your answers in your project file. Include a paragraph that outlines your plan.

- Decide on the number of employees your business will employ for the months of July and August. Think about how much work you will be able to find. Also consider how many other people you would have the time to manage.
- Will you have any part-time staff? Any on-call workers who will work just when they are needed?
- What skills or qualities should your employees have?
- Decide what the regular working hours for the day and week will be. Will there be weekend work? Any work on statutory holidays?
- Research the minimum wage in your province or territory (see p. 63 for more information about minimum wage). For this project, pay your summer employees the minimum wage for your province or territory.
- Will you offer any benefits to your staff, for example, a bonus if they keep working throughout the summer?

These students in Victoria, BC do yardwork in the summer to earn money.

FINAL PRESENTATION CHECKLIST

You will present a payroll plan in a business-like presentation folder or binder or create a slide show using presentation software. Your payroll plan will include the following items:

- a paragraph that outlines your plan;
- a spreadsheet or table that contains a list of positions, the gross pay, deductions, and net pay, with a total for the pay period;
- an equation that describes your regular weekly salary costs;
- a sample pay statement for one employee, with a list of deduction amounts and a statement of net pay; and
- a memo you have written to your staff about payroll policies.

2.1 Wages and Salaries

MATH ON THE JOB

Joseph Galloway lives in a group home for men with schizophrenia in North Battleford, Saskatchewan. He recently finished his high school diploma, taking classes offered to adults with mental illnesses at the Saskatchewan Hospital, where he is an outpatient.

Joseph works at four part-time jobs to earn his spending money. He works one 4-hour shift a week as a short-order cook at McDonald's. He also works one 4-hour shift a week at the Saskatchewan Hospital canteen, selling drinks and snacks. He works one 8-hour day on a work crew organized by the hospital, helping elderly people in North Battleford with chores such as snow shovelling and lawn mowing. From May to October, Joseph works two 3-hour shifts a week at the local golf course selling golf balls and other golf accessories. Joseph is paid the **minimum wage** at the canteen, on the work crew, and at the golf course. In Saskatchewan, this rate is $8.60 an hour. At McDonald's, Joseph recently was given a raise, and he now earns $8.75 an hour. How much does Joseph earn each week during the winter months? During the golfing season?

Joseph Galloway works at this golf course in Saskatchewan during the summer months.

EXPLORE THE MATH

minimum wage: the minimum amount a worker must be paid an hour; this rate varies, depending on which province or territory you live in

gross pay: the total amount of money earned; also called gross earnings

Have you worked at a job where you have earned money? Did you earn a fixed amount paid hourly or weekly? Many tradespeople and people who work in service industries earn wages calculated this way. Other people earn salaries, which are often expressed as an annual amount but are paid monthly, semi-monthly, or biweekly. What are some occupations where people earn an annual salary?

The total amount people earn is called their **gross pay**. Later in this chapter, you will learn about deductions that are made from gross pay.

There are occasions when people are asked by their employers to work extra hours in addition to their normal hours. What are some situations where employees may be asked to work **overtime**? How much is a reasonable amount to increase the rate of pay for overtime hours?

ACTIVITY 2.1
INTERPRETING PAY STATEMENTS

Work in a small group to complete this activity. Your friend Jolie has started a job as an apprentice elevator repairperson. Study her first **pay statement**, which is shown below. Pay statements are provided by the employer.

pay statement: a form an employer gives an employee that shows earnings and deductions from earnings for a defined pay period

Employee Name: Jolie		
Company: ABC Elevator Repair	Pay Begin Date:	10/13/2010
	Pay End Date:	10/19/2010

General			
Employee ID: 999999		Job Title:	Elevator repair apprentice
Address:		Pay Rate: Annual:	$19.00/h

Hours and Earnings			
Description	Rate	Hours	Gross Earnings
Regular	19.00/h		$712.50

1. How many days does the pay period cover?

2. If Jolie's gross earnings are $712.50, how many hours did she work?

3. Did she earn more or less than the minimum wage in your province or territory?

4. Develop a formula Jolie could use to calculate her earnings for any given pay period.

DISCUSS THE IDEAS
TYPES OF EARNINGS

Working with a partner, discuss the following questions:

1. Make a list of the different ways people are paid.

2. What are several different types of jobs that fall into each category of pay?

3. Is there an advantage to being paid weekly rather than monthly? Why do you think most workers are not paid weekly?

4. If you worked at a job in which you earned an annual salary that was paid monthly, and you worked more than 40 hours in a week, how might you be compensated for your overtime work?

Chapter 2 Earning an Income

Example 1

Each summer, Rick works at the Pacific National Exhibition in Vancouver as a parking lot attendant. His wages this year are $9.76 an hour and his hours of work vary from week to week. He worked 25 hours for the week August 14–20 and 35 hours for the week August 21–27.

Rick's pay statement is shown below. Check it for accuracy and correct any errors you find.

Employee Name: Rick			
Company: Pacific National Exhibition		Pay Begin Date:	14/08/2010
		Pay End Date:	27/08/2010

General			
Employee ID:	999999	Job Title:	Parking lot attendant
Address:		Pay Rate: Annual:	$9.76/h

Hours and Earnings			
Description	Rate	Hours	Gross Earnings
Regular	$8.76	60	$525.60

SOLUTION

His pay rate is shown as $8.76 when it should be $9.76. His gross earnings are $585.60, not $525.60.

Mental Math and Estimation

How many hours are there in a work week that is made up of five 7.5-hour days? How many hours would that be in a year?

Example 2

Zhong was hired to be the office clerk at an insurance company. His annual salary will be $34 756.00.

a) Why is Zhong not paid annually for his work?

b) Would he earn more each pay period if he were paid **semi-monthly** or **biweekly**?

semi-monthly: twice a month

biweekly: every two weeks

SOLUTION

a) Being paid annually would create hardship because Zhong would have to work an entire year before he was paid. Most people prefer to get regular pay so they can set monthly budgets to meet their expenses and plan for savings.

b)
$12 \times 2 = 24$ To find the number of semi-monthly pay periods in a year, multiply the number of months in a year by 2.

$52 \div 2 = 26$ To find the number of biweekly pay periods in a year, divide the number of weeks in a year by 2.

Since the same annual salary will be paid in 26 pay periods for biweekly pay as in 24 pay periods for semi-monthly pay, for each pay period Zhong would earn more if he were paid semi-monthly. However, he would get 2 extra paycheques a year if he were paid biweekly.

ALTERNATIVE SOLUTION

To determine whether Zhong would earn more each pay period if he were paid semi-monthly or biweekly, you could calculate his semi-monthly and biweekly gross pay.

$\$34\,756.00 \div 24 = \$1448.17$ Divide the annual salary by 24 pay periods for semi-monthly pay.

$\$34\,756.00 \div 26 = \$1336.77$ Divide the annual salary by 26 pay periods for biweekly pay.

Zhong would earn more each pay period if he were paid semi-monthly.

Example 3

Laura's regular rate at her job in a warehouse is $9.86 an hour. She works 8 hours a day. She has to work an extra shift on a holiday, and her overtime rate is time and a half.

a) What are Laura's gross earnings for the holiday?

b) What is her hourly rate on the holiday?

Laura earns a higher wage when she works at the warehouse on a holiday.

SOLUTION

a) First, find Laura's regular daily rate. Why is the answer in dollars?

$9.86/h × 8 h = $78.88

$78.88 × 1.5 = $118.32   Multiply Laura's regular daily rate by "time and a half" or 1.5.

Laura's gross earnings for the holiday are $118.32.

b) $118.32 ÷ 8 = $14.79   Divide her holiday gross earnings by the number of hours in a work day.

Laura's hourly rate on the holiday is $14.79.

ALTERNATIVE SOLUTION

First, solve b) by finding the hourly overtime rate.

$9.86 × 1.5 = $14.79   Multiply Laura's regular hourly rate by 1.5.

Then solve a).

$14.79 × 8 = $118.32   Multiply the hourly overtime rate by the number of hours in a work day.

Laura's gross earnings for the holiday are $118.32.

> **HINT**
>
> To calculate overtime, convert the rate to a decimal. For example, double time is 2.0, or twice the rate of pay.

Example 4

Gregor works as a glazier, a person who cuts and fits glass, at a window manufacturing company in Steinbach, MB. He earns $19.99/h for 37.5 hours a week and time and a half for any hours over that. Gregor examines the schedule for the upcoming week, shown here.

WEEKLY SCHEDULE

Employee Name	Day	Start time	End time
Gregor	Sunday		
	Monday	8:00 am	4:00 pm
	Tuesday	8:15 am	4:00 pm
	Wednesday	8:00 am	3:30 pm
	Thursday	8:00 am	4:00 pm
	Friday	9:00 am	4:15 pm
	Saturday	8:30 am	6:30 pm

a) Describe your strategy for determining the number of hours Gregor will work each day and express these amounts as decimals.

b) How many hours of overtime will he work?

SOLUTION

a) To calculate how many hours and minutes Gregor will work each day, you can calculate the number of hours he will work in the morning and add the hours he will work in the afternoon.

First, convert the start and end times from hours and minutes to hours expressed as decimals. For example:

8:15 = 8.25 hours

3:30 = 3.5 hours

Next, subtract the start time from 12:00 noon to determine the morning hours, and add the end time to 0 to determine the afternoon hours (because 12:00 noon is 0 hours pm).

A glazier uses a level to ensure that the window will be straight.

You might want to add another column to the table, showing hours worked, as shown in the following table.

WEEKLY SCHEDULE

Employee Name	Day	Start time	End time	Hours worked
Gregor	Sunday			
	Monday	8:00 am	4:00 pm	8.0
	Tuesday	8:15 am	4:00 pm	7.75
	Wednesday	8:00 am	3:30 pm	7.5
	Thursday	8:00 am	4:00 pm	8.0
	Friday	9:00 am	4:15 pm	7.25
	Saturday	8:30 am	6:30 pm	10.0

b) Calculate the total number of hours Gregor will work.

8.0 + 7.75 + 7.5 + 8.0 + 7.25 + 10.0 = 48.5

Then, find the number of overtime hours.

48.5 − 37.5 = 11   Subtract normal weekly hours from total hours.

Gregor will work 11 hours of overtime.

ACTIVITY 2.2
MIND MAPPING FOR TRADES

Working in small groups, draw mind maps that show ways in which you would use math in three trades or occupations. Then discuss these questions with your group.

1. How much overlap did you find in the kinds of math that different trades use?

2. Have you worked in any jobs or done chores that required you to use math? If so, give some examples.

Mental Math and Estimation

An office assistant who earns $10.00 an hour was paid $120.00 for 10 hours of work. How is this possible?

Gaming industry employees use math in their job.

BUILD YOUR SKILLS

1. Rachel works 40 hours a week as a journeyman printer. She earns $23.68 an hour.

   a) What are her gross weekly earnings?

   b) If she works 49 weeks a year and receives 3 weeks of paid holidays, what are her gross annual earnings?

2. What is the difference between biweekly and semi-monthly pay periods? What advantage does one method have over the other?

3. Luc earns $497.12 a month and works 12 hours a week. Explain how you would calculate his hourly pay. (Hint: $10.36 an hour is not correct.)

4. You are cutting lawns for your summer job. One customer gives you the option of being paid $11.00 an hour or a flat fee of $35.00 each time you cut the lawn. What factors would you take into account in deciding which option to choose?

5. If Arielle is paid $9.56 an hour as a swimming lifeguard and she works 12 hours a week, what is her average monthly wage? If she asked for a raise to $12.50 an hour, would her monthly earnings increase by more or less than $100.00?

60 MathWorks 10

6. Brandon is paid 150% of his regular hourly rate for overtime hours. He is paid $45.00 an hour for overtime hours. What is his regular hourly rate?

7. Sholeh works as a welder at a jewellery workshop. She receives annual cost-of-living raises. Her salary before receiving a raise is $29 535.00.

   a) One year, Sholeh receives a cost-of-living raise of 3.4%. What is her new salary?

   b) If Sholeh receives cost-of-living raises of 2.8% the following year and 3.2% the year after that, what will her salary be after the three cost-of-living raises?

8. Examine the following table, which records the hours worked by an employee who uses a punch-card system to log her hours.

   a) How many hours and minutes did this employee work each day?

   b) What are these amounts expressed as decimals?

   c) If the employee's rate of pay is $9.60/h, how much did she earn for the week?

   d) Why is it preferable to start and end at the specified times in a job that logs exact log-in times?

HINT

Employers don't usually pay for every minute. Round off the hours to the nearest quarter hour, then calculate the pay.

Time Card

Employee Number: 67891
Employee Name: Navreet Kooner
For Week Ending: 19/11/10
Approval: *N. Kooner*

Date	Morning IN	Morning OUT	Afternoon IN	Afternoon OUT	Overtime IN	Overtime OUT	Hours REG	Hours OT	Total Hours
Nov 15	9:03	12:05							
Nov 16			4:02	9:06					
Nov 17	8:58	12:00							
Nov 18			4:30	10:01					
Nov 19	8:32	12:00							

9. Examine the following pay statements.

   a) Franco worked 5 days, from 6:00 pm to 1:00 am, with a 30-minute unpaid dinner break each day. He earns $8.95/h. Fix the mistakes on his pay statement.

Employee Name: Franco		
Company:	Pay Begin Date:	21/05/2010
Silver Screen	Pay End Date:	15/05/2100

General			
Employee ID:	999999	Job Title:	Theatre attendant
Address:		Pay Rate: Annual:	$8.95/h

Hours and Earnings			
Description	Rate	Hours	Gross Earnings
Regular	$8.95/h	30.0	$268.50

b) In one week, Christine worked three 4-hour shifts, one 5-hour shift, and one 6.5-hour shift. She is paid $9.54/h. Fix the mistakes on her pay statement.

Employee Name: Christine		
Company:	Pay Begin Date:	14/07/2010
Whole Earth Gardens	Pay End Date:	20/07/2010

General			
Employee ID:	999999	Job Title:	Cashier
Address:		Pay Rate: Annual:	$9.45/h

Hours and Earnings			
Description	Rate	Hours	Gross Earnings
Regular	$9.54/h	23.5	$222.08

c) If you noticed an error on your pay statement, what would you do?

Extend your thinking

10. You are comparing two options for summer jobs. One job is as a summer camp counsellor for 10-year-olds and takes place at your local community centre. The pay is $240.00 a week for a period of 6 weeks. The other job is working as a house painter. It would require you to commute to different locations and pays a rate of $11.50/h. You can work 8.5 weeks at this job.

   a) What factors would you consider in choosing between the two jobs?

   b) What additional information would you need to project your earnings from each job?

   c) Which job might involve working some overtime? Explain why.

   d) Under what circumstances would working overtime appeal to you? Why might you choose not to work overtime?

THE ROOTS OF MATH

THE MINIMUM WAGE IN CANADA

In Canada, there is a minimum wage that guarantees a minimum level of income for employees. The minimum wage is set by the provinces and territories and varies from one province or territory to another. Although the minimum wage is intended to guarantee a basic living wage for less skilled positions, there are several sectors in the economy, such as the service industry, where the minimum wage is the norm, no matter how much experience an individual has. The minimum wage is used as a benchmark for other wages. When the minimum wage rises in response to rising costs of living, other wages also rise.

Until the twentieth century, there was no minimum wage standard anywhere in Canada. Employers could offer people whatever wages they chose to. Many people who worked in factories or in service industries were paid at very low levels and worked very long hours to make enough money to survive.

In 1919, more than 30 000 workers took part in the Winnipeg General Strike to protest poor working conditions, lack of bargaining power, and low wages.

Achieving laws that require a minimum wage level was the work of tradespeople who joined together in trade unions in the late nineteenth century. They worked together to improve their working conditions and rates of pay. By 1912, 160 000 Canadians belonged to trade unions, and the first minimum wage legislation was passed in British Columbia and Manitoba in 1918. In 1920, Ontario, Quebec, Nova Scotia, and Saskatchewan passed minimum wage laws. Gradually, all the provinces and territories passed minimum wage laws. The last to do so was Prince Edward Island, in 1960.

While most provinces and territories state their minimum wage as an hourly rate, some also have weekly and monthly minimums. Alberta, for example, has a minimum weekly and a minimum monthly wage standard. These apply to certain types of jobs, such as salespeople and domestic workers.

1. What is the minimum wage in your province or territory? How does it compare to the rates in other provinces or territories?

2. What is the annual wage paid in your province or territory if someone earns the minimum wage and works 40 hours a week?

3. Do you think it is sensible to have laws that govern minimum wages?

2.2 Alternative Ways to Earn Money

MATH ON THE JOB

Carl Howard is a Red Seal carpenter, which means he is certified to work in any province or territory in Canada. He works as a kitchen cabinet installer on the Sunshine Coast in British Columbia. He is a **self-employed** journeyman who is paid on a **piecework** basis by the cabinet companies he works for.

In the piecework system used by one company, each installed cabinet is assigned a point value. For example, a standard upper or lower cabinet is worth one point. This includes hanging the cabinet and installing its door and hardware such as hinges and door handles. Larger cabinets are worth two points, for example, tall pantry cabinets. The toe kick for each lower cabinet is worth $\frac{1}{2}$ point and so is the crown moulding installed along the top of the upper cabinets. One point is assigned a dollar value, in this case, $16.00, and the whole kitchen installation payment is calculated by adding up the number of points and multiplying by the dollar value of a point.

If Carl installs a kitchen that contains 6 standard upper cabinets with crown moulding, a pantry cabinet with crown moulding and a toe kick, and 5 standard lower cabinets, each with a toe kick, how much will he be paid for installing that kitchen?

Carl must keep accurate records of his work to ensure he is paid correctly.

EXPLORE THE MATH

self-employed: a person who works for him- or herself rather than for an employer

piecework: when someone is paid a set rate for an amount produced

commission: an amount, usually a percentage, paid to someone for a business transaction

contract: a legal agreement that outlines terms, conditions, and payments for work to be done

Not every working person earns wages or a salary. What kinds of jobs do you think may be paid in each of the following ways:

- on a **commission** basis?
- with a base salary plus commission?
- by **piecework**?
- through a **contract**?

In piecework, people are paid according to the number of items they complete. For example, a person may deliver promotional flyers at five cents a flyer, or a berry-picker may pick organic raspberries for $0.65 a pound. The number that can be completed in an hour will determine the hourly amount earned.

A contract is an agreement between two or more parties that describes

64 MathWorks 10

the amount and type of work and the amount to be paid. There is often a schedule of payments, with payment at each stage of a job as it is completed. With a contract you get paid the same amount regardless of how many hours the job takes. Can you think of a situation where you would prefer to get paid by a contract amount rather than by the hour?

Self-employed people often work on a contract basis with their clients, and they may run their own businesses. What are some advantages and disadvantages of owning your own business?

ACTIVITY 2.3
PIECEWORK VERSUS HOURLY RATES

Work in small groups. Your flyer distribution business offers local stores a contract for delivering promotional flyers to a specified number of households. Four stores each pay you $0.08 per flyer to deliver flyers on a weekly basis, and you hire two people to work for you.

1. What method of payment would you offer your workers?

2. How would you determine whether a piecework rate or an hourly rate will lower your costs?

3. Write an algebraic formula you could use to calculate how much the four stores will pay you.

DISCUSS THE IDEAS
HOME RENOVATION CONTRACTS

You have a home renovation business that specializes in adapting existing homes for people with disabilities.

1. How would you calculate how much to charge customers for the renovations they are requesting?

2. If you bid on a contract with a price of $14 500.00 and your potential client requests a reduction of 8% to match a lower bid, what would your new bid be?

3. Would you consider making this reduction? Why or why not? What factors would you take into account?

Installing ramps makes homes more accessible for people who use wheelchairs.

4. What would you set as a payment schedule? What is your reasoning?

5. Why do you think the homeowner would prefer to pay on a contract basis rather than an hourly basis?

DISCUSS THE IDEAS
CUSTOM WORK

Artisans—craftspeople who specialize in decorative arts such as weaving and pottery—are often self-employed. They earn money by selling their crafts, including custom work. When a customer hires an artisan to produce a unique piece for an agreed-upon price, this is known as custom work.

A handwoven 100% wool Métis sash is one item that may be custom-made by an artisan. Manitoba, Saskatchewan, Alberta, and British Columbia have all created the Order of the Sash, which recognizes members of the Métis community and non-Métis people who have made cultural, political, or social contributions to the Métis people. Unique ceremonial sashes are given to recipients as part of their award.

1. If a weaver receives an order for 5 custom-made 196 cm sashes that cost $95.00 and 2 custom-made 224 cm sashes that cost $125.00, how much will the weaver earn, not including taxes?

A handwoven Métis sash.

2. If you compare the prices of the shorter and longer sashes, which length do you think earns the artisan more? What additional information do you need to accurately answer this question?

3. If a work is custom ordered and then the customer declines the finished piece, the artisan may choose to sell it at a discount. Estimate the price of a 224 cm sash if it is sold at a 15% discount.

Example 1

Manjit is a self-employed aesthetician. She offers European facials for $85.00 each. She sells skin-care products to her customers at an average markup of 45%. Customers who buy skin toners, protective creams, masks, and related products that total more than $95.00 receive a 20% discount on both the facial and the skin-care products.

a) How much does Manjit earn in half a day if she gives 3 facials and sells one customer moisturizers and skin creams totalling $125.00? Calculate her gross earnings, without taking into account her costs.

b) How much does Manjit earn from the sale of skin creams during this half day?

c) If all the customers had paid the full price for the same services and products, how much more would Manjit have earned? Would you advise her to offer the 20% discount? Why or why not?

SOLUTION

a) Calculate Manjit's earnings from the customer who takes advantage of the discount.

$$\$85.00 \times 0.80 = \$68.00$$

$$\$125.00 \times 0.80 = \$100.00$$

$$\$68.00 + \$100.00 = \$168.00$$

Total the income from all three customers.

$$\$85.00 + \$85.00 + \$168.00 = \$338.00$$

Manjit earns $338.00 during this half day.

b) $\$125.00 \times 0.8 = \$100.00$ Calculate what Manjit charges the customer after a 20% discount.

    $\$125.08 \div 1.45 = \$86.21$ Calculate Manjit's cost before markup.

    $\$100.00 - \$86.21 = \$13.79$ Subtract the costs from the discounted price.

Manjit earns $13.79 profit from the sale of the skin-care products.

c) $(\$85.00 \times 3) + \$125.00 = \$380.00$ Calculate the full-price option.

    $\$380.00 - \$338.00 = \$42.00$ Subtract the discounted rate from the full price.

Manjit would earn $42.00 more if she offered no discount. Offering the discount is probably worthwhile because customers are more likely to buy skin-care products if they get them at a discount. In addition, the markup on the products is high enough that Manjit still earns a profit after discounting them 20%.

Example 2

Gwen works as a sales clerk in a clothing store. She earns a base salary of $8.00/h plus a 15% commission on the price before taxes of each item she sells. Her work day is 8 hours. One day, Gwen sells a suit with a price of $625.00, a sweater priced at $95.00, 3 T-shirts that cost $45.00 each, and a raincoat priced at $225.00. How much does she earn that day?

SOLUTION

$8 \text{ h} \times \$8.00/\text{h} = \$64.00$ First, calculate Gwen's base salary.

$\$625.00 \times 0.15 = \$93.75$ Then calculate the commission on each item she sells. Convert the commission rate to a decimal.

$\$95.00 \times 0.15 = \$14.25$

$\$45.00 \times 0.15 \times 3 = \$20.25$

$\$225.00 \times 0.15 = \$33.75$

Add the commission amounts and the base salary to find her total earnings for the day.

$\$64.00 + \$93.75 + \$14.25 + \$20.25 + \$33.75 = \$226.00$

Gwen earns $226.00 that day.

ALTERNATIVE SOLUTION

Alternatively, you could add the prices of all the items together and multiply by 0.15, then add that amount to the base salary.

Example 3

Hien is a painting contractor. He negotiates a contract with a homeowner to paint the exterior siding on a house at a rate of $30.00/h plus the cost of materials. It takes Hien six 8-hour days to prepare and paint the siding, and he uses 15 gallons of paint that cost $45.00 each. What is the total value of the contract?

SOLUTION

First, calculate the value of Hien's time.

$6 \times 8 \times \$30.00 = \$1440.00$ Multiply the number of days by the number of hours per day and then by the amount per hour.

Hien's time on this job is worth $1440.00.

Next, calculate the cost of materials.

$15 \times \$45.00 = \$675.00$ Multiply the number of gallons of paint by the price of one gallon.

The cost of materials is $675.00.

Add the two amounts to find the total price.

$1440.00 + $675.00 = $2115.00

The total value of the contract is $2115.00.

Mental Math and Estimation

Jagdish earns $800.00 a week as an autobody technician. His work week is 40 hours. If he works only 35 hours one week, how much will he get paid?

BUILD YOUR SKILLS

1. Suggest two benefits self-employed people might enjoy. Suggest two disadvantages of self-employment. On balance, would you prefer to be self-employed? Why or why not?

2. Ginpon, an aluminum fabricator in Richmond, BC, accepts a contract to make an aluminum gate for $500.00.

   a) If the cost of materials and labour to make the gate is $425.00, how much is his profit on this gate?

   b) What is this amount expressed as a percentage of the contract?

   c) If the cost of materials were to increase after the contract was signed, could Ginpon adjust the price? Explain your reasoning.

3. Leo is a self-employed plumber. One month, his plumbing business had three contracts for $2500.00, $7000.00, and $275.00. The cost of Leo's expenses and materials to complete these contracts was $7200.00.

   a) How much did Leo earn an hour based on a 40-hour work week?

   b) Suggest two ways in which Leo could raise his hourly rate to $20.00.

4. Ling works as an assistant to a florist. She can be paid $2.75 for every arrangement or $13.25/h. Ling estimates she could create about five arrangements an hour. Which payment scheme would you recommend and why?

One of a plumber's tasks is to remove roots from drains with a snake.

Chapter 2 Earning an Income 69

5. Marlene is a website designer. In January, she creates a website for a new client, charging $13 000.00. Marlene bids on and obtains a maintenance contract for the balance of the year that will pay her $200.00/month, beginning in February.

   a) How much will the maintenance contract be worth?

   b) How many hours a month do you think would be reasonable to spend on website maintenance, given the contract amount?

   c) How much will Marlene earn this year from this client?

Website designers often work on a contract basis.

6. William is a salesperson at an electrical supply company. He earns a base salary of $24 000.00 a year plus a commission of 12% on electrical supplies such as wire, switches, and fixtures. If William aims to earn a total of $32 000.00 a year, how many dollars' worth of electrical supplies will he need to sell?

7. Dorothy, a cabinet installer, earns income on a piecework basis. When she has to return to a customer's home on a service call to make changes or repairs, she is paid by the hour. The service-call rate is $30.00 an hour.

   a) If Dorothy installs 6 upper cabinets at a rate of $15.00 each, 6 lower cabinets at a rate of $15.00 each, and returns twice for service calls that each take 3 hours, how much will she earn in all from this job?

   b) Think of two ways that piecework benefits a working person.

   c) What advantages or disadvantages might piecework have for an employer?

Extend your thinking

8. You are a painting contractor who has been asked to provide a quote for painting the living room in a customer's home. The room has a fireplace and a glass patio door. The fireplace and marble mantel is 1.75 m wide and is as high as the room. The patio door is 3.5 m wide and extends from floor to ceiling.

   a) What measurements would you need to take?

   b) What other calculations are involved in producing the quote?

   c) Write two formulas, one for calculating total costs and one for calculating percentage of profit.

PUZZLE IT OUT

A WEIRD WILL

A wealthy lawyer owned 11 expensive cars. When he died, he left a weird will. It asked that his 11 cars be divided among his three sons in a particular way. Half of the cars were to go to the eldest son, one-fourth to his middle son, and one-sixth to the youngest.

Everybody was puzzled. How can 11 cars be divided in such a way?

While the sons were arguing about what to do, a mathematics teacher drove up in her new sports car.

"Can I be of help?" she asked.

The teacher used her sports car and her math skills to help the three sons.

After the sons explained the situation, she parked her sports car next to the lawyer's 11 cars and hopped out. "How many cars are there now?" The sons counted 12.

Then she carried out the terms of the will. She gave half of the cars, 6, to the oldest son. The middle son got one-fourth of 12, or 3. The youngest son got one-sixth of 12, or 2.

"6 plus 3 plus 2 is 11. So, one car is left over, and that's my car."

She jumped into her sports car and drove off. "Glad to be of service!"

Can you solve a similar will with 17 cars?

2.3 Additional Earnings

MATH ON THE JOB

Emiko works for an art gallery that sells works of art such as sculptures, paintings, photographs, and prints and also rents them to businesses and individuals to decorate their offices and homes. Emiko took a certificate course in business administration at a college, specializing in marketing.

Emiko advises corporate and private clients on art rentals and promotes her gallery's collection. She maintains a computerized database of artists her gallery represents. This database contains biographical information about the artists and records of the works the gallery carries for rental and sale.

Emiko earns a base salary of $26 000.00 a year, but she is able to earn extra money when she makes sales. Emiko's employer pays her a **bonus** of 15% of the first month's rental whenever she signs up a new client for a long-term rental. She also receives a bonus of 3% of the sale price when a rented work is sold outright to a client.

These alabaster beluga whales were carved by Joe and Sam Ashoona, Inuit carvers who live in Yellowknife.

If Emiko arranges a rental of an Inuit stone carving with a new client and the rental rate is $60.00/month, what will Emiko's bonus be? If the customer later decides to purchase the carving for $4250.00, what bonus will Emiko earn?

EXPLORE THE MATH

bonus: extra pay earned when certain conditions of employment have been met or exceeded

shift premium: extra payment for non-standard work hours

In certain jobs, people earn additional money beyond their basic wage or salary. You might have contributed to these additional earnings. If you have a pizza delivered, do you tip the delivery person? When you get a great haircut, do you give the hairdresser a tip to show your appreciation? It is common for people in service industry jobs to earn tips from satisfied customers.

Another form of additional earnings that is often related to job performance is a bonus. For example, employers may pay bonuses to staff who exceed sales targets or sign up new customers.

Some people earn extra money based on their work environment or the time of day they work. People who work in remote areas might earn an isolation allowance. People who work in potentially dangerous situations, such as members of the armed forces, may earn danger pay. If you work non-standard hours, your employer might pay you a **shift premium**. What hours would be considered non-standard? Can you think of jobs in which shift premiums might be paid? How else might employees earn money in addition to their basic rate of pay?

ACTIVITY 2.4
A BABYSITTING SERVICE

For the summer months, you have decided to work at a neighbourhood babysitting service. The service requires you to have your Red Cross babysitting certification and to provide your own transportation to the clients' homes. When you work between the hours of 08:00 am and 5:00 pm, you earn $10.00 an hour. You receive a shift premium of an additional $1.50 an hour for every hour you work beyond the standard hours. You can also earn a $7.00 bonus each shift if you ensure your client's house is tidy before you leave.

The job doesn't pay overtime. You can work up to 10 hours a day. You are able to work two shifts in a day, but only if there's at least an hour break between them.

WEEKLY SHIFT SCHEDULE

Client	Monday	Tuesday	Wednesday	Thursday	Friday
Bains	12:00 pm – 4:00 pm	8:00 am – 12:00 pm	8:00 am – 12:00 pm	8:00 am – 12:00 pm	8:00 am – 12:00 pm
Mitchel	10:00 am – 2:00 pm	10:00 am – 4:00 pm	10:00 am – 2:00 pm	9:00 am – 3:00 pm	10:00 am – 2:00 pm
St. Germaine			4:00 pm – 6:00 pm	8:00 am – 6:00 pm	
Longriver	8:30 am – 4:30 pm	8:30 am – 4:30 pm	8:30 am – 4:30 pm	8:30 am – 4:30 pm	8:30 am – 4:30 pm
Lee	7:00 am – 11:00 am	3:00 pm – 5:00 pm	7:00 am – 11:00 am	7:00 am – 11:00 am	

1. What is the most money you can earn on a Monday?

2. What's the most money you can earn in a week?

3. If you only want to work 20 hours a week, which shifts would you choose? How much would you earn from these shifts?

4. What expenses might you ask the babysitting service to pay for?

5. On Wednesday you earned $68.50. You worked one shift premium hour and earned one bonus. Which shifts might you have worked?

DISCUSS THE IDEAS
EARNING TIPS

People who work in restaurants usually earn some of their income in the form of tips, often paid in addition to the minimum wage. Because many people's first jobs are as servers, this is an important type of income to understand. Many people also make a lifelong career in the restaurant industry. Consider the following questions about income from tips.

Servers often share tips with kitchen staff.

1. Your restaurant gives 5% of the tips received in a shift to employees working in the kitchen. If $2100.00 is received in tips, and there are 5 people working in the kitchen, how much will each person receive?

2. You worked a four-hour shift as a server and your customer bills totalled $2500.00 before tips. Your rate of pay is $8.75/h.

   a) If all your customers tipped you 10%, how much did you earn an hour in wages and tips?

   b) If all your customers tipped you 15%, how much did you earn an hour in wages and tips?

   c) If all your customers tipped you 20%, how much did you earn an hour in wages and tips?

3. Do you think certain working hours would be better for earning tips? Which hours? Why?

Example 1

Kyle works in a bookstore selling books. He also sells customers reward cards for $30.00 that will give them a discount on future purchases. His employer gives him a bonus of 10% of the amount received if he sells more than 20 cards in a month. If his regular wages are $1883.77 and he sells 27 reward cards one month, what will Kyle's wages be including the bonus?

SOLUTION

Find the bonus amount.

$30.00 × 27 = $810.00   Multiply the cost of one card by the number of cards sold.

$810.00 × 0.10 = $81.00   Find 10% of the total sales amount.

$81.00 + $1883.77 = $1964.77

Kyle will earn $1964.77.

Example 2

Jacob works as a stock clerk for a grocery store in Moose Jaw, SK. His regular pay is $12.00 an hour, but he earns a shift premium of $2.00 an hour for any hours he works between 5:00 pm and 8:00 am. Jacob also earns 1.5 times his pay rate in overtime for any hours he works above 35 hours a week. His timesheet is shown below.

A stock clerk refills grocery shelves with fresh produce as needed.

a) What percentage of Jacob's weekly hours are regular hours?

b) What percentage of his weekly earnings are paid at the regular rate?

Monday	Tuesday	Wednesday	Thursday	Friday	Saturday
12:00 am – 8:00 am	12:00 am – 8:00 am	4:00 pm – 12:00 am	6:00 am – 11:00 am	6:00 am – 11:00 am	8:00 am – 3:00 pm

SOLUTION

a) Calculate the percentage of regular hours Jacob worked this week.

   8 h ÷ 41 h = 0.195   Divide the number of regular hours by the total hours Jacob worked.

   19.5% of Jacob's hours were at the regular rate.

b) First, calculate the percentage of Jacob's earnings that were at the regular rate.

   8 h × $12.00/h = $96.00   Calculate Jacob's regular pay.

   6 h × $18.00/h = $108.00   Calculate his overtime pay.

   27 h × $14.00/h = $378.00 Calculate his shift premiums.

   $96.00 + $108.00 + $378.00 = $582.00

   $96.00 ÷ $582.00 = 0.165   Divide the amount Jacob earned at his regular rate by his total earnings.

   16.5% of Jacob's weekly earnings will be paid at his regular rate.

   Why do you think the percentage of regular rate earnings is different from the percentage of regular hours worked?

ALTERNATIVE SOLUTION

Calculate the percentages by graphing them on pie charts.

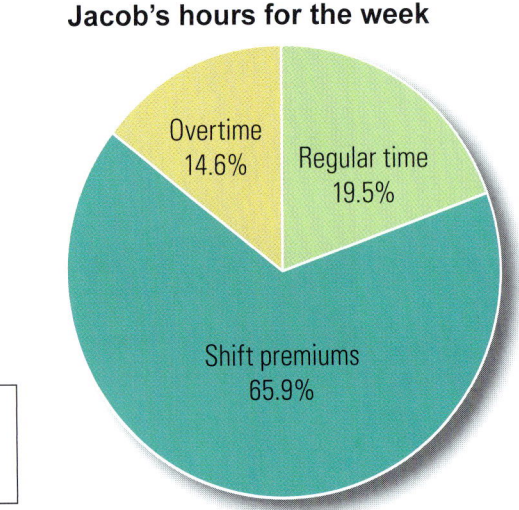

Jacob's hours for the week

- Overtime 14.6%
- Regular time 19.5%
- Shift premiums 65.9%

Jacob's earnings for the week

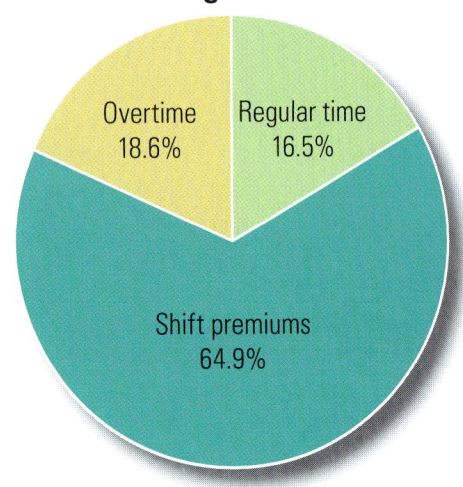

- Overtime 18.6%
- Regular time 16.5%
- Shift premiums 64.9%

Legend:
- Regular time
- Shift premiums
- Overtime

19.5% of Jacob's hours were at the regular rate.

16.5% of Jacob's weekly earnings will be paid at his regular rate.

BUILD YOUR SKILLS

1. Julia was a participant in the Department of National Defence's RAVEN program for Aboriginal youth. Now, she is a naval weapons technician in the Canadian Armed Forces. Julia is posted to a war zone and will earn $1900.00/month in danger pay on top of her annual salary of $51 250.00.

    a) What will her annual salary be, including danger pay?

    b) What will her monthly pay be?

2. David works as a dishwasher at a private club. He receives 1% of the tips collected in the club during his shift. If the total amount of tips collected is $760.00, how much will David's portion be?

3. Tristan works as a restaurant server. He is paid $8.50/h and works a 5-hour shift, 4 days a week. On a typical day, his customer bills total $650.00 before tips, and almost every customer tips him 15%. Estimate how much Tristan will earn in wages and tips in 4 weeks.

4. Layla works as a barista, someone who makes and serves coffee in a specialty coffee shop. She earns the minimum wage of $8.00 an hour, as well as an equal share of any tips that customers leave in a jar by the till.

76 MathWorks 10

a) Develop a formula to figure out Layla's gross earnings in a shift, including tips.

b) During Layla's 6-hour shift, the total in tips is $53.62. There are three people working at the time. Layla determines that she earned $68.21 for that shift. Is she correct?

5. Ivan gets an annual bonus of 15% of his base salary if he exceeds sales quotas by $10 000.00. If his base salary is $42 000.00 and he exceeds the sales quota by the required amount, what is his bonus? What is his total salary for that year?

6. Francis applies for a job as a commercial transport inspector in Tête Jaune, BC. He receives a starting salary of $38 901.76 and an isolation allowance. If Francis grosses $41 610.52 for the year, what would his monthly isolation allowance be?

7. Rishma works as a security guard at Watson Lake Airport, YT. Her regular work shift is 3:00 pm to 11:00 pm. At this airport, a shift premium of $2.00 an hour is paid on any hours worked between 5:00 pm and 8:00 am.

a) For how many hours per shift is Rishma paid a shift premium?

b) If Rishma's regular hourly rate of pay is $17.36, how much is her gross pay for one shift?

c) If Rishma works 5 days a week, what percentage of her weekly wage is at the shift premium rate?

d) What percentage of her weekly schedule is regular hours?

Extend your thinking

8. Rosa is a community wellness nurse in Fort Simpson, NT. She attends a meeting of the Deh Cho Health & Social Services Authority in Fort Providence. To attend the meeting, she drives her own car 325.3 km. Her employer will reimburse her at a rate of $0.605/km.

a) How much will Rosa receive as reimbursement for her trip?

b) Is this fair compensation for the use of your own car for work? Why or why not? What factors would you consider?

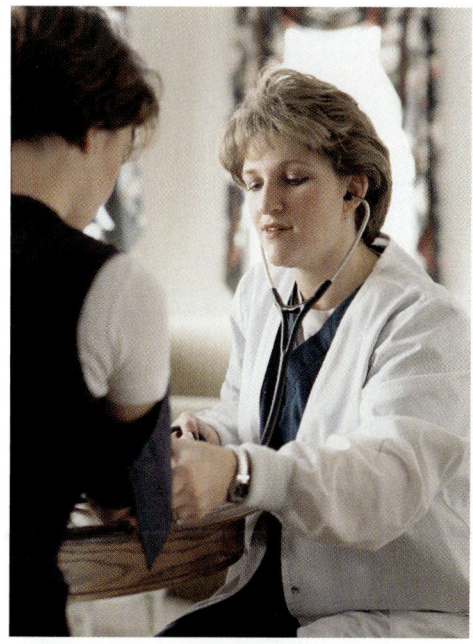

This home-care nurse travels to her patients. She must keep a record of her travel so that she can request reimbursement from her employer.

PROJECT—A PAYROLL PLAN FOR A SUMMER BUSINESS

PREPARING A PAYROLL POLICY

Earlier, you wrote a paragraph describing your plans for the number of staff you plan to hire and how much you will pay them. You have now learned more about how income is calculated and about extra payments working people may earn. Do you want to revise your paragraph, considering what you have learned?

You will now add some more information to your project file.

- Develop a formula that describes your regular payroll costs for a week. If you decided to include an on-call person, don't include that person's wages because his or her hours will vary.

- Write a short policy memo to your employees so they understand what their income will be, what benefits you will offer, if any, and whether the rate of pay will change if they work weekend or overtime hours. Include the following items:

  - the regular work day hours and the days they will work;
  - the regular hourly rate of pay (the minimum wage for your province or territory);
  - overtime rate, if you have one, and which hours it will be paid for; and
  - a list of any benefits that you will offer.

You might need to provide employees with safety equipment or tools.

Deductions and Net Pay

2.4

MATH *ON THE JOB*

Eric works as an administrative assistant at a mining company. He has a certificate in business administration from a college. At work, Eric does a variety of financial transactions, including the payroll for the company employees. Eric has to calculate the gross wages of each person and then subtract deductions for government programs, such as income tax, the Canada Pension Plan, and Employment Insurance, and for company programs, such as a dental plan. Eric relies on the Canada Revenue Agency instructions for calculating these amounts.

Eric also has to deduct union dues from the employees' paycheques. If an employee earns $32.50/h, works 40 h/week, pays 2.4% in union dues, and is paid weekly, how much are the weekly union dues? What is the hourly rate?

Eric has to calculate a number of deductions from the miners' wages, including union dues.

EXPLORE THE MATH

As you learned earlier, the total amount of money a person earns at his or her job is called gross pay. Working people are not usually paid their gross pay, however. Instead, they take home their **net pay**. Net pay refers to the amount left after certain deductions have been made by an employer.

net pay: also known as take-home pay; refers to the money paid to an employee after deductions have been made

Look at the pay statement shown here. What categories of deductions are made from gross pay?

Employee Name: Hermione			
Company:	Pay Begin Date: 09/08/2010		Net Pay:
	Pay End Date: 15/08/2010		Cheque Date: 16/08/2010

General	
Employee ID:	**Job Title:** Appliance Repair Apprentice
Address: 123 Main Street Dawson City, YT	Pay Rate: $650.00/wk Annual: $33 800.00

Taxes Data	
Description	Federal
Claim Code	1

Hours and Earnings			
	Current		
Description	Rate	Gross Earnings	
Regular	$650.00/wk	$650.00	

Before-Tax Deductions	
Description	Amt.
Union Dues	$14.10
Pension	$20.50
Total	$34.60

Taxes	
Description	Amt.
Federal	$61.15
Provincial	$28.70
CPP	$28.43
EI	$11.25
Total	$129.53

Chapter 2 Earning an Income 79

Based on the amounts deducted for union dues and pensions, what percentage of Hermione's gross pay does she pay in union dues and what percentage does she contribute to a pension?

Do you think deductions are the same for everyone? Why or why not?

Look in the Taxes portion of the pay statement. What do CPP and EI stand for? Why do most working Canadians contribute to these plans?

The federal and provincial deductions on the pay statement are income tax payments. The amount of income tax you pay varies according to your personal circumstances and the province/territory in which you live.

When you begin a new job, your employer requires you to complete a TD1 form (Personal Tax Credits Return) to determine the amount of income tax you should pay. From your TD1 exemption claims, you determine your claim code, which your employer uses to calculate your tax deductions. Many people are only able to claim the basic personal exemption, which is TD1 claim code 1.

benefits: a range of programs that benefit employees; these vary from employer to employer

In addition to paying taxes, many people pay amounts from their gross pay for a wide range of **benefits** and programs, such as dental plans and savings plans.

What are some pros and cons for having deductions like these made directly from your paycheque?

When all deductions have been made, the amount remaining—the net pay—is paid to the employee.

DISCUSS THE IDEAS
LIFESTYLE BENEFITS

Some workplaces provide lifestyle benefits to their employees that are connected to the nature of the business or organization. For example, educational institutions may offer free tuition to their employees for courses they offer. What other lifestyle benefits might be offered to employees, for example, at a ski resort or a golf course?

You have a 16-week contract as a lift operator at Marmot Basin in Jasper, and you will be working between 12 and 20 hours a week. Your employer offers you a choice in how you are paid: a straight wage of $10.50/h or $8.50/h plus a weekday season pass that has a value of $679.00. Which one would you choose? What factors would you consider in your choice?

People sometimes choose a job because of its attractive lifestyle benefits.

ACTIVITY 2.5
PROS AND CONS OF DEDUCTIONS

Work in pairs for this activity. If all workers received their gross pay without any deductions, what might the consequences be? Construct a table that shows the pros and cons of contributing to the Canada Pension Plan and Employment Insurance and paying federal and provincial/territorial taxes.

Example 1

You need to calculate the Canada Pension Plan deduction for Amanda, whose pay statement is shown here. In 2008, the CPP contribution rate was 4.95% of any gross earnings above $3500.00.

Employee Name: Amanda					
Company:	Pay Begin Date: 08/17/2008			Net Pay:	
	Pay End Date: 08/23/2008			Cheque Date:	

General			
Employee ID:		Job Title:	
Address: 123 Main St. Cochrane, AB		Pay Rate: $500.00/wk Annual: $26 000.00	

Taxes Data	
Description	Federal
Claim Code	1

Hours and Earnings		
	Current	
Description	Rate	Gross Earnings
Regular	$500.00/wk	$500.00

Before-Tax Deductions	
Description	Amt.
Union Dues	
Pension	
Total	

Taxes	
Description	
Federal	
Provincial	
CPP	?
EI	
Total	

SOLUTION

First find the basic pay-period exemption that applies in this case.

$3500.00 ÷ 52 weeks = $67.31

$500.00 − $67.31 = $432.69   Subtract the basic exemption from the gross pay.

$432.69 × 0.0495 = $21.42   Multiply by the CPP contribution rate.

The CPP deduction is $21.42.

ALTERNATIVE SOLUTIONS

There are several other ways to find the amounts of the CPP deduction. The Canada Revenue Agency has an online calculator that employers may use. It also publishes a series of payroll deduction tables that employers may consult, electronically and on paper. Employers may also use specialized computer software that has built-in deduction formulas that calculate deductions automatically, once the basic exemption and payroll procedures are entered.

Example 2

Referring to Amanda's pay statement on p. 81, calculate the Employment Insurance premium that will be deducted from her weekly pay. In 2008, the EI premium rate was 1.73% of gross earnings.

SOLUTION

$500.00 × 0.0173 = $8.65   Multiply the insurable earnings by the EI premium rate.

The EI deduction will be $8.65.

ALTERNATIVE SOLUTIONS

As outlined in Example 1, the Canada Revenue Agency provides several tools that can assist employers to find the deduction amounts. Information on methods of calculating EI premiums can be found at www.cra-arc.gc.ca/tx/bsnss/tpcs/pyrll/clcltng/ei/menu-eng.html.

Example 3

> **HINT**
>
> Remember that you need to select the income tax tables for the province or territory discussed in each problem.
>
> The CRA website is at http://www.cra-arc.gc.ca/
>
> Select "Payroll" under the "Business" heading and then select "Payroll Deductions Online Calculator."

a) Calculate the amount of income tax to deduct from Amanda's paycheque. Her TD1 claim code is 1, and she lives in Alberta.

b) Calculate her net pay.

c) Fill in all the deductions that will be entered on her pay statement.

SOLUTION

a) First, find the online Payroll Deductions Tables for your province or territory on the Canada Revenue Agency website. In this example, we use the Alberta Payroll Deduction Tables effective January 1, 2008.

b) Look up two amounts in the tables, a federal amount and a provincial amount. Use the amount ($500.00), the pay period (weekly), and the TD1 claim code (1) to locate the amount of tax to deduct.

Federal tax payable is $40.15.

Provincial tax payable is $15.90.

Subtract CPP, EI, and federal and provincial taxes from the gross wages.

$500.00 − $21.42 − $8.65 − $40.15 − $15.90 = $413.88

Amanda's net pay will be $413.88.

c)

Employee Name: Amanda				
Company:	Pay Begin Date: 08/17/2008		Net Pay: $413.88	
	Pay End Date: 08/23/2008		Cheque Date: 08/23/2008	

General			
Employee ID:		Job Title:	
Address: 123 Main St. Cochrane, AB		Pay Rate: $500.00/wk Annual: $26 000.00	

Taxes Data	
Description	Federal
Claim Code	1

Hours and Earnings		
	Current	
Description	Rate	Gross Earnings
Regular	$500.00/wk	$500.00

Taxes	
Description	**Current**
Federal	$40.15
Provincial	$15.90
CPP	$21.42
EI	$8.65
Total	$86.12

ALTERNATIVE SOLUTIONS

You can also calculate the federal and provincial/territorial income tax amounts manually by looking up the percentage rates in the tax tables and multiplying by the income amount. The Canada Revenue Agency also has an online calculator available at www.cra.gc.ca/pdoc. Many businesses use software that automates the calculation of government deductions.

Mental Math and Estimation

You know that all your deductions add up to approximately 38% of your gross pay and you earn $950.00 a week. Estimate what your net pay will be.

ACTIVITY 2.6
COMPARING DEDUCTIONS

Francine, a cook who worked in a diner in Aubigny, MB, moved to Fort McMurray, AB to work as a cook on an oil rig. In Aubigny she earned $427.00 a week. In Fort McMurray she earned $2300.00 a month. She was paid twice monthly at both jobs.

a) For each job, calculate her gross pay for each pay period. Then use the payroll deductions online calculator to determine deductions for CPP, EI, and federal and provincial taxes. What was her net pay at each job?

b) On two blank pay statements, fill in all the relevant information for both jobs: gross earnings, all deductions, and net pay.

c) How much more did Francine pay in taxes at the Alberta job?

This cook is preparing desserts for a work crew.

Example 4

taxable income: income on which federal and provincial/territorial tax is paid

Some benefit deductions are not taxable. For example, union dues and pension contributions are not **taxable income**.

a) In the pay statement shown on p. 85, what is the person's taxable income?

b) How much income tax will he or she pay?

c) Using the CPP and EI amounts from Examples 1 and 2 and the income tax amount in this example, find the net pay. Assume the TD1 claim code is 1, the province is British Columbia, and the tax tables were from January 2008.

Employee Name:					
Company:	Pay Begin Date: 08/17/2008			Net Pay: $413.88	
	Pay End Date: 08/23/2008			Cheque Date: 08/23/2008	

General

Employee ID:		Job Title:	
Address:		Pay Rate: $500.00/wk	
		Annual: $26 000.00	

Taxes Data

Description	Federal
Claim Code	1

Hours and Earnings

		Current
Description	Rate	Gross Earnings
Regular	$500.00/wk	$500.00

Before-Tax Deductions

Description	Amt.
Union Dues	$1.38
Pension	$43.00
Total	?

Taxes

Description	Current
Federal	?
Provincial	?
CPP	?
EI	?
Total	?

Paycheque Summary

Gross Earnings	Taxable Gross	Total Taxes, CPP, and EI	Total Deductions	Net Pay
$500.00	?	?	?	?

SOLUTION

a) $500.00 − $1.38 − $43.00 = $455.62   Subtract the benefit deductions from the gross income.

The taxable income is $455.62.

b) Look up the taxable income in the federal and provincial tax tables (remember to use the British Columbia tax tables for this example).

The federal tax is $33.40.

The provincial tax is $10.40.

c) Subtract the CPP, EI, and income tax from the taxable income to find the net pay.

$455.62 − $2.42 − $8.65 − $33.40 − $10.40 = $400.75

The net pay is $400.75.

ALTERNATIVE SOLUTIONS

As was the case in the other examples in this section, the Canada Revenue Agency provides a number of tools to assist people in calculating government deductions.

PROJECT—A PAYROLL PLAN FOR A SUMMER BUSINESS

CREATING A PAY STATEMENT

It is time to calculate the deductions that will reduce your employees' weekly gross pay.

Create a spreadsheet or table to record your calculations and add it to your project file. Assume that your employees, who are likely fellow students, will have a TD1 claim code of 1.

Include the following items:

- gross pay for each employee;
- deductions for CPP, EI, and income tax;
- net pay; and
- a totals column for each category of deduction.

T Now, design a sample weekly pay statement that lists gross pay, deduction amounts, and net pay. You can use a spreadsheet or other layout software to create this statement.

Employee Name:			
Company:	Pay Begin Date:		Net Pay:
	Pay End Date:		Cheque Date:

General

Employee ID:	Job Title:
Address:	Pay Rate:
	Annual:

Taxes

Description	Current
Federal Tax	
Provincial Tax	
CPP	
EI	
Income Tax	
Total	

Hours and Earnings

Description	Rate	Hours	Gross Earnings

SAMPLE

Paycheque Summary

	Gross Earnings	Total Deductions	Net Pay

86   MathWorks 10

BUILD YOUR SKILLS

1. What is the difference between taxable income and gross income?

2. Two friends work similar jobs at two different companies. One gets paid $1458.00 twice a month and the other one gets paid $1346.00 biweekly.

   a) Which person has a higher annual salary?

   b) In what ways would their payroll deductions differ?

3. Lianne is paid $750.00 biweekly for her part-time job as a dental assistant. Explain how you can determine what her EI premium will be.

4. Helen is paid $3170.06 semi-monthly. She pays deductions of $17.12 for union dues and $126.40 for the company pension plan.

   a) What is her taxable income?

   b) Explain which is higher, her taxable income or her net pay.

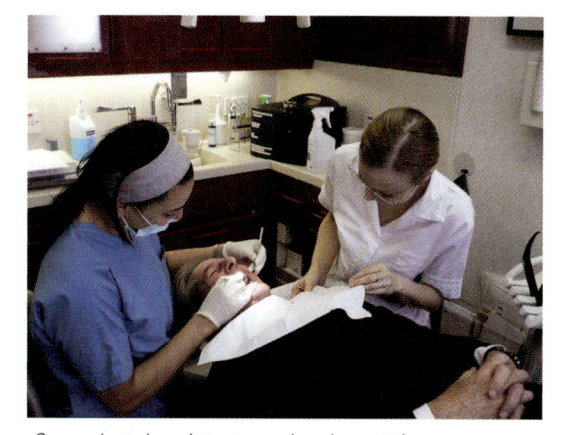

5. Amber works as a cashier and earns $960.00 biweekly. Each pay period, her employer deducts $69.50 for federal tax, $21.91 for provincial tax, and 1.73% for EI premiums. The CPP contribution rate is 4.95%, and the CPP annual exemption is $3500.00. What is Amber's net pay?

Some dental assistants work only part time.

6. Ruaridgh is a boat salesperson. He works part-time at a marina in Prince Rupert, BC where he earns $2500.00 a month, paid monthly. He has a second part-time job at another marina nearby on the Skeena River, where he earns $2500.00 a month, paid semi-monthly. His TD1 claim code is 1. (See Hint on p. 82.)

   a) What will Ruaridgh's monthly CPP deduction be for each job?

   b) What will his monthly EI premiums be?

   c) How much income tax will be deducted monthly from Ruaridgh's earnings from both his jobs?

   d) What is his net pay each month?

7. Pierre earns $3461.54 a month, paid semi-monthly. Each pay period, his employer deducts $172.98 federal tax, $69.82 territorial tax, $78.45 for CPP, and 1.73% for EI premiums. Pierre drives his car to work, so he purchased an annual staff parking permit for $750.00. He pays for the permit by monthly payroll deductions, which are made at the end of each month.

a) On the 15th of last month, Pierre's take-home pay was $1379.58. Was he paid the correct amount? Explain how you know.

b) On the 31st of last month, Pierre's take-home pay was $1254.58. Was he paid the correct amount? Explain how you know.

Extend your thinking

8. Gerry's employer has a dental plan for employees that covers Gerry, his spouse, and their child. The dental plan will pay 100% for routine checkups and cleaning and basic procedures such as fillings. It pays 70% for a crown and 65% for braces. One year, the following dental work is done:
   - each member of the family has a routine checkup and cleaning that costs $165.00 for each person;
   - Gerry gets a crown that costs $900.00; and
   - the child has a filling that costs $125.00 and gets braces that cost $4250.00.

   a) How much is the total bill?

   b) What amount will the insurance company pay?

PROJECT—A PAYROLL PLAN FOR A SUMMER BUSINESS

MAKE A PRESENTATION

You are now ready to gather your information and documents and prepare a final presentation.

T Compile the materials you have prepared in a business-like presentation folder or binder or create a slideshow using presentation software. Be sure to include the following items:

- a paragraph that outlines your plan;
- **T** a spreadsheet or a table that contains a list of positions, the gross pay of each employee, deductions, and net pay, with a total payroll amount for the pay period;
- an equation that describes your regular weekly payroll costs;
- a sample pay statement for one employee, with a list of deduction amounts and a statement of net pay; and
- a memo you have written to your staff that describes the payroll policies.

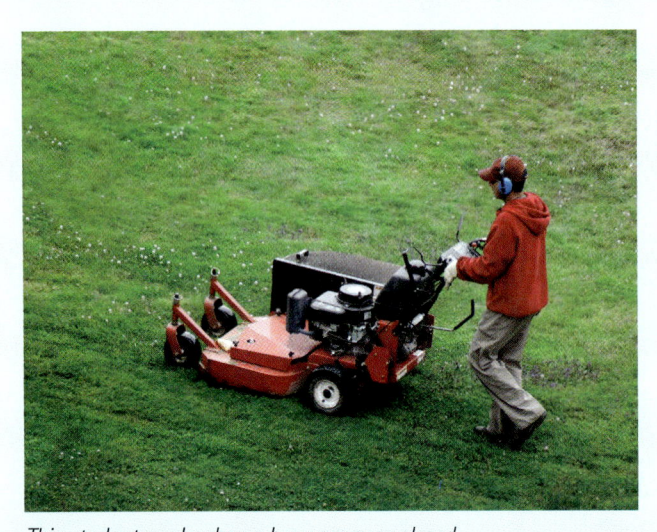

This student worker has a busy summer ahead.

REFLECT ON YOUR LEARNING

EARNING AN INCOME

Now that you have finished this chapter, you should be able to

- ❐ calculate gross pay given a rate of pay and amount of time worked;

- ❐ calculate total time worked from a weekly work schedule;

- ❐ describe various methods of earning income and give examples of jobs that fall into different categories;

- ❐ calculate earnings that combine a base salary plus commissions, bonuses, or tips;

- ❐ calculate income based on piecework;

- ❐ describe the advantages and disadvantages of a given method of earning an income, such as contract work, piecework, salary, or commission;

- ❐ determine CPP, EI, and income tax deductions for a given gross pay and calculate the net pay.

In addition, you have completed a project in which you have produced pay statements and payroll deductions in the context of a summer business.

PRACTISE YOUR NEW SKILLS

1. Tiffany works in a clothing store in Calgary. She earns $1454.88 gross pay each month. If she works 40 hours a week, how much is her hourly rate?

2. The dining room at the faculty club at the University of Saskatchewan in Saskatoon has 5 waiters on a Thursday dinner shift and 6 on a Friday dinner shift. Their hourly wages are $9.50 and they work 7 hours on Thursday and 6 hours on Friday. If the total tips are $225.50 on Thursday and $310.00 on Friday, on which night will the waiters earn more? Explain the steps in your solution.

3. Alex works as a crane operator in Langley, BC. His hourly rate of pay is $21.00 and his regular work week is 40 hours.

    a) If he works an extra 8-hour shift on Canada Day and his overtime rate is time and a half, what are his gross earnings for the holiday?

    b) How much more is this than a regular day's pay?

4. Henri is a self-employed bricklayer. One month he had four contracts for $1100.00, $4500.00, $2600.00, and $925.00. The cost of materials was $3850.00 and wages for himself and his part-time assistant were $3200.00.

   a) How much did the business earn for the month?

   b) What are these earnings expressed as a percentage of the total contracts?

   c) With this percentage of earnings, is this business likely to succeed? Explain.

5. Pierrette works as a salesperson in a car dealership in Kelowna, BC. She gets paid a base salary plus commission on each vehicle she sells. The commission is 25% of the profit the company makes on the sale. If Pierrette sells a new vehicle on which the markup was $3500.00 but the customer negotiates $1500.00 off the list price, how much commission will Pierrette earn?

6. Explain what information you need in order to calculate a person's net pay. What tools and/or equipment would you use to do the calculations?

7. Use the portions of the federal and provincial tax deductions tables shown here to answer these questions.

Federal tax deductions
Effective January 1, 2008
Biweekly (26 pay periods a year)
Also look up the tax deductions in the provincial table

Pay Rémunération From Less than De Moins de		0	1	2	3	4	5	6
						Deduct from each pay Retenez sur chaque paie		
1088 -	1104	148.55	93.15	87.60	76.50	65.40	54.30	4
1104 -	1120	150.80	95.40	89.85	78.75	67.65	56.55	4
1312 -	1328	179.90	124.50	118.95	107.85	96.75	85.65	7
1328 -	1344	182.15	126.75	121.20	110.10	99.00	87.90	7
1344 -	1360	184.35	129.00	123.45	112.35	101.25	90.15	7
1360 -	1376	186.60	131.25	125.70	114.60	103.50	92.40	8
1376 -	1392	188.85	133.45	127.90	116.80	105.70	94.60	8
1392 -	1408	191.10	135.70	130.15	119.05	107.95	96.85	
1408 -	1424	193.35	137.95	132.40	121.30	110.20	99.10	
1424 -	1440	195.55	140.20	134.65	123.55	112.45	101.35	
1440 -	1456	197.80	142.45	136.90	125.80	114.70	103.60	
1456 -	1472	200.55	145.15	139.60	128.50	117.40	106.30	
1472 -	1488	203.90	148.50	142.95	131.85	120.75	109.65	

Alberta provincial tax deductions
Effective January 1, 2008
Biweekly (26 pay periods a year)
Also look up the tax deductions in the federal table

Pay Rémunération From – Less than De – Moins de	0	1	2	3	4	5
1316 – 1332	124.20	62.05	57.50	48.45	39.35	30.25
1332 – 1348	125.70	63.55	59.00	49.90	40.85	31.75
1348 – 1364	127.20	65.05	60.50	51.40	42.30	33.25
1364 – 1380	128.70	66.55	62.00	52.90	43.80	34.70
1380 – 1396	130.20	68.05	63.50	54.40	45.30	36.20
1396 – 1412	131.70	69.55	65.00	55.90	46.80	37.70
1412 – 1428	133.20	71.00	66.50	57.40	48.30	39.20
1428 – 1444	134.65	72.50	67.95	58.90	49.80	40.70
1444 – 1460	136.15	74.00	69.45	60.35	51.30	42.20
1460 – 1476	137.65	75.50	70.95	61.85	52.75	43.70
1476 – 1492	139.15	77.00	72.45	63.35	54.25	45.15
1492 – 1508	140.65	78.50	73.95	64.85	55.75	46.65
1508 – 1524	142.15	80.00	75.45	66.35	57.25	48.15
1524 – 1540	143.65	81.50	76.95	67.85	58.75	49.65
1540 – 1556	145.15	82.95	78.40	69.35	60.25	51.15

Provincial claim codes/Codes de dem
Deduct from each pay
Retenez sur chaque pai

a) If a hotel reservations clerk in Banff, AB earns $1392.00 biweekly and his TD1 claim code is 2, how much federal tax will be deducted from each pay?

b) How much provincial tax will be deducted from each pay?

c) If this worker earned the same amount in Fernie, BC, what information would you need to determine whether the deductions would be different?

8. Chandra works as a flight dispatcher at the Calgary airport. Her annual salary is $37 000.00 and her TD1 claim code is 2.

a) Calculate her biweekly gross pay.

b) What will her deductions be for CPP, EI, and income tax for each pay period? Use the federal and provincial tax tables shown above.

c) What will her net pay be?

9. Would you rather work on a straight commission basis or a salary plus commission basis? Why? What are the advantages and disadvantages of each?

Chapter 2 Earning an Income 91

Chapter 3

Length, Area, and Volume

GOALS

Measurement is an essential skill that everyone uses every day to make sense of the physical world. In the workplace, you will need to know how to take accurate measurements and how to estimate measurements. In this chapter, you will use your knowledge of fractions, decimals, ratios, and estimation to learn about measurement using both the Système international d'unités (SI) and the imperial system of measurement. You will learn how to

- convert measurements from SI to imperial units and from imperial to SI units;
- calculate perimeter, circumference, and area in imperial units; and
- calculate the surface area and volume of three-dimensional objects in imperial units.

KEY TERMS

- base unit
- capacity
- conversion factor
- foot (ft)
- geometric net
- imperial system
- inch (in)
- mile (mi)
- referent
- surface area
- Système international d'unités (SI)
- volume
- yard (yd)

PROJECT—DESIGN AN ICE-FISHING SHELTER

START TO PLAN

PROJECT OVERVIEW

Have you ever gone ice fishing or seen an ice-fishing shelter? Imagine trying to ice fish for many hours without a shelter to protect you from the cold. In this chapter, your project will be to design an ice-fishing shelter and estimate the cost of its construction.

You will design a small ice-fishing shelter that can seat 2 to 3 people. Your shelter will be sheathed with plywood, and it must have a door, at least one window, a portable propane heater, a flat roof, 2 or 3 fishing holes, interior seating, and a painted exterior.

This ice-fishing shelter seats two people and has a wood-burning stove.

GET STARTED

To begin your project, plan the design of your shelter. You can use the internet and books on construction to research ice-fishing shelters and other shed-like designs. Make a list of all the things you will need to consider. For example:

- What dimensions are needed to fit 2 to 3 people?
- What size of heater will you need for your shelter?
- How will you design your seating?
- Where will you drill the holes in the floor?
- What will be the dimensions of your door and window?

Visualize your shelter and make a list of all the materials you will need to construct the shelter. How will you attach the plywood? How will you attach the door? What other hardware and materials will you need?

FINAL PRESENTATION CHECKLIST

You will make a final presentation when you have completed this project. Your presentation will include the following:

- a description of your materials, quantities, and costs;
- an accurate two-dimensional floor plan; and
- a three-dimensional scale model.

Chapter 3 Length, Area, and Volume

3.1 Systems of Measurement

MATH ON THE JOB

Stéphanie Klassen is an animal health technologist at Central Animal Hospital in Saskatoon, Saskatchewan. After graduating from École régionale Saint-Jean-Baptiste in Saint-Jean-Baptiste, Manitoba, she obtained a diploma in animal health technology from Red River College in Winnipeg. As an animal health technologist, Stéphanie knows how to handle and restrain animals, perform initial examination procedures, and identify injuries and possible signs of abuse. She is knowledgeable about animal nutrition, diseases, and illnesses. She takes X-rays, puts animals under general anaesthetic, takes and runs blood tests, and assists the veterinarian with ultrasound examinations. She is informed about animal vaccinations and diets, and she can perform simple surgeries such as neutering cats and extracting teeth.

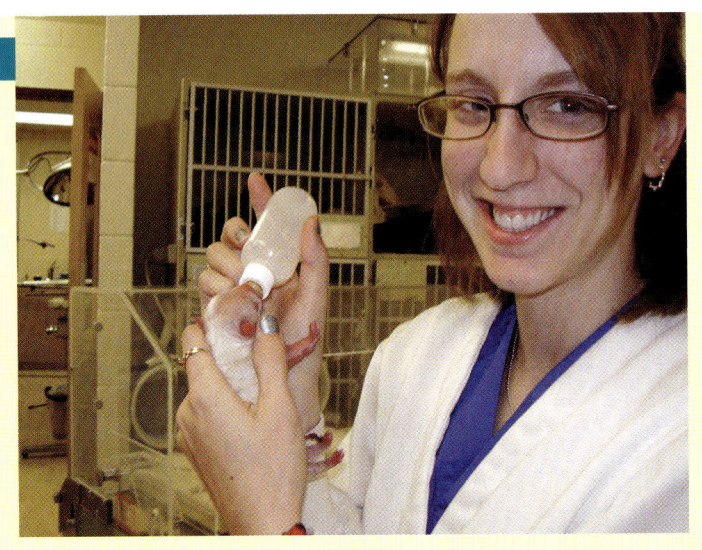

This newborn Shih Tzu puppy needs to be fed six times a day. Understanding the nutritional needs of animals is an important skill for an animal health technologist.

One task that Stéphanie performs daily is feeding the animals. Stéphanie needs to calculate how much dog food to give a full-grown husky dog. She knows that the husky needs 1250 kilocalories (kcal) of food energy a day. The dog's food contains 254 kcal in 250 mL. How many millilitres of dog food should Stéphanie feed the husky in one day? Round your answer to the nearest mL.

EXPLORE THE MATH

base unit: a unit of measurement on which other units are based

volume: the amount of space a solid occupies

In Canada, we use two systems of measurement: the Système international d'unités (SI) and the imperial system. Although we use the SI most often in our daily lives, the imperial system is used in many trades. For example, plumbers and carpenters typically take measurements in inches and feet, which are imperial units. To work in the trades, you need to be familiar with both the SI and imperial systems.

In the SI, the **base unit** for measuring length is the metre (m). The base unit for measuring **volume** is the litre (L).

The SI is a decimal system because it is based on multiples of 10. Any measurement stated in one SI unit can be converted to another SI unit by multiplying or dividing by a multiple of 10. Multiples of the base units are indicated by SI prefixes. For example, the prefix centi means one-hundredth, so 1 centimetre is one-hundredth of a metre. The prefix kilo means 1000, so 1 kilometre equals 1000 metres. What other SI prefixes do you know?

In the imperial system, the base unit for measuring length is the foot and the base unit for measuring volume is the pint.

The imperial system is not a decimal system. Because the imperial units were developed at different times to meet different needs, each group of units has a particular relationship. For example, there are 12 inches in 1 foot, and there are 3 feet in 1 yard. Figure 3.1 shows the most commonly used imperial units for length.

FIGURE 3.1
Some Common Imperial Units

Length

Unit	Abbreviation
inch	in or "
foot	ft or '
yard	yd
mile	mi

In order to solve an imperial measurement problem, you may have to convert the given measurements into common units. To convert from one imperial unit to another imperial unit, you use a unit **conversion factor**. A unit conversion factor is a fraction that is equal to 1. The numerator of the fraction contains the units to which you want to convert. The denominator of the fraction contains the original units in which the measurement was taken. What would the conversion factor be for feet to inches?

conversion factor: a number by which a quantity expressed in one unit must be multiplied to convert it to another unit

DISCUSS THE IDEAS
DART

The Disaster Assistance Response Team (DART) is a team of 200 Canadian armed forces personnel that provides assistance to disaster-affected regions around the world. In addition to providing basic medical assistance, DART's main goal is to produce safe drinking water.

1. DART's water purification system can purify 150 000 litres of water a day. If DART has a three-week mission to help in a disaster zone, how many litres of water can it purify?

2. An adult needs at least 4 litres of water a day for drinking, food preparation, and hygiene. For how many days would DART have to be on-site to produce a 3-week supply of clean drinking water for a community of 7000? What assumptions have you made in arriving at your answer? Would the location of the community or the type of disaster change your answer?

Chapter 3 Length, Area, and Volume

3. In the problem above, if DART was only available to be at the disaster location for 3 days, how long would the community have to get its own water systems working again (or to re-establish its access to clean water)?

ACTIVITY 3.1
EXPLORING IMPERIAL MEASUREMENT

In this activity, you will work with a partner to take imperial measurements and create an imperial conversion table.

1. Before you start measuring, look at the division markers on your imperial measuring tools. Imperial rulers and tape measures are marked in fractions of an inch. What is the smallest fraction indicated on each of your measuring tools?

2. With your partner, select 9 objects and distances to measure:

    - 3 objects that fit in your hand

    - 3 objects that are larger than your desk

    - 3 distances that are longer than and outside of the classroom

3. Measure each of your objects and distances and record your answers. Take as many measurements of the objects as are necessary to give the object's dimensions. How did you decide on the appropriate measuring tool to use for each of your measurements? Record your measurements in a table like the one below.

4. How could you estimate these measurements if you didn't have a ruler, measuring tape, or other tool? A referent is an object that represents approximately one unit of measurement. For example, an object that is about one inch long could be used as a referent to estimate inches. Working independently from your partner, find referents that you could use to estimate one inch, one foot, and one yard. Record the referent you used and its approximate length. Compare your referents with your partner's and share your reasons for choosing each referent.

IMPERIAL MEASUREMENTS

Item	Measurements (imperial units)	Referent estimate	Difference

SAMPLE

5. Use your referents to estimate the measurements of the objects and distances you selected in question 2. Record your estimates.

6. Compare your estimates with your partner's. Calculate and record the differences between your estimates and the actual imperial measurements. Whose estimates were closer, yours or your partner's? Which referents were most accurate?

7. Copy the table below in your notebook and fill in the missing information to create an imperial conversion table.

IMPERIAL CONVERSION TABLE

1 foot = _____ inches	
1 yard = _____ feet = _____ inches	
1 mile = 1760 yards = _____ feet	

Example 1

Maxime is a finishing carpenter who is replacing the case moulding around a double French door and the baseboards around the 4 walls of a living room. The dimensions of the rectangular living room are 20′ × 15′. The French door is along one of the 20′ walls, and the door frame measures 72″ wide and 84″ high. Case moulding costs $9.50 a linear foot and baseboard costs $4.50 a linear foot. These items must be purchased in whole feet. If Maxime's labour charge is $8.50 a linear foot, what will be the total cost of this job?

SOLUTION

$20' + 20' + 15' + 15' = 70'$ Calculate the perimeter of the room.

Baseboard will not be installed in front of the French door, so the width of the French door must be subtracted from the perimeter to find the number of linear feet of baseboard needed.

$72'' \times \dfrac{1'}{12''} = 6'$ Convert the door width from inches to feet.

$70' - 6' = 64'$ Maxime will need 64′ of baseboard.

Case moulding will be installed along the top and two sides of the doorframe.

$72'' + 84'' + 84'' = 240''$

$240'' \times \dfrac{1'}{12''} = 20'$ Convert 240″ to feet to find the number of linear feet of case moulding.

HINT

The numerator of the conversion factor is the unit to which you want to convert. The denominator is stated in the original units in which the measurement was taken.

Maxime will install 64′ of baseboard and 20′ of case moulding. His labour charge is $8.50 a linear foot. Calculate the labour cost.

$$64' + 20' = 84'$$

$$84' \times \$8.50/\text{foot} = \$714.00$$

Labour cost is $714.00.

Calculate the cost of the baseboard and moulding and add it to the labour cost.

$$\$4.50/\text{foot} \times 64' = \$288.00$$

$$\$9.50/\text{foot} \times 20' = \$190.00$$

$$\$714.00 + \$288.00 + \$190.00 = \$1192.00$$

The total cost of the job is $1192.00.

ALTERNATIVE SOLUTION

Conversions can also be done using division.

$$72'' \div 12 = 6'$$

Convert the door width from inches to feet by dividing by 12.

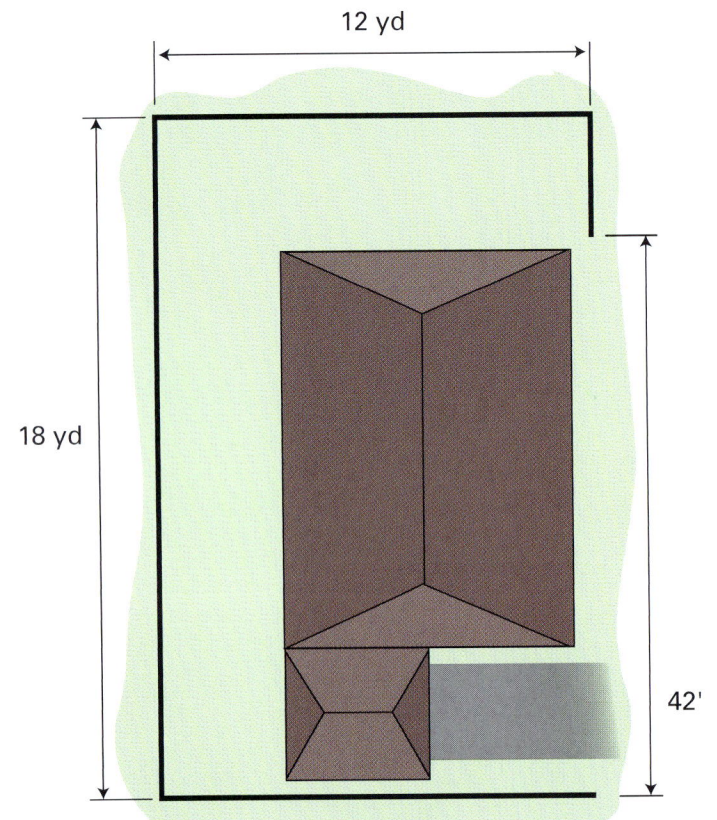

Example 2

Kiri needs to replace the wooden fence that surrounds her yard. She measured her property, and it is 18 yards wide and 12 yards deep. There is no fence in front of her house, and the gap in the fence at the front of the property is 42 feet, as shown in the diagram. Kiri plans to replace the existing fence pickets with 5-foot-long cedar boards placed vertically. The boards are $5\frac{1}{2}$ inches wide and will be spaced $\frac{1}{4}$ inch apart. She placed an order for 275 boards. Did she order enough boards?

SOLUTION

The fence boards will be spaced $\frac{1}{4}''$ apart. Rewrite $5\frac{1}{2}$ as $5\frac{2}{4}$.

$$5\frac{2}{4} + \frac{1}{4} = 5\frac{3}{4}$$ The $\frac{1}{4}''$ spacing must be added to the width of one board to find the total space needed for each board.

Kiri needs to allow $5\frac{3}{4}''$, or 5.75" for each board.

Find the total length of the fence in yards.

The front of the property has a 42-foot gap in the fence.

$$42 \times \frac{1}{3} = 14$$ Convert 42 feet to yards using the conversion factor $\frac{1 \text{ yard}}{3 \text{ feet}}$.

The gap is 14 yards wide.

$$18 - 14 = 4$$ Subtract the width of the gap from the width of the property.

The fence at the front of the property is 4 yards long.

$$18 + 12 + 12 + 4 = 46$$ Calculate the total length of the fence.

The total length of the fence is 46 yards.

To find the number of boards needed, first convert 46 yards to inches. This conversion can be done in two steps.

$$46 \text{ yards} \times \frac{3 \text{ feet}}{1 \text{ yard}} = 138 \text{ feet}$$

$$138 \text{ feet} \times \frac{12 \text{ inches}}{1 \text{ foot}} = 1656 \text{ inches}$$

$$\frac{1656}{5.75} = 288$$ Divide 1656 inches by the space needed for one board to find the total number of boards needed.

Kiri will need approximately 288 boards, so she has not ordered enough boards.

ALTERNATIVE SOLUTION

You can also find the number of boards needed by converting the board width to yards.

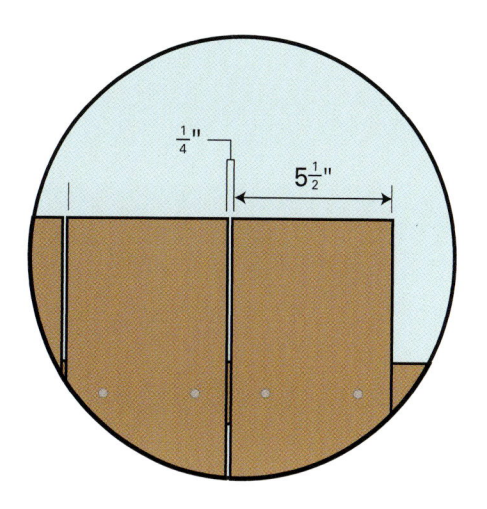

Chapter 3 Length, Area, and Volume

The total space needed per board is $5\frac{3}{4}$ inches, or 5.75 inches.

$5.75 \div 36 = 0.16$ Convert 5.75 inches to yards by dividing by the number of inches in 1 yard.

The total space needed per board is 0.16 yards.

$\frac{46 \text{ yards}}{0.16 \text{ yards}} = 287.5$ Divide the length of the fence by the space needed for one board to find the total number of boards needed.

Kiri will need approximately 288 boards, so she has not ordered enough boards.

Example 3

Julie, a baker, specializes in wedding cakes. She would like to calculate the cost of decorating a 3-tiered circular cake with fresh flowers around the base of each level. The bottom cake has a 14″ diameter, the middle layer has a 10″ diameter, and the top layer has a 6″ diameter. All three layers are stacked on top of each other without spacers. If the cost of $1\frac{1}{2}$″ wide red roses is $0.99 each and the cost of $2\frac{1}{2}$″ wide red roses is $1.49 each, which size of roses should Julie decorate with to give her client the best price?

SOLUTION

First find the circumference of each cake layer.

$C = \pi d$ Use the formula for the circumference of a circle.

$C = \pi(6 \text{ in})$ Calculate the circumference of the top layer.

$C = 18.85$, rounded to 19 in   Julie would round up the measurement to ensure that enough flowers are ordered.

$C = \pi(10 \text{ in})$ Calculate the circumference of the middle layer.

$C = 31.42$ in, rounded to 32 in

$C = \pi(14 \text{ in})$ Calculate the circumference of the bottom layer.

$C = 43.98$ in, rounded to 44 in

$19 + 32 + 44 = 95$ The total circumference of the cake is 95 in.

Bakers need math to create elaborate cakes.

Find the number of roses needed by dividing the circumference by the width of one rose.

$\frac{95}{1.5}$ = 63.33, rounded to 64   Julie would need 64 of the 1.5" roses to surround the cake.

64 × $0.99 = $63.36   The 1.5" roses would cost $63.36.

$\frac{95}{2.5}$ = 38   Julie would need 38 of the 2.5" roses to surround the cake.

38 × $1.49 = $56.62   The 2.5" roses would cost $56.62.

Julie should decorate with the 2.5" roses.

ACTIVITY 3.2
VISUALIZING A MEASUREMENT

You have baked a rectangular cake that measures 9 in × 13 in. You need to cut 5 large pieces (4 in × 3 in) and at least 12 small pieces (2 in × 2 in) for your guests (whole pieces only).

1. Working with a partner, use an imperial ruler and an 11" × 17" sheet of paper to determine how to cut the cake. Do you have enough cake for your guests? Support your answer with a scale drawing.

2. Is there more than one way to cut the cake? Support your answer with a scale drawing.

ACTIVITY 3.3
DESIGNING A TIN CAN LAYOUT

Cylindrical tin cans are manufactured from tin-plate sheets. The body of the can is cut from one tin-plate sheet, and the lid and bottom of the can are cut from another sheet. After the pieces are cut out and shaped, the can is assembled and seals are applied to the top, bottom, and side seams.

You have been hired to design the layout for fabricating cans that are 2.5 inches in diameter and 4.5 inches high. The tin-plate sheets measure $2\frac{1}{2}$ yards by $1\frac{1}{2}$ yards. One sheet of tin plate is used for making lids and bottoms, and two sheets are used for making the body of the can. Three seals are applied to each can. The cost of the tin plate is $13.20 a sheet, and each seal costs $0.28 to make.

Work in a small group and use a ruler, compass, and a large sheet of paper to answer the following questions.

1. How many cans can be made from the three tin-plate sheets? Create a diagram to illustrate your answer. Describe the strategies you used to find your solution.

2. What is the cost for each can?

Mental Math and Estimation

The Canadian Football League record for the longest field goal is held by Paul McCallum. In 2001, while playing for the Saskatchewan Roughriders, he kicked a 62-yard field goal. How many feet is that?

BUILD YOUR SKILLS

1. Convert the following measurements.

   a) Convert 3520 yd to miles.

   b) Convert $10'\frac{3}{16}''$ to inches.

   c) Convert $8\frac{3}{4}$ yards to feet.

2. René is a florist who uses 10 inches of ribbon to tie each bouquet of flowers he creates. He has a roll of ribbon 100 yards long. How many bouquets can he make with the roll of ribbon (assuming no wastage)?

3. Calm Air will accept carry-on luggage if its length, width, and height add up to no more than 46 inches. Beverly's suitcase has the following dimensions: length 2 ft; width 1 ft 4 in; and height 9 in. Will Calm Air allow her to carry her suitcase on board?

4. You have decided to build a small hockey rink in your backyard, as shown in the diagram. You want to use plywood to build rink boards that are 48" high. Exterior $\frac{1}{2}$" plywood is sold in 4' × 8' sheets that cost $14.15 a sheet.

   a) How many sheets of plywood will you need to surround the rink?

   b) What will be the cost of the plywood, before taxes?

5. A landscape gardener has designed a circular herb garden with 4 sectors, shown on the left. The radius of one sector is 4'3". Each sector will be surrounded with plastic lawn edging that costs $9.99 for a 20' roll. How much will it cost to put edging around the herb garden? Assume that you cannot buy partial rolls.

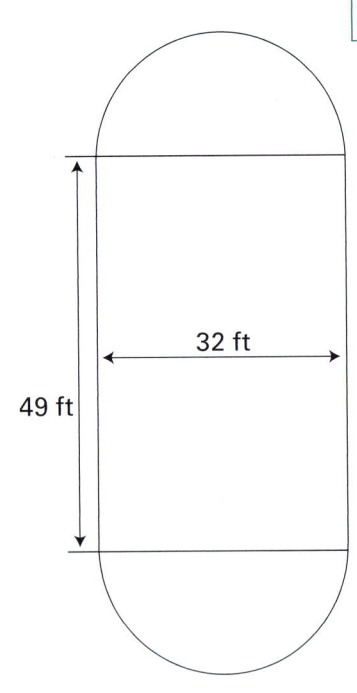

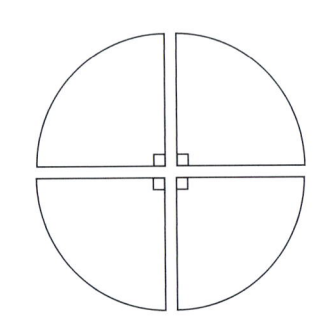

6. In professional theatres, there is a catwalk called a fly gallery that runs along the four walls above the stage. Stagehands stand on the fly gallery to raise and lower scenery on and off stage. A structural steel fitter has been asked to replace the inside safety rail of a fly gallery. The space above the stage is 109′ 6″ long and 48′ 9″ wide. The fly gallery is $2\frac{1}{2}'$ wide. If the fitter uses rails that are 20 feet long, how many rails will she need?

7. Noah is designing new drapes for a client's living room window that is 9′ wide and 4′ high. The finished drapes will have two panels so they can be opened in the centre. The drapes will be twice as wide as the window and they will be 6′ long. The drape fabric is 60″ wide.

   a) How many yards of fabric must be purchased to make these drapes? Disregard seam allowances and hems in your calculations.

   b) How much will the drapes cost if the price of the fabric is $15.00/yard?

8. A finishing carpenter is working on a partial home renovation project, and the homeowner has asked the carpenter how much it would cost to replace the baseboards in the bathroom. The floor plan of the bathroom is shown on the right. The carpenter bills his time at a rate of $45.00/h and he charges a markup of 15% on materials. Baseboard costs $6.50 a linear foot and the carpenter estimates it will take him two-and-a-half hours. How much does he tell the homeowner it will cost? List any assumptions you made in your calculations.

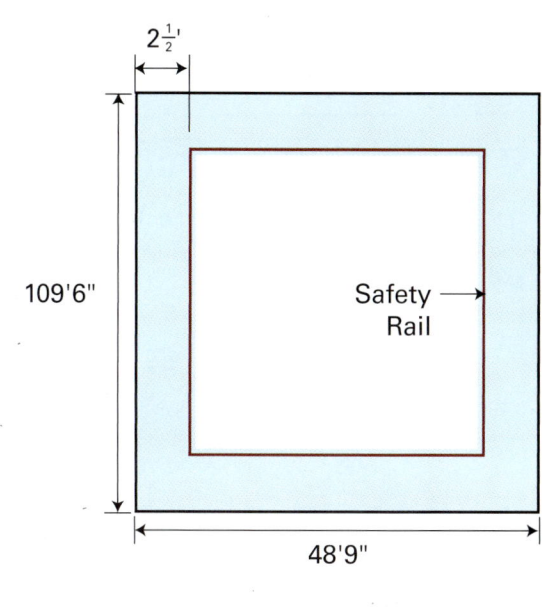

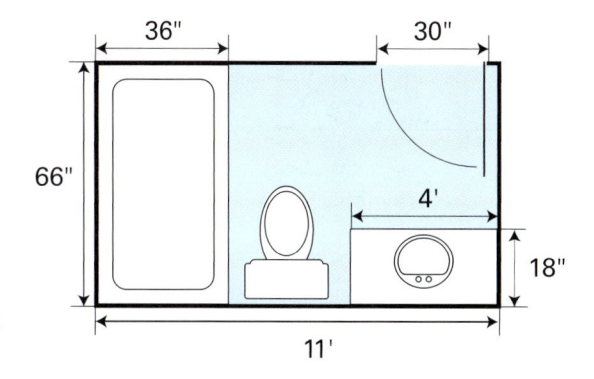

Extend your thinking

9. An insulator has a contract to insulate a residential garage that measures 24′ × 24′. The interior walls are 8′ high, the garage door is 16′ wide and 7′ high, and the door in the wall opposite the garage door is 36″ wide and 80″ high. The garage is framed with wall studs spaced 16″ apart. The insulator is using fiberglass insulation that comes in batts that measure 16″ wide and 47″ long. If there are 18 batts in one package, how many packages of insulation will she need?

THE ROOTS OF MATH

THE ORIGINS OF STANDARD MEASUREMENT

Humans have always needed to use measurement to make comparisons and to perform tasks such as building shelters or trading goods. But for thousands of years, there was no universal system of measurement. Instead, measurement units developed according to custom and usage.

The first measurement units were based on dimensions of the human body. People used their arms, hands, and fingers to measure length. For example, ancient Egyptians used a unit of measurement called the cubit. A cubit was the distance from a person's elbow to the tip of his or her middle finger. When smaller units of measure were needed, the digit, or width of a finger, and the palm, or width of a hand, were used.

The cubit was the unit of measurement the ancient Egyptians used to construct the pyramids.

The imperial measurement system we use today also originated from units based on the human body. In England during the Middle Ages, measurement units included the ynce, the foot, the ulna, and the fathom. The ynce was the width of a thumb, and the foot was the length of a human foot. An ulna was the distance from the tip of a person's nose to the end of the middle finger of his or her outstretched arm. A fathom was the distance across a person's outstretched arms, from fingertip to fingertip.

Clearly, the results of this type of measurement would vary depending on who was doing the measuring. Sometimes, that didn't matter. If you built a table for your own use, you could use your hands and arms to take measurements. But what if you were hired to build a table for someone else, and she told you the table had to be eight feet long? Whose "foot" would you use to take the measurements?

In the thirteenth century, King Edward of England decided that his country needed standard measurement units. He decreed that one ynce was equal to the length of three grains of barley, 12 ynces equalled 1 foot, and 3 feet equalled 1 ulna. He created a master ulna made of iron to be used as the standard throughout the country.

Some units of measurement based on the human body are still used today. A horse's height is measured in hands, which has been standardized at 4 inches. Sailors still use the 6-foot fathom to measure the depth of water. And although today we use the words inch and yard instead of ynce and ulna, the ratios between the inch, foot, and yard set by King Edward remain the basis of the imperial system of measurement.

1. Why do we need standard units of measurement?

2. What are the advantages of using non-standard forms of measurement to describe something?

104 MathWorks 10

PROJECT—DESIGN AN ICE-FISHING SHELTER

DRAW A FLOOR PLAN

Earlier, you planned the design of your ice-fishing shelter. It is now time to put your plans on paper and draft a floor plan.

- Write a description of your ice-fishing shelter. Include details about everything that will be inside the shelter and describe the exterior.

- Sketch a rough draft of the floor plan of your fishing shelter. Is your shelter large enough to seat two or three people? Is the shelter small enough to be moved to the fishing location?

- Create an accurate floor plan of the shelter, using your rough sketch as a guide. Show all the measurements of the dimensions of the floor, door, and window openings in imperial units. State your scale.

You must measure accurately when you draw a scale floor plan.

3.2 Converting Measurements

MATH ON THE JOB

Manuel Marques is an automotive service technician who owns Lube King Service Centre in Winnipeg. Manuel inspects, diagnoses, repairs, and services the mechanical and electrical systems of vehicles. As a business owner, Manuel supervises employees and apprentice automotive technician students. He uses mathematics to calculate resistance and voltage when working with electronic components. He also converts between imperial and SI units when servicing American-made vehicles or using equipment, such as his air conditioning refrigerant capture machine, that was made in the US.

Manuel uses math every time he repairs a vehicle.

Manuel needs to order a supply of hose clamps with a minimum diameter of 32 mm. He found an online auto parts company in the US that sells hose clamps with a maximum diameter of $\frac{7}{8}$ inch. Would the US clamps be the correct size?

EXPLORE THE MATH

In 1983, a Boeing 767 ran out of fuel on a flight from Montreal to Edmonton. The aircraft was able to glide to a safe landing in Gimli, Manitoba, and no one was hurt. An investigation revealed that the aircraft ran out of fuel because the ground crew used the wrong conversion factor to convert gallons to litres. Because of this error, the pilot took off from Montreal with 12 598 litres of fuel, instead of the 27 770 litres of fuel he needed to reach Edmonton.

Not all conversion errors have such potentially serious consequences, but in many jobs you need to know how to convert from SI units to imperial units. For example, the United States, which is Canada's largest trading partner, uses imperial units, so if you are doing business with a US company, you need to know the imperial equivalent of SI units.

In this section, you will use proportional reasoning and conversion factors to convert between SI and imperial units.

ACTIVITY 3.4
CONVERTING BETWEEN SI AND IMPERIAL UNITS

In this activity, you will work with a partner to create a conversion table you can use to convert between linear imperial and SI units. You will need a ruler and metre/yard stick.

1. Compare the metric and imperial units on your ruler. Approximately how many centimetres are in one inch?

2. Compare the metric and imperial units on your metre/yard stick. Which is longer, one yard or one metre? Approximately how many inches are in one metre? Approximately how many feet are in one metre?

3. Proportional reasoning can be used to convert a measurement from imperial to SI units. In a table like the one below, fill in the missing information to create an imperial–SI conversion table.

CONVERSION FACTORS BETWEEN SI AND IMPERIAL UNITS

SI to imperial	Imperial to SI
1 mm = ___ in	1 in = ___ mm
1 cm = ___ in	1 in = 2.54 cm
1 m = ___ ft	1 ft = ___ m
1 m = 1.0936 yd	1 yd = ___ m
1 km = ___ mi	1 mi = 1.6093 km

DISCUSS THE IDEAS
INSTALLING A CHANDELIER

Yori was hired to install a chandelier in the foyer of a home with a 9-foot ceiling. The homeowner, who is 180 cm tall, cannot decide on the length of the chandelier that he wishes to hang.

1. Calculate some possible lengths of the chandelier.

2. What factors should the homeowner consider before deciding on the length of the chandelier?

Example 1

Giselle would like to replace the carpet in her living room. She used her imperial tape measure to measure the room, and the dimensions were 12 ft by 15 ft. When she went to the carpet store, she found the price of the carpet was $24.99/m² (taxes included). She cannot order less than a full square metre of carpet.

a) How much carpet should she order?

b) How much will the carpet cost?

SOLUTION

a) Convert the room dimensions from imperial units to SI units. Because 1 metre equals 3.2808 feet, the conversion factor used to convert feet to metres is $\frac{1}{3.2808}$.

$$\frac{1}{3.2808} = \frac{x}{12}$$

Use the conversion factor to convert the width of the room from feet to metres.

$$12\left(\frac{1}{3.2808}\right) = 12\left(\frac{x}{12}\right)$$

Multiply each side of the equation by 12 to isolate x.

$$3.658 = x$$

The room is 3.658 metres wide.

$$\frac{1}{3.2808} = \frac{x}{15}$$

Convert the length of the room from feet to metres.

$$15\left(\frac{1}{3.2808}\right) = 15\left(\frac{x}{15}\right)$$

Multiply each side of the equation by 15 to isolate x.

$$4.572 \text{ m} = x$$

The room is 4.572 metres long.

$$3.658 \times 4.572 = 16.724$$

To find the number of square metres of carpet Giselle needs to order, find the area of the living room.

The area of the room is 16.724 m². Giselle must order full square metres of carpet, so she should order 17 m².

b) 17 m² × $24.99/m² = $424.83   Find the cost of 17 m² of carpet.

Her order will cost $424.83.

Before installing the new carpet, Giselle removes the old flooring.

Example 2

Samir is the cost estimator for a landscape company. He has to calculate the amount of material needed to construct a circular outdoor patio built from paving stones. The diameter of the patio is 13 m. One bundle of paving stones covers 116 ft². Samir has ordered 11 bundles of paving stones. Did he order enough paving stones?

SOLUTION

Convert the diameter of the patio from metres to feet using proportional reasoning and the conversion factor 1 ft equals 0.3048 m.

$$\left(\frac{1 \text{ ft}}{0.3048 \text{ m}}\right) = \left(\frac{x \text{ ft}}{13 \text{ m}}\right)$$

$13\left(\frac{1}{0.3048}\right) = x$ — Multiply both sides of the equation by 13 to isolate x.

$42.6509 \text{ ft} = x$ — When you are estimating material, it is best to round up to ensure that enough material is purchased.

The diameter of the patio is approximately 43 ft.

Use the formula for the area of a circle to find the area of the patio.

$A = \pi r^2$

$A = \pi(21.5)^2$ — The diameter is 43 feet, so the radius is 21.5 feet.

$A = 1452.20$ — The area of the patio is 1452.20 ft².

$\left(\frac{1452.20}{116}\right) = 12.5$ — Divide the area of the patio by the coverage of 1 bundle of paving stones.

Samir ordered 11 bundles, so he did not order enough paving stones.

When complete, the patio will look similar to this design.

ACTIVITY 3.5
DESIGNING A CFL FIELD LOGO

Most football teams have their logo and team name painted on the surface of the field. Imagine that your high school has been chosen to create the field logos for the next Canadian Football League (CFL) Grey Cup Championship. Working with a partner, you will design field logos for a CFL team and create a scale drawing.

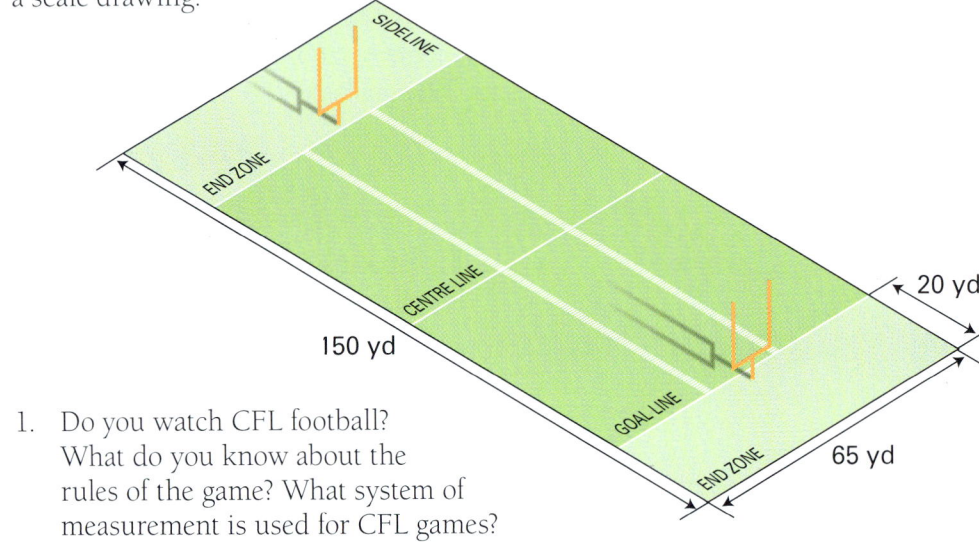

The rules of Canadian football are different from those of American football, but both countries use the same system of measurement in the game.

1. Do you watch CFL football? What do you know about the rules of the game? What system of measurement is used for CFL games?

2. Why do you think the CFL has not converted its game to the SI? Make a list of the impacts converting to the SI would have on the game.

3. The CFL playing field is a rectangle that is 150 yards by 65 yards. At each end is an end zone, with a goal line 20 yards from the end of the field. How many yards long is the playing field between the two goal lines? How many yards is it from the goal line to the centre line?

4. Create a scale diagram of the CFL field on 1-inch graph paper. Record the scale you used.

5. Design your logos and place them on your scale diagram using the following design specifications:

    a) 2 end zone logos, each 10 yards × 35 yards

    b) 2 large field logos, each 10 yards × 10 yards

    c) 2 small field logos, each 5 yards × 10 yards

    d) 1 centre field logo, centred on the 55-yard line, with a maximum radius of 5 yards

6. Calculate the amount of paint that will be needed to paint all the logos if one 3.8-litre can of paint covers 37 m².

DISCUSS THE IDEAS
LAKE WINNIPEG

Lake Winnipeg is the world's tenth largest freshwater lake. In 1999, researchers began documenting the effects of the buildup of blue-green algae blooms caused by excess nitrogen, phosphorus, and other pollutants in the lake. Researchers analyze water samples, observe lake water colour, and document marine species to determine changes to the toxicity of the lake. For some calculations, researchers need to know the area of the lake, but because it is an irregular shape, its area cannot be found using a standard formula.

Given a map of Lake Winnipeg, what strategies could you use to find the approximate area of the lake in both km² and mi²?

Mental Math and Estimation

The distance a plane travels from Calgary to Edmonton is approximately 277 km. Estimate this distance in miles.

BUILD YOUR SKILLS

1. A low bridge has a posted maximum vehicle height of 7′6″. Your truck is 2.3 m high. Will it fit under the bridge?

2. David works for a company that is developing a high-accuracy altimeter for skydivers that measures and records their velocity and other measurements during a jump. The system that it has developed uses SI measurements. David must give a presentation on the device in San Francisco, showing the data the company obtained from several jumps from an altitude of 4200 metres. What is this altitude in feet?

3. Valerie wants to apply for a driver's licence. The application asks her to state her height in cm. Valerie is 5′8″ tall. What is her height in cm?

4. Sandy has been asked to give an estimate for replacing a countertop in a client's kitchen. The countertop measures 2′ × 6′ and the client wants Sandy to install 4″ × 4″ tiles that cost $3.50 each. Sandy has estimated her labour charge will be $350.00. What is the total cost of tiles and labour?

5. The Vancouver Parks Board wants to install grass sod on a playground that measures 20 m × 40 m. Two companies have bid on the job. Company A's bid was $4.00/yd² installed. Company B put in a bid of $2.50/m² plus $2000.00 for installation. Which company should get the job based on the best price?

Scale (km)
0 20 40 60

This map of Lake Winnipeg shows its irregular shape.

Chapter 3 Length, Area, and Volume **111**

6. Shelley is trying to decide whether to put hardwood flooring or carpet on her living room floor. The dimensions of the room are 22 ft by 16 ft. The hardwood flooring costs $18.99/m² with an installation cost of $1500.00. The carpet costs $21.95/yd² with an installation cost of $1350.00. Which type of flooring costs less?

7. Irina purchased a farm in Saskatchewan. She wants to plant balsam fir seedlings, and she estimated the field measures 72 yards by 65 yards. The tree nursery manager told her that each seedling requires an area of 64 ft² to grow properly. The seedlings cost $0.65 each. The nursery sells them in bundles of 20, and she cannot order partial bundles.

   a) How many seedlings can Irina plant on her acre of land?

   b) How much will it cost to purchase the seedlings?

8. Dejan was hired to lay vinyl flooring in the kitchen, meeting room, and foyer of the local Friendship Centre. He used the measurements in the diagram below to estimate the job. The flooring material comes in rolls 10 ft wide and is sold by the running foot, and Dejan needs to purchase enough flooring to ensure the pattern will match in all three rooms. He will also add 15% to his order to compensate for wastage. One running foot of vinyl flooring costs $12.50. Dejan estimates his labour charge will be $560.00. What is the total estimate for vinyl flooring and labour?

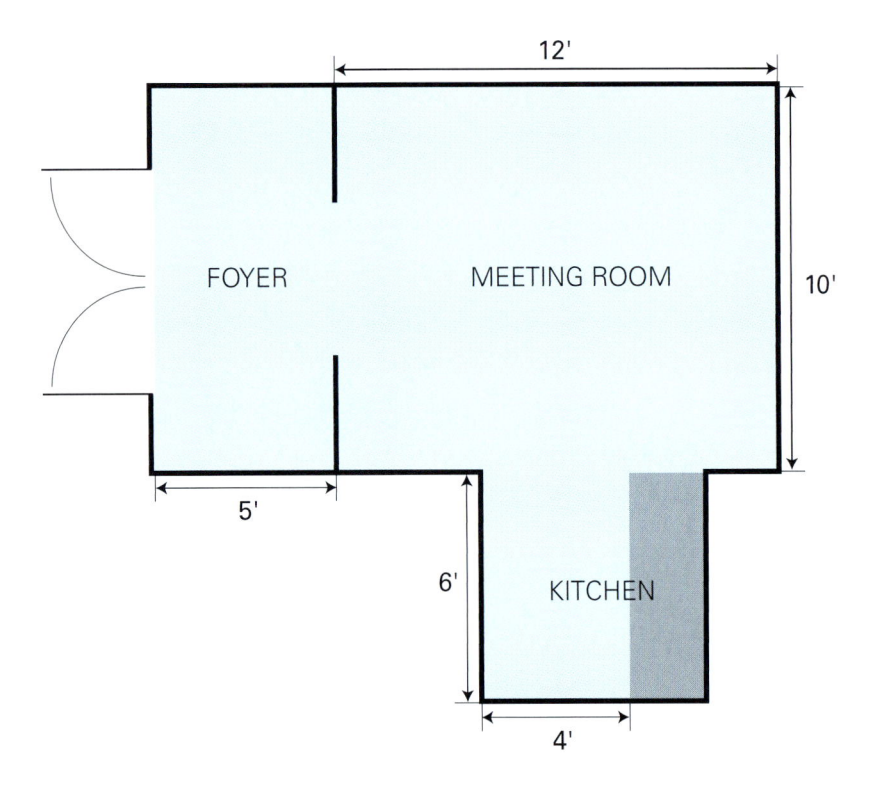

Extend your thinking

9. Lesa plans to carpet her sunroom with indoor-outdoor carpeting. She measured the room and made a sketch, shown below. When she went to the store, she discovered that the bolts of carpeting are 12 feet wide and cost $22.95/yd^2. The carpet will be attached with double-sided tape around the perimeter and along all seams. A 30-foot roll of double-sided tape costs $4.85. Lesa wants to lay out the carpet so the nap is running in the same direction, with the minimum number of seams. What will be the total cost of tape and carpet?

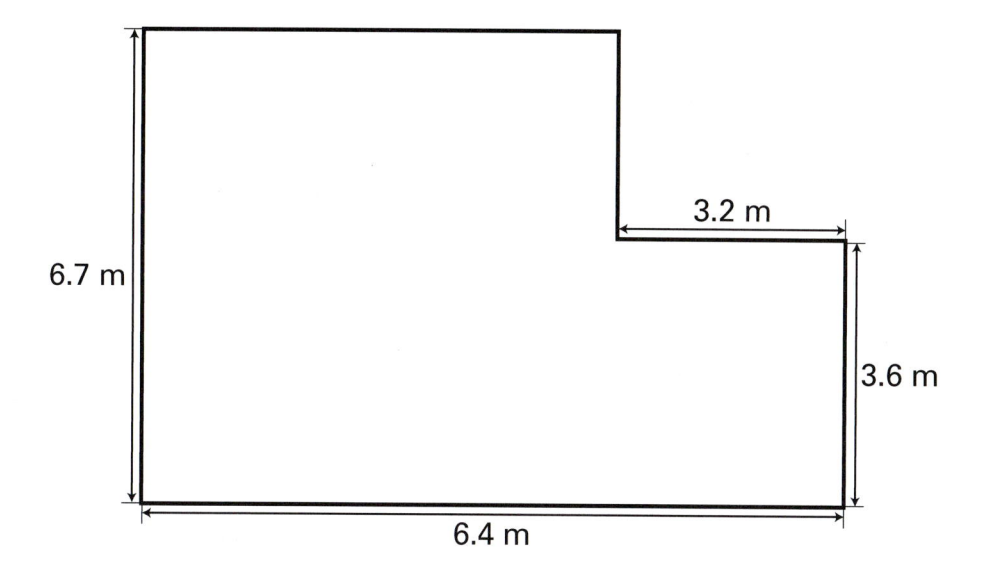

PROJECT—DESIGN AN ICE-FISHING SHELTER

ESTIMATE MATERIALS AND COSTS

In the first part of the project, you listed the materials you would need to build your ice-fishing shelter. In this project activity, you will estimate the quantities and the costs of the materials you will need. Record your calculations and research on charts similar to the ones below. You may want to use spreadsheet software to organize your information.

1. First, review your lists to ensure that you have listed all the materials you will need. Is there anything else that you thought of while you were drawing your floor plan?

2. The exterior of your shelter, the roof, and the floor will be sheathed with plywood. Plywood is sold in 4 ft by 8 ft sheets. Estimate the number of sheets of plywood you need to buy.

Use your floor plan to calculate how much paint and plywood you need.

3. A one-litre can of paint will cover 100 ft^2. Estimate the number of litres of paint you need to buy to paint the exterior of your shelter with one coat of paint. Will you paint the door?

4. Using the internet, local newspapers, or flyers, find the cost of your materials. How much will your shelter cost to build? Are there ways that you can save money?

SHELTER DIMENSIONS

	Length	Width	Area
Wall 1			
Wall 2			
Wall 3			
Wall 4			
Floor			
Roof			
Door			
Window(s)			

SAMPLE

MATERIALS AND COSTS

Materials	Quantity needed	Unit price	Cost before taxes	Taxes (GST and PST)	Total cost
Paint					
Plywood					
Propane heater					
Window					

SAMPLE

114   MathWorks 10

Surface Area 3.3

MATH *ON THE JOB*

David Kattegatsiak is the community economic development officer for Chesterfield Inlet, Nunavut. David provides information to his community about government resources and writes business proposals for local community members. He assists management with grant proposals and acts as a liaison between the community, municipal government, and various consultants. David helps plan and facilitate hamlet council meetings, creates budgets, and analyzes cash flow financial statements. One of David's duties is to do preliminary planning work with surveyors, architects, and engineers for construction projects in the community. In order to receive government grants to construct or renovate a building, David must take measurements at the site, calculate how much material or landfill is needed for the site, and create a budget for the project.

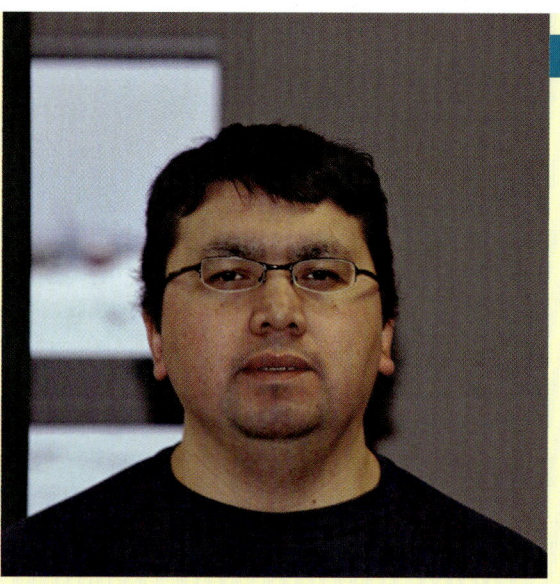

Measuring and budgeting are two of the ways that David Kattegatsiak uses math in his job.

David is creating a budget for a renovation project. He needs to calculate how much paint to buy to paint the walls of a school classroom. The classroom is 32 feet long and 25 feet wide, with a 10-foot ceiling. Paint is sold by the litre, and one litre of paint covers 12 square metres. Approximately how many litres are needed for one coat of paint?

EXPLORE THE MATH

Have you ever noticed the many types of packaging used to contain household goods? Cereal, detergent, and tissue are sold in rectangular boxes. Soup and tuna come in cylindrical cans. What other packaging shapes have you seen? Why do you think manufacturers choose different packaging shapes for their products?

In order to know how much packaging material is required for a product, its **surface area** must be calculated. Tradespeople such as machinists also need to calculate surface area to determine the amount of material they need to fabricate parts.

One way to find the surface area of a three-dimensional object is to create a **geometric net**. A geometric net is created by imagining that you are cutting open a three-dimensional object and laying it out flat to create a two-dimensional figure. The surface area can then be found by summing the areas of each side, or face, of the two-dimensional net.

surface area: the total area of the surface of a three-dimensional object

geometric net: a two-dimensional pattern used to construct three-dimensional shapes

DISCUSS THE IDEAS
SCALE FACTOR

scale factor: the ratio of the lengths of corresponding sides of two polygons

Sarita manufactures cardboard boxes. One of her clients would like her to double the lengths of the sides of a box that is currently 3 in long, 2 in wide, and 1 in high.

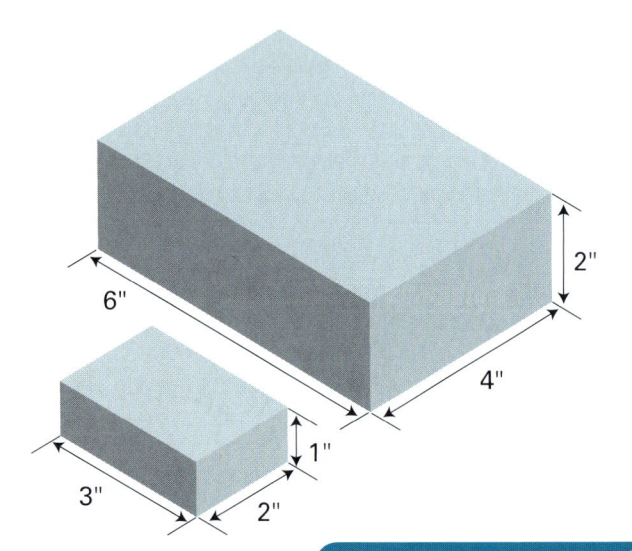

1. What **scale factor** will Sarita use to create the new box?

2. What will be the surface area of the new box?

3. What effect does doubling the length of the sides have on the surface area of the box?

4. What effect would tripling the length of the sides have on the surface area of the box? What if the lengths were quadrupled?

5. Write a formula that you can use to find the surface area of a scaled object when you know the original surface area and the scale factor.

ACTIVITY 3.6
DESIGNING A TOOL BOX

A welder needs to make a rectangular aluminum tool box for the bed of a pickup truck. The inside dimensions of the truck bed are $78\frac{5}{8}''$ long × $62\frac{3}{8}''$ wide × 21″ high.

a) Working in a group of 3, design a tool box for the truck bed. What factors influenced your design?

b) Sketch your tool box design and label its dimensions.

c) How many square feet of aluminum would be needed to make your tool box? What formula did you use to arrive at your answer?

ACTIVITY 3.7
SURFACE AREA FORMULAS

In this activity, you and your partner will examine the geometric nets of common three-dimensional shapes and develop formulas for their surface area. Your teacher will provide you with the required nets.

1. Cut out the geometric nets for the rectangular prism, triangular prism, cylinder, and cone. Describe the nets. How many faces are the same on each net? Record your answers in a table like the one below.

DESCRIBING GEOMETRIC NETS

Description	Rectangular prism	Triangular prism	Cylinder	Cone
Total number of faces				
Number of each type of face				
Area of each type of face				
Total surface area				
Formula for total surface area				$\pi r s + \pi r^2$

2. Measure the nets with an imperial ruler and calculate the area of each face. How can you use the area of the faces to find the total surface area of the object? Calculate the total surface area of each shape and record it in your table.

3. Assemble the geometric nets, using tape to hold them together. Write a formula that you can use to find the total surface area of a rectangular prism, triangular prism, and cylinder.

4. A triangular pyramid, or tetrahedron, is a pyramid with a triangular base, as shown.

    a) Which of the following are geometric nets of a triangular pyramid (all are congruent triangles)?

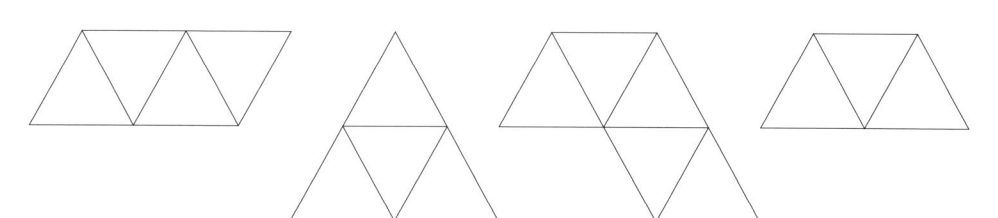

    b) If the area of one face of a triangular pyramid is 8 in², what is the total surface area of the triangular pyramid?

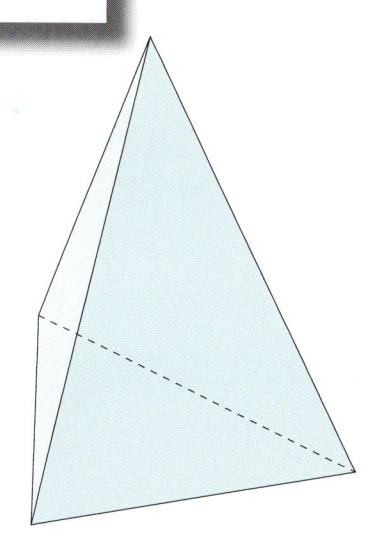

Example 1

A cannery has redesigned the size of the can for its canned salmon. The diameter of the new can is 4″ and its height is 5.5″. How much tin will be needed to construct one can?

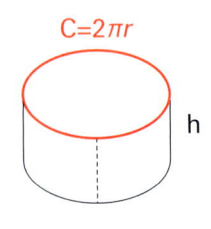

SOLUTION

A can is a cylinder. To find the amount of tin, you need to find the surface area of the cylinder.

$A = \pi r^2$	Use the formula for the area of a circle to find the area of the top of the can.
$A = \pi (2)^2$	The radius is half the diameter. The diameter of the can is 4″, so the radius is 2″.
$A = 12.57 \text{ in}^2$	
$2(12.57) = 25.14 \text{ in}^2$	Multiply the result by 2 to find the total area of the top and bottom of the can.

The side of a cylinder is a rectangle. The length of the rectangle is equal to the circumference of the top of the cylinder.

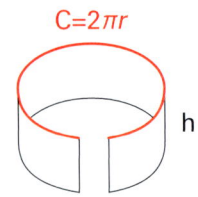

$C = 2\pi r$	Use the formula for the circumference of a circle to find the length of the rectangle.
$C = 12.57 \text{ in}$	The rectangle is 12.57 in long.
$A = 12.57 \times 5.5$	Use the formula for the area of a rectangle to find the area of the side of the can.
$A = 69.14 \text{ in}^2$	
$25.14 + 69.14 = 94.28$	Find the sum of the areas of the top, bottom, and side of the cylinder.

The amount of tin needed to construct one can is 94.28 in².

Example 2

Taizo manufactures and sells farm implements in Winkler, MB. One piece of equipment that he sells is a 3-point spreader that attaches to a tractor to spread grass seed, wheat seed, or fertilizer. The hopper of the spreader is a cone with a diameter of 40″ and slant height of 45″. How many square feet of plastic is needed to form one hopper?

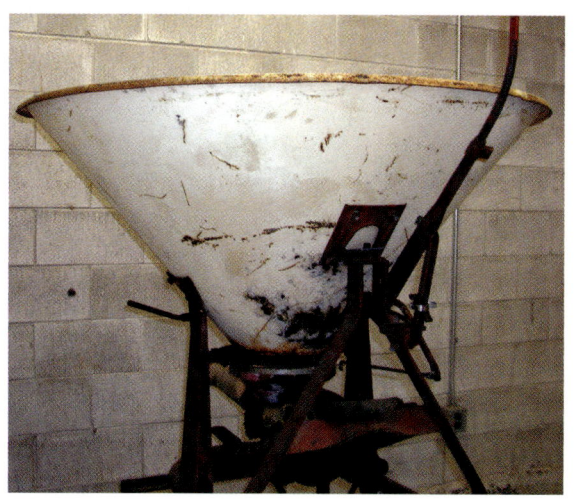

This is an older style hopper made of metal instead of plastic.

SOLUTION

The hopper is a cone without a base, so to calculate the amount of plastic, you only need to calculate the surface area of the side. The formula for the surface area of the side of a cone is $A = \pi r s$, where r is the radius of the base and s is the slant height, or length of the side.

Convert the hopper dimensions from inches to feet using the conversion factor $\frac{1 \text{ ft}}{12 \text{ in}}$.

$$\frac{1 \text{ ft}}{12 \text{ in}} = \frac{x \text{ ft}}{20 \text{ in}}$$

Convert the radius from inches to feet. The diameter of the hopper is 40″, so the radius is 20″.

$$20\left(\frac{1}{12}\right) = 20\left(\frac{x}{20}\right)$$

Multiply both sides of the equation by 20 to isolate x.

$$1.67 = x$$

The radius of the hopper is 1.67 ft.

$$\frac{1}{12} = \left(\frac{x}{45}\right)$$

Convert the slant height from inches to feet.

$$45\left(\frac{1}{12}\right) = 45\left(\frac{x}{45}\right)$$

$$3.75 = x$$

The slant height of the hopper is 3.75 ft.

$$A = \pi(1.67)(3.75)$$

Rewrite the formula, substituting the known values, and multiply.

$$A = 19.67$$

The amount of plastic in one hopper is 19.67 ft².

ACTIVITY 3.8
A REDECORATING PROJECT

You have added a new bathroom in your house, shown in the diagram below. You have installed the vanity and bathtub. You want to tile the floor before the toilet is installed and then paint the walls. The walls are 9 feet and the door is 7 feet high. The height of the bathtub is $1\frac{1}{2}'$ and the height of the vanity is 36". Work with 1 or 2 partners to answer the following questions.

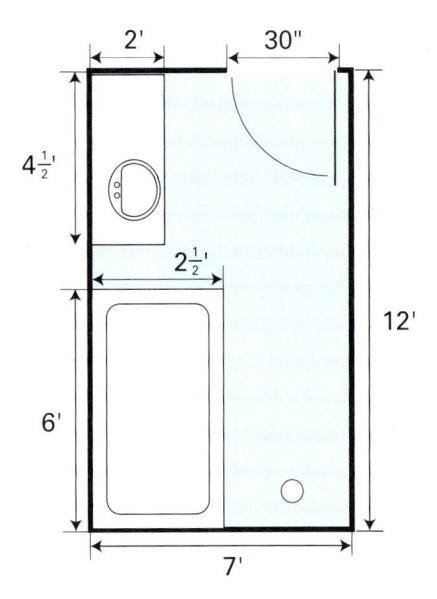

1. The floor will be tiled with 12" × 12" tiles. The area under the tub and vanity will not be tiled. Tiles cost $6.99 each. What will be the total cost of the tiles?

2. The door and the wall area that is covered by the tub and vanity do not need to be painted. The walls require 2 coats of paint. The second coat will require $\frac{2}{3}$ as much paint as the first coat. If a 4-litre can of paint covers 400 ft^2 at a cost of $46.99, and a 1-litre can covers 100 ft^2 at a cost of $17.99, what combination of cans of paint should you buy to minimize the cost of painting the bathroom?

3. You have a budget of $600.00 for the entire bathroom. After adding taxes (GST and provincial or territorial PST) to your materials cost, do you have any money left over to purchase a new mirror for the vanity?

Painters calculate surface area to determine how many cans of paint they need to buy.

Mental Math and Estimation

The surface area of a cube is 24 ft^2. Find the area of one face and the length of one side of the cube.

BUILD YOUR SKILLS

1. Vedran is a landscaper who builds custom garden ponds. Most of his clients want a circular pond that is 1.5 feet deep and has a 4-foot diameter. Vedran lines the ponds with synthetic rubber liner, which he buys in 10′ × 15′ rolls that cost $149.00.

   a) How many pond liners can be made from one roll?

   b) How much does it cost to line one pond?

2. A company manufactures aluminum beverage cans in two sizes: Can A has a diameter of 2.5 inches and a height of 4.5 inches. Can B has a diameter of 3 inches and a height of 3 inches. Which can requires more aluminum to manufacture?

3. Jashandeep is refinishing a wooden child's storage bench. She has two options for finishing the bench. Her first option is to treat the bench with 2 coats of wood stain. A one-litre can of stain costs $12.99 and will cover 15 m². Her second option is to paint the bench with 2 coats of latex paint. A one-quart can of paint costs $14.99 and will cover 100 ft². She drew the sketch at the right so she could estimate how much paint or stain she will need. Which option is less expensive?

4. A seed hopper in the shape of a cylinder has a diameter of 3.5 yd and a height of 4.7 yd. Both ends of the cylinder are capped with a cone that has a slant height of 2.73 yd. Find the number of square yards of sheet metal required to build the hopper (assume the hopper is hollow inside).

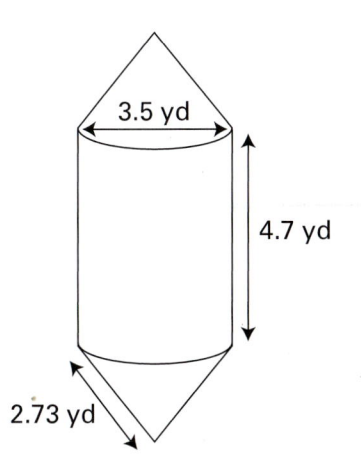

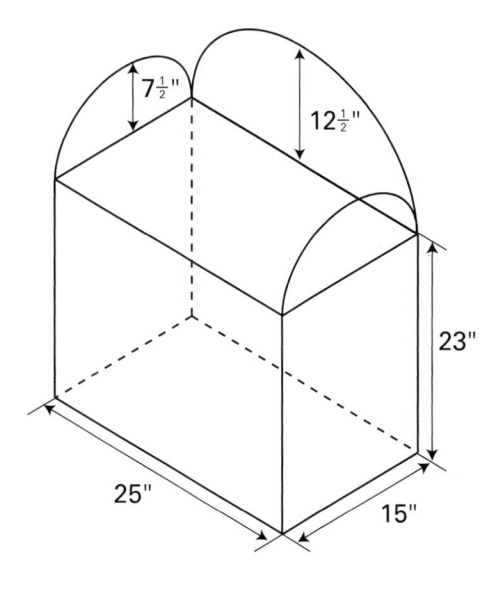

Chapter 3 Length, Area, and Volume

5. Francine wants to build a rectangular barbeque in her parents' backyard. The barbeque will be 40" wide, 32" deep, and 26" high and will be open at the front. She has decided to use bricks for the three walls and the floor. Bricks cost $0.80 each. Francine learned that bricklayers often estimate the number of bricks they need by calculating 48 bricks/yd^2 and then adding 5% for cutting and breakage.

   a) How many bricks should Francine buy?

   b) How much will the bricks cost?

6. A packaging company received a special order to design and manufacture boxes that measure 3" long, 1" wide, and 1" high. The boxes will be cut from sheets of cardboard that measure 1 yd × 1 yd. Draw a diagram to illustrate how you could cut 72 boxes from 1 sheet of the cardboard.

Extend your thinking

7. Benoit built an elaborate scratching post for his cats. It consists of three poles of different lengths topped with circular platforms for the cats to lie on. The poles are 2" in diameter and 2', 3', and 4' long. Each circular platform is 12" in diameter and 3" high. At the base of the structure is a cylindrical playhouse $1\frac{1}{2}'$ high with a 12" diameter. The cats get into the playhouse through a 6" diameter hole. The base of the structure is 2' × 2' × 2". Now Benoit wants to completely cover the scratching post with carpet. All sides of the poles, platforms, playhouse, and base will be covered. The carpet he has chosen costs $5.60/ft^2. How much will it cost to carpet the scratching post?

PROJECT—DESIGN AN ICE-FISHING SHELTER

BUILD A THREE-DIMENSIONAL MODEL

A three-dimensional model will help you visualize your ice-fishing shelter. Here is one way that you can build a scale model without a roof (so that you can see inside it). You will create a two-dimensional geometric net of your ice-fishing shelter, and then you will fold the net to create a three-dimensional model.

- Obtain a large piece of Bristol board or cardboard and measure its dimensions.

- Choose a scale that will enable you to copy your floor plan in the centre of the Bristol board and draw your 4 walls connected to the floor. Draw the window and door. Your drawing should look like the geometric net of a rectangular prism without the top (roof).

- Cut out your two-dimensional geometric net and fold up the walls to create a three-dimensional model. Tape the sides together.

- What is inside your shelter? Use the same scale factor to create any of the amenities that you plan to include. For example, include the seats, the heater, and the fishing holes in the floor. You can also provide additional materials to illustrate your design, such as paint samples or photos.

This student is creating a three-dimensional model based on her floor plan.

3.4 Volume

MATH ON THE JOB

Anthony is a warehouse technician in the City of Yellowknife Public Works Department. His job is to manage storage, shipping, and inventory of government assets such as furniture and office supplies. He inspects the items that arrive at the warehouse, decides where to store them, and uses a computer database to keep track of the number and location of the items in the warehouse. In order to make the best use of his warehouse space, Anthony uses math to plan how and where to store his inventory.

Anthony needs to know how many boxes can be stored in a storage bay in his warehouse. The storage bay is 24 feet long and 12 feet wide. The maximum height that boxes can be stacked is 9 feet. Each box is 24 inches × 36 inches × 18 inches. What is the maximum number of boxes that will fit in the storage bay?

Anthony needs to know the dimensions of the warehouse in order to store the inventory efficiently.

EXPLORE THE MATH

capacity: the maximum amount that a container can hold

In the SI, the base unit for measuring volume is the litre. The litre is also the base SI unit for measuring **capacity**. A litre is one-thousandth of a cubic metre. Why is volume measured in cubic units? What is the formula for calculating volume?

In the imperial system, the base unit for measuring volume and capacity is the pint, but volume can also be measured in cubic inches, cubic feet, or cubic yards.

In Canada, we use the term imperial units to mean British imperial units. The United States also uses an imperial system, but the sizes of its units for volume and capacity are different from the British units. Britain redefined its volume measurements after the United States had become an independent country that set its own standards. A British gallon is equal to 4.54609 litres; a US gallon equals 3.785 litres. Because British and US gallons are different sizes, so are all the related volume and capacity measures. For example, a British pint is 20 fluid ounces, while a US pint contains 16 fluid ounces.

Figure 3.2 lists the abbreviations for some common imperial units of volume and capacity.

FIGURE 3.2
Imperial Units of Volume and Capacity

Unit	Abbreviation
ounce	oz
fluid ounce	fl oz
pint	pt
quart	qt
gallon	gal

In many industries, volume and capacity are measured in imperial units rather than SI units. For example, in the food industry, ingredients are often measured in teaspoons, cups, and ounces. Other industries use both the imperial system and the SI. A building contractor estimating the amount of concrete needed for a job may find one supplier who delivers concrete by the cubic metre and another who delivers it by the cubic yard. The contractor would need to know how to convert between the two systems to ensure that she is getting the best price for her client.

In this section, you will develop methods to convert between the imperial system and SI for volume and capacity measurements.

DISCUSS THE IDEAS
PACKAGING

Over the years, beverage companies have marketed soft drinks in cans and bottles with different capacities. In Canada, a standard-size can of pop contains 355 mL. Why do you think pop is sold in containers of this size?

1. The table below lists three of the pop can sizes sold in the US and the equivalent sizes of cans sold in Canada. Working with a partner, copy the table in your notebook and fill in the ratios for the three sizes of cans.

RATIOS OF POP CAN SIZES

US pop can	Canadian pop can	Ratio fl oz: mL
8 US fl oz	237 mL	
12 US fl oz	355 mL	
16 US fl oz	473 mL	

Chapter 3 Length, Area, and Volume

2. Using the ratios from question 1, create a formula you can use to convert from mL to US fl oz. Do your results suggest a reason for the Canadian packaging sizes?

3. Copy the table below in your notebook and use your information from questions 1 and 2 to fill in the missing information and create a conversion chart.

CONVERTING US IMPERIAL TO SI UNITS

US Imperial	SI
1 fl oz	____ mL
1 pt = 16 fl oz	____ L
1 qt = 2 pt	____ L
1 gal = 4 qt	____ L

ACTIVITY 3.9
CONVERTING A RECIPE

You are making a batch of raisin bannock to take to a community feast. Your grandmother has given you her recipe, but the ingredients are in imperial units and you only have SI measuring equipment.

1. Examine your teaspoon and measuring cup. What SI and imperial markings are on them? Use the two items and work with a partner to convert the following recipe.

RAISIN BANNOCK RECIPE

Imperial	Ingredients	SI
3 cups	flour	____ mL
$1\frac{1}{2}$ teaspoons	baking powder	____ mL
$\frac{1}{2}$ teaspoon	salt	____ mL
$\frac{1}{4}$ cup	shortening	____ mL
$1\frac{1}{4}$ cups	water	____ mL
1 cup	raisins	____ mL

2. Copy the table below in your notebook and fill in the missing information to create a conversion chart.

CONVERTING COMMON COOKING UNITS	
Imperial	SI
$\frac{1}{4}$ teaspoon	____ mL
$\frac{1}{2}$ teaspoon	____ mL
1 teaspoon	____ mL
1 tablespoon (3 teaspoons)	____ mL
1 cup	____ mL
1 pint	568.2614 mL
1 quart (2 pt)	1.1365 L
1 gallon (4 qt)	4.5461 L

Example 1

Nigel imported a vehicle that was made in Britain. The capacity of the gas tank is 22 gallons. If the price of gasoline is $1.20 a litre, how much will it cost Nigel to fill his tank when it is empty?

SOLUTION

Because 1 British gallon equals 4.5461 litres, the conversion ratio used to convert gallons to litres is $\frac{4.5461}{1}$.

$\frac{4.5461 \text{ litres}}{1 \text{ British gallon}} = \frac{x \text{ litres}}{22 \text{ gallons}}$ Set up a proportion.

$22\left(\frac{4.5461}{1}\right) = 22\left(\frac{x}{22}\right)$ To isolate x, multiply both sides of the equation by 22.

$22 \times 4.5461 = x$

$100.0142 = x$

The capacity of the gas tank is 100.0142 L.

$100.0142 \times \$1.20 = \$120.02$

It will cost $120.02 to fill Nigel's gas tank.

Nigel may find it difficult to drive his British, right-hand drive car on Canadian roads.

Example 2

The cooling system of a car's 6-cylinder, 250-cubic-inch displacement engine has a capacity of $3\frac{1}{2}$ gallons. To protect the engine against freezing temperatures, an antifreeze solution of $\frac{3}{8}$ ethylene glycol and $\frac{5}{8}$ water is added to the cooling system. If the cooling system is filled to capacity with the antifreeze solution, how many quarts of ethylene glycol are in the cooling system?

SOLUTION

First find the capacity of the cooling system in quarts. Because 4 quarts equals 1 gallon, the unit conversion factor is $\frac{4 \text{ quarts}}{1 \text{ gallon}}$.

$$\frac{x}{3.5} = \frac{4}{1}$$
Convert $3\frac{1}{2}$ to a decimal and set up a proportion.

$$\frac{x}{3.5}(3.5) = \frac{4}{1}(3.5)$$
Multiply both sides of the equation by the common denominator to isolate the variable.

$$x = 4 \times 3.5$$

$$x = 14$$

The cooling system has a capacity of 14 quarts.

Find the number of quarts of ethylene glycol the cooling system contains.

$$0.375 \times 14 = 5.25$$
Convert $\frac{3}{8}$ to a decimal and multiply by the capacity of the cooling system.

The cooling system contains 5.25 quarts of ethylene glycol.

Example 3

Reshma built 24 wood planters for her garden. The inside of each planter measures 4′ long, 2′ deep, and $1\frac{1}{2}$′ wide. She needs to order soil to fill the planters. At K & R Soils, potting soil sells for $17.00/yd³, while Bob's Best Buy sells potting soil for $21.50/m³. Where should Reshma buy her soil?

SOLUTION

To find the cost of buying the potting soil from K & R Soils, convert the dimensions of one planter from feet to yards.

$$\left(\frac{x \text{ yd}}{4 \text{ ft}}\right) = \left(\frac{1 \text{ yd}}{3 \text{ ft}}\right)$$
Set up a proportion to convert the length to yards.

Antifreeze prevents water from freezing and expanding in the cooling system.

$$4\left(\frac{x}{4}\right) = 4\left(\frac{1}{3}\right)$$

$$x = \left(\frac{4}{3}\right)$$ Convert the fraction to a decimal.

$$x = 1.33 \text{ yd}$$

$$\left(\frac{x \text{ yd}}{2 \text{ ft}}\right) = \left(\frac{1 \text{ yd}}{3 \text{ ft}}\right)$$ Set up a proportion to convert the depth to yards.

$$2\left(\frac{x}{2}\right) = 2\left(\frac{1}{3}\right)$$

$$x = \frac{2}{3}$$ Convert the fraction to a decimal.

$$x = 0.67 \text{ yd}$$

$$\left(\frac{x \text{ yd}}{1.5 \text{ ft}}\right) = \left(\frac{1 \text{ yd}}{3 \text{ ft}}\right)$$ Convert the fraction to a decimal and set up a proportion to convert the width to yards.

$$1.5\left(\frac{x}{1.5}\right) = 1.5\left(\frac{1}{3}\right)$$

$$x = 0.5 \text{ yd}$$

$$V = 1.33 \times 0.67 \times 0.5$$ Use the formula for volume to calculate the cubic yards of soil needed for one planter.

$$V = 0.45 \text{ yd}^3$$ One planter requires 0.45 yd³ of soil.

$$24 \times 0.45 = 10.8$$ Multiply by 24 to find the cubic yards of soil needed to fill all the planters.

Reshma would need 10.8 yd³ of potting soil.

$$10.8 \times \$17.00 = \$183.60$$ The soil from K&R Soils would cost $183.60.

To find the cost of buying the potting soil from Bob's Best Buy, convert the dimensions of one planter from feet to metres.

$$\frac{x \text{ m}}{4 \text{ ft}} = \frac{1 \text{ m}}{3.2808 \text{ ft}}$$ Use the conversion factor 1 m = 3.2808 feet to convert the length of the planter to metres.

$$4\left(\frac{x}{4}\right) = 4\left(\frac{1}{3.2808}\right)$$

$$x = 1.22 \text{ m}$$

Reshma will be able to add a wide variety of flowers to her planters.

$$\frac{x \text{ m}}{2 \text{ ft}} = \frac{1 \text{ m}}{3.2808 \text{ ft}}$$ Convert the depth to metres.

$$2\left(\frac{x}{2}\right) = 2\left(\frac{1}{3.2808}\right)$$

$$x = 0.61 \text{ m}$$

$$\left(\frac{x \text{ m}}{1.5 \text{ ft}}\right) = \left(\frac{1 \text{ m}}{3.2808 \text{ ft}}\right)$$ Convert the width to metres.

$$1.5\left(\frac{x}{1.5}\right) = 1.5\left(\frac{1}{3.2808}\right)$$

$$x = 0.46 \text{ m}$$

$$V = 1.22 \times 0.61 \times 0.46$$ Use the formula for volume to calculate the cubic metres of soil needed for one planter.

$$V = 0.34 \text{ m}^3$$ One planter requires 0.34 m³ of soil.

$$24 \times 0.34 = 8.16$$ Multiply by 24 to find the cubic metres of soil needed to fill all the planters.

Reshma would need 8.16 m³ of potting soil.

$$8.16 \times \$21.50 = \$175.44$$ The soil from Bob's Best Buy would cost $175.44.

Reshma should buy her potting soil from Bob's Best Buy.

ACTIVITY 3.10
DRIVEWAY CONSTRUCTION

Maynard has decided to pave his driveway, which measures 74 ft × 18 ft. He has narrowed his choices to concrete or paving stones.

EXCAVATION AND PAVING COSTS

Item	Cost
Soil excavation and removal	$75.00/yd³
Gravel	$12.00/yd³
Sand	$30.00/yd³
Concrete	$135.00/yd³
Crushed limestone	$35.00/yd³
Paving stone	$6.50/yd³

a) If the driveway is paved with concrete, he will need 4 inches of concrete on top of 8 inches of gravel.

b) If he uses paving stones that are $2\frac{1}{2}''$ thick, they will need a foundation of $3\frac{1}{2}$ inches of sand and 12 inches of crushed limestone. He will also need to add 10% to his paving stone order to allow for breakage and cutting.

The costs of excavation and materials are shown on the previous page. Working in your small group, compare the cost of paving the driveway with concrete and with paving stones. Write a report with an itemized cost analysis for both options.

PUZZLE IT OUT

THE DECANTING PUZZLE

You have two empty containers. One has a capacity of 5 units and the other has a capacity of 3 units. Neither container has any unit markings. Your job is to fill one of the containers with exactly 4 units of water. You can fill a container, empty a container, and pour water from one container to the other, without spilling over.

Find the fewest number of pours needed to reach your goal.

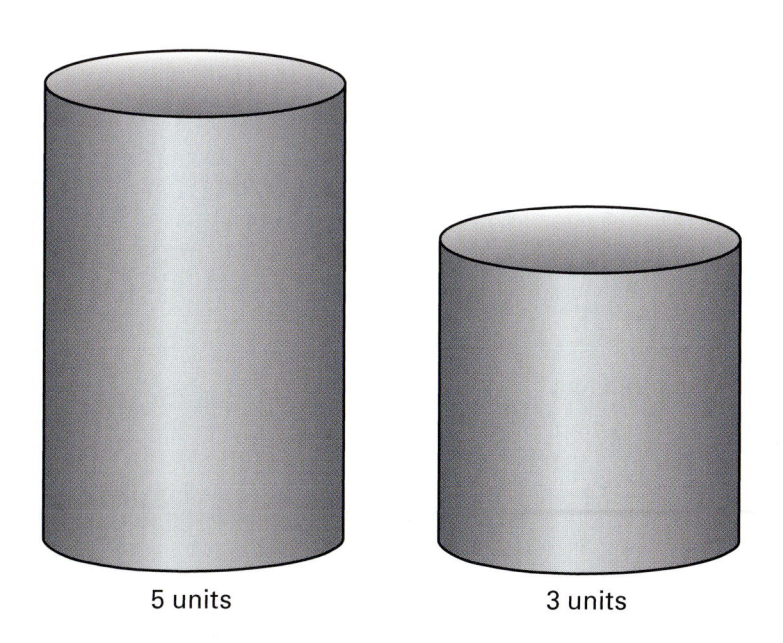

5 units   3 units

Chapter 3   Length, Area, and Volume   131

BUILD YOUR SKILLS

1. A baker needs to double a recipe that requires 3 cups of milk, but he only has SI measuring utensils. How many mL of milk will he need?

2. A convenience store in the US sells 4 different sizes of slushy drinks: 12 US fl oz, 16 US fl oz, 28 US fl oz, and 40 US fl oz. What would be the equivalent sizes in millilitres? Do the millilitre sizes correspond to the drink sizes in your neighbourhood?

3. Anne-Laure is a toy manufacturer. She imported a supply of boxes from the US with the dimensions 12″ × 6″ × 8″. She needs a box for a game that measures 20 cm × 11 cm × 16 cm. Will the game fit in the boxes she imported?

4. An American tourist has crossed the Canadian border. His vehicle has a 15-gallon capacity and he has $\frac{1}{8}$ tank of gas left. If the price of gas is $1.10 a litre, how much will it cost him to fill his tank?

5. Everett owns and operates an auto repair shop. He wants to pour a concrete pad 24′ × 22′ × 4″ in front of the garage. J & L Concrete sells concrete for $145.00/yd^3 and M & W Concrete sells concrete for $165.00/m^3. How much will each company charge? Which company should Everett buy his concrete from?

6. Elann is a bridgeworker who needs to calculate the amount of concrete required to repair concrete spalls on a bridge deck. Spalls are shallow holes where fragments of concrete have broken off due to freezing, use of road salt, or wear. There are three concrete spalls on the bridge deck. The spalls are rectangular and each is $2\frac{1}{2}$ in deep. The first spall measures $6\frac{1}{2}$ ft by 3 ft. The second is 16 ft by 6 ft. The third is $15\frac{1}{2}$ ft by 9 ft. She needs to order enough concrete to fill the spalls, plus an extra $\frac{1}{2}$ yd^3 to compensate for any waste. How many cubic yards of concrete should she order?

Extend your thinking

7. Jamal wants to buy a fuel-efficient vehicle. He knows that in countries that use the SI, fuel efficiency is measured by the number of litres of fuel the vehicle uses in 100 km. He can use litres per 100 km to compare fuel efficiency. The vehicle that uses the least fuel per 100 km is the most fuel efficient. Jamal saw an ad for a car that averages 45 miles to 1 US gallon and an ad for a minivan that uses 10 litres per 100 km. Which vehicle is more fuel efficient?

Driving a fuel-efficient car is economical and environmentally responsible.

PROJECT—DESIGN AN ICE-FISHING SHELTER

MAKE A PRESENTATION

You are now ready to present your ice-fishing shelter. Start by planning your presentation. What information will you include? How can you best communicate the information you have gathered and present your shelter? Presentations are often made using illustrated posters or handouts, or you could use presentation software. Be sure to include the following items in your presentation:

- a description of your materials, quantities, and costs;
- an accurate two-dimensional floor plan; and
- a three-dimensional scale model.

Include pictures of your materials and the amenities you have found for your shelter. You may also want to explain why you have chosen certain materials or amenities.

Share ideas with your classmates about the best way to present your project.

REFLECT ON YOUR LEARNING
LENGTH, AREA, AND VOLUME

Now that you have finished this chapter, you should be able to

- ❒ understand the relationships between units in the SI and imperial system;
- ❒ convert a given measurement from SI units to imperial units;
- ❒ convert a given measurement from imperial units to SI units;
- ❒ estimate measurements using a referent;
- ❒ calculate perimeter, circumference, and area in imperial units;
- ❒ calculate the surface area and volume of a three-dimensional object in imperial units.

In addition, you have completed a project that applied your new skills in a practical context.

Chapter 3 Length, Area, and Volume **133**

PRACTISE YOUR NEW SKILLS

1. A walking trail in Stanley Park in Vancouver is 10.8 km long. The Parks Board wants to install benches every 600 m along the trail. The benches cost $350.00 each, and labour will cost $1500.00. How much will it cost to install the benches?

2. Brenda was hired to replace the wood case moulding on a window frame that measures 90 inches by 48 inches. If the moulding costs $3.25 a linear foot and her labour charge is $8.50 a linear foot, how much will it cost to replace the mouldings?

3. A family room is 21 ft × 12 ft with four 8-foot walls. It has one door to the deck outside that is 30 in wide and 7 ft high and two windows that each measure 5 ft × 3 ft. The interior walls are to be painted. The painter charges $6.95/ft^2. How much will the painter charge to do this job?

4. Antoine needs to buy metal primer to rust proof a cylindrical fuel storage tank. The tank has a diameter of 15'6" and a height of 18'. A 3.8 L can of metal primer costs $47.13 and covers 40 m^2. What will be the total cost of the metal primer? (Assume that the bottom of the storage tank will be painted.)

5. A snack bar advertises ice cream by displaying an oversized ice-cream cone on its roof. The cone is made of aluminum and has a 12-inch diameter, a height of 36 inches, and a slant height of 36.50 inches. How many square feet of aluminum were used to make the cone?

6. An American tourist crossing the border into Canada notices a sign that states, "227 km to the next service station." There is a service station across the road from the sign. Her car's 18-gallon fuel tank is $\frac{1}{2}$ full, and she knows her vehicle gets 28 miles to the gallon. Should she stop for gas now or fill up at the next service station? Show the evidence for her decision.

7. Blueberry farmers use peat moss as mulch around blueberry bushes to conserve moisture and prevent weeds. A farmer has a blueberry field that is 30 ft long and 18 ft wide. He wants to lay 6 in of mulch on the field. He can buy a 1 yd^3 bale of peat moss for $39.00 or a 3.8 ft^3 bale for $12.49. Which size bale would give the farmer the best total price?

Putting mulch around blueberry plants is an environmentally friendly method of encouraging their growth.

134   MathWorks 10

8. Dawai is creating a flower bed alongside his house. The bed will be 15 ft by 3 ft, and he needs to add soil to a depth of 12 in. Dirt for Less sells garden soil for $15.99/yd^3, and Rocks and Soils sells soil for $18.99/m^3.

   a) If he can buy fractions of a cubic yard or metre, where should he buy the soil?

   b) If he must buy whole cubic yards or metres, where should he buy the soil?

9. Steve is building an 8-inch-thick concrete retaining wall that is 75 feet long and $2\frac{1}{2}$ feet high. Concrete is made by mixing one part cement, two parts sand, and four parts gravel with water.

   If Dawai chooses to plant tulips, he should plant each bulb 8 inches deep.

   a) How many cubic yards of the following ingredients will Steve need to build the wall?

      i) cement

      ii) sand

      iii) gravel

   b) Sand costs $18.00/yd^3, gravel costs $8.99/yd^3, cement costs $65.00/yd^3, and Steve is charging $1500.00 for labour. How much will the job cost?

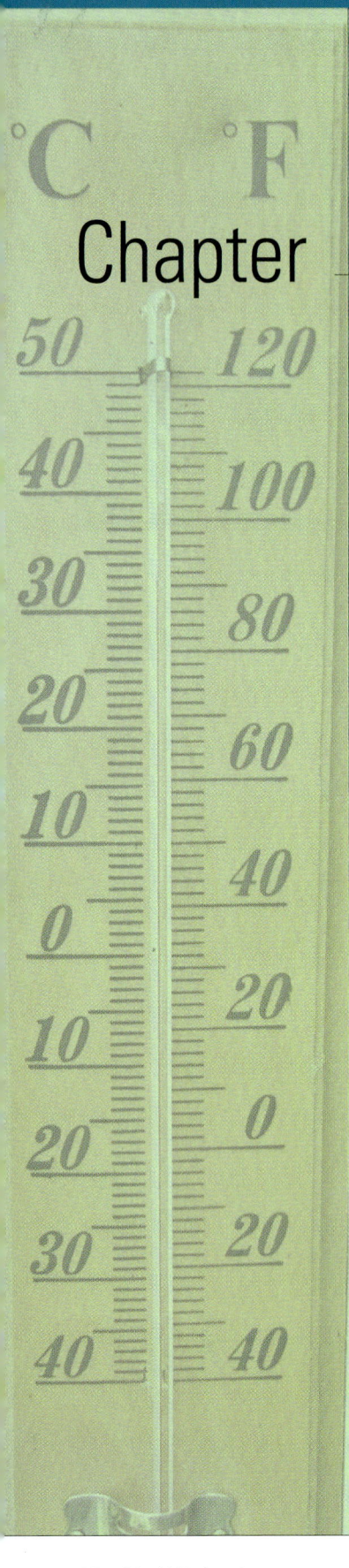

Chapter 4

Mass, Temperature, and Volume

GOALS

In this chapter, you will consider temperature in the Celsius and Fahrenheit scales and measures of weight and mass in the Système internationale (SI) and imperial system. In the workplace and in everyday life, these measurements are applied in a variety of contexts, including cooking, medicine, farming, and building construction. In this chapter, you will build on your prior mathematical skills and knowledge to

- compare and make conversions within and between Celsius and Fahrenheit temperature scales and between imperial and SI units of mass/weight;
- examine the differences between mass and weight in each system; and
- perform other conversions that are important in the workplace, such as conversions between mass and volume.

KEY TERMS

- Celsius (°C)
- conversion factor
- Fahrenheit (°F)
- gram (g)
- kilogram (kg)
- mass
- ounce (oz)
- pound (lb)
- temperature
- ton (tn)
- tonne (t)
- weight

PROJECT—CULINARY COMPETITION

START TO PLAN

PROJECT OVERVIEW

You may have seen cooking competitions on television where chefs challenge one another in the kitchen for fame and status. Can you think of some examples? In this chapter, you will plan a menu that could be submitted to an international cooking competition.

For this project, you will plan a menu consisting of an appetizer, main course, and dessert. You will also need to research all the recipes. Since this is an international competition, you must include ingredient amounts and cooking temperatures in both SI and imperial units. Finally, you will design a printed menu and a recipe booklet for submission and judging by your classmates.

*A la cuisine!**

GET STARTED

To begin your project, research recipes from different countries to see how they measure ingredients (by weight, by volume, or by both?). Next, plan your menu and find recipes for each dish. Decide on the number of guests you will feed. You will be assigned two ingredients that you must use. The rest is up to you.

You can either create your own recipes or use cookbooks, the internet, or other resources. When choosing your dishes and recipes, be sure to keep the following in mind:

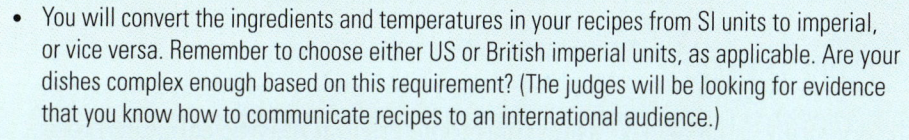

- Do your dishes work together? Are they interesting and do they incorporate several ingredients? Do they incorporate the theme ingredients?

- You will convert the ingredients and temperatures in your recipes from SI units to imperial, or vice versa. Remember to choose either US or British imperial units, as applicable. Are your dishes complex enough based on this requirement? (The judges will be looking for evidence that you know how to communicate recipes to an international audience.)

These competitors are preparing the final course of their gourmet meal.

FINAL PRESENTATION CHECKLIST

You will present your menu and recipe booklet to your class and your teacher for evaluation. Each person in your class will vote, by secret ballot, for his or her top three favourites. Your final presentation must include the following:

- a menu with a brief description of each of the dishes; and
- a recipe booklet that includes
  - a recipe for each dish,
  - conversion tables for the various ingredients, and
  - a shopping list of all the ingredients with amounts converted into either SI or imperial units.

---

* *A la cuisine!* means "To the kitchen!" in French.

Chapter 4 Mass, Temperature, and Volume 137

4.1 Temperature Conversions

MATH ON THE JOB

Denise Sparrow, a citizen of the Musqueam First Nation, is the owner/operator of Salishan Catering in Vancouver, BC. In 1993, Denise began to package and sell salmon. Her business flourished and was transformed into a catering business that fuses traditional Musqueam cultural knowledge and foods with modern foods. Denise credits her success to her grandmother and her mother, who taught her the ways of her ancestors.

Denise's company offers many different kinds of catering services such as potlatch platters, family feasts, buffets, and full service six-course dinners for any number of people, sometimes with servers wearing traditional clothing. Denise also enjoys sharing her knowledge of traditional cultural food preparation with schools.

Denise's catering company offers specialties like smoked salmon eggs on grilled bannock and pemmican buffalo jerky strips.

Denise is planning a banquet for 400 people. She is serving appetizers of alder-smoked salmon, buffalo sausage, and BBQ bannock. The main course will include venison, seaweed, wild rice, sea asparagus, and a green salad. Wild berry and whipped soapberry dessert will finish off the meal. Denise is used to working in degrees Fahrenheit but the refrigerator and oven at the banquet facility use degrees Celsius. She knows that cold foods must be kept below 40°F and hot foods must be kept above 140°F. What will Denise need to know in order to convert from Fahrenheit to Celsius?

EXPLORE THE MATH

Temperature is measured using thermometers that may be calibrated to different scales. In Canada, temperature is measured using the Celsius scale, but there are some cases where the Fahrenheit scale is also used. What examples can you think of? If you have travelled to the United States, you may have heard temperatures stated in degrees Fahrenheit. The Celsius and Fahrenheit scales are the two scales most commonly used in daily life and in the workplace. For instance, tradespeople who work outdoors have to know the external temperature in order to calculate the setting times of solvents, adhesives, or paint. In what other jobs might you need to measure temperatures?

In the SI, temperatures are measured using the Celsius scale. Because the Celsius system is a 100-step scale from the freezing to the boiling point of water, it is sometimes referred to as centigrade, from the Latin words meaning 100 steps.

ACTIVITY 4.1
PREPARE A TEMPERATURE GRAPH

On the Celsius scale 0° is the freezing point of water, while on the Fahrenheit scale, water freezes at 32°. Other equivalencies that exist are shown in the chart below:

EQUIVALENCIES IN FAHRENHEIT AND CELSIUS UNITS

Example	°F	°C
Bitterly cold day	−22	−30
Mild day	59	15
Hot day	81	27
Normal body temperature	98.6	37
Boiling water	212	100

1. Use the above information to sketch a graph from which you can determine the Fahrenheit temperature that corresponds to any Celsius temperature between 0° and 100°.

2. What type of relationship appears to exist between the two temperature scales?

3. Use the graph to determine the approximate Fahrenheit equivalent for 20°C, 40°C, 60°C, and 80°C.

4. Each pair of Celsius temperatures above differs by 20°C. What do you notice about the differences in Fahrenheit?

5. How can you use the graph to determine the degrees Celsius that correspond to a given Fahrenheit temperature?

6. Use the graph to determine the approximate Celsius equivalent of −10°F.

ACTIVITY 4.2
DEVELOP A CONVERSION FORMULA

1. Work with a partner and use the information from Activity 4.1 to estimate the safe temperatures in the Math on the Job on the previous page.

2. Using the fact that 0°C and 100°C are the freezing and boiling points of water respectively on the Celsius scale and that the corresponding temperatures on the Fahrenheit scale are 32°F and 212°F, develop a formula for converting degrees Fahrenheit to degrees Celsius.

3. Use your understanding of equations to adapt this formula so that you can convert directly from degrees Celsius to degrees Fahrenheit.

HINT

When substituting a number for a letter in a formula, use brackets around the number, including its sign, so you don't confuse the operation symbol with the number sign.

4. Since one must be very careful in handling food, use the formulas you have developed to determine the exact values for safe storage of food in the Math on the Job. Were your estimates based on the graph close enough?

Mental Math and Estimation

The thermometer on the outside of your house reads 20°F. Estimate what the temperature would be if expressed in degrees Celsius.

DISCUSS THE IDEAS
SEPARATION OF CRUDE OIL

When crude oil is refined, it is heated and separates into different fuels, such as gasoline, kerosene, diesel oil, and fuel oil. As the crude oil is heated, it turns into vapour. When the vapour cools, the different fuels condense at predictable temperatures.

Measurement coordinators are responsible for maintaining temperature records during the oil separation process. Like many tradespeople who convert measurements on a regular basis, measurement coordinators often use a formula containing decimals rather than fractions. Sian is a measurement coordinator at a Saskatchewan oil refinery. She has recently been consulting with a colleague in the US and would like to send him a report about fuel condensation points, giving him the data in degrees Fahrenheit.

These are the temperatures she wants to include:

FUEL CONDENSATION POINTS

Fuel	Condensation point (°C)
Gasoline	150
Kerosene	200
Diesel	300
Fuel oil	370

1. Rewrite the conversion formula $F = \frac{9}{5}C + 32$ using decimals.

2. Convert the four fuel condensation points from Celsius to Fahrenheit using decimals.

3. Use your understanding of equations to solve for C so that Sian can convert directly from Fahrenheit to Celsius.

4. What advantage is there to using decimals rather than fractions in conversion formulas?

Example 1

Harpreet is transporting frozen food from Los Angeles to Vancouver in a refrigerated truck. The external temperature in Los Angeles is 90°F when he leaves. He knows that the safest temperature for preserving the frozen food is between 0°F and −4°F. When he arrives at the Canadian border, the border guard determines the temperature of the truck to be −19°C. Is this within the acceptable range of temperature for preserving frozen food? Give your answer to the nearest half a degree.

Harpreet must ensure that his cargo remains frozen or it won't be safe to eat.

SOLUTION

Use the formula for converting degrees Fahrenheit to degrees Celsius.

First, convert −4°F to degrees Celsius.

$$C = \frac{5}{9}(F - 32)$$

$$C = \frac{5}{9}[(-4) - 32] \qquad \text{Substitute −4 for } F.$$

$$C = \frac{5}{9}\left(\frac{-36}{1}\right)$$

$$C = \frac{5}{\cancel{9}_{1}} \times \frac{\cancel{-36}^{-4}}{1} \qquad \text{Simplify.}$$

$$C = 5(-4)$$

$$C = -20$$

Therefore, −4°F is equivalent to −20°C.

Next, change 0°F to degrees Celsius using the same method.

$$C = \frac{5}{9}(F - 32)$$

$$C = \frac{5}{9}[(0) - 32]$$

$$C = \frac{5}{9}\left(\frac{-32}{1}\right)$$

$$C = \frac{-160}{9}$$

$$C \approx -17.78$$

Therefore, 0°F is rounded to −18°C.

The Celsius thermometer should read between −18° and −20°. Since Harpreet's truck is at −19°C, it falls within the safe range.

Example 2

While travelling in the US, Jennifer and Richard are concerned because their daughter Isabella has a temperature of 39°C, so they take her to a medical clinic. The nurse takes Isabella's temperature on the Fahrenheit scale. What will Isabella's temperature be in degrees Fahrenheit?

SOLUTION

Use the formula $F = \frac{9}{5}C + 32$ plus your calculator to convert Isabella's temperature.

$$F = \frac{9}{5}(39) + 32 \qquad \text{Substitute 39 for } C.$$

$$F = 102.2$$

Isabella has a fever of 102.2°F. Normal body temperature is about 37°C or 98.6°F.

ACTIVITY 4.3
COOKING AT HIGHER ALTITUDES

The definitions of freezing and boiling points for water have been established at sea level. Due to differences in atmospheric pressure, these change with altitude. At higher elevations, water will "boil" at a lower temperature but may not be hot enough to make coffee. The pressure difference also affects the preparation of food.

T You and a partner have planned an excursion for a party of eight to Abbot Pass on the British Columbia-Alberta border. You will have breakfast at a hut 2925 metres above sea level. Use the internet to research how you may need to change your breakfast preparations.

1. At what temperature will water boil? Express your answer in degrees Celsius.

2. At sea level, it takes 3 minutes to prepare a soft-boiled egg. How many minutes will it take to prepare a soft-boiled egg at the hut on Abbot Pass?

Abbot Pass is located in the Rockies between Mount Lefroy and Mount Victoria, shown here.

BUILD YOUR SKILLS

1. Cooked meat must reach a recommended internal temperature before it is safe to eat. A cookbook contains a list stated in degrees Fahrenheit.

   FIGURE 4.1
   Recommended Internal Temperatures

Meat	Temperature
ground meats	160°F
beef (medium rare)	145°F
beef (well-done)	170°F
chicken (whole)	165°F

   Determine the corresponding temperatures in degrees Celsius.

2. Mandy supervises a road construction crew. She knows that she must modify the asphalt paving mixture her crew uses if temperatures drop below 21°C. What is this temperature in degrees Fahrenheit? Why would temperature have an effect on the paving mixture?

Chapter 4 Mass, Temperature, and Volume 143

Crews usually pave in the summer because the asphalt needs warm temperatures to set properly.

3. Chan works at a building construction site. His boss told him that he does not have to work if the temperature is above 105°F or below −15°F. Chan has a Celsius thermometer. What are the limits the boss has stipulated for him in degrees Celsius? Why might Chan's boss state these temperatures? What other factors, other than straight temperature, might affect Chan's and his boss's decision to work on the construction site on a particular day?

4. Pedro purchased a new crimper for his hair salon. The regulations state that the surface temperature, when in use, will be (230 ± 10)°C. What is this in degrees Fahrenheit? Express the answer in the form $(T \pm t)$°C.

5. In the summer, Bev turns on her air conditioner to keep her house cool, but in the winter, she turns on the furnace to warm it up.

   a) Check your thermostat at home to determine the temperature. Be sure to note if it is °C or °F. Convert the temperature to the other scale.

   b) Compare your home's temperature with that of at least 3 other students. What is the range of temperatures in the homes of you and your friends in °C? °F?

   c) If Bev likes to keep the inside temperature between 18°C and 22°C, what would the Fahrenheit temperatures be?

Extend your thinking

6. Use the conversion formulas to determine the temperature(s) at which degrees Celsius equal degrees Fahrenheit.

THE ROOTS OF MATH

MEASURING TEMPERATURE

People have intuitively known about temperature—the measurement of heat and cold—since the beginning of time. Fire is hot and ice is cold! People gained more knowledge about temperature as they started working with metals and needed to determine the level of heat required to melt them. However, people's understanding of temperature remained subjective for a long time. The thermoscope was one of the first instruments developed to indicate that one thing was hotter or colder than another. In 1592, the Italian scientist and mathematician Galileo invented an air thermoscope that was very sensitive to changes in temperature, but it was also subject to changes in air pressure. This meant that the thermoscope could indicate when there was a change in temperature, but it could not measure temperature itself. Another Italian scientist, a doctor named Santorio Santorio, is credited with being the first person to apply a number scale to the thermoscope in 1612, thus making the first useful thermometer.

Daniel Gabriel Fahrenheit produced the first alcohol thermometer in 1709 and the first mercury thermometer in 1714 in Amsterdam, Netherlands. In 1724, he wrote an article, introducing his new temperature scale. Although no one is completely sure how Fahrenheit set the scale, it is commonly thought that he set the starting point, or 0°, as the point to which the mercury in the tube descended when it was placed in a mixture of ice and salt, which was the coldest measurable substance at the time. Using a 12-point scale (similar to a foot-long ruler), Fahrenheit set the upper point of the scale at normal body temperature, which he determined was 96°. He then set the thermometer in water that was turning into ice. Fahrenheit determined that the temperature at which the water froze was 32°. Using his scale, Fahrenheit's successors determined the boiling point of water to be 212°. They also made slight changes to his calculations, but they maintained the 12-point scale.

This is a modern-day thermometer based on Galileo's thermoscope.

Anders Celsius, from Uppsala, Sweden, is acknowledged to be the inventor of the Celsius scale, although history tells us that he worked with a group of colleagues. The Celsius scale was first used in 1742. Celsius determined that the freezing and boiling points of water depend on atmospheric pressure, and for this scale, he set the freezing point and boiling point of pure water at sea level to be 0° and 100° respectively. In 1954, the 10th Conférence générale des poids et mesures (CGPM) defined these points to be taken at the atmospheric pressure at mean sea level at the latitude of Paris, France because, for practical purposes, this pressure reflects that of many industrialized cities around the world.

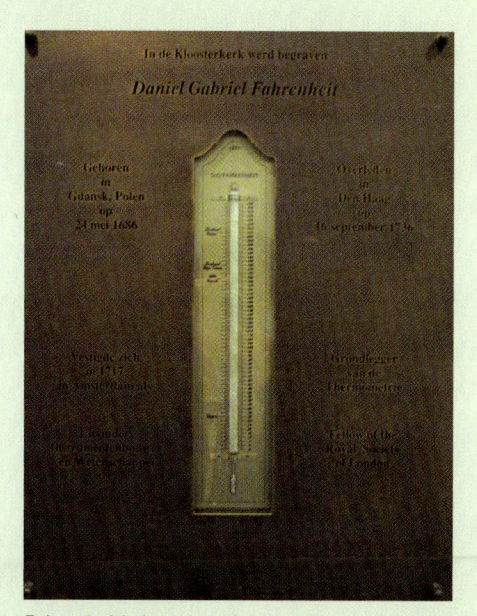

Fahrenheit's burial marker includes an example of his thermometer.

1. Is a degree the same from one scale to another?

2. How do you think a thermometer works? Why does the liquid in a thermometer rise and fall?

3. Celsius used the boiling and freezing points of water to calibrate his scale. Can you think of other calibration points that could be used? Can you explain why Celsius and Fahrenheit used two points?

Chapter 4 Mass, Temperature, and Volume **145**

4.2 Mass in the Imperial System

MATH *ON THE JOB*

Craig and Genevieve own and manage a pet food store in Saskatoon, Saskatchewan. In order to keep their business profitable, they need a wide range of financial and computer skills. They must also be familiar with all the different products they sell, so they will know which ones to recommend to their customers.

Some of Craig and Genevieve's suppliers are in Canada, but others are in the US. Products ordered from the US are weighed in pounds and ounces. There are 16 ounces in 1 pound. Because many of their customers are elderly and prefer the imperial system of measurement, Craig and Genevieve often package their pet foods in imperial units.

These dog treats are sold in bulk and priced by the pound.

Craig and Genevieve purchased 288 pounds of cat food at $2.50 a pound. They plan to sell it to their customers in 12-ounce packages. To cover overhead and to make a profit, they have calculated that they must charge 175% of what they paid. How many packages of cat food will there be and what must they charge for each one, not including taxes?

EXPLORE THE MATH

mass: a measure of the quantity of matter in an object

weight: a measure of the force of gravity on an object

Although people often use the terms mass and weight interchangeably, there is a difference between them. **Mass** refers to the quantity of matter in an object. Mass is usually measured using a balance to compare a known amount of matter to an unknown amount of matter. **Weight** is a measure of the force of gravity on an object. Weight is therefore a measurement of the heaviness of a body, the force with which a body is attracted to a celestial body (planet or moon, for example), and is equal to the product of the object's mass and the acceleration of gravity.

But what does this mean? Simply stated, it means that wherever an object is, its mass will remain constant. However, the further away it is from the centre of gravity, the less it will weigh. You may have studied planets in science and know that on another planet, because the force of gravity is different than it is on earth, an object would weigh a different amount. Recall how astronauts in space look the same as they do on earth—they have the same size and shape—but they are weightless! On the moon, you would weigh about $\frac{1}{6}$ of what you weigh on earth.

Measuring weight and mass are necessary tasks for many trades. For example, crane and hoist operators weigh material to determine whether it can be lifted safely and they often use imperial measures.

In the imperial system, the slug is the unit of mass and the pound is the unit of weight. The slug is not often used, and we have come to use the pound as the basic unit for both mass and weight. Although Canada converted from imperial units to SI units in the 1970s, many Canadians measure weight in pounds. Some trades still measure weight in pounds, too, including forklift operators and building contractors.

In the imperial system, there are three commonly used units of weight: the ounce, the pound, and the ton. The pound is the basic unit of weight.

1 ton (tn) = 2000 pounds	A ton is sometimes referred to as a short ton. An adult bison may weigh 1 tn.
1 pound (lb)	A football weighs approximately 1 lb.
16 ounces (oz) = 1 pound	One slice of bread weighs about 1 oz.

Crane operators often weigh their loads in imperial units.

HINT

A pound is slightly less than ½ a kilogram. This can be useful when making an estimate or doing a mental calculation.

Pound is abbreviated lb because it comes from the Latin word for pound, *libra*. Ounce is abbreviated oz because it comes from an old Italian word for ounce, *onza*.

In order to define what one pound is, we need a standard with which to compare it. The pound is actually defined in terms of the SI system as the rounded value of 0.453 592 37 kilograms.

DISCUSS THE IDEAS
THE WEIGHT OF WASTE

Imagine that you work at a waste management plant. You are responsible for managing the process of getting the loose recycled materials that you receive ready for shipping to the companies that actually recycle the materials (for example, that melt glass down so that it can be made into new glass products). You must consider many variables in determining how you will prepare the materials for shipment. One important thing to consider is the volume vs. the weight of the materials in different forms. See Figure 4.2 for some examples.

1. Why would you need to consider the weight and the volume of the materials?

2. What factors would affect the weight of the materials, other than their volume?

Recycled material is measured in both cubic yards and pounds.

FIGURE 4.2
Volume to Weight Conversion Table for Recyclable Materials

Material	Volume	Estimated weight (pounds)
computer paper—uncompacted	1 cubic yard	655
computer paper—compacted and baled	1 cubic yard	1310
refillable soft drink bottles	24 bottles	22
glass bottles—whole	1 cubic yard	500–700
glass bottles—crushed	1 cubic yard	1800–2700
cans—whole	1 cubic yard	150
cans—compacted	1 cubic yard	850
finished compost	1 cubic yard	600
used motor oil	1 gallon	7

ACTIVITY 4.4
CHOOSING IMPERIAL UNITS

When weighing objects, it is important to think about what units to use. For example, in weighing a load of bricks, you would probably use tons because they are very heavy. A grown person usually weighs him/herself in pounds, whereas a newborn baby's weight is measured in pounds and ounces. Working with a partner, determine 5 objects that you encounter in daily living that would be weighed in ounces, 5 that would be weighed in pounds, and 5 that would be weighed in tons. Justify your choices. Other than a young baby, can you think of objects that might be weighed in pounds *and* ounces?

Babies are usually measured in pounds and ounces.

Example 1

Stephan is building a rectangular water cistern on an acreage outside Beausejour, Manitoba so that he can collect rainwater for his garden. The inside dimensions of the finished cistern will be 10 feet 8 inches by 8 feet 4 inches by 4 feet 6 inches. A cubic foot of water weighs about 62 pounds 8 ounces. If the cistern is completely filled with water, what will be the weight of the water expressed in tons?

SOLUTION

Since 12 inches equals 1 foot, we can convert the amounts expressed in inches to feet by dividing by 12 and simplifying.

$$\frac{8}{12} = \frac{2}{3}$$ Eight inches is $\frac{2}{3}$ of a foot.

$$\frac{4}{12} = \frac{1}{3}$$ Four inches is $\frac{1}{3}$ of a foot.

$$\frac{6}{12} = \frac{1}{2}$$ Six inches is $\frac{1}{2}$ of a foot.

The dimensions of the cistern can, therefore, be stated as $10\frac{2}{3}$ feet by $8\frac{1}{3}$ feet by $4\frac{1}{2}$ feet.

The volume of a rectangular prism is found by multiplying length times width times height.

$$V = l \times w \times h$$

Calculate the volume of water in the cistern using this formula.

$$V = 10\tfrac{2}{3} \times 8\tfrac{1}{3} \times 4\tfrac{1}{2}$$

$$V = \tfrac{32}{3} \times \tfrac{25}{3} \times \tfrac{9}{2}$$

$$V = \tfrac{7200}{18}$$

$$V = 400 \text{ cubic feet}$$

If 1 cubic foot weighs 62 pounds 8 ounces, then 400 cubic feet weigh 400 times this amount.

Convert 62 pounds 8 ounces to pounds.

$$\tfrac{8}{16} = \tfrac{1}{2} \text{ pound}$$

Water thus weighs $62\tfrac{1}{2}$ pounds per cubic foot.

Calculate the weight of the water.

$$400 \text{ ft}^3 \times 62\tfrac{1}{2} \text{ lb/ft}^3 = 400 \times \tfrac{125}{2} \text{ lb}$$

$$400 \times \tfrac{125}{2} \text{ lb} = 25\,000 \text{ lb}$$

Convert the number of pounds to tons by dividing by 2000.

$$25\,000 \div 2000 = 12.5 \text{ tons}$$

The weight of the water in the cistern would be $12\tfrac{1}{2}$ tons.

Example 2

George estimates that each bale of hay in his field weighs 62.5 pounds on average. There are 892 bales to be picked up. If his truck can carry 8 tons on one trip, how many trips will he have to make to move his bales?

Farmers usually bale hay in the middle of the day, so the hay is not damp from dew.

SOLUTION

Find the total weight of the bales in pounds by multiplying the number of bales by the weight per bale.

892 bales × 62.5 pounds/bale = 55 750

55 750 ÷ 2000 = 27.875 tons

Next, find the number of trips George will need to make.

27.875 ÷ 8 ≈ 3.5

George will need to make 4 trips.

Mental Math and Estimation

Annalise works as a fishing guide in the Northwest Territories. On a recent trip, her client caught two chinook salmon. One salmon weighed 20 lb 7 oz and the other weighed 21 lb 9 oz. What is the total weight, in pounds, of the two salmon?

Annalise's client caught two average size chinook salmon.

BUILD YOUR SKILLS

1. Choose the correct item to go with each weight. About how much do you think each of the other items weighs?

   a) About 1 ounce:

   i. pat of butter   ii. loaf of bread   iii. house cat

   b) About 1 pound:

   i. sofa   ii. small basket of raspberries   iii. gallon of water

   c) About 1 ton:

   i. refrigerator   ii. large dog   iii. blue whale

Chapter 4   Mass, Temperature, and Volume   151

What unit would you use for the weight of a hippopotamus?

2. Which unit—ounce, pound, or ton—would you use to express the weight of the following? Give an alternate choice, if suitable, and justify your answer.

   a) brick

   b) plasma TV

   c) box of chocolates

   d) hippopotamus

   e) duck

   f) box of books

   g) tractor-trailer truck

3. At birth, Johan weighed 7 pounds 9 ounces.

   a) Why are newborns' weights given in pounds and ounces and not rounded to the nearest pound?

   b) What would Johan's weight be in ounces?

   c) Why are newborns' weights not given in ounces alone?

   d) Marc, the nurse on the maternity ward, told Dawn that her baby would lose about 10% of his weight in the first week. Then the baby would likely gain about 5 ounces a week for the next four weeks. What should Dawn expect Johan to weigh at 5 weeks of age if he weighed 7 pounds 9 ounces at birth?

   e) How does Johan's weight at 5 weeks compare to his weight at birth?

   f) Would the comparison be different if he had weighed more or less at birth?

4. A contractor is building a patio behind Polli's house. The cement slab will be 9 feet 8 inches long, 7 feet 3 inches wide, and 4 inches thick. If the concrete weighs 150 pounds a cubic foot, what is the weight of the concrete in Polli's patio?

5. Coffee is the second most highly traded commodity in the world. Hon owns a coffee shop. He buys fresh fair-trade coffee beans because he knows that this helps protect the coffee farmer's income. The beans he buys weigh 35 pounds a cubic foot, and after he roasts them, they weigh only 27 pounds a cubic foot. He sells his coffee for $17.95 a pound.

a) What do you think is the most highly traded commodity in the world?

b) Assume that the farmer selling the beans got a market floor price of $1.35 a pound. If Hon buys 25 cubic feet of coffee beans, and sells it at $17.95 a pound after roasting, compare the income of the farmer with Hon's selling price.

Coffee beans are lighter after roasting because they lose moisture during the process.

Extend your thinking

6. Think about question 5 above.

   a) Do you think the farmer received a fair price? Why or why not?

   b) Do you think Hon paid $1.35/lb for the beans? Why or why not?

7. Pete can carry a maximum of 8 tons in his truck. He has been hired by the waste management plant that he works for to transport 105 cubic yards of compacted computer paper to be recycled. Sam measures the box of Pete's truck and notes that it will hold 24 cubic yards. He therefore reasons that Pete will need to make 4.375 trips, after dividing 105 yd^3 by 24 yd^3. Explain what is wrong with Sam's reasoning and determine the correct number of trips Pete will need to make.

4.3 Mass in the Système International

MATH *ON THE JOB*

Jeff and Winona work as emergency medical professionals in Whitehorse, Yukon. In an emergency, they are often the first on the scene.

Jeff and Winona completed a Primary Care program approved by the Canadian Medical Association. This program included courses on basic anatomy and vital statistics, legal and ethical behaviour, how to deal with trauma, and even proper vehicle operation.

When responding to an emergency situation, Jeff and Winona may need to administer a treatment or drug based on presented conditions and treatment charts. For example, if a patient is thought to have suffered a cardiac arrest (heart attack), Jeff or Winona would usually administer an appropriate drug. The recommended concentration of one such drug is 1:10 000 and its recommended dosage is 0.01 to 0.03 mg/kg of a person's weight.

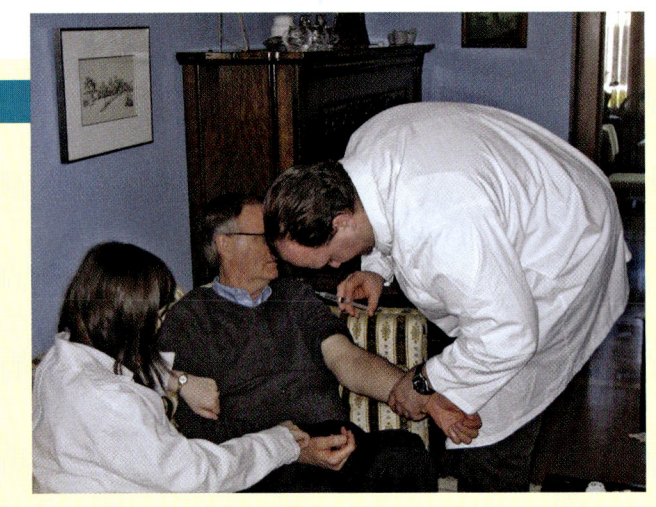

Jeff and Winona must know their patient's weight to calculate the correct dose of medicine to administer.

Jeff and Winona respond to a 911 call. The symptoms of the 52-year-old patient indicate a cardiac arrest. His wife tells them that her husband weighs about 70 kg. Use proportional reasoning to calculate the acceptable dosage of this drug for Jeff and Winona to administer.

EXPLORE THE MATH

kilogram: the mass of one litre of water at 4°C

In the last section, you discussed the differences between mass and weight and determined that in the imperial system, we tend to use the term pound—a unit of weight—for both mass and weight. In the SI units, we do the opposite. The correct term for a unit of weight is the newton, but we use the term **kilogram**, a unit of mass, to refer to both mass and weight.

ACTIVITY 4.5
USING SI PREFIXES

Since the kilogram is the basic unit of mass in the SI system, use your understanding of the prefixes you know to determine:

1. the number of grams in a kilogram
2. the name for 1000 kilograms
3. the name for $\frac{1}{1000}$ of a gram

ACTIVITY 4.6
EQUIVALENT MASSES

Work with a partner to discuss the following two situations. Write a justification of your solutions. The megagram is generally referred to as a **tonne**, a metric ton, or a long ton.

tonne: a metric ton; 1000 kilograms

1. Use your understanding of weights to determine a referent for:

    a) 1 tonne (t)

    b) 1 kilogram (kg)

    c) 1 gram (g)

    d) 1 milligram (mg)

2. 2.8 t, 2800 kg, and 2 800 000 g are equivalent masses. Each represents the mass of a truck. Which would be the most appropriate unit to use if you were discussing the mass of a truck? Why?

3. When you are cooking, there is more than one way to determine how much of an ingredient to use. Some recipes give amounts in volume and others use mass, especially those from Europe. If you use a measuring cup, you are measuring volume. To measure mass, you need a kitchen scale.

It would be unusual to give a truck's weight in grams.

You are measuring the amount of flour you need to make a cake, but some of your batter has splashed on your recipe and hidden the unit of measurement. You can see that the number is 250. Would this be tonnes, kilograms, grams, or milligrams? Give examples of items that might weigh each of these amounts. Do not use the referents suggested above.

Example 1

You and your 5 friends want to use your motorboat to cross the bay and you are the only one who can pilot the boat. The maximum capacity for your boat is listed as 0.55 tonnes. You weigh 75 kg and your friends weigh 76 kg, 82 kg, 63 kg, 68 kg, and 78 kg respectively. You also have 104 kg of supplies. How many trips will you have to make in order for everyone (and your supplies) to get across the water safely? Give reasons for your answer.

SOLUTION

Convert 0.55 tonnes to 550 kg. This is the maximum load for your motorboat. Find the total weight of you, your friends, and the supplies.

75 + 76 + 82 + 63 + 68 + 78 + 104 = 546 kg

Strictly speaking, your boat has the capacity to carry the total weight in one trip. However, since the weight is so close to the capacity limit, you might consider making two trips because your clothes weigh something, the water might be rough, and so on.

DISCUSS THE IDEAS
GROSS VEHICLE WEIGHT RATING

Truckers and others who transport loads in their vehicles need to be aware of their Gross Vehicle Weight Rating (GVWR). The GVWR is the maximum recommended weight of a vehicle, including everything it is carrying: the vehicle itself, cargo, passengers, other accessories, and fuel. The base curb weight is the weight of the vehicle with a full tank of fuel. The difference between these two weights is the cargo capacity.

You and your friend rent a truck with a 3016 kg GVWR and a base curb weight of 2255 kg, so that you can help your friend haul a load of bricks for a construction project. The combined weight of you, your friend, and your accessories is 160 kg. If one brick weighs 2.7 kg, how many bricks can your truck carry?

ACTIVITY 4.7
PROTEIN VS FAT CONTENT

Your health food store carries several different brands of nutritional bars. The bars come in different sizes and they have different proportions of nutrients. A woman between the ages of 19 and 30 requires about 0.8 grams of protein per kilogram of weight and about 48 grams of fat every day.

A 24-year-old who weighs 55 kg tells you she would like to get her daily required intake of protein from nutritional bars, but she is worried about the amount of fat in them.

1. How many grams of protein does she need each day?

2. Using at least 3 different types of nutritional bars, determine how many bars of each type she would have to eat in a day to get her allotted amount of protein and how much fat she would consume. Record your findings on a table like the one that follows.

NUTRITIONAL BAR PROTEIN AND FAT CONTENT

Type of bar	Grams of protein per bar	Grams of fat per bar	Number of bars needed for protein	Total amount of fat in bars
NG	2	3.4		
EM	15	4.5		
LT	15	11.1		

3. Based on your findings, which bar would you advise your client to buy?

ACTIVITY 4.8
ESTIMATING MASS

Every day we have to estimate the weight of objects. Choose an object you use fairly regularly that you think weighs approximately 1 kilogram. This object will be your referent for weight.

1. Using your referent for comparison, find objects with the following estimated weights:

    a) 2 kg

    b) 5 kg

2. Use a balance to determine the actual weight of your referent. Was it more or less than 1 kg? As a result, do the objects you chose weigh more or less than your estimate?

3. Would this method of estimation be a good way to estimate the weight of a heavy object? Why or why not?

DISCUSS THE IDEAS
MASS/WEIGHT CONVERSION BETWEEN IMPERIAL AND SI

There are many important conversion factors that you use daily. For example, earlier you used a conversion formula to convert degrees Celsius to degrees Fahrenheit and vice versa. You also explored conversions in chapter 3. Think about the relationship between pounds and kilograms.

1. In Europe, the term "pound" is often used to mean half a kilogram. Is this an appropriate use of the term? Why or why not? Use your understanding of pound and kilogram to discuss the relationship between them. List three items you sometimes hear talked about in pounds.

2. Stores sometimes list prices of vegetables by both the pound and by the kilogram. If they only gave the price per pound, how would you determine the price per kilogram? Explain your reasoning.

3. Sometimes the price for items is listed as dollars per 100 grams.

    a) Why would the store price items this way rather than per kilogram?

    b) What types of items would likely be priced in this way?

4. A bag of sand is labelled as 20 kg and also as 44 lb. Use this information to develop a conversion formula from kilogram to pound and pound to kilogram (round to the nearest tenth).

5. Research the approved use of the various units of weights permitted in Canada on the internet.

Some of these items are measured in grams, some in kilograms, and others in tonnes.

Mental Math and Estimation

What is the approximate weight of:

a) a 5 pound roast, expressed in kilograms?

b) a 62 kg person, expressed in pounds?

BUILD YOUR SKILLS

1. Choose the correct item to go with each measure of mass.

    a) About 1 gram

        i. a brick   ii. a penny   iii. a book

    b) About 1 kilogram

        i. this textbook   ii. a dime   iii. an MP3 player

    c) About 1 gram

        i. a thumbtack   ii. a cat   iii. a chair

    d) About 1 tonne

        i. a bull   ii. two men   iii. a laptop computer

2. Read each statement and judge whether the estimate makes sense. If you disagree with the statement, justify your solution by estimating the approximate weight of the object.

   a) A loaded truck has a mass of about 500 kg.

   b) A small boy has a mass of about 100 g.

   c) A hockey puck has a mass of about 2 kg.

   d) A headache tablet has a mass of 1 mg.

   e) Two loaves of bread have a mass of about 1 kg.

   f) A piece of gum has a mass of about 1 g.

   g) A two-tonne truck weighs about 2200 pounds.

   h) A five-pound roast weighs about the same as a 5 kg roast.

3. Drugs come in different strengths, so the doctor decides what dosage to give you based on your symptoms, age, and weight. The drug penicillin V has a strength of 250 mg per pill, and you have been prescribed a dosage of 0.5 g three times a day for five days.

   a) How many pills will you have to take at one time?

   b) How many milligrams of the drug will you take over the five days?

   c) How many kilograms of the drug is this amount?

4. A gardener wants to mix his own fertilizer so that the strength is 6-7-5. This means that 6% of each tonne is nitrogen, 7% is phosphorus, and 5% is potassium. How many kilograms of nitrogen, phosphorus, and potassium will there be if he mixes 0.5 tonnes of fertilizer?

5. It is estimated that the air in a glass tank weighs 1.29 g a litre. The tank is 2.5 metres by 3.4 metres by 4.1 metres. What is the weight of the air in the tank?

HINT

1 litre equals 1000 cm^3.

6. You have a recipe for a cheese dip that calls for $1\frac{1}{4}$ lb of Stilton cheese. The store has packages that weigh 253 g, 421 g, 97 g, 398 g, and 124 g. Which packages will you purchase so that you have enough Stilton at the lowest cost?

7. Max must transport 20 sheets of drywall and 480 six-inch by six-inch tiles to a building site. He knows that the drywall weighs 1.7 lbs a square foot, and each sheet is 4 feet by 8 feet. The tiles weigh 2.4 pounds a square foot. What is the total weight of his load, expressed in kilograms?

Astronauts weigh 83.5% less on the moon than they do on earth.

Extend your thinking

8. In 1969, Neil Armstrong became the first person to walk on the moon. His crewmates were Buzz Aldrin, who also walked on the moon, and Michael Collins, who remained in the spacecraft.

   The three astronauts had the same mass on the moon as they had on earth, but they weighed less. The weight you feel on a different planet or moon is affected by the mass of the planet or moon, how far you are from its centre, and your own mass. The greater the mass of the planet, the more you will weigh.

   Use your knowledge of the planets to judge:

   a) on which planet you will weigh the most;

   b) on which planet you will weigh the least.

   T Use the internet to determine your weight on the planets where you weigh the most and the least, and calculate a conversion factor.

PUZZLE IT OUT

THE COUNTERFEIT COIN

You have 12 golden coins that look identical, but one of them is counterfeit. Using a balance, and at the most 3 weighings, how can you determine which coin is counterfeit?

You can use a balance to compare the mass of two objects.

PROJECT—CULINARY COMPETITION

CREATE CONVERSION TABLES

Now that you have created your menu and decided on your recipes, you can begin work on the other components of your recipe book.

You may have noticed that many recipe books include conversion charts for common ingredients. In your booklet, you will create a conversion chart for your ingredients.

First, write a list of all the ingredients that your recipes require. Next, choose a standard unit of measurement (100 grams, for example) on which to base your conversions. Finally, make a chart and complete it for each ingredient. You will have to calculate the amounts in SI and imperial units for mass and volume for each ingredient.

T Note that when converting between weight and volume, the conversion will not be the same for every ingredient. For example, one cup of flour will weigh a different amount than one cup of sugar. Use the internet or other resources to find the volume and weight equivalencies for your different ingredients. If using the internet, you may want to check a couple of different websites to make sure that what you find is accurate.

After you have listed your ingredients and determined equivalent conversion amounts for each one, convert the amount of each that your recipes require. Complete a table showing the amounts given by your recipe, then perform the conversions into the other units of this amount. This will serve as a shopping list for anyone who would like to make the dishes in your menu.

You now have two tables for your recipe booklet.

Many cookbooks contain conversion charts for common ingredients.

Chapter 4   Mass, Temperature, and Volume

4.4 Making Conversions

MATH *ON THE JOB*

Louise Niwa is the operations manager for a family business, Niwa Ranching Company, in Acadia Valley, Alberta. She completed a science program at the University of Saskatchewan in 2000 and worked in feed formulation/nutrition at a feed mill before moving back to the farm. "For my science degree, I was required to take some math courses. Now that I am back on the farm, it seems that I use a lot of basic algebra. And conversions are vital to our operations!"

Jim purchased some rolled barley from the Niwa Ranching Company to feed his cattle. Rolled barley is barley that is processed to make it more digestable. The price of barley at the time was $3.60/bushel plus $0.22/bushel for rolling and delivery. GST of 5% is added to the rolling and delivery charge, but not to the barley. The barley was rolled out of a grain bin directly into a 3-tonne truck. One tonne of barley contains 45.9 bushels. The mass of the full truck was 12 100 kg. The mass of the empty truck was 5550 kg. How much must Jim pay the Niwa Ranching Company for his rolled barley?

As the operations manager of Niwa Ranching Company, Louise uses algebra and conversion calculations on a regular basis.

EXPLORE THE MATH

In the past, you have converted from one unit into another, either within a measuring system or between the imperial and SI systems. In the Math on the Job above, a different type of conversion occurred. Grain is measured and sold in bushels, a volume measure, even though the SI measurement for grain in Canada, the tonne, is a measure of mass or weight. A bushel is a unit of volume or capacity equivalent to approximately 2220 cubic inches. The word bushel comes from a fourteenth-century word, *buschel* or *busschel*, meaning box.

In order to solve this problem, you needed to know the conversion factor to convert tonnes of barley to bushels of barley. Since grains weigh different amounts per bushel, a farmer needs to know the correct conversion factor for the grain he is buying or selling. Fortunately, many of these factors have been worked out for you and are available on the internet or in reference books.

DISCUSS THE IDEAS
AGRICULTURAL CONVERSION FACTORS

In the Math on the Job problem at the beginning of this section, you needed the conversion factor of 45.9 bushels per tonne of barley to help Jim determine how much to pay for the barley. Farmers grow many other types of grain, such as wheat, flax, oats, and mustard. A different conversion factor is needed for each type of grain. Why do you think this is the case? Search the internet to find conversion factors for these other grains.

Using your experience in daily life, think of other times when you make conversions that are between volume and weight. List as many as you can and determine the conversion factor if possible. When might it be more appropriate to use volume? When would you use weight?

Barley is just one of the many grains farmers grow in Canada.

ACTIVITY 4.9
USING CONVERSION FACTORS

The Niwa Ranching Company has an old rectangular wooden bin in which Louise stores grain. To calculate the crop insurance she needs, she must determine the volume of oats the bin holds. Louise measured the bin and determined that it was 15 feet long by 12 feet wide by 9 feet high.

1. How many bushels of oats will the bin hold?

2. For transporting the grain, Louise needs to know the weight of the oats. How many tonnes are in the bin?

Work with a partner to solve this problem. See if you can find at least two different approaches.

Example 1

Rain is catering a dinner for 20 people. She consults a cookbook that tells her she will need approximately $\frac{3}{4}$ lb of beef for each person and that it will take approximately 20 minutes per pound to cook at 350°F.

a) Approximately how many kilograms of beef should Rain buy?

b) At what approximate temperature Celsius should she cook it?

c) Approximately how many minutes per kilogram will she have to cook the roast?

HINT

Remember that 1 kg is equal to about 2.2 lb.

SOLUTION

a) Determine how many pounds of beef Rain needs to buy.

$$\frac{3}{4} \text{ lb/person} \times 20 = 15 \text{ lb}$$

2.2 lb are approximately 1 kg. Find the number of kilograms by dividing 15 pounds by 2.2.

$$\frac{15}{2.2} = 6.82$$

Rain should buy a roast that is almost 7 kg.

b) Convert 350°F to degrees Celsius.

$$C = \frac{5}{9}(F - 32) \quad \text{Use the formula for converting Fahrenheit to Celsius.}$$

$$C = \frac{5}{9}(350 - 32)$$

$$C = \frac{5}{9}(318)$$

$$C = \frac{1590}{9}$$

$$C = 176.7$$

The oven temperature will be 176.7°C, rounded to 180°C.

c) To estimate the minutes per kilogram Rain will have to cook the roast, use the conversion estimate 1 kg = 2.2 lb.

$$\frac{20 \text{ min}}{1 \text{ lb}} = \frac{x \text{ min}}{2.2 \text{ lb}} \quad \text{Set up a proportion.}$$

$$(2.2)\frac{20}{1} = \frac{x}{2.2}(2.2) \quad \text{Multiply by 2.2 to isolate the variable.}$$

$$2.2 \times 20 = x$$

$$44 = x$$

It will take approximately 44 minutes per kilogram to cook the roast.

ALTERNATIVE SOLUTION

a) Find out how many kg/person is required by dividing $\frac{3}{4}$ or 0.75 by 2.2, then multiplying this by 20 people.

$$0.75 \div 2.2 = 0.34$$

$$0.34 \times 20 = 6.8 \text{ kg}$$

Rain must calculate the cooking time and temperature for her roast beef.

ACTIVITY 4.10
HOW MUCH CAN A FORKLIFT LIFT?

You work for a construction company that is about to embark on a new project. Your task is to source 4 forklifts for the job. You have been asked to research and present several classes of forklifts with information on how much weight they can lift. Your findings will be distributed to the project managers, and they have requested that the lift information be supplied in tons, metric tonnes, pounds, and kilograms—so you may need to do some conversions. You should also indicate whether the forklift is intended for indoor or outdoor use. Use the internet to research forklifts and complete a table like the sample below.

This forklift is used outdoors for moderate loads of construction material.

FORKLIFT MAXIMUM LOAD LIMIT RESEARCH

Forklift brand and model name	tons	tonnes	pounds	kilograms

SAMPLE

What other things might you want to consider when purchasing a forklift?

BUILD YOUR SKILLS

1. A box of baseballs arrives at Vinny's sporting goods store. The box of balls weighs 266 oz and there are 50 baseballs in the box. Vinny discards the box, which weighed 1 pound. What is the weight of each baseball in grams?

2. In her restaurant, Hana uses 25 lb of sugar each day. She asks Raj, her stock clerk, to order enough for the month of January. The sugar comes in 10 kg bags. How many bags of sugar must Raj order to be sure they have enough?

3. Hong is a building contractor. The building code in his area requires that roofs be built to withstand 30 pounds of weight per square foot of horizontal area.

   a) How many kilograms per square metre is this?

   b) After a snowfall, a square foot of flat roof covered with snow has a weight of 18.1 pounds pressing on it. If the flat area of the roof of a house is 1700 square feet, what is the weight of the snow on the roof:

      i. in pounds?   ii. in kilograms?

4. Krystina is stacking flats of 355 mL bottles of water on a shelf. If there are 24 bottles in a flat, how much will 12 flats weigh? Ignore the weight of the plastic bottles and the cardboard flat.

   a) in kilograms?

   b) in pounds?

5. Craig and Genevieve have purchased 26 cases of birdseed. Each case contains 16 boxes that weigh 20 ounces each. How much do the 26 cases weigh:

   a) in pounds?

   b) in kilograms?

6. The conversion factor for changing cubic metres of wheat to tonnes is 0.778. Frank has been told that he can estimate the volume of grain dumped on the ground by using the formula $V = l \times w \times h \times 0.5$. If the length of the pile is 25 feet, the width is 15 feet, and the height is approximately 7 feet, how many bushels of wheat are in the pile? (See diagram; 1 tonne of wheat contains approximately 36.744 bushels.)

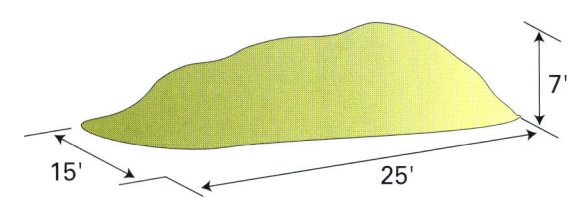

7. Jason is having a new elevator installed in the four-storey apartment building he manages. Although many people will use the stairs, he knows that at times 5 or 6 people will be on the elevator, and more importantly, it will be used to move furniture. He estimates that the heaviest piece of furniture that people will move will be an upright grand piano. He has checked with movers and has found that pianos can weigh up to 545 kg. He assumes that two strong people would be needed to move a piano and they would ride with it in the elevator. To be on the safe side, Jason estimates that they will weigh about 90 kg each. The elevators he is considering have ratings of no more than 1000, 2000, 3000, 4000, 5000, or 6000 pounds. What is the lowest-rated elevator that Jason should install?

Extend your thinking

8. A recent trend is for people to purchase goods and foods produced locally and when possible directly from the producer—often limiting themselves to a 100 km radius. This may mean that they have to buy larger quantities at one time. For example, they may buy beef by the "side" directly from a rancher, although the meat must still be properly processed by a licensed butcher. However, a side of beef is a lot of meat and so people sometimes share a side between two or three families.

   Arduk and his family shared a side of beef with two other families. Their share was:

   48 lb of ground beef

   7 lb 9 oz chuck roast

   6 lb 12 oz sirloin roast

   9 lb 14 oz grilling steak

   7 lb 4 oz T-bone steak

   4 lb stewing meat

   Even if you live in an urban area, you can buy locally grown produce at markets like The Forks in Winnipeg.

   The cost of the meat was $1.75/lb; cutting and wrapping cost an additional $0.42/lb.

   a) How much did Arduk pay for the meat?

   b) What was his cost per kilogram including cutting and wrapping?

   c) How many kilograms (to the nearest tenth) of each type of meat did Arduk buy?

   d) Check the prices of similar cuts of meat at your local grocery store or butcher. How much would you pay for the same amount of meat at the store? Did Arduk save money compared to buying at the local store?

   e) What are some other direct-buy products that you could buy in your neighbourhood?

   f) What reasons, other than cost, might people have for choosing to purchase their beef or other goods directly from the producer?

PROJECT—CULINARY COMPETITION

COMPILE YOUR WORK AND PREPARE A PRESENTATION

Adding pictures will make your booklet more attractive.

You should now have the following information for your project:

- a menu
- a recipe for each dish
- a conversion table for your ingredients
- a table that lists all of your ingredients with amounts

Design your menu. Be creative! Next, compile the last three items in the above list into a booklet that is both attractive and useable. You may want to look at a variety of cookbooks first to get some ideas for the layout. Will you include pictures? How will you organize the elements in your booklet? What page size will you use, and how many pages will your booklet have? Include your converted ingredient amounts with your recipes, not just in the table. Also, be sure to provide conversions for any cooking temperatures that are given in the recipes.

Once you have completed and printed a copy of your menu and your booklet, it is time to start the judging. Evaluate your classmates' menus and booklets according to the judging criteria. May the best menu win!

REFLECT ON YOUR LEARNING
MASS, TEMPERATURE, AND VOLUME

Now that you have finished this chapter, you should be able to

- ❒ understand the difference between the Celsius and the Fahrenheit temperature scales;
- ❒ convert from degrees Celsius to degrees Fahrenheit and vice versa;
- ❒ understand the difference between mass and weight and understand why we often use the terms interchangeably;
- ❒ calculate mass and weight in both the SI and the imperial systems;
- ❒ convert mass and weight within each system and between systems;
- ❒ use conversion factors to convert between volume and mass.

In addition, you have completed a project that applied your new skills in a practical context.

PRACTISE YOUR NEW SKILLS

1. Canada's prairie provinces are known for their extreme temperatures—hot summers and cold winters. Midale and neighbouring Yellow Grass, both in Saskatchewan, recorded Canada's record high temperature on July 5, 1937. It was 113°F. The previous year, on February 16, Midale recorded its lowest ever temperature at −55°F. What would these temperatures have been in degrees Celsius? What do you notice about the differences in these temperatures?

2. The coldest temperature ever recorded in Canada was in Snag, Yukon on February 3, 1947. It was officially recorded as −63°C. What is this in degrees Fahrenheit?

3. Your mother has asked you to water some plants and she has given you a 5-US gallon pail of water.

   a) By first converting US gallons to litres, use your knowledge about the weight of 1 litre of water to determine the weight of a 5-US gallon pail of water. Refer to p. 127 for the volume conversion factor.

   b) How much would 1 m³ of water weigh?

4. Your school has been running a nickel drive to raise money for a sister school in Africa. A nickel weighs approximately 5 g. A roll of nickels is worth $2.00. You have collected a total of $135.65 in nickels.

   a) How much will your nickels weigh?

   b) What is the weight of a roll of nickels?

   c) How many rolls would you need to make 1 kg?

5. A carpenter is installing a floor in an upper room of a house. He is debating whether to install cherrywood, which weighs 35 pounds a cubic foot, or cork, which weighs 15 pounds a cubic foot. If the area of the floor is 180 square feet and the flooring is $\frac{1}{2}$-inch thick, what is the difference between the weight of the cherrywood floor and the weight of the cork floor?

6. A drugstore buys bleach by the skid. Each skid weighs approximately 46.3 lb and holds 48 cases of bleach. Each case contains six 5.38-litre bottles. If one litre of bleach weighs about 847.5 grams, what is the weight of a loaded skid of bleach stated in kilograms? In pounds?

Wild rice is actually a cereal grain.

7. Many farmers use anhydrous ammonia to fertilize their crops. Anhydrous ammonia is a chemical composed of hydrogen and ammonia. It contains 82% nitrogen by weight. It is potentially a very hazardous chemical and must be handled appropriately. If the desired rate of application is 100 lb of nitrogen per acre, how many tonnes of anhydrous ammonia must a farmer order to fertilize 860 acres?

8. You are at a worksite and need to determine the weight of the rocks that you will use to finish the front entrance of the house. You do not have a scale, but you have a number of bags of cement that weigh 20 kg each. Explain how you could use them to determine the weight of the rocks.

9. Wild rice is a traditional food of many Aboriginal peoples of western Canada. Today, wild rice is grown and harvested in a number or places, including in numerous northern lakes in Saskatchewan. After the rice is harvested, it is dried, heated, and the hulls are removed before it is packaged and sold. Northern Lights Foods is a company owned and operated by the Lac La Ronge Indian Band that sells certified organic wild rice to the United States, Japan, and European markets.

   a) If the average annual production of wild rice in Saskatchewan is 2.5 million pounds and Aboriginal producers are responsible for one-third of the province's annual crop, how many kilograms of wild rice do Aboriginal harvesters produce?

   b) If there are 25 lb of processed wild rice in a US bushel and Northern Lights Foods sells 8500 lb to a customer in Hawaii, how many cubic feet of rice are they shipping? One bushel contains 1.24 ft^3.

   c) If a wild rice harvester sells 600 kg of green rice to Northern Lights Foods and they process it and sell it to a customer in Florida, how many pounds of processed rice will they ship if 10 lb of raw green rice yield 5 lb of processed rice?

170 MathWorks 10

Extend your thinking

10. Jean-Luc decided to make tourtière for his mother for Mother's Day from his grandmother's old recipe. His mother loved this "secret" family recipe and how each ingredient was in perfect proportion with the others. He assembled the ingredients on the counter and, realizing that he did not have the thyme, asked his sister Lucie to carefully measure and mix the other filling ingredients while he popped out to the store. Lucie looked at the recipe and figured it would be simple.

TOURTIÈRE
18 oz ground beef
20 oz ground pork
8 oz potatoes, boiled and mashed
6 oz of onion, finely chopped
large pinch of thyme
pastry for double pie crust

Tourtière is a French-Canadian food traditionally served at Christmas.

But Lucie got a little bit confused. She put 18 oz of pork and 20 oz of beef into the bowl, instead of the other way around. She also mixed up the potatoes and onion, using 8 oz of onion and 6 oz of potatoes. Then she mixed all the ingredients together. Luckily, she noticed her mistake. But it is difficult to un-mix.

So now she has to get the recipe back to its proper proportions. And she hopes that the filling will still fit into the crust! What is the smallest quantity of whatever has to be added to get the recipe back to its original proportions?

Chapter 5

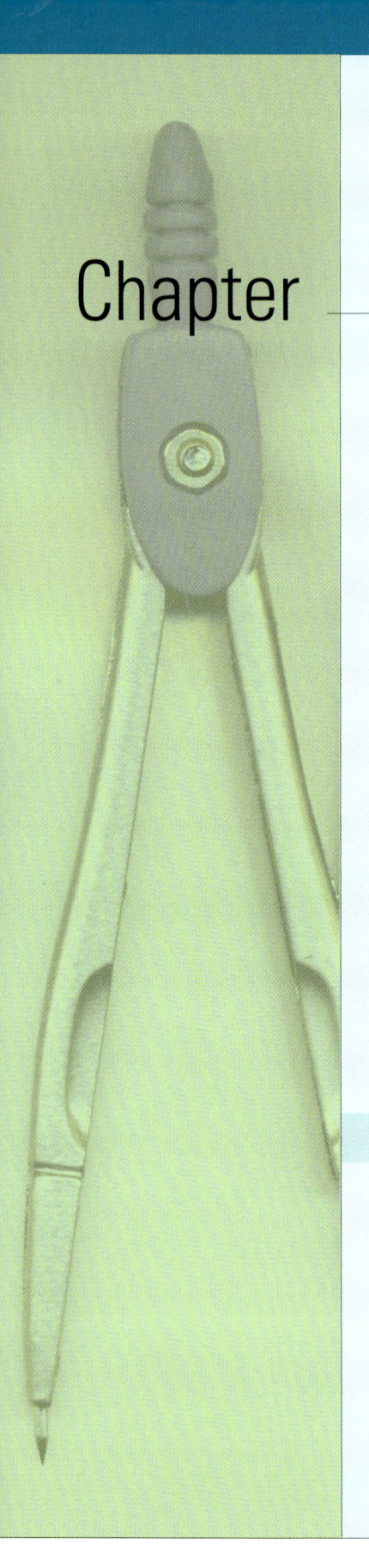

Angles and Parallel Lines

GOALS

Every day, in our homes, at work, or when travelling from one place to another, we encounter angles and parallel lines. They can be found in buildings, furniture, graphic designs, city layouts, and many other places. In this chapter, you will learn about how angles are measured and created for workplace applications and how combinations of angles and lines can be used to create parallel and non-parallel lines. You will use your mathematical skills and knowledge to

- measure, draw, and describe angles;
- estimate the measure of angles;
- use certain angles to determine whether two lines are parallel; and
- solve problems involving angles and pairs of angles, and parallel, non-parallel, perpendicular, and transversal lines.

KEY TERMS

- angle
- angle measure
- degree
- parallel lines
- perpendicular lines
- transversal

PROJECT—CREATE A PERSPECTIVE DRAWING

START TO PLAN

PROJECT OVERVIEW

Three-dimensional (3-D) drawings are found in advertisements, comic books, architectural blueprints, and film mockups. Can you think of other examples?

Although software has been created for the purpose of making 3-D drawings and animations, many artists draw by hand to achieve an effect that is difficult or impossible to create with computer graphics software. For this project, you will learn how to create 3-D perspective diagrams of buildings.

Your task will be to create a 3-D perspective diagram of a city street for the cover of a new comic book featuring a superhero, Theta*. The cover will have Theta standing steadfastly in the centre of a street lined with buildings.

GET STARTED

Before you start, think about the questions below. Record your decisions in a project file.

- What type of material will you draw on? Paper? Card stock?
- How large will your diagram be?
- What type of pencil(s) or pen(s) will be best for drawing?
- What type of tools will you need to draw straight lines and parallel lines?

FINAL PRESENTATION CHECKLIST

Make a display that includes the following items:

- all preliminary sketches/diagrams used to develop the final drawing; and
- the final cover drawing itself.

Be sure to sign your name, and the name of any partner(s) involved in the creation of this drawing, in the bottom right corner of each item.

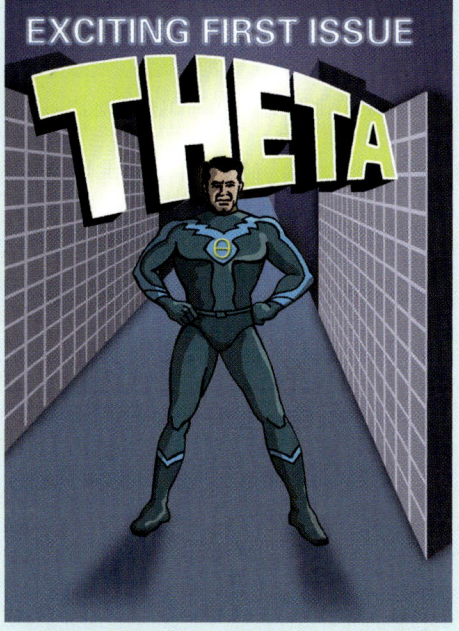

This is an example of a comic book cover that uses several vanishing points.

---

* Theta is the Greek symbol often used to name angles.

Chapter 5 Angles and Parallel Lines

5.1 Measuring, Drawing, and Estimating Angles

MATH ON THE JOB

Sunny (Sunje) Petersen and her husband Werner own and run South Nahanni Outfitters, a Whitehorse, Yukon-based company that organizes big game hunting trips to the Mackenzie Mountains. Sunny grew up in northern Germany near the Baltic Sea and Werner was raised in the Austrian Alps.

Sunny helps her husband outfit, organize, and guide hunting expeditions for people from all over the world. To do this, she uses her math skills for bookkeeping, paying wages, calculating the weight and volume of supplies that can fit on a bush plane, determining the weight and amount of fuel the plane needs to reach its destination, writing invoices for clients, and calculating the amount of ingredients she will need when she cooks for large hunting parties. Close encounters with wolves, mountain goats, and moose are also part of the job.

Sunny Petersen takes people from all over the world heli-hiking in Canada's north.

Guiding heli-hikers (hikers flown to remote locations in a helicopter) is also part of Sunny's job. Before flying the heli-hikers into the wilderness, Sunny and Werner plot the course the helicopter will take to reach its destination.

As they fly, aircraft change direction many times. Using five or more line segments, plot a course that Sunny and Werner could take in order to reach the towering granite cliffs known as the Cirque of the Unclimbables. Determine the direction of each line segment that comprises your route. Use the eight main directions of a compass to describe the directions used in your course. These are north, northeast, east, southeast, south, southwest, west, and northwest.

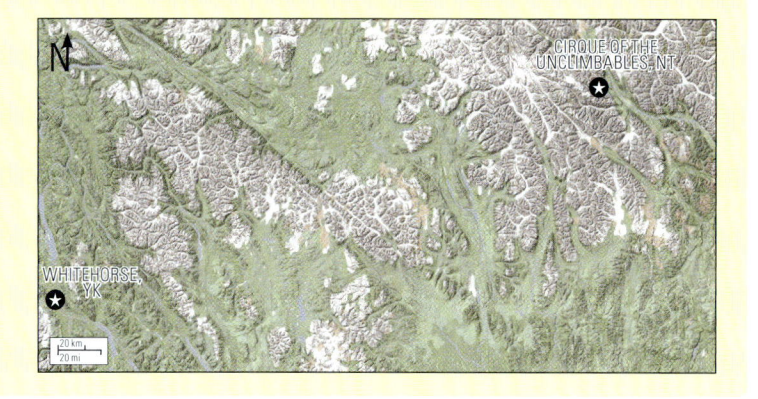

angle: two rays that meet at a point called the vertex

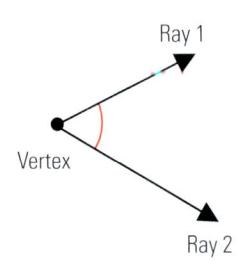

EXPLORE THE MATH

Take a moment to look at the structures in your classroom that contain **angles**. Consider who would have been involved in creating the structures that have those angles, for example, architects, designers, surveyors, and carpenters. Angles are also useful to people who do not make structures. Aircraft pilots and boat pilots use angles for navigation. Astronomers use angles to locate objects in the sky.

So, what exactly is an angle? An angle is formed when two rays meet at a common endpoint called a vertex. Angles are measured with tools, such as a protractor, that are marked in degrees.

174 MathWorks 10

Visualize an angle that is used to express direction in navigation and mapping, such as east. In this case, the angle is measured relative to true north, which is 0° and may be expressed as a bearing. A **true bearing** describes the number of degrees, measured clockwise, between an imaginary line pointing towards true north (geographic north) and another imaginary line pointing towards an intended direction or along a pathway. East is represented in land navigation and mapping at a 90° angle from true north.

true bearing: the angle measured clockwise between true north and an intended path or direction, expressed in degrees

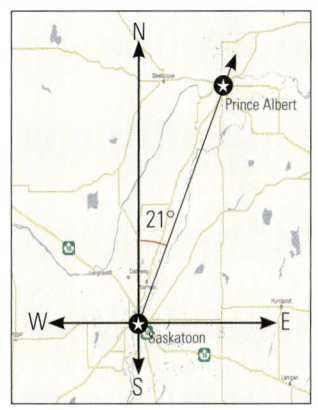

Angle measures can be estimated by using **referents**, which are common measurements like 90°, 45°, 30°, and 22.5°.

How can we draw angles? The tools used to measure angles can also be used to draw or replicate angles having specific measures. Tools have been designed to measure and create angles having only one or two specific measures, such as a set square used in technical drawings to draw right angles.

You have used a protractor and ruler to draw angles. You can also draw certain angles with a ruler and compass, and you can replicate any angle with these tools.

angle measure: a number representing the spread of the two rays of an angle, expressed in degrees

angle referent: a common standard of angle measure, for example, 90°, 45°, 30°, and 22.5° used to estimate angles

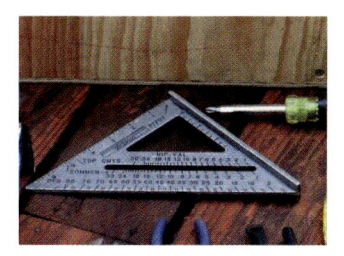

A rafter-angle square is used to lay out and create angles in carpentry.

Example 1

Use a ruler and compass to create the following angles.

   a) Draw a 90° angle.

   b) Replicate any existing angle.

   SOLUTION

   a) To draw a 90° angle, follow these steps.

   Draw a line segment, then mark where you want the 90-degree angle to go.

Chapter 5   Angles and Parallel Lines   175

Put the compass point at the mark you made. Open the compass slightly and make two more marks on each side of the first mark. Ensure they are the same distance from the first mark.

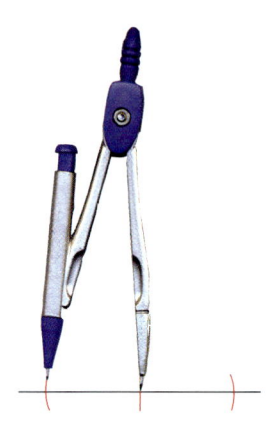

Widen the compass a bit more, and place the compass point at one of the new marks. Make a small arc, then do the same thing after placing the compass point at the other new mark. Ensure the two arcs intersect each other.

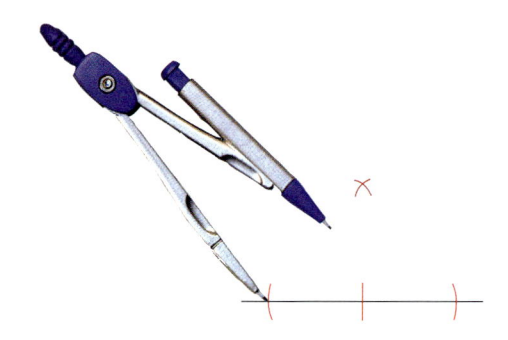

Draw a line segment that goes between or through the point where the arcs intersect and the first mark you made. The two line segments are perpendicular to each other, and therefore form a 90° (right) angle.

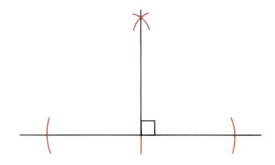

b) To replicate any existing angle, follow these steps.

Use a compass to lightly draw an arc centred at the vertex of the original angle.

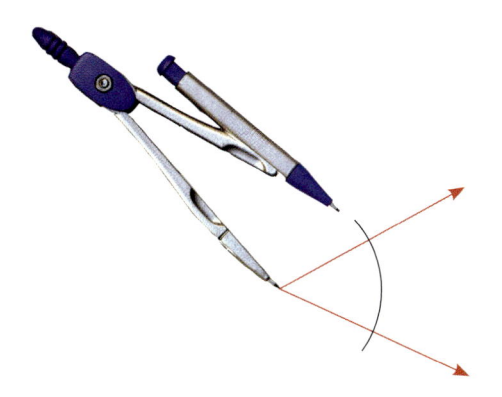

Use a ruler to draw one side of the new angle, and draw an arc of the same radius and arc length as the one you just drew on the original angle.

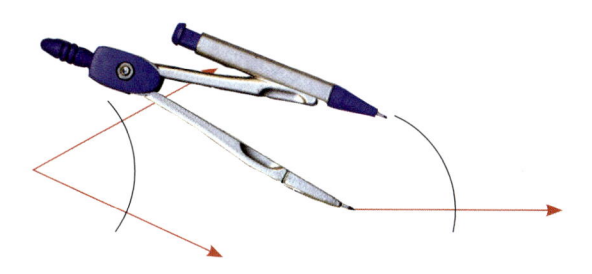

Bring the compass up to the original angle, and set it so that its point and the tip of the pencil touch the points where the original arc intersects the sides of the angle.

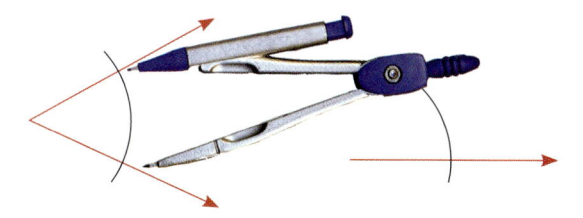

Place the compass point over to the point of intersection of the side of the new angle and the new arc. Draw a short arc through the new arc.

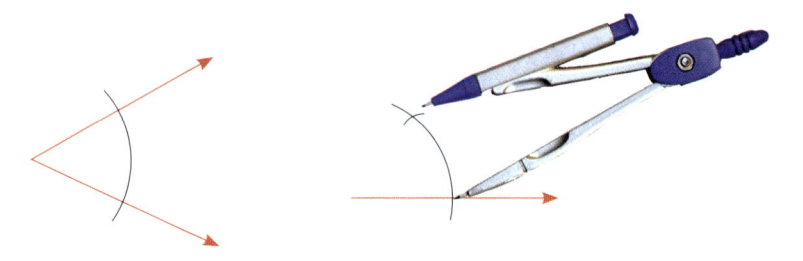

Use the ruler to draw the other side of the angle, from the left end of the first side (the vertex) through the point of intersection of the two arcs. The result is a new angle with the same measure as the original.

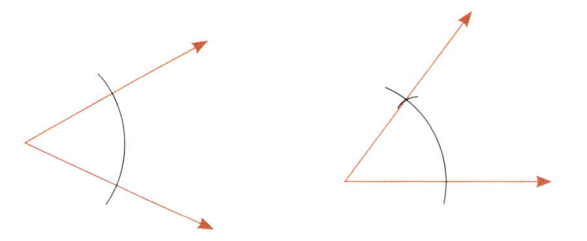

DISCUSS THE IDEAS
ESTIMATION OR MEASUREMENT?

Skilled carpenters can estimate the amount of wood, nails, and joist hangers needed to build a set of shelves.

Many trades require the construction and measurement of angles. Carpenters constantly check angles to ensure, for example, that a foundation is level, a stud is perpendicular to the floor, or a staircase is the right size.

1. Working in small groups, identify five distinct trades that use angles. Start by thinking about the people you know and the trades they work in. For each of the five trades you think of, suggest an example of how the tradesperson creates and measures angles on the job.

2. Do the types of angles your group listed need to be precisely measured and created? This is true in trades such as surveying or manufacturing. Would estimations be adequate, as they may be in landscaping, for example?

ACTIVITY 5.1
FIVE ANGLES

Angle measures range from 0° to 360°. On a piece of paper, draw five angles of various measures, labelling the rays, vertices, and angle. (The rays can be about 5 cm long.)

Trade your angle drawings with a partner. Create a chart for drawing, measuring, and describing each of the five angles, as follows:

- angle: measure the angle you've been given and redraw it yourself, to the same angle measure;
- angle measure: state the angle measure in degrees;
- kind of angle: identify the type of angle, for example, "acute" or "obtuse" and explain how you know this;
- example: give an example of where you might see an angle like this in the real world, for example, a rooftop or a vault for gymnastics.

Then check and discuss your work with your partner.

HINT

Degrees represent a scale that can be used to measure angles or temperature.

Mental Math and Estimation

Estimations are made in many trades that use angles. Imagine that you are working as a tradesperson in the situations below and make the following estimations (aim to be within 5°).

a) a landscaper estimating the angle of the corner of a garden bed

b) a surveyor estimating the angle of a property boundary line on a map

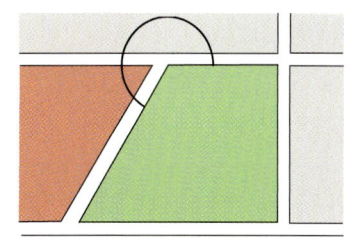

c) a roofer estimating the angle of the peak of a roof

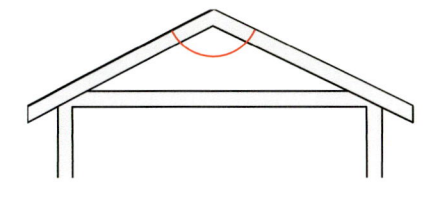

d) a cabinet-maker estimating the angles of two corners of a shelf

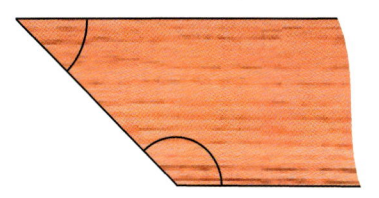

Example 2

Estimate the measure of this angle without using a measuring device.

Before this staircase was built, its angle, or incline, was calculated to ensure that it meets building codes.

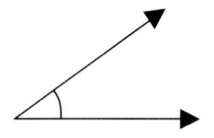

SOLUTION

Look closely at the angle, then do some mental mathematics. This is clearly an acute angle since it is less than half the size of a right angle. A close estimate is therefore less than one half of 90°, or about 30° to 35°.

ALTERNATIVE SOLUTION

Compare the angle to a known, real-life referent. This angle looks similar to the angle of a standard staircase. Standard staircases are often constructed at an angle of 33° but may be constructed to a maximum of 42°. A close estimate is therefore 30° to 35°.

Example 3

Estimate the measure of this angle without using a measuring device.

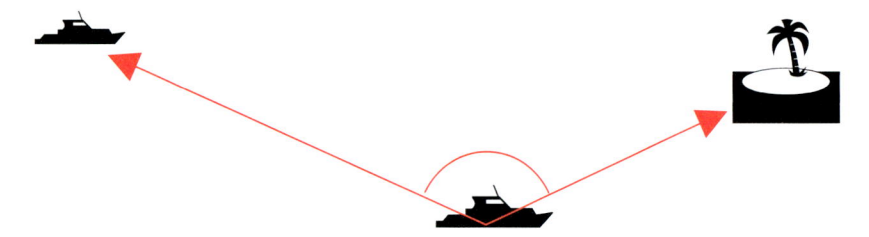

SOLUTION

Look closely at the angle, then do some mental mathematics. This is an obtuse angle, since it is bigger than 90° but smaller than 180°. It looks as if it is about one and a half times the size of a right angle. A good estimate is therefore 135° (90° plus 45°).

ACTIVITY 5.2
CREATE A REFERENTS DIAGRAM

A referents diagram shows angles from 0° to 360°.

Use only a pencil, ruler, protractor, and/or compass drawing tool. Work with a partner to create your own referents diagram.

Choose an angle whose measure divides exactly into 360° that you think could be useful in estimating angle measures.

Create a diagram featuring referents by drawing a series of radii at angles that are multiples of that angle going from 0° to 360°.

HINT

A clock face is an example of a referents diagram.

Example 4

Sort the following angles into pairs of **complementary** and **supplementary angles**.

∠1 = 42°   ∠5 = 121°

∠2 = 107°   ∠6 = 31°

∠3 = 59°   ∠7 = 19°

∠4 = 48°   ∠8 = 73°

complementary angles:
two angles that have measures that add up to 90°

supplementary angles:
two angles that have measures that add up to 180°

SOLUTION

The added measure of angles 1 and 4, and of angles 3 and 6, is 90°, so those two angle pairs are complementary.

The added measure of angles 2 and 8, and of angles 3 and 5, is 180°, so those two angle pairs are supplementary.

ACTIVITY 5.3
USING ANGLES IN WEATHER REPORTING

Compass roses, such as the one shown to the right, were originally created to navigate at sea. Although marine navigators now use other technologies, compass roses are still used extensively today to describe weather patterns and wind directions relative to true north.

A compass rose includes the four cardinal directions, N, E, S, and W, plus twelve intermediate directions.

HINT

Cardinal direction N is bearing 0°.

Create your own table of compass-point directions and related bearings stated in degrees. In the first column, list the sixteen cardinal and intercardinal directions, beginning with N (North) and going clockwise to NNW. In the second column, list the true bearing for that direction. The difference in degrees between one point and the next will equal $\frac{1}{16}$ of 360°.

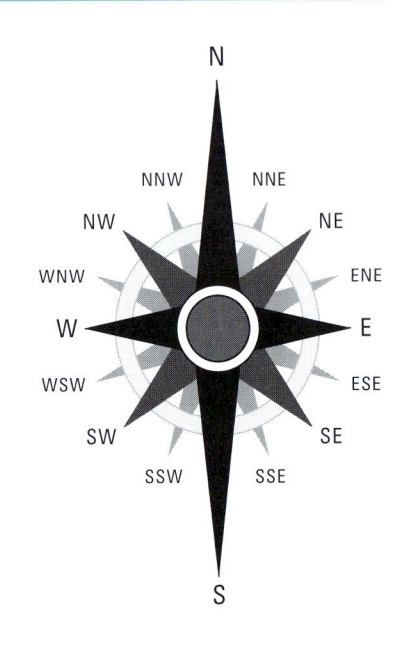

Example 5

a) Determine the true bearing between A and B.

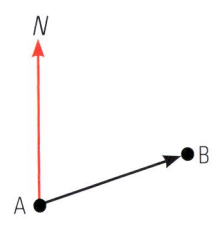

SOLUTION

HINT

Some protractors, such as full-circle and navigational protractors, can measure angles of up to 360°.

First estimate the angle, using the compass rose above as a guide. It looks as if the bearing is ENE, or about 66°. Using a protractor, measure the angle between direction N and ray AB. The angle measure is 72°, so the true A-to-B bearing is 72°.

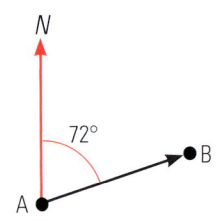

b) Determine the true bearing between A and B.

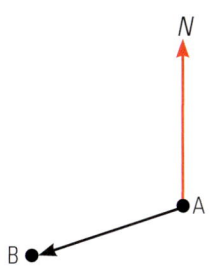

SOLUTION

The common semicircular protractor only includes angles from 0° to 180°. To use it to measure angles greater than 180°, complete the following steps.

1. Mark off an angle of 180° from N.

2. Measure the angle from that mark to ray AB. This angle is 72°.

3. Add the measure of the first angle (180°) and the second angle (72°). The sum is 252°, so the true A-to-B bearing is 252°.

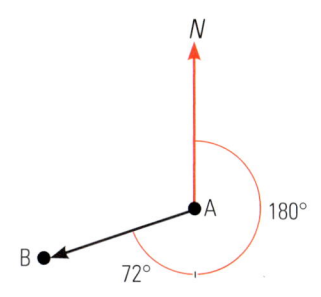

ALTERNATIVE SOLUTION

A common protractor usually has two sets of angles, the inner set going from 0° (on the left) to 180° and the outer set going from 180° (on the left) to 0°.

1. Using the outer circle of a protractor, measure the interior angle (108°).

2. Subtract the measure of the interior angle from 360°.

3. The difference is 252°, so the true A-to-B bearing is 252°.

BUILD YOUR SKILLS

1. Estimate the measure of the indicated angles, to within approximately 5°.

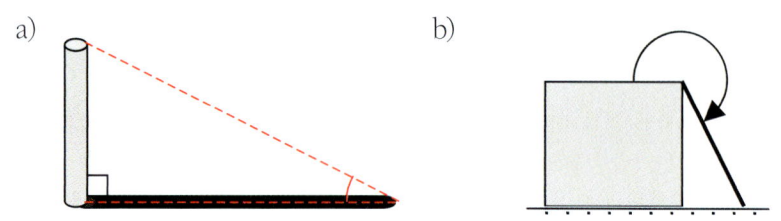

   a)

   b)

2. Look closely at the indicated angles and predict what relationships may exist among them. Measure the indicated angles in this king post truss to confirm your predictions.

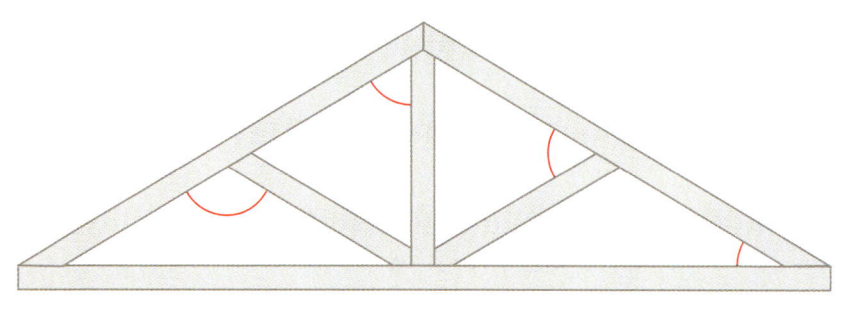

3. Atzuko is making a picture frame for her favourite picture, a reproduction of an abstract painting by Charles Daudelin. She cuts the bottom piece of the wooden frame with 50° angles. If Atzuko wants 90° corners on the frame, at what angle must she cut the bottom ends of the side pieces?

4. A woodworker is given the following diagram of an octagonal panel that will have to be cut from a rectangular piece of wood. At what approximate angles will the cuts have to be made, either to the vertical or the horizontal sides?

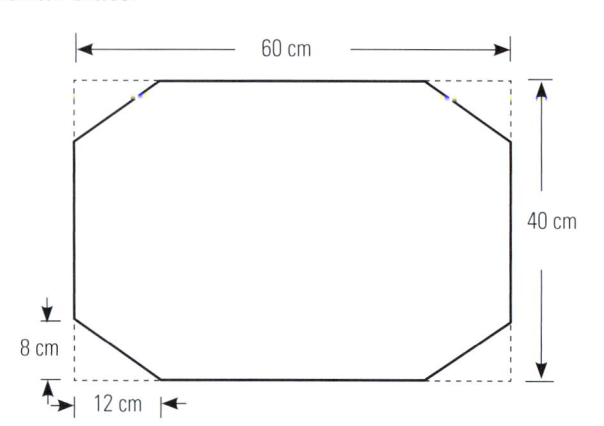

5. Draw a vertical ray that points upward to depict the direction north (bearing 0°). From the end point of that ray, draw more rays that depict the following true bearings: 65°, 140°, 220°, and 315°. (The angles should be measured clockwise from north.)

6. Sketch a map featuring several locations, without using any tools. Estimate the distances and directions. First draw an X, which will be the reference point for the other locations. From X, draw the following:

    - a small house symbol 2 km SSW of X;

    - an observation tower 3.5 km with a true bearing of 80° from X; and

    - a hill 5 km to the northwest of X.

    Use a scale for the map in which 1 cm equals 1 km on land. After you have finished, compare your estimated angle and distance measures using a protractor and ruler.

A compass needle points towards magnetic north, which varies by location.

Extend your thinking

7. Magnetic declination is the difference between true north (the direction to the North Pole) and magnetic north (the direction a compass needle actually points towards). A park ranger is using a compass that cannot be adjusted for magnetic declination. From the starting point on her map, she must walk at a true bearing of 54°, then at a true bearing of 195°, and finally in that a true bearing of 107°.

    The magnetic declination on her map is 6° east of true north.

    The park ranger wants to convert the true bearings on her route (which are based on true north) to the compass readings she will read from her compass.

    a) How should the park ranger calculate the compass readings?

    b) What compass reading should she use for each true bearing?

    To visualize the park ranger's route, draw a rough map showing the three bearing directions.

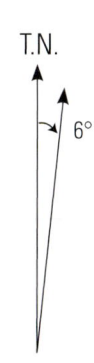

Chapter 5   Angles and Parallel Lines   **185**

PROJECT—CREATE A PERSPECTIVE DRAWING

DRAW A BUILDING IN 3-D

When we look at buildings, the vertical edges remain vertical (and thus parallel to each other). But when we look at horizontal edges they seem to be at an angle to each other, converging at a single point called a vanishing point. When you draw a 3-D diagram of a building in perspective, the horizontal edges appear to converge at a vanishing point.

For this project you will create a one-point perspective diagram, so-called because it has only one vanishing point. In this type of perspective diagram, the horizontal edges of the front and rear faces of buildings remain horizontal, so the faces are rectangular. The horizontal edges of the left and right faces, however, are drawn at various angles that all go towards the vanishing point.

You may or may not have had experience with drawing diagrams in perspective. Here are some simple steps you can follow to get some experience with creating a one-point perspective diagram of one or more buildings.

STEP 1: Very lightly draw a horizon, and mark a vanishing point somewhere along it. (For this project it should be in the centre.)

STEP 2: Draw the front face of the building, a rectangle.

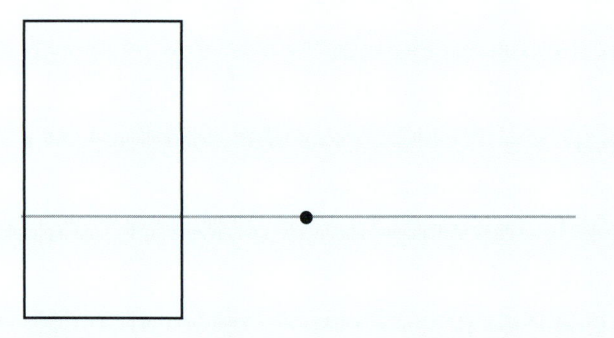

STEP 3: Very lightly draw guide lines going from the four corners of the front face to the vanishing point. These guide lines are horizontal lines drawn in perspective. The top and bottom edges of the right and left faces will be drawn on them.

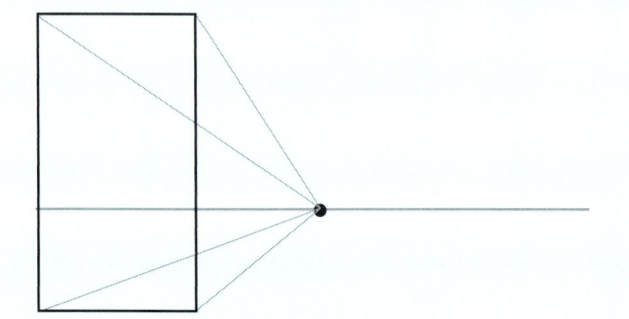

STEP 4: Draw where the rear of the building is, and draw in the edges that form the faces of the building. (Hidden edges are drawn with dashed line segments, and will eventually be erased. They will help set the widths of buildings behind this one.) Make sure that the vertical edges are parallel to each other.

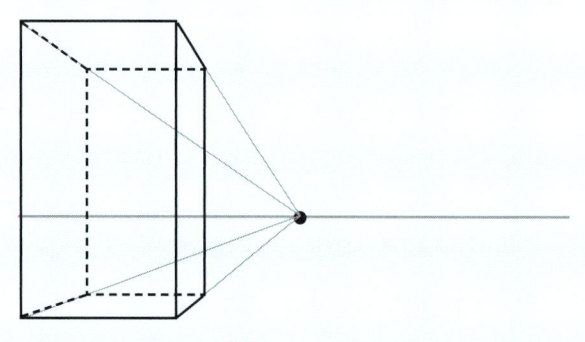

Draw two more buildings behind this one. You will need to create some space between each building for streets and sidewalks. Also, remember that as the buildings get further away, their faces must be less wide than the closer ones. Your finished drawing should resemble this one. (The relative heights of the buildings in your diagram, however, can be different.)

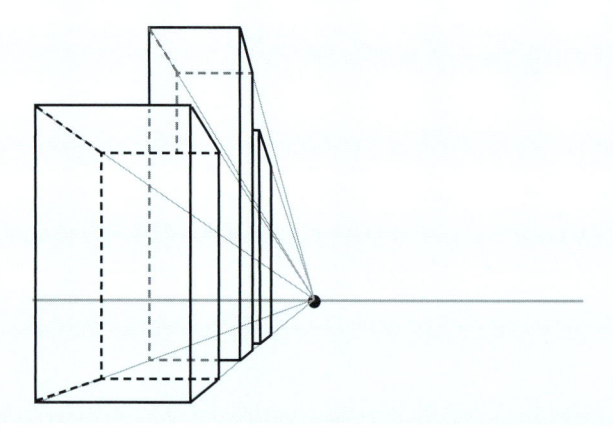

Angle Bisectors and Perpendicular Lines

5.2

MATH ON THE JOB

Yiman (James) Zhan grew up in Bejing, China. He attended No. 58 High School and has a college certificate. He now lives in Vancouver, British Columbia. He and his wife, who trained as a baker, own a small pizzeria, Kinross Pizza, where they make and sell pizzas and desserts. Yiman (James) Zhan bakes dozens of pizzas and cuts hundreds of slices every day at Kinross Pizza.

When he slices pizza, James cuts slices that are all roughly the same size, with angles that are roughly equal in measure. Typically, he cuts large pizzas into 8 slices, medium pizzas into 6 slices, and small pizzas into 6 slices. Customers who order pizzas often ask that the slices be cut in half, usually to make them easier for small children to eat.

One morning James gets an order for one large and one small pepperoni pizza to be picked up for a party at a preschool. He is asked to cut the slices so that they are half their regular size.

James spends much of his day cutting pizza wedges.

What are the approximate sizes of the central angles of regular slices from both a large and a small pizza? What are the approximate sizes of the central angles of the slices from the pizzas for the party order?

EXPLORE THE MATH

Bisecting an object involves dividing it into two congruent (equal) parts. When you bisect an angle you divide it into two angles of equal measure. For example, when bisected, a 76° angle is divided into two 38° angles. The line, line segment, or ray that separates the two halves of a bisected angle is called the **angle bisector**. Depending on the material that makes the angle, bisecting the angle can be done using measuring tools (such as protractors and compasses) and/or by manipulating the material itself (for example, by folding paper or fabric).

A right (90°) angle can be thought of as a bisected straight (180°) angle. Perpendicular lines and line segments form right angles. Look around your desk and classroom. Can you identify any perpendicular lines or line segments? You can probably identify several rectangular or square objects that contain them.

angle bisector: a segment, ray, or line that separates two halves of a bisected angle

framing square: a metal tool used to lay out right angles

A framing square can be used to find the length of a roof rafter, the slope of a set of stairs, or the measure of a bisected angle.

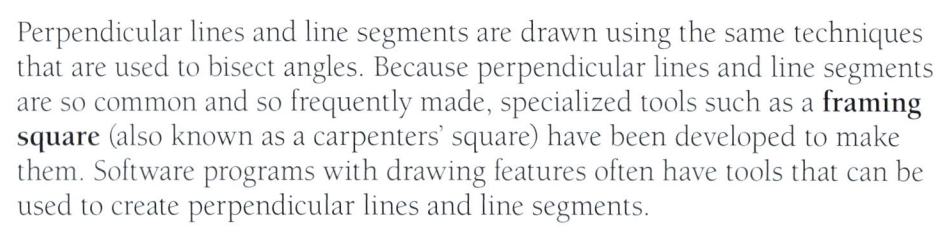

Perpendicular lines and line segments are drawn using the same techniques that are used to bisect angles. Because perpendicular lines and line segments are so common and so frequently made, specialized tools such as a **framing square** (also known as a carpenters' square) have been developed to make them. Software programs with drawing features often have tools that can be used to create perpendicular lines and line segments.

Finishing carpenters, cabinetmakers, and other woodworkers often make mitre joints, where the ends of two pieces of wood are cut with angles having the same measure. When the ends are joined, the two pieces of wood form a right angle, with the mitre joint acting as a bisector. Mitre joints are made using mitre saws or radial arm saws, because the cuts must be very precisely made. What would the result be if the angles of the cuts were even slightly off? How would this affect the right angle formed by the two pieces of wood?

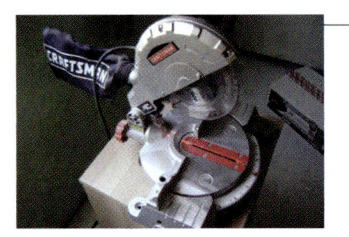

Mitre saws are used to cut accurate angles. They are often used by people constructing picture frames, baseboards, or doorframes.

DISCUSS THE IDEAS
WAYS TO BISECT ANGLES

Alexandre is a glazier who cuts and installs glass. He has been hired to replace some windows at Ecole King George in Prince Albert, Saskatchewan. As part of the job, he must cut a square piece of glass into two equal triangles. He will do this by making one cut that bisects the top left angle and bottom right angle of the square. What visual cues could Alexandre use to divide these two angles into approximately equal parts? How could he accurately bisect the angles? What measuring devices could he use to bisect the angles?

When two pieces of material meet to form a corner, craftsmen often cut the ends at a 45° angle and join them together to form a mitre joint.

Example 1

Accurately bisect an angle like the one shown here.

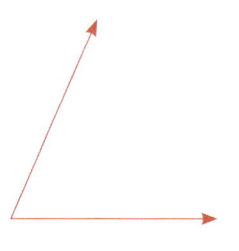

SOLUTION

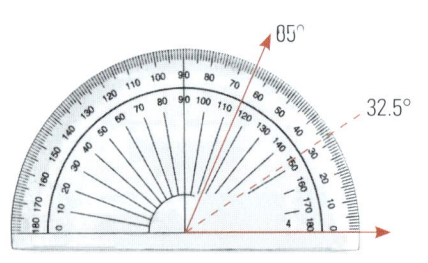

Measure the angle using a protractor. Divide that measure by 2.

The angle measure is 65°.

65 ÷ 2 = 32.5

Use a protractor to measure and mark off a 32.5° angle.

Draw a line segment from the vertex to the mark you made.

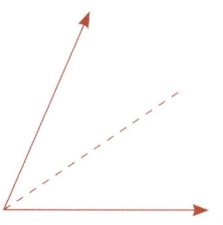

The angle has been successfully divided into two equal parts.

ALTERNATIVE SOLUTION

Trace the angle on p. 188 onto a sheet of paper. Place one side of the angle over the other side, creating a fold that goes through the vertex of the angle. The angle has been successfully divided into two equal parts.

ALTERNATIVE SOLUTION 2

Replicate the angle drawn in the previous solution. Set a compass so that the gap between the pivot point and pencil is a few centimetres. Put the pivot point on the vertex. Mark each side of the angle with the pencil.

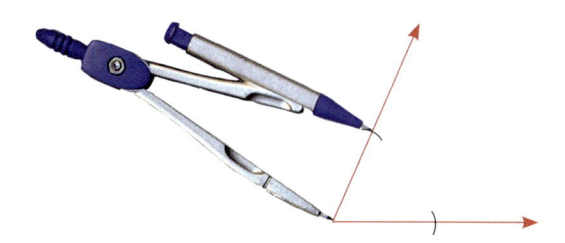

Adjust the compass so that the gap between the pivot point and pencil is over half the distance between the two marks on the sides of the angle. Put the pivot point on one mark and mark off a short arc inside the angle. Put the pivot point on the other mark and mark off another short arc inside the angle, to intersect with the first arc.

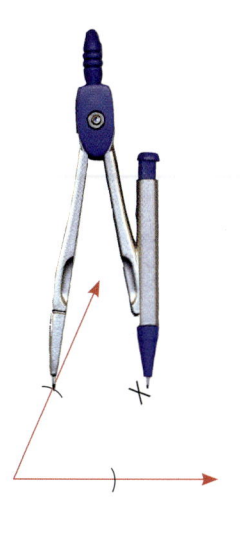

Chapter 5　Angles and Parallel Lines

Draw a line segment from the vertex to the point of intersection.

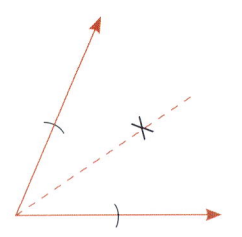

ACTIVITY 5.4
DRAW A KITCHEN COUNTERTOP PLAN

House designers, carpenters, and cabinetmakers frequently need to make items with bisected angles. For example, countertops often run along two, three, or four walls in a kitchen, with the ends of the countertop sections meeting at mitre joints that bisect the angles formed in the corners.

In this activity, you and a partner will act as kitchen designers. On a sheet of blank or graph paper, collaborate on drawing a 1:12 scale (where 1 inch equals 1 foot) countertop plan for a kitchen with the dimensions shown below. Show the mitre joints in your drawing.

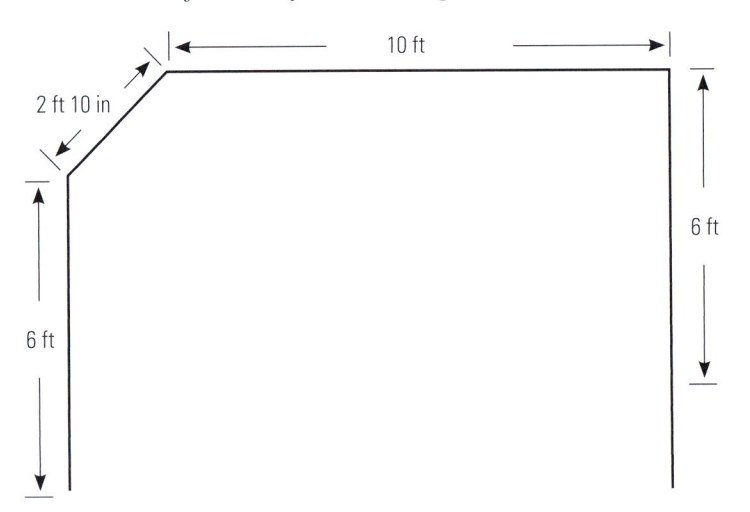

New kitchen countertop can be cut to the correct size with a jigsaw. If the countertop contains a sink, silicone sealant must be applied where the countertop and sink meet.

There is one 90° corner and two 135° corners in this kitchen at which mitre joints will have to be made. The ends of the countertop (the start and finish) will be perpendicular to the walls in your plan. Except for the areas around the mitre joints, the countertop will have, from start to finish, a width of 2 feet.

Follow these steps to make your plan:

a) Draw an outline of the kitchen to scale, using the diagram above as a guide.

b) Draw a perpendicular line from the wall, to scale, where the countertop starts and ends.

c) Bisect the three angles formed by the corners, using a protractor or other tool, and draw the angle bisector lines.

d) Draw four lines parallel to the walls representing the countertop.

e) The angle bisectors show where the sections of countertop will be cut. Write the angle measure of each angle that the sections make at the wall.

The carpenter will follow your plan to cut the countertop sections with angles that meet your specifications.

Once you and your partner have drawn your countertop plan, check it for accuracy. Ensure that:

- the dimensions of the wall are to scale;
- the extreme ends of the counter are perpendicular to the walls; and
- that the mitre joints bisect the corners.

ACTIVITY 5.5
CROSS-BRACING AND CROSS-STITCHING

Cross-bracing is used to erect safe, stable scaffolding. When working high above the ground on a construction project, builders rely on the stability provided by the triangular supports that are used to cross-brace the scaffolding. Box-stitching and cross-stitching are often found in sewn items such as backpacks, postal bags, camera bags, and other bags that are used to carry heavy materials. Box- and cross-stitching enhances durability in the spots that are subjected to a lot of stress from various angles.

Imagine that you are designing a piece of scaffolding that contains cross-bracing for a construction site. Work with a partner. Have one person draw a square and the other a rectangle, on separate sheets of paper. Then draw line segments connecting the opposite corners of the shape. Identify and name each angle with a unique number. Then identify the following items.

1. the pairs of adjacent angles that are complementary;
2. the pairs of adjacent angles that are supplementary;
3. the pairs of line segments that are perpendicular;
4. the line segments (if any) that are angle bisectors.

Switch papers with your partner and confirm with each other that your answers are correct.

This fabric has been strengthened by cross-stitching.

BUILD YOUR SKILLS

1. Luisa is a tile setter who works in The Pas, Manitoba. She is installing some tile in a science lab at the University College of the North. When installing tile, Luisa has to cut pieces of tile to fit the surface she is covering. Below are shown the angles of some pieces of tile that Luisa must cut.

   For each of these angles, measure the angle. Then determine the measure of the resulting angles after each of the original angles has been bisected.

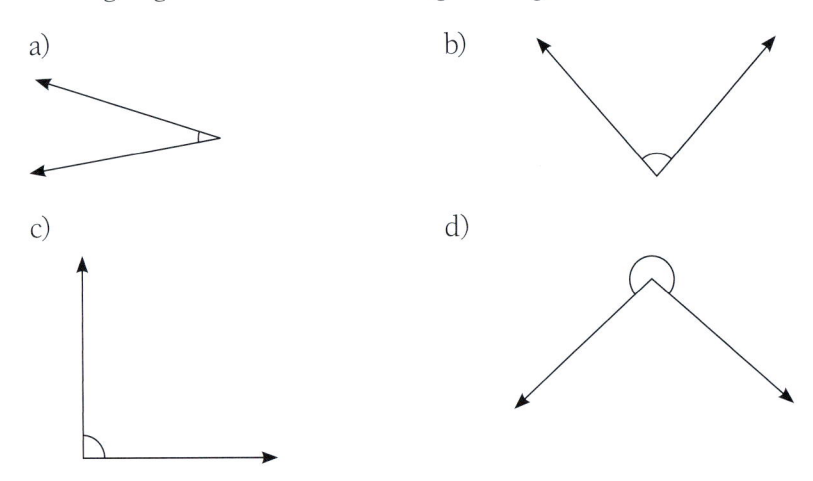

   a)

   b)

   c)

   d)

2. Jung Min has worked as a sheet metal worker for over 10 years. He has been hired to install work tables in the kitchen of St. Boniface General Hospital. These work tables need stainless steel edging bolted to their edges in order to reduce wear. Below is a scale (1:10) drawing of the stainless steel edging Jung Min will bolt over the top edges of one table. The edging has three mitred joints.

   a) Measure each angle.

   b) Determine the measure of the bisector of each angle.

   c) Determine at what angle each end of each strip should be cut.

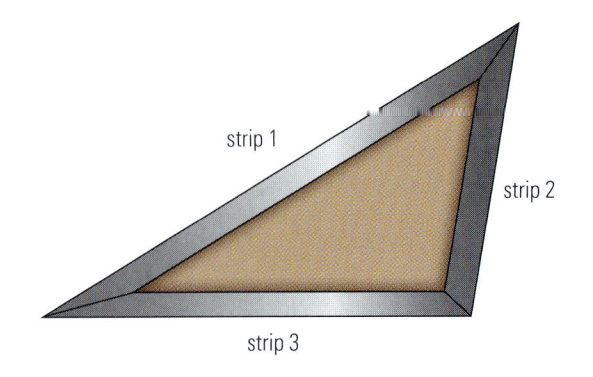

   strip 1

   strip 2

   strip 3

192 MathWorks 10

3. Imagine that you are a furniture-maker and have been asked to build a wood and glass tabletop according to the design shown here. Your client wants the outside to be made of wood, with an octagonal piece of glass in the centre. The tabletop is to be made of eight identical pieces of wood that have an arc on the outside edge, a straight side on the inside edge, and angled ends.

   The pieces of wood have to be cut so that their ends form mitre joints. If the mitre joints bisect the reflex angles outside of the octagon, at what angle relative to the straight sides of the wood must the ends be cut?

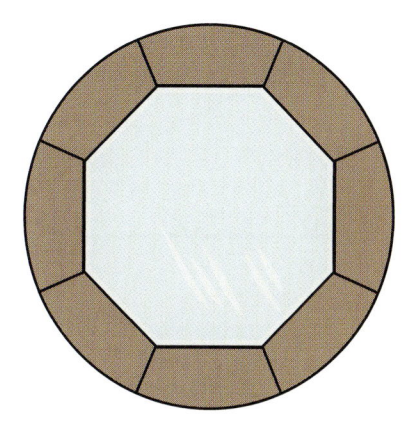

4. Jurek is a welder working on the construction of a pedestrian bridge in Cold Lake, Alberta. He is welding together bridge railing. As a decorative element to the rail, Jurek will weld four metal strips on each side of the figure, from the middle of each of the four marked angles to the edge of the piece of metal in the centre. A scale drawing of the plan is shown. Determine the measure of each angle bisector for angles A, B, C, and D.

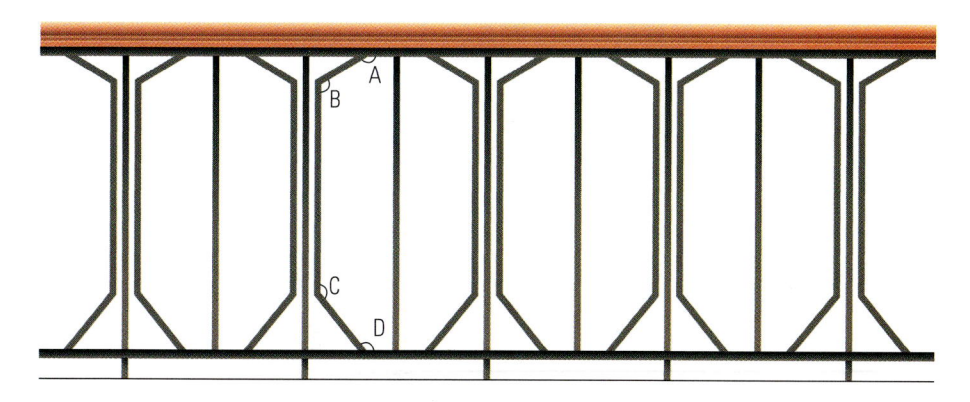

Chapter 5 Angles and Parallel Lines 193

5. When a ray of light is reflected from a flat surface, the light strikes the surface at an angle (the angle of incidence) that is equal to the angle of reflection. Both of these angles are measured from a line that is perpendicular to the surface (called the normal).

   Using the diagram below, measure the total angle between each pair of incident and reflected rays in the left, middle, and right rays. Then determine the angles of incidence and reflection for each ray.

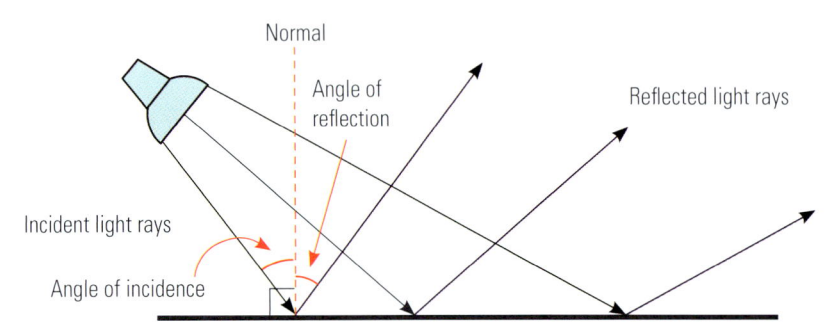

6. A carpenter needs to cut a 2-by-4 piece of wood that will fit in a corner, as shown in the diagram below. If one end of the wood forms a 50° angle with one wall, at what angle must the other end be cut (at the indicated angle) to lay flat against the other wall? Why must that end be cut to that measure?

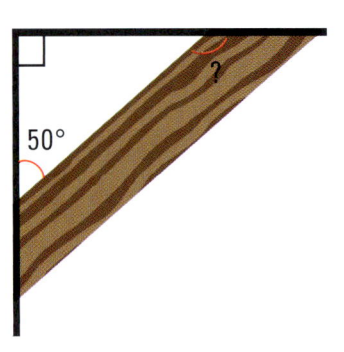

7. Suppose that you are creating a graphic design for a logo that is made up of a reflex angle at the top of a square area, similar to the one shown below, with the reflex angle divided into sixteen equal angles. Copy the design below onto a piece of paper. Use your knowledge of bisecting angles to draw line segments that divide the reflex angle into sixteen equal angles. What strategy will you use?

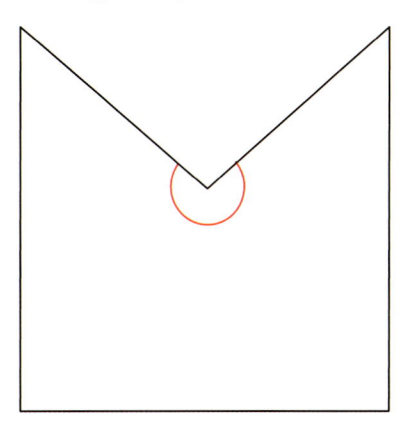

Extend your thinking

8. Lan works as a portrait photographer in Watson Lake, Yukon. When taking photographs, Lan uses a flat reflector to brighten the shadow areas. The main light illuminates the front and left side of the subject, but leaves the right side in shadows. The reflector is supposed to bounce some of the light rays from the far right side of the main light source towards the right side of the subject (shown by the dashed ray). With the reflector in its present orientation (parallel to the right wall), those light rays will miss the subject (shown by the solid reflected ray).

    Assume that the diagram below is an accurate scale diagram of Lan's studio. Determine how many degrees and in what direction (clockwise or counterclockwise) the reflector should be swivelled to ensure the right side of the subject's face is properly illuminated? (Consider how to change the direction of the normal line to the reflector so that the angle of incidence equals the angle of reflection depicted by the dashed ray.)

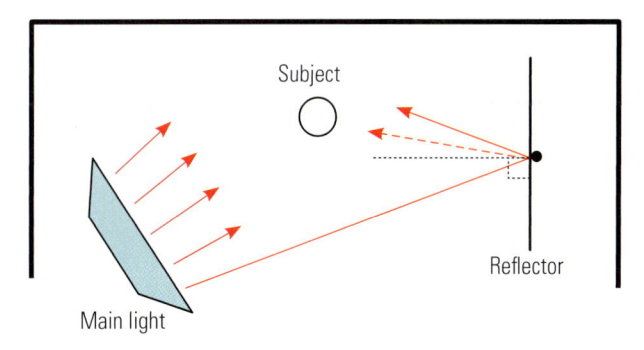

Chapter 5   Angles and Parallel Lines   195

PROJECT—CREATE A PERSPECTIVE DRAWING

DRAW DETAILS OF BUILDINGS IN 3-D

Buildings in city centres typically have features that are vertical and horizontal. The closest buildings in a perspective diagram should have a fair amount of detail. Buildings that appear further away will be too small for you to effectively draw fine details. Details on those buildings can be less fine.

To help determine what detail to draw on buildings, create a profile sketch of the buildings with details (as shown in the example below). Notice that the building on the left (closest to the viewer) has more detail than the other two buildings.

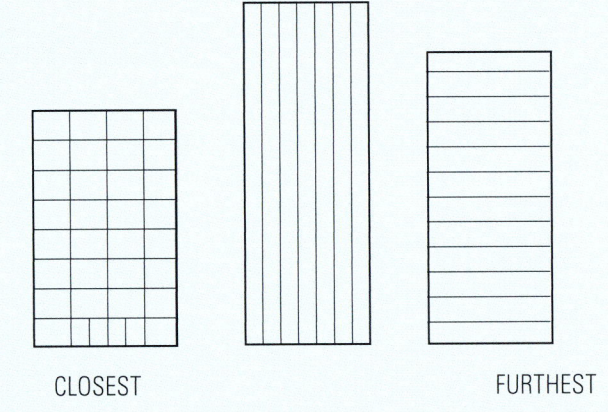

CLOSEST   FURTHEST

Go back to the sketch of the buildings you previously made. Here is how you can draw vertical and horizontal details of a building in perspective.

STEP 1: Draw the main vertical details on the front face. Then start drawing the verticals on the right face by very lightly drawing a diagonal guide line between opposite corners on that face. Then very lightly draw three evenly-spaced marks on the right front vertical edge of the building.

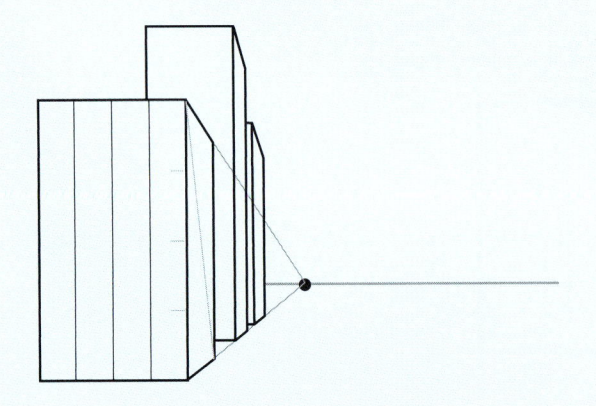

STEP 2: Finish the verticals on the right face by very lightly drawing guide lines from those marks on the right front edge towards the vanishing point. Draw the verticals through the points where these new guide lines meet the diagonal. Drawn correctly, the verticals on the right face should get progressively closer together as you go from left to right. When finished, carefully erase the diagonal.

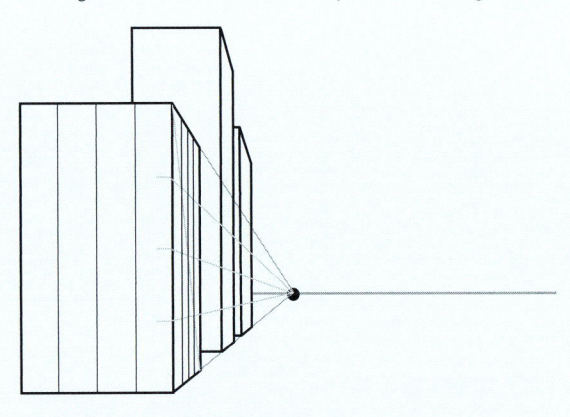

STEP 3: Draw the horizontal details. There are seven horizontals spaced evenly apart. Draw them first on the front face. Then draw the horizontals on the right face in perspective, going towards the vanishing point.

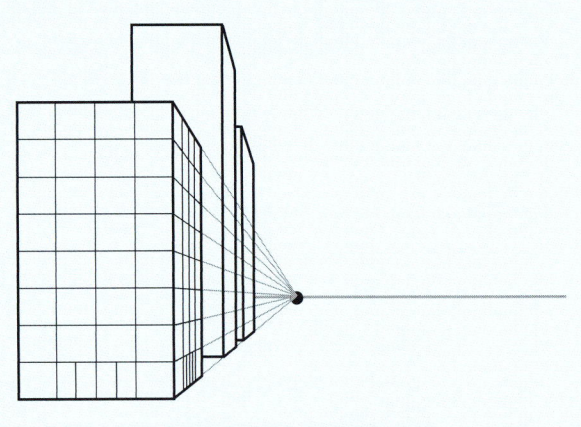

STEP 4: Draw in any smaller details, like the doors.

Now, draw details on the other two buildings. You could draw primarily vertical details on the second building, and primarily horizontal details on the third building.

THE ROOTS OF MATH

GEOMETRIC PERSPECTIVE IN ART

The School of Athens, completed by Raphael in 1511, is famous for its use of perspective.

Panels painted with olive trees and placed behind stage actors were some of the first artistic attempts to make closer objects appear larger and distant objects appear smaller, or to produce perspective. This occurred in fifth-century Greece. Medieval and Byzantine art also incorporated perspective in paintings.

Renaissance artists such as Michelangelo are most frequently celebrated for their use of perspective, since they were the first to use the same principles of perspective and scale that artists use today. Between the fourteenth and seventeenth centuries, Renaissance artists used geometric perspective to create the appearance of three-dimensional space within two-dimensional paintings.

Geometric perspective uses four elements to create a three-dimensional effect, the first being a horizon line. It is often found at the viewer's eye level, and represents the horizon. The second is a vanishing point, a spot on the horizon line where the parallel lines in the painting converge and seem to disappear. Perspective lines—those drawn from the edges of objects and leading back into the distance—and angular lines are also used. Geometric scale also allows artists to create perspective by accurately representing the size of one object in relation to another.

1. Think about a photograph you took, a painting you like, or a poster you own. In what ways does it represent geometrical perspective? Identify parallel lines, a vanishing point, or a horizon line that it contains.

2. How could a picture have more than one vanishing point? Is it possible for a picture not to have a vanishing point? Explain your reasoning.

3. How would you define the term "parallel lines"? Describe a method you could use to prove whether or not two lines are parallel.

5.3 Non-Parallel Lines and Transversals

MATH *ON THE JOB*

An interior designer needs to know which textures and colours complement each other. Being able to place furniture so that it makes a large living room seem cozy or a cramped kitchen seem spacious is another necessary talent. Listening to and incorporating a client's ideas and preferences is also important—hot pink suede couches and leopard print rugs aren't for everyone. Michelle Diaz helps customers improve their living spaces by using her design, communication, and math skills. Michelle manages a showroom of designer fabrics in Winnipeg, Manitoba.

After going to school at Winnipeg's West Kildonan Collegiate, Michelle obtained her interior decorating diploma. Today, she works in sales, customer service, and order administration. Her job involves calculating the yardage needed for drapery and upholstery orders, calculating the length of drapery tracks, setting prices, and writing up invoices. As an interior designer, Michelle also needs to be able to produce polished drawings of design ideas to present to clients.

Using her client's ideas and her own skills, an interior decorator can transform office space, hotel lobbies, or rooms in a house.

For an order, Michelle must cut square pieces of coloured cloth into six asymmetrical sections. The pieces will be stitched together to form multi-coloured cushion covers. To cut the fabric accurately, Michelle uses chalk to mark off the angles of the shapes she will cut.

The first line Michelle draws is horizontal and bisects the square. Next, she draws two vertical lines. The first vertical line forms four angles where it intersects with the horizontal line. Michelle draws this line so that the upper left angle that is formed measures 115°. She draws the second vertical line so that the lower right angle that is formed with the horizontal line measures 72°. What are the measures of the other six angles?

EXPLORE THE MATH

vertically opposite angles: angles created by intersecting lines that share only a vertex

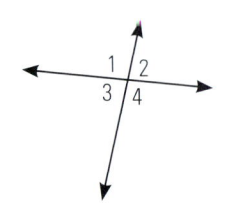

A variety of objects and materials such as trusses, railroad tracks, and fabrics contain intersecting lines. The measures of certain angles created by intersecting lines and the ability to identify types of angles can indicate whether these lines are parallel or non-parallel.

When two lines intersect each other, four distinct angles are created. The angles that share a side are adjacent angles. Angles that share only a vertex are **vertically opposite angles**.

Consider this diagram. Pick an angle and identify the two angles that are adjacent to it and the one that is vertically opposite to it. What type of angle do any two adjacent angles make? How do the measures of vertically opposite angles seem to compare to each other?

Suppose that there are two main lines (l_1 and l_2) and a third line (t) intersects both of them. That third line (t) is a **transversal**. Pairs of angles formed by the intersections of these lines fit into categories based on their relative positions to each other.

Angles that have the same corresponding positions at the two intersections are corresponding angles. In the diagram below, one pair of **corresponding angles** is highlighted. Identify the three other pairs.

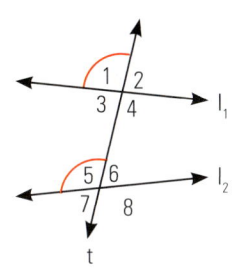

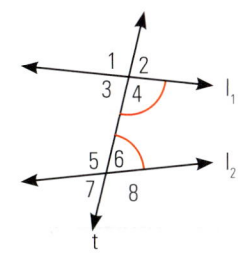

transversal: a line that intersects two or more lines

corresponding angles: angles that occupy the same relative position in two different intersections

alternate interior angles: angles in opposite positions between two lines intersected by a transversal

Angles between the two main lines are interior angles. Two interior angles that are on alternate sides of both the transversal and the interior of the main lines are called **alternate interior angles**. One pair of alternate interior angles is highlighted in the diagram below. Identify the other pair.

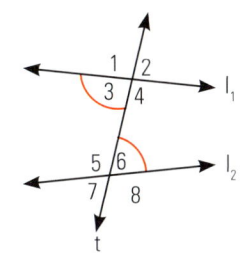

In the following diagram, two interior angles on the same side of the transversal have been highlighted. Identify the other pair of interior angles on the same side of the transversal.

Chapter 5   Angles and Parallel Lines   **199**

alternate exterior angles: angles in opposite positions outside two lines intersected by a transversal

Angles outside the two main lines are exterior angles. Alternate interior angles have exterior counterparts called **alternate exterior angles**. Alternate exterior angles are angles on the outside of two lines intersected by a transversal and are highlighted in the diagram below. Identify the other pair of alternate exterior angles.

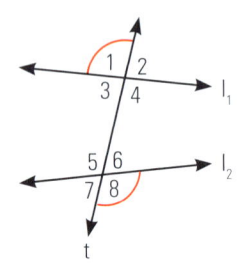

Two exterior angles on the same side of the transversal are highlighted in the diagram below. Identify the other pair of exterior angles on the same side of the transversal.

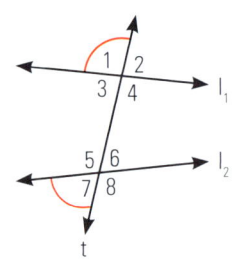

DISCUSS THE IDEAS
LINES AND TRANSVERSALS

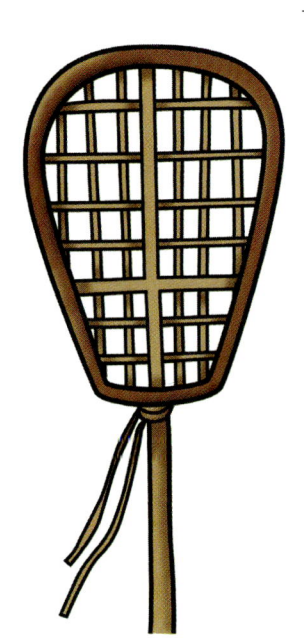

Lacrosse has many other names, including *baggataway* (Anishinabe) and *tewaarathon* (Mohawk). This game was first played by First Nations peoples. Today, many people play lacrosse for the great cardiovascular workout it provides. They also play to develop the coordination needed to manipulate the lacrosse stick and pass and shoot the ball accurately.

Lacrosse sticks contain parallel and non-parallel lines as well as transversals. These can be found in the top of the stick that holds the ball, which is called the head.

Work with a partner. You will each draw a diagram of a lacrosse stick, complete with netting (which looks similar to cross bracing), like the one shown.

On one of the diagrams pick any two of the line segments as the main line segments, and one more that is a transversal to the other line segments. Next, identify the following types of angles (if they exist) based on those line

200 MathWorks 10

segments and transversal: two corresponding angles, two alternate interior angles, and two interior angles on the same side of the transversal.

Follow the same steps for the second diagram, but pick a different pair of main line segments and transversals. Measure the angles you have identified and discuss the following questions.

1. Are the measures of corresponding angles of non-parallel line segments and a transversal equal or different? Explain your reasoning.

2. Are the measures of alternate interior angles of non-parallel line segments and a transversal equal or different? Explain your reasoning.

3. Are the interior angles formed on the same side of the transversal by non-parallel line segments supplementary? Explain your reasoning.

ACTIVITY 5.6
MAPPING AN AIRPORT RUNWAY

Large airports often have multiple runways positioned so they run parallel to the direction in which winds typically blow. It is essential for airplanes to take off into the wind to help them gain lift during takeoff. The runway with the direction that most closely matches the direction of the prevailing wind at a given time is the one that is used for takeoffs and landings. The diagram shows the runway layout of a Winnipeg airport.

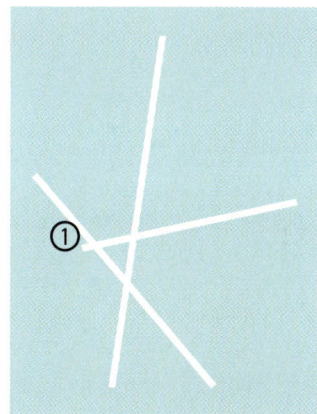

Winnipeg's James Armstrong Richardson International Airport has three intersecting runways.

Work with a partner to complete the following steps.

1. Place a sheet of tracing paper over the runway diagram and copy it.

2. Starting from 1, number each of the exterior and interior angles on your copy of the runway layout, going from left to right and top to bottom.

3. Select two of the runways to be main line segments and label them l_1 and l_2. The remaining runway will be the transversal, t.

4. Identify and list all pairs of the following types of angles: corresponding, alternate interior, interior angles on the same side of the transversal, alternate exterior, exterior angles on the same side of the transversal, and vertically opposite angles. Explain your reasoning for identifying each pair.

5. Measure the exterior angles, then compare the alternate exterior angles. Do any two alternate exterior angles have the same angle measure? Explain your conclusion.

6. Add up the measures of the exterior angles on the same side of the transversal. Are the angles in each pair supplementary angles? Explain your reasoning.

Example 1

Below is a side diagram of a verandah that is attached to a house.

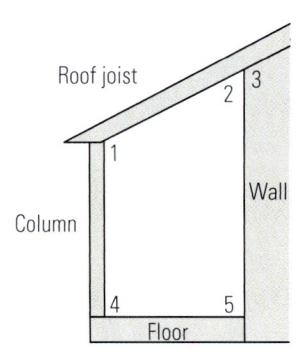

For each pair of angles listed below, identify the kind of angle pair as well as the parts of the verandah that make up the angle pair's lines and transversals.

    a) ∠1 and ∠4

    b) ∠3 and ∠5

    c) ∠1 and ∠3

SOLUTION

a) ∠1 and ∠4 are inside the lines and on the same side of the transversal, so they are interior angles on the same side of the transversal. The roof joist and floor are the lines and the column is the transversal.

b) ∠3 and ∠5 are on alternate sides of a transversal, so they are alternate interior angles. The roof joist and floor are the lines and the wall is the transversal.

c) ∠1 and ∠3 are in the same position relative to two lines and a transversal, so they are corresponding angles. The column and wall are the lines and the roof joist is the transversal.

Example 2

Lattice towers are free-standing structures that have cross-bracing to give the structures the strength and rigidity needed to stand by themselves without additional support. The lattice that exists on each side of a lattice tower is essentially a series of pairs of line segments and transversals. The diagram below shows a small part of one such tower.

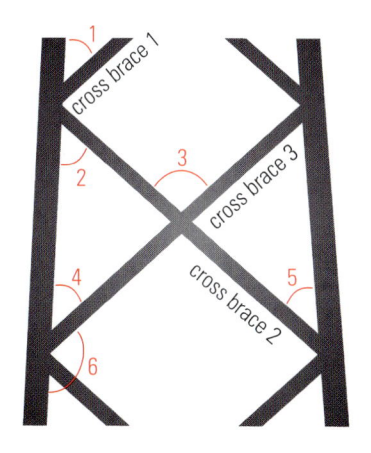

Transmission towers often use a lattice steel pylon design to support cables and conductors.

The following list contains three pairs of angles and the type of angle each pair is. Determine which two parts of the tower make up the main line segments, and which part makes up the transversal that forms each of these pairs of angles.

a) Angles 3 and 4 are corresponding angles.

b) Angles 2 and 5 are alternate interior angles.

c) Angles 1 and 6 are exterior angles on the same side of the transversal.

SOLUTION

a) Angles 3 and 4 are both above cross brace #3, and to the right of cross brace #2 and the left side of the tower respectively. The transversal is cross brace #3, and the main line segments are cross brace #2 and the left side of the tower.

b) Angles 2 and 5 are in between the left and right sides of the tower. They are also on alternate sides of cross brace #2. In this case, the transversal is cross brace #2, and the two main line segments are the left and right sides of the tower.

c) Angle 1 is above cross brace #1, and to the right of the left side of the tower. Angle 6 is below cross brace #3 and also to the right of the left side of the tower. This makes the left side of the tower the transversal, and cross braces #1 and #3 the main line segments.

BUILD YOUR SKILLS

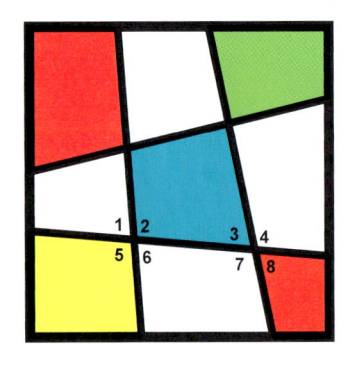

1. Aimée is an artist who makes stained-glass items. She lives and works in the small town of Jean Marie River, NT, but sells many of her items over the internet. Currently, Aimée is working on a window whose outer dimensions are 0.5 m by 0.5 m. The design consists of 9 glass panels of different colours bound by the square frame and non-parallel dividers, as shown in the diagram.

    The two dividers going from the top side to the bottom side of the frame are the main line segments, and the bottom divider going from the left to the right side of the frame is the transversal.

    a) Determine which angle is vertically opposite to angle 1. Measure it, along with angle 1. Is the measure of angle 1 equal to its vertically opposite angle?

    b) Determine which angle is the alternate exterior angle to angle 4. Measure these two angles. Do these alternate exterior angles have equal measures?

    c) Determine which angle is the corresponding angle to angle 6. Measure the two angles. Are the measures of these corresponding angles equal?

    d) Angle 2 is one of a pair of interior angles on the same side of a transversal. Which angle is the other angle in this pair? Measure both angles. Are the measures of these angles supplementary or not?

2. Pitseolak lives in Pelly Bay, Nunavut. She is an avid kayaker and is building a small shed to store her new kayak and fishing equipment in. Before building, she draws a plan for the shed. Consider her sketch of the shed's roof, which will be supported by a king post roof truss.

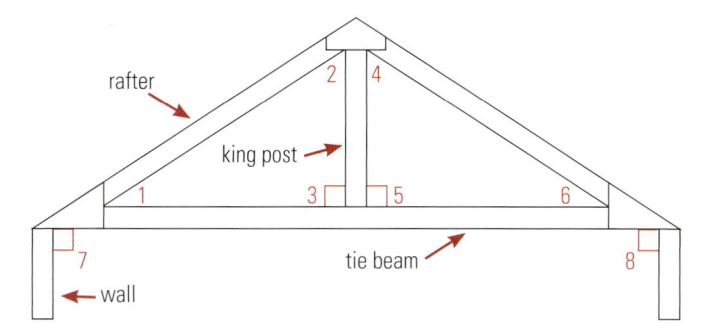

a) If the right rafter and the left rafter make up the two main line segments, name one possible transversal for the rafters.

b) What type of angles are angles 3 and 5?

c) If the walls are the line segments and the tie beam is the transversal, what type of angles are angles 7 and 8?

d) If angles 1 and angles 2 and 4 combined are a pair of interior angles on the same side of a transversal, which components of the truss must form the two main line segments and the transversal?

3. Laurence is an apprentice furniture-maker trying to make a chair with a side profile like the one below. The seat and runners are not parallel to each other. The main support and back is to be slanted 12° from an imaginary vertical line, and the seat should be 7° above an imaginary horizontal line. Do the following.

a) Consider what parts would make up the two main line segments and the transversal.

b) State the type of angles (corresponding, alternate interior, interior angles on the same side of the transversal, alternate exterior, or exterior angles on the same side of the transversal) that angles 1 and 2 are.

c) Determine what the degree measures of angles 1 and 2 should be. (Do not measure directly with a protractor because the diagram is not to scale.)

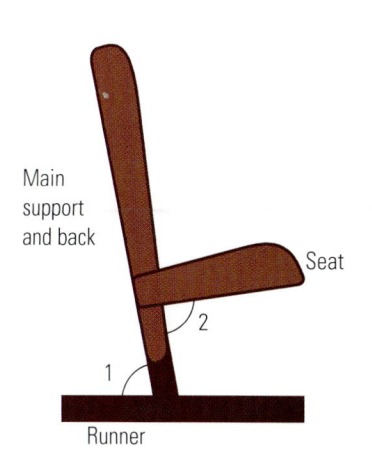

Chapter 5   Angles and Parallel Lines   205

Extend your thinking

The railings and supports of this bridge are reinforced with right triangles.

4. Below is a diagram of a Pratt truss, which is used in the construction of many bridges. A Pratt truss contains components that are parallel and non-parallel, perpendicular and non-perpendicular.

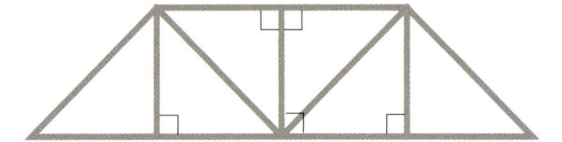

   a) Consider these components—a vertical and a diagonal member form the two main (non-parallel) line segments, and the bottom line segment forms the transversal. Measure angles 1, 2, and 3, then do the following analysis. Explain your reasoning for each question.

      i) Compare the measures of the corresponding angles, ∠1 and ∠3. Is ∠1 equal to, less than, or greater than ∠3?

      ii) Add the measures of the interior angles on the same side of the transversal (∠2 and ∠3) together. Are angles 2 and 3 supplementary angles or not? Explain your reasoning.

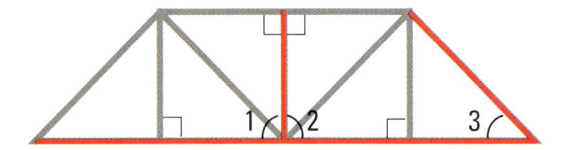

   b) Consider these components—two diagonal members form the two main (parallel) line segments, and the bottom line segment forms the transversal. Measure angles 1, 2, and 3, do the following analysis, and explain your reasoning for each.

      i) Compare the measures of the corresponding angles, ∠1 and ∠3. Is ∠1 equal to, less than, or greater than ∠3?

      ii) Add the measures of the interior angles on the same side of the transversal (∠2 and ∠3) together. Are angles 2 and 3 supplementary angles or not? Explain your reasoning.

206 MathWorks 10

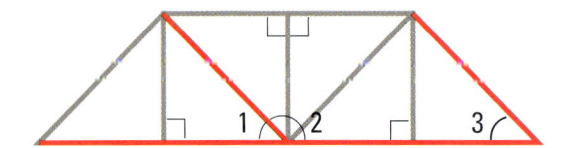

c) Consider the results for parts a) and b).

   i) What did you notice about the measures of corresponding angles for parallel line segments that was not true for non-parallel line segments?

   ii) Are either pair of interior angles on the same side of the transversal, one formed by two parallel line segments and one formed by non-parallel line segments, supplementary angles or not? Explain your reasoning.

The Victoria Bridge in Saskatoon, Saskatchewan, crosses the South Saskatchewan River.

Chapter 5 Angles and Parallel Lines 207

PROJECT—CREATE A PERSPECTIVE DRAWING

DRAW A STREET SCENE IN 3-D

The drawings you have made so far have been of buildings on one side of the street. This project requires an entire street scene to be done. Complete the street scene by drawing the right side of the street, which will primarily show the left faces of the buildings drawn in perspective. The same vanishing point must be used. The spacing between buildings should be the same as the other side of the street, so that streets crossing the one in the diagram are aligned.

Draw details on these buildings as you see fit. Use the same techniques for drawing horizontal and vertical detail you used earlier. Draw a sidewalk on each side of the street. When finished, use this diagram as the basis of your project diagram.

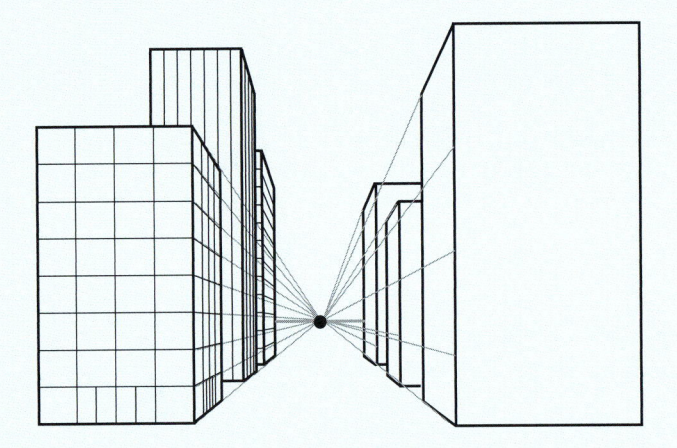

Parallel Lines and Transversals

5.4

MATH *ON THE JOB*

June Peterson is a member of the Sturgeon Lake Cree Nation and lives in Sturgeon Lake, Alberta. After graduating from Hillside High School, she took the pre-trades program through the Northern Alberta Institute of Technology (NAIT). Since she has always loved building things, she focussed on the carpentry aspect of the program and worked with a local contractor on a new housing project at Sturgeon Lake.

June often works on wood-framed houses and buildings. The frames are made of studs (parallel, vertical pieces), and wall plates (pieces that are attached along the top and bottom of the studs). Frames are usually constructed on the ground or floor and then erected. The wall plates hold the studs in position.

Part of June's job is to make sure that the studs are exactly perpendicular to the bottom wall plate and parallel to each other. To do this, she uses a measuring device such as a carpenters' square, which is used to measure and mark off 90° angles.

Carpenters often make rough sketches of structures they work on.

June is constructing a partial wall for the side of a staircase. The top of the wall follows the slope of the staircase. A partial diagram of the framing for the staircase is shown here.

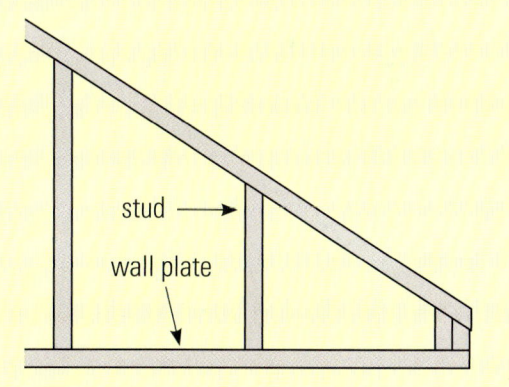

- Decide upon a reasonable angle for the staircase. Staircase angles range between 33° and 42°.
- To make the studs parallel, what angle measure will June need to make between the studs and the bottom wall plate?
- To make the ends of the studs align with the top wall plate, what angle will June need to make between the studs and the top wall plate?

EXPLORE THE MATH

Two lines are parallel if they never intersect each other. This only happens when the lines are a constant distance from each other. Imagine a case where you find parallel lines, then imagine what would happen if those lines were not parallel. For example, lines drawn on roads to define lanes should be parallel. What would happen if those lines became closer and closer together? In houses, the studs that support walls should be vertical and parallel to each other. What would happen to a wall if the stud at one end of a wall was vertical but the other studs were not parallel to this one and to each other?

If two lines are parallel and are intersected by a transversal, the corresponding angles, alternate interior angles, interior angles on the same side of a transversal, alternate exterior angles, and exterior angles on the same side of a transversal all have certain properties. Whether lines are parallel or not can be confirmed if these angles have certain measures.

Look at the pair of corresponding angles, ∠1 and ∠5, in the diagram below. Measure them. How do the measures of the angles compare? Are they equal or different? Is this also true of the other pairs of corresponding angles?

Look at the pair of alternate interior angles, ∠3 and ∠6, in the diagram below. Measure them. Are the measures the same or different? Is the same true of the other pair of alternate interior angles? What about the pairs of alternate exterior angles?

Look at the pair of interior angles on the same side of the transversal, ∠3 and ∠5, in the diagram below. Measure them. What is the sum of the angle measures? Is this true of the other pair of interior angles on the same side of the transversal, and the two pairs of exterior angles on the same side of the transversal?

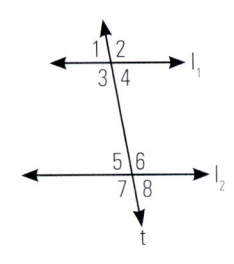

Craftsmen use tape measures to measure and create accurate angles.

What you should have found by measuring the angles above is that when two lines are parallel and intersected by a transversal:
- The measures of corresponding angles, alternate interior angles, and alternate exterior angles will be equal. (If such angles do not have equal measures, then the lines are not parallel.)
- Interior and exterior angles on the same side of a transversal will be supplementary. (If they are not, then the lines are not parallel.)

HINT

In a diagram of two lines and a transversal, if the corresponding angles are equal, the lines are *not* parallel.

DISCUSS THE IDEAS

DRAWING PARALLEL LINE SEGMENTS

Wooden drying racks are used by many peoples to dry and smoke fish and meat. The racks are made of parallel rods, over which strips of scored meat or filleted, scored fish are hung. A smoldering smoky fire is lit on the ground in the middle of the structure. It can take from twelve hours to several days for the fish or meat to be ready.

Some First Nations peoples build drying racks in square or rectangular shapes. Square-shaped drying racks are made of a square held up by four vertical posts. Parallel horizontal poles are fastened across the square. Triangular drying racks look like a triangular tent with parallel poles fastened horizontally, end-to-end.

Imagine you are out on a fishing trip and catch many fish. You would like to smoke some of it at your camp, in order to preserve it. Would you build a triangular or rectangular drying rack? Explain your reasoning.

Drying fish was traditionally used as a way of preserving meat for consumption during the winter.

Work with a partner. Choose the shape of rack you would build and draw a construction diagram. One partner can draw the horizontal line segments and the other can draw the parallel lines. You can draw the sides of the racks separately or in three dimensions. Choose a scale factor to use, such as 1:48.

While you are working on this task, determine how to ensure that the parallel line segments remain parallel. Discuss how much space you need to leave between each segment of the rack that fish will be draped over, so that air and smoke can circulate evenly. (Fish fillets are often around 30 cm long.) What would be the best type of material to make your rack from? How would you fasten the poles together? How could you discourage animals and insects from coming near the fish?

Chapter 5 Angles and Parallel Lines 211

ACTIVITY 5.7
DESIGN A FRENCH PATTERN TILE FLOOR

When tile is laid in a French pattern, the result is a mosaic that connects square and rectangular tiles of different sizes. The pattern is random, but each stone must be flush with the ones beside it. The vertical sides of all the tiles should be parallel with each other, as should the horizontal sides. Traditionally, marble and travertine, a type of limestone, were used to make a French pattern tile floor. A French pattern tile floor can be made using different-sized squares that were made to the same scale.

Imagine you are installing tile on a kitchen floor in a French pattern. On a sheet of graph paper, measure off a square that is 15 cm by 15 cm. Draw in tiles in the French pattern. Start with one tile that is 3 cm by 4 cm. Use a scale of 1.5:1. (You can round your measurements up to one decimal place.) Add two tiles that were enlarged using this scale and two that were reduced. Add a tile that is 1 cm by 1 cm. Use a scale of 3:1. Add two tiles that were enlarged using this scale. Fill in the rest of the paper with tiles of different sizes. Make sure the horizontal and vertical sides are parallel.

Think about how a craftsperson would make sure the horizontal and vertical sides of the tiles are parallel to each other. What tools could you use to help you do this? Ensure that the lines are parallel by making the interior and exterior angles on the same side of a transversal add up to 180°.

Different-sized tiles are used to set tile in the French pattern.

Example 1

A cable stay bridge is made of a support tower and cables that reach down to the bridge deck. The cables, which can be parallel or angled, suspend the bridge above water. One of Canada's most well-known cable stay bridges is the Esplanade Riel in Winnipeg.

Consider the diagram below. Determine which of the four indicated cables are parallel to each other and which ones are not. Explain how you came to your conclusion.

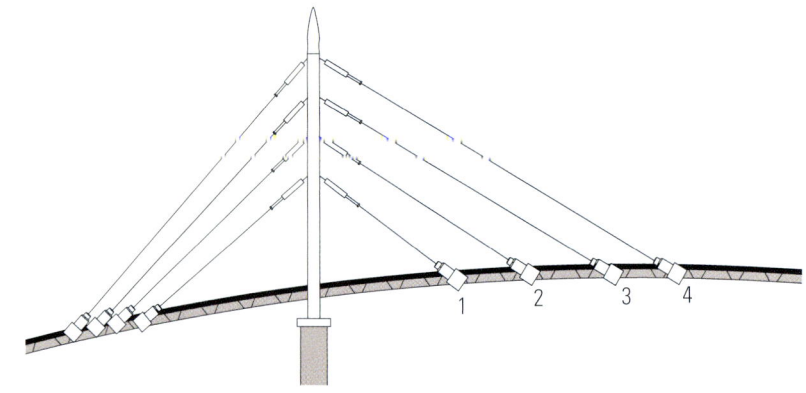

Winnipeg's Esplanade Riel is a side-spar cable-stay bridge designed for pedestrian use. It crosses the Red River to connect downtown Winnipeg with St. Boniface.

SOLUTION

You could measure the bottom angles between the right side of the vertical tower and each cable. Since these angles all have the same positions relative to the points where the cables intersect the tower, these angles are corresponding angles. Those angles, from bottom to top, should have the measures 54°, 58°, 60°, and 60°. The only two corresponding angles that have equal measures are the ones under Cable 3 and Cable 4 (both 60°), making Cables 3 and 4 the only cables that are parallel to each other. The other cables are not parallel to each other because the measures of their corresponding angles do not equal the measures of other corresponding angles.

Example 2

Danielle is a sheet metal worker. She specializes in installing sheet metal roofs in her hometown of La Ronge, Saskatchewan. The sheet metal roofing Danielle uses contains parallel ridges. It can be purchased in segments, snapped into place, and secured with screws or nails.

Below is a diagram showing two segments of sheet metal roofing. The horizontal line, or transversal, represents where the two segments meet. The vertical lines are ridges. One angle is given. State the measures that angles 1, 2, and 3 must have if the ridges are parallel to each other. Explain why they must have those measures.

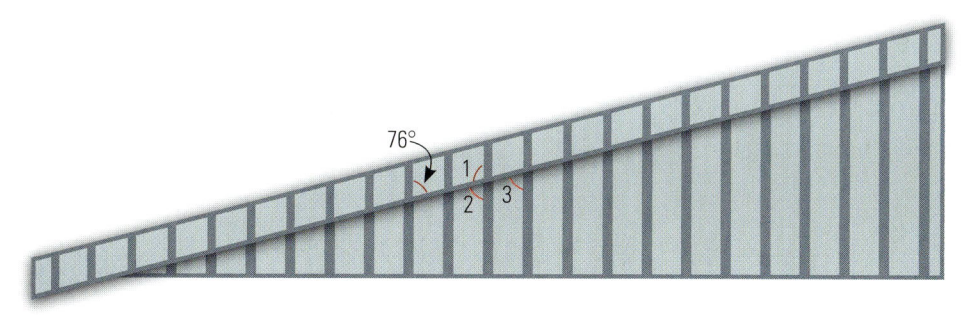

SOLUTION

Angle 1 forms a pair of interior angles on the same side of a transversal with the 76° angle. These two angles must be supplementary, so the measure of Angle 1 must be 180° minus 76°, which equals 104°.

Angle 2 is an alternate interior angle to the 76° angle. These two angles must have equal measures, so the measure of Angle 2 must equal 76°.

Angle 3 is another alternate interior angle to the 76° angle, and is a corresponding angle to Angle 2. These angles must all have equal measures, so the measure of Angle 3 must also equal 76°.

BUILD YOUR SKILLS

1. After graduating from high school, Jamila worked for her uncle's flooring business in Port Hardy, British Columbia, and learned how to install electric radiant heating. Electric radiant heating consists of criss-crossing parallel lines of conductive wires that are installed underneath the floor. When she works, Jamila needs to ensure the wires are parallel, so that the heating is distributed evenly. Sketch how a radiant heat system might look by drawing three lines that are parallel. Then, draw three parallel transversals.

2. Railroads in Canada are typically made out of parallel steel rails that are held in place by wooden ties. State two ways that rail workers could ensure that the rails run parallel to each other.

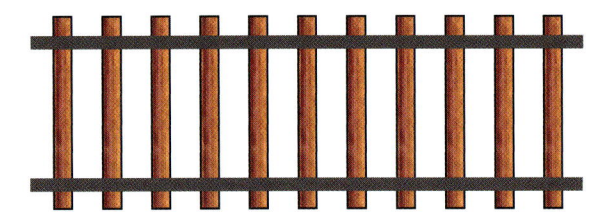

3. Sometimes optical illusions can make lines look parallel when they are not, and non-parallel when they are. Look at two line segments in each of the drawings below. Judge whether they are parallel. Describe two different techniques you would use to determine whether or not they are parallel.

   a)

b)

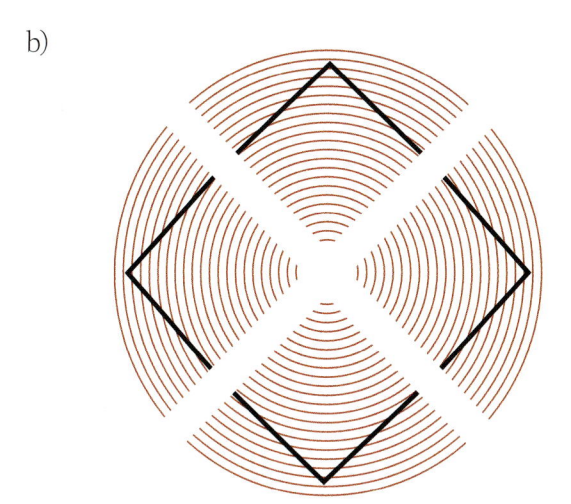

4. To make sure his grandmother can get upstairs safely, Robert is installing a new banister on her stairs. Vertical posts, called spindles, attached to the handrails of a banister must be parallel to each other. What is the degree measure of *x*? Explain how you determine that measure.

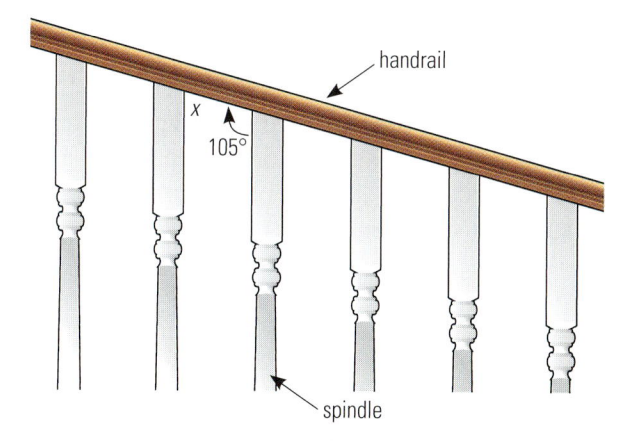

5. The front face of a concrete block is shown in the diagram below. Consider the indicated angle measures to determine which edges (if any) are parallel, and which edges (if any) are not parallel.

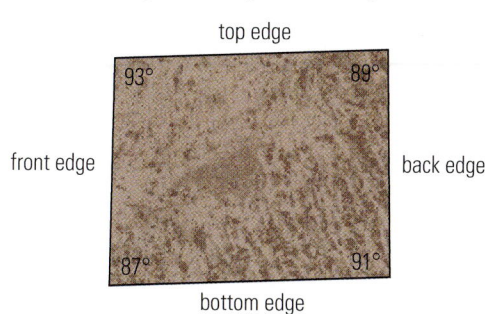

Chapter 5 Angles and Parallel Lines 215

6. Giang gives boat tours along the Yukon River. When on the river, he tries to stay 10 m away from, and run parallel to, other boats on the river for safety reasons. If Giang's boat is travelling on a bearing of 193° while another boat is travelling at a bearing of 201°, by how many degrees starboard (right) or port (left) must Giang adjust his boat's course to make it parallel to the other boat's course?

7. An architect designs a wall of a building with line segments that make up a lattice. Which of the numbered line segments is parallel to other(s)? In each case, state how you can tell the line segments are parallel.

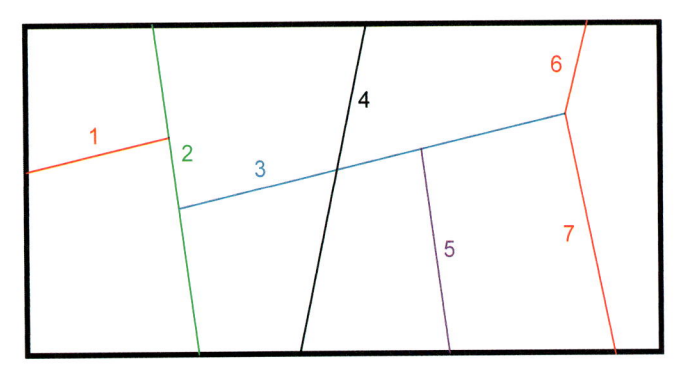

Extend your thinking

8. A client has asked a shop that specializes in mirrors to create a full-length roof mirror to be used by people standing in front of it. (A roof mirror is so named because it is shaped like the roof of a house). A roof mirror reverses a reflection so that people looking at themselves see their reflections oriented as others see them rather than oriented as a standard mirror image. (The left side of your body will appear on the right side of the reflection.)

   A roof mirror can be created by joining two full-length rectangular mirrors vertically so that their reflecting surfaces are perpendicular and facing inwards. The perfectness of the right angle can be tested by shining a narrow beam of light straight towards the roof mirror. If, when viewed from above, the reflected beam is parallel to the incident beam (as shown in the ray diagram below), then the mirrors are perpendicular to each other, and a roof mirror will work as expected.

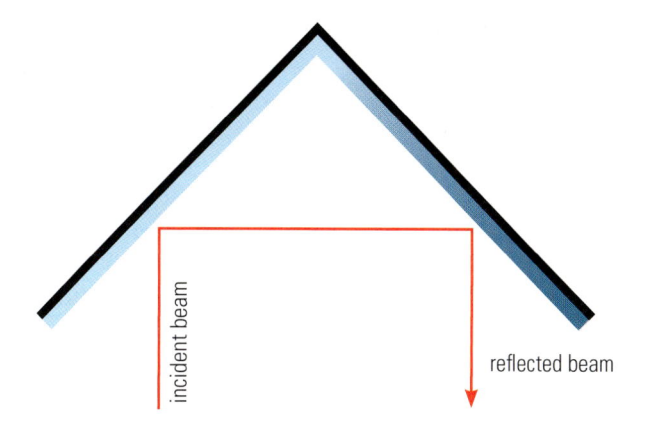

a) Think about how you would ensure the mirrors could be held in place to form a 90° angle.

b) Draw a ray diagram similar to the one above, but with an angle between the mirrors measuring less than 90°. Do you think that the same orientation effect can be achieved? Explain your reasoning.

c) Do the same as in part b) of this question, but use an angle that is greater than 90°.

If possible, obtain two small rectangular mirrors to see how light is reflected off of them.

PUZZLE IT OUT

THE IMPOSSIBLE STAIRCASE

This drawing of an impossible object, the first of its kind, was created by the English geneticist Roger Penrose. It is a two-dimensional depiction of a staircase in which the stairs make four 90° turns as they ascend or descend. Yet they form a continuous loop, meaning that a person could climb them forever and never get any higher (or lower). The staircase is impossible in three dimensions, but looks possible in two dimensions because of distorted perspective.

Follow the staircase around. Can you determine the lowest or highest step? What happens when you go around in a clockwise direction? In a counter-clockwise one? Try creating your own neverending staircase (without tracing this image).

Explain how this illusion works, using what you have learned about parallel lines.

PROJECT–CREATE A PERSPECTIVE DRAWING

CREATING 3-D PERSPECTIVE

You must now create the street scene that will appear on the front cover of THETA. Use your preliminary drawings as guides for making the final drawing. Create a cover drawing that is as close to publishable quality as you can make it. Ensure that all edges and details are easy to see, and that all temporary lines are fully erased.

Make a display that includes the following items:

- all preliminary sketches/diagrams used to develop the final drawing; and
- the final cover drawing itself.

Be sure to sign your name, and the name of any partner(s) involved in the creation of this drawing, in the bottom right corner of each item.

A graphic artist's studio.

REFLECT ON YOUR LEARNING

ANGLES AND PARALLEL LINES

Now that you have finished this chapter, you are able to

- ❒ draw, measure, and describe angles of various measures;
- ❒ determine whether pairs of angles are complementary, supplementary, or neither;
- ❒ use referents to estimate angle measures;
- ❒ bisect angles;
- ❒ identify corresponding, alternate interior, and alternate exterior angles around lines and transversals;
- ❒ identify interior and exterior angles on the same side of a transversal; and
- ❒ determine whether or not lines are parallel.

You will also have finished a chapter project that allowed you to apply these skills in a practical way to a real-world task.

PRACTISE YOUR NEW SKILLS

1. As her first job as a designer, Martine was asked to create a large decorative panel for a café in Medicine Hat. The panel will be suspended from a ceiling by cables, to partially hide exposed pipes and electrical conduits. To show what the panel will look like from the front of the coffee shop, make a 1:24 scale front-view diagram in which 1 inch equals 2 feet. The diagram should depict the panel suspended 2 feet below the ceiling. The room is 16 feet wide and 12 feet tall. The panel is to be 11 feet wide by $\frac{1}{2}$ foot tall. Two cables will hold up the panel on each of its sides, which will have 95° and 110° angles (relative to the top of the panel) when viewed from the front.

2. A standard door in a floor plan is drawn as a line segment with the arc swept by the door's edge (typically a quarter circle representing 90°) when it is fully swung open.

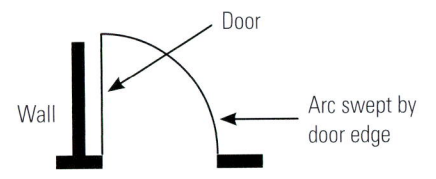

   On a sheet of paper, draw a similar diagram of a door that will open as wide as 125° to rest along a wall that is at a 125° angle to the adjoining wall, rather than the standard 90°.

3. Suppose that you are the skipper of the boat depicted by the white symbol in the map below. Place a sheet of paper over the map. Draw a clockwise course made up of three legs that will take you just past each of the buoys (marked in red), to a spot right beside the boat (depicted in black). Use the vertical gridlines, which point north, to determine what true bearing the boat must be on during each leg, and record those bearings.

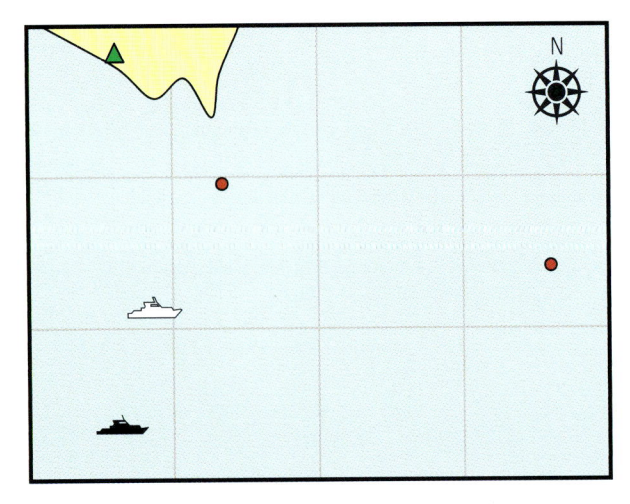

4. Garnett is a draftsman, and part of his job consists of making floor plans. He has been asked to create a small meeting room to add to the Makkuttukkuvik Youth Centre in Iqaluit. Imagine that you have Garnett's job. Draw a sketch so you can show the staff of the centre what you propose.

- The front wall has a length of 16 feet.

- The left wall has a length of 12 feet, and the right wall a length of 10 feet. Both walls are perpendicular to the front wall.

- The back wall also has a length of 12 feet and is perpendicular to the left wall.

- There is a fifth wall that joins the back and right walls at an angle.

Use this information to draw that sketch. Then analyze the diagram to estimate the length that the fifth wall will have, along with the measures of the angles it makes with the back and right walls. Also draw in a door on the side of the fifth wall that will open fully to the maximum angle. What is that angle?

5. You are a contractor in charge of building a house with exterior walls that face the four cardinal directions—N, E, S, and W. A meteorologist's report shows that strong winds in that area most likely come in from the NW, WSW, and SSE directions. You had intended to have double-pane windows installed in all exterior walls. But to make the house more energy efficient, you now want to install triple-pane windows with extra insulating properties on the two walls most likely to be hit by cold winds. Draw a sketch of the house, and label the directions from which the strong winds typically blow. Then determine which of those two walls should get the triple-pane windows.

Installing multi-paned windows will make a house more energy efficient.

Chapter 5 Angles and Parallel Lines 221

6. Binh makes custom windows. He is asked to make a pair of windows shaped like right triangles that will be installed side by side in the top floor of an A-frame house. The two halves of the ceiling meet at a 70-degree angle. The sloped side of each window runs parallel to the ceiling. The diagram below roughly depicts the arrangement. Determine the following measures:

   a) the measures of the top and bottom angles; and

   b) the measures of the angles needed to cut the pieces of window frame to form mitre joints at each vertex.

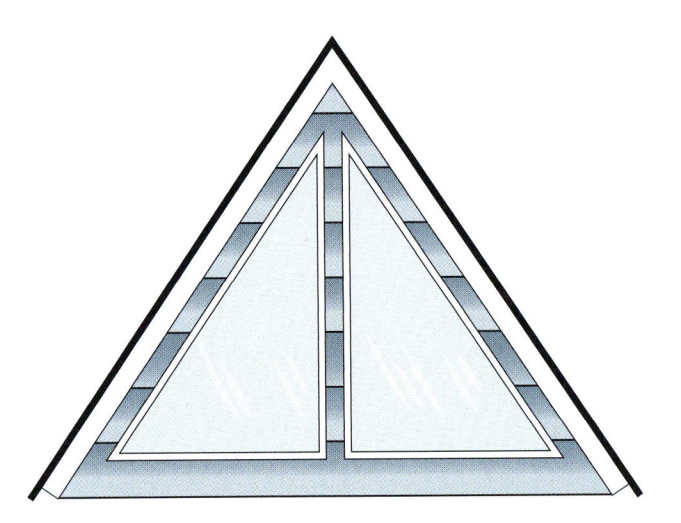

7. A gusset is an angled reinforcing plate that is glued and either nailed or bolted onto a joint where pieces of wood meet end to end. A gusset helps reinforce this type of joint. Suppose that you are a roofer who wants to make a series of identical gussets like the ones depicted below from a sheet of $\frac{3}{4}$-inch plywood. To ensure that the gussets have a consistent shape, make a template on paper or cardstock. The template will be used to draw outlines of the gussets on the plywood. Use your knowledge of parallel lines and angle bisectors to draw a gusset template that meets the following criteria. Each gusset is to precisely fit over two 2-by-6 boards that meet in a mitre joint at a 120° angle. Each "wing" of the gusset must be exactly $5\frac{1}{2}$ inches wide, and at least 8 inches long. The ends of the gusset should be parallel to each other.

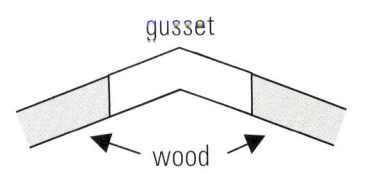

When mitre joints are under pressure or need added stability, gussets are used to reinforce the joint

8. The following diagram shows part of the framing in a wall, with 2-by-4 studs nailed into a bottom wall plate. The double stud on the left side is perfectly perpendicular to the wall plate. Which of the numbered studs are perpendicular to the bottom plate? Which of the studs need to be moved before they are nailed to the top plate? Explain how you identified which studs are parallel to the left side, and which are not.

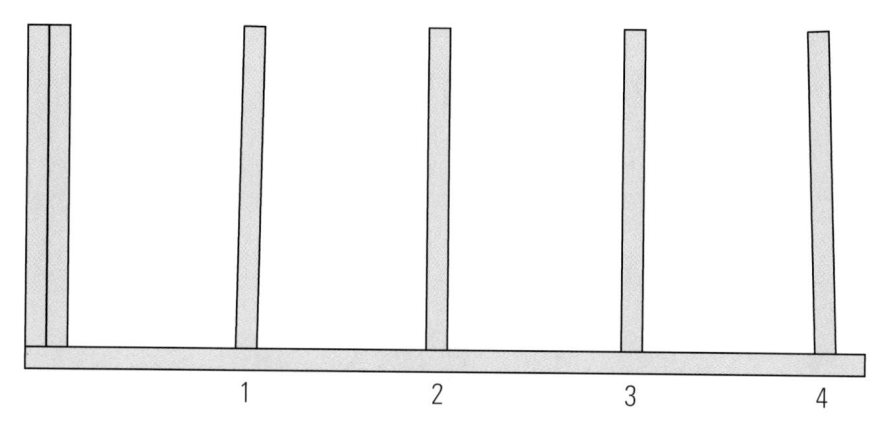

9. Suppose that one aircraft travels at 120 km/h due west, and another at 100 km/h due south. They take off from the same airport at roughly the same time.

   a) Calculate how far each of the aircraft will travel in 30 minutes.

   b) Without using measuring tools, draw a rough sketch showing the approximate positions of the aircraft from the airport after 30 minutes.

Chapter 6

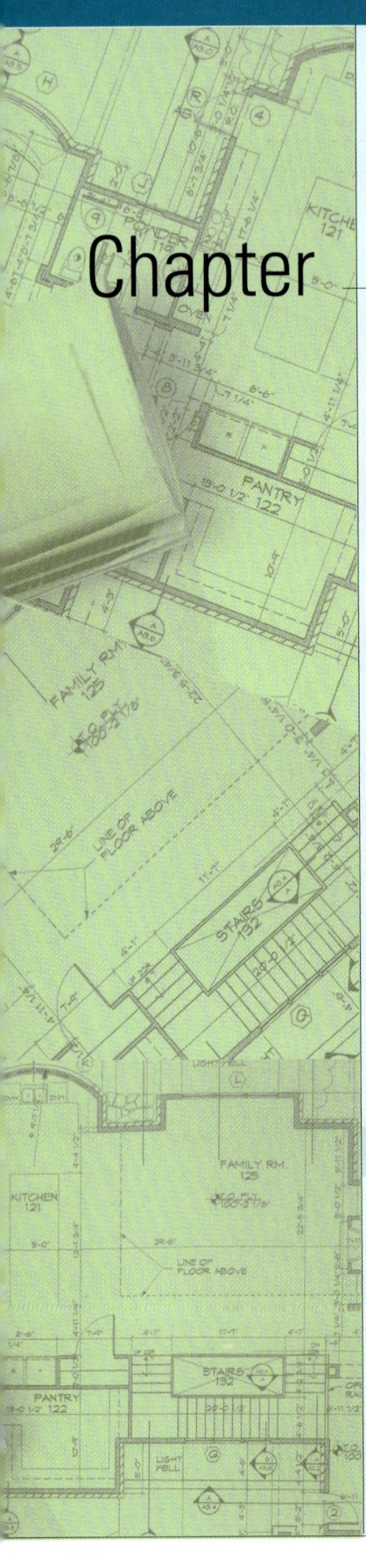

Similarity of Figures

GOALS

When you draw an image of something that is larger or smaller than the original, you create an image that is similar to the actual object. Architects, engineers, and construction workers use blueprints and plans that are smaller than the real buildings they create. Microbiologists and computer engineers use diagrams that are larger than the real-life items they study or make. Toy and furniture makers create scale drawings of toys and furniture to help customers assemble these items from parts.

In this chapter, you will learn what makes two figures similar to help you

- identify similar polygons;
- identify images that are *not* similar to the original diagrams;
- draw a polygon similar to another polygon; and
- understand what characteristics make triangles similar.

KEY TERMS

- congruent
- convex polygon
- corresponding angles
- corresponding sides
- proportional
- similar figures

PROJECT – DESIGN A COMMUNITY GAMES ROOM

START TO PLAN

PROJECT OVERVIEW

Have you ever been to a community games room? A community games room may be part of a youth centre, a friendship centre, or at a seniors' facility. Some common equipment in a community games room includes card tables, air hockey tables, shuffleboards, foosball tables, pinball machines, and chess or croquinole boards.

For this project, you will be part of a committee that uses scale drawings to plan and design a new community games room. The proposed room will have an area of about 70–80 square metres. Your sketch will be 50 times smaller than the actual room and will look like a floor plan. In your room, you must include at least four pieces of community game equipment. You can include any other items you would like in your community games room.

A community games room is a good place to relax, visit with friends, or work on your pool or dart skills.

GET STARTED

To begin your project, start thinking about how you will arrange the items in your community games room and how you will create the floor plan. When people build a new building, they think about the following questions.

- Who will use the room, and at what times of the day?
- What games will you include for the community games room?
- Will you need places for people to sit?
- Is there enough space for people to move around?
- What other elements can you put in your community games room to make it original and interesting?
- How will you present your design? Will it be on a poster, or perhaps in a virtual tour created with computer-assisted design software? Will you colour in the community games room to show your colour choices?

FINAL PRESENTATION CHECKLIST

Your final presentation will be displayed at a community meeting and members will decide on their favourite design. Your presentation should include:

- A sketch or computer-generated visual tour of your community games room.
- A separate sheet of paper with your calculations. Include the actual measurements of each piece of community game equipment or furniture in your room, as well as the sizes on your scale diagrams and an explanation of how you calculated those sizes.

Chapter 6 Similarity of Figures

6.1 Similar Polygons

MATH ON THE JOB

Paul Messier is a francophone cabinetmaker who lives in Calgary, Alberta. He designs, builds, and installs fine cabinets in kitchens, bedrooms, and living spaces as part of renovations that people do to improve their older homes. In his work, he creates scale diagrams to help the clients visualize what the new cabinets will look like in the old space. The plans show exactly what the new installation will look like, because he draws them to scale, or with the exact same proportions and angles. He is very good at drawing plan views of three-dimensional objects, and he is careful to always duplicate the angles on the diagram to be exactly the same as the angles that will be in the actual space.

Paul plans to create a bank of cabinets that will be 10 feet long and 3 feet high. He is creating a scale diagram on graph paper with measurements that are one-twelfth of the real-life measurements. What will the size of the cabinets be on the diagram? How can he be certain that they will look similar to the real cabinets?

Paul Messier uses scale diagrams in his work as a cabinetmaker.

EXPLORE THE MATH

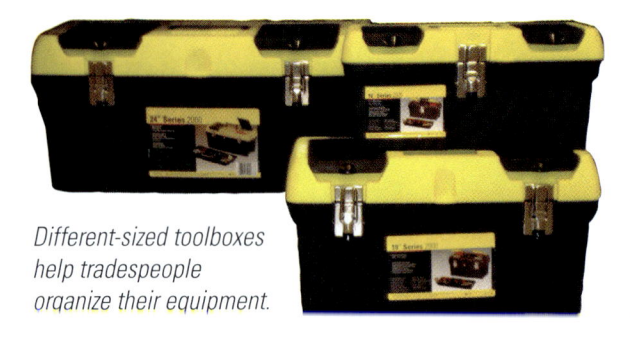

Different-sized toolboxes help tradespeople organize their equipment.

When two figures are similar, one figure has dimensions (length and width) that are proportional to the other figure. A set of toolboxes, such as the one shown on the left, can be placed inside each other to save space (and therefore shipping costs) when shipping the toolboxes to retailers. These toolboxes may have dimensions that are proportional; each box has length and width dimensions in the same proportion, or ratio, as the next larger size.

If the largest toolbox has a length of 600 mm and a width of 300 mm, and each smaller box is $\frac{4}{5}$ the size of the box before it, what would be the length and width of the second and third toolboxes? What would be the length and width of the fourth toolbox in the series?

DISCUSS THE IDEAS
SIMILAR FIGURES

Similar figures have the same shape but are usually different sizes. Starting at the top left corner, label the four corners of your classroom board A, B, C, and D. Now take a piece of writing paper and hold it up. Is it the same shape as the board? Label its corners A′, B′, C′, and D′, again starting at the top left corner. Angle A and angle A′, both 90° angles, are **congruent**. They are also both at the top left corner of the shapes. In similar figures, **corresponding angles** refers to two congruent angles in separate similar shapes that occupy the same relative position.

For the paper and the board to be truly similar figures, their **corresponding sides** would have to be proportional, or in the same ratio all around. Measure the top of the blackboard (side AB), and the top of your piece of paper (side A′B′). Now measure the left side of each figure. The figures are proportional if the following is true.

$$\frac{AB}{A'B'} = \frac{AD}{A'D'}$$

The symbol ~ can be used to mean similar. If rectangle ABCD is similar to rectangle EFGH, this is written as ABCD ~ EFGH.

similar figures: figures that have the same shape

corresponding angles: two angles that are congruent and occupy the same relative position in similar figures

congruent: the same, or equal, shape and size

corresponding sides: two sides that occupy the same relative position in similar figures

HINT
A′ is another way to name a point, and is pronounced "A prime."

Example 1

Debbie works for a magazine and is adjusting the dimensions of some images to fit into an article. She is not certain that she has changed the length and the width by the same amount and wants to find out if she has used the same ratio for each direction.

1. Look at the original photo on the left and the changed image. What is the ratio of the lengths (the horizontal measurement)?

2. What is the ratio of their widths (the vertical measurement)?

3. Has the same ratio been used in both cases?

4. Are the two photographs similar to each other? Explain why.

SOLUTION

1. Compare the length of the enlargement with the length of the original. The enlargement is 6 cm long and the original is 4 cm long. The ratio of the lengths is 6:4 or 3:2.

2. Compare the width of the enlargement with the width of the original. The ratio of the widths is 3:2.

3. Yes, a ratio of 1.5 has been used in both cases.

4. The two photographs are similar to each other because the angles are congruent and the ratios of the corresponding sides are equal.

Example 2

A family built a home in Regina, Saskatchewan and designed a backyard garden in the shape of a trapezoid. Over the years, they loved the design they had created, and when they moved to a larger property in Avonlea, Saskatchewan, they decided to use the same shape for their new backyard garden. They mapped what they did in the first garden, then created a map of a trapezoid that would fit in the new space.

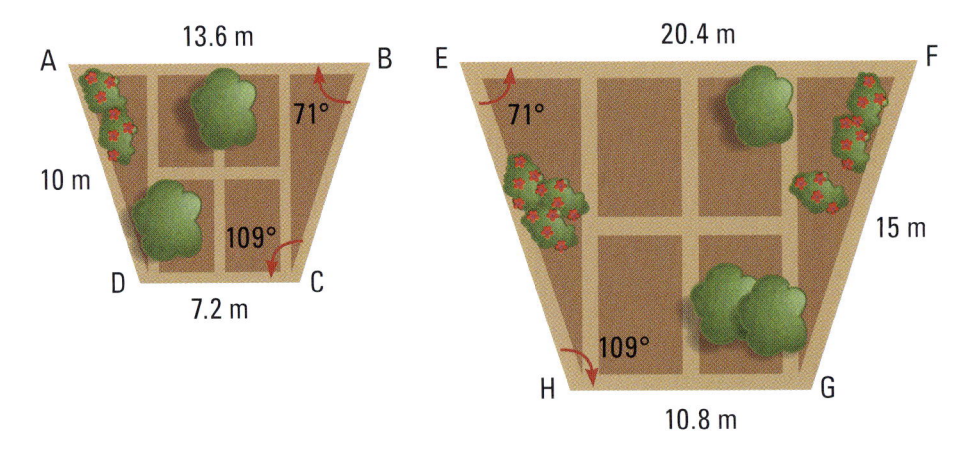

a) If the family uses the plan they have sketched for the new garden, will the shape of their two backyards be similar to each other?

b) Do you think laying out the trees and flowers in an exactly similar way makes the most sense? Explain why or why not.

SOLUTION

a) For two figures to be similar, the measures of the corresponding angles need to be congruent and the measures of the corresponding sides need to be proportional.

The angles in the first figure are represented by the letters A, B, C, and D. The angles in the second figure are represented by the letters E, F, G, and H.

- Angle A in the first figure corresponds with angle E in the second figure because they are in the same positions. Angle A is congruent to angle E because they both have measures of 71°.
- Angle B corresponds to angle F and they are congruent with measures of 71°.
- Angle C corresponds to angle G and they are congruent with measures of 109°.
- Angle D corresponds to angle H and they are congruent with measures of 109°.

Determine the length ratios of the corresponding sides.

$$\frac{EH}{AD} = \frac{15}{10}$$
$$\frac{EH}{AB} = 1.5$$

$$\frac{EF}{AB} = \frac{20.4}{13.6}$$
$$\frac{EF}{AB} = 1.5$$

$$\frac{HG}{DC} = \frac{10.8}{7.2}$$
$$\frac{HG}{DC} = 1.5$$

There are many names for gardens designed in geometrical shapes. For example, a formal French garden, or jardin à la française, has shrubbery and plants cultivated to form triangles and diamonds, and arranges paths in geometric patterns.

Since the measures of the corresponding angles are congruent and the measures of the corresponding sides are proportional, we know that ABCD is similar to EFGH. We can write this as ABCD ~ EFGH.

b) Making the new garden in exactly the same proportions, but larger, may not be the most sensible design. This could result in some vegetables or flowers having too much area, and it could also make it harder to reach to the centre of the garden beds to do the weeding.

Mental Math and Estimation

A poster has a length of 3′1″ and a width of 2′4″. Kerri plans to create a reproduction of the poster by enlarging each dimension by a scale factor of 2.

Estimate the length of framing wood she will need to build a frame for the enlarged poster.

HINT

When you estimate how much material you will need for a project, you should always overestimate instead of underestimate.

Example 3

A tissue company creates tissues for their dispensers in the shape of rectangles. Each tissue has a length of 9 cm and a width of 10 cm. They want to increase the length of their tissues by a factor of 1.7 but keep the same width so they can still fit in their dispensers.

a) Draw a sketch of the original tissue with its dimensions and a sketch of the new tissue with its dimensions.

b) Do the figures in your sketches represent similar figures? Why or why not?

SOLUTION

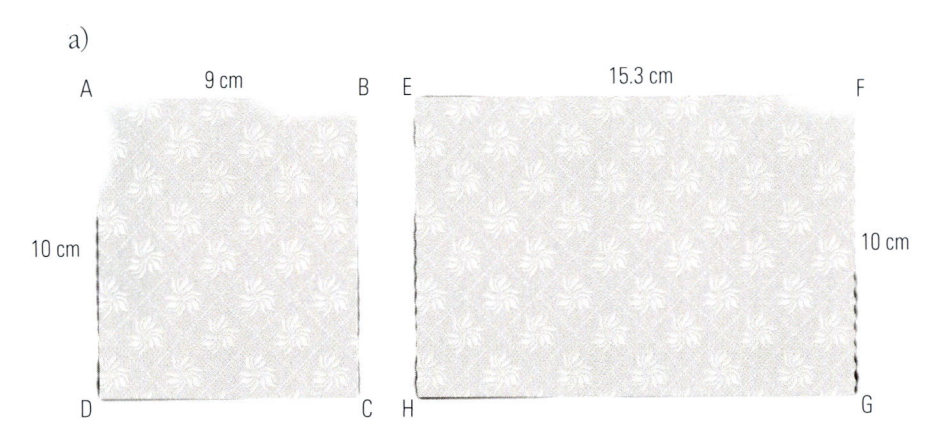

a)

The tissues are drawn to scale because their actual dimensions restrict drawing these figures. The original tissue has dimensions of 10 cm by 9 cm. The new tissue will keep the same width, but will have a length that is 1.7 times longer.

9 cm × 1.7 = 15.3 cm

So the new tissue will have dimensions of 10 cm by 15.3 cm.

b) All of the angles in ABCD that correspond with the angles in EFGH are congruent and are equal to 90°.

But since only the corresponding lengths of ABCD and EFGH were increased and the widths were not increased by the same amount, the ratios of corresponding sides are not equal. Therefore, these figures are not similar.

ALTERNATIVE SOLUTION

To determine if the tissues represent similar figures, you can create a similar version of the original tissue using the factor 1.7 to increase the dimensions. The length of the new tissue would be 9 times 1.7, which is 15.3 cm. The width of the new tissue would be 10 times 1.7, which is 17 cm.

Since the width of the new tissue is 10 cm and not 17 cm, the two figures will not be similar.

ACTIVITY 6.1
ENLARGING BLUEPRINTS

Three summer students were working together on a landscaping project in Winkler, Manitoba. Their boss asked them to enlarge the blueprint before they lay out the hexagonal gazebo on the lawn. The sides need to be doubled, while keeping the shape exactly the same.

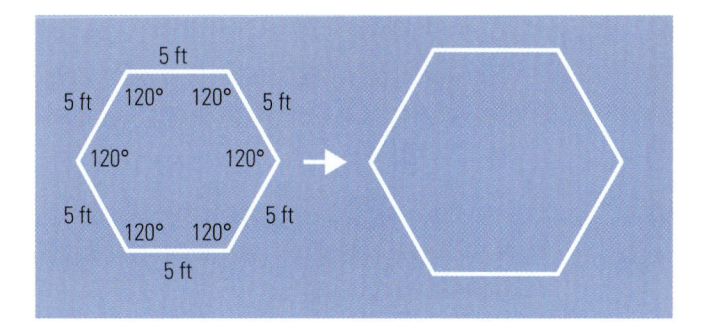

After the students discussed the problem, they each suggested their own strategy for drawing out the larger hexagonal blueprint.

Student 1: Double the length of each side and double the measure of each angle.

Student 2: Keep all of the lengths the same and double the measure of each angle.

Student 3: Keep all of the angles the same and double the length of each side.

In a group of three people, have each person choose one of the strategies above. Show what shape each strategy produces and explain why the strategy works or does not work.

BUILD YOUR SKILLS

1. Suppose you create a similar polygon using each of the given scale factors below. How will the side lengths and angle measurements compare to those of the original?

   a) doubled

   b) tripled

   c) halved

2. Maxime has entered a contest to design a logo for a local basketball team. After she drew her logo below, she found out that for it to meet the contest criteria, she had to increase its dimensions.

   Which of the following rules could she use to create a similar figure that is an enlargement of the original?

   a) Use side lengths that are one-third the length of the original figure and keep the angle measurements the same.

   b) Use angle measurements that are double the size of the original figure and keep the side lengths the same.

   c) Use side lengths that are triple the size of the original figure and keep the angle measurements the same.

   d) Use side lengths that are 8 cm longer and keep the angle measurements the same.

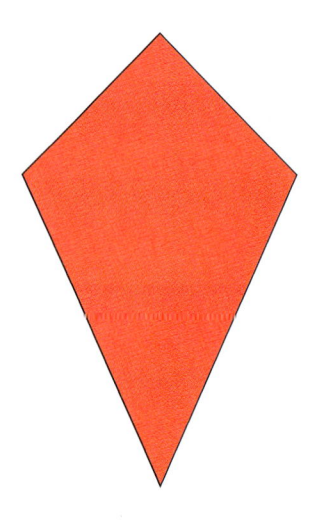

An all-star basketball player needs good shooting, defense, and ball-handling skills.

3. Duane drew the two figures shown.

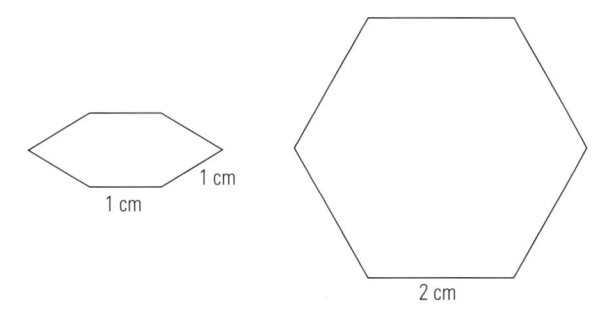

   Duane thinks the two shapes are similar because the side lengths of the larger figure are twice as long as those of the smaller figure. How would you explain to Duane why the two figures are not similar?

4. Talise created a blueprint of her garden with rectangular plots to plant different vegetables. She created 3 different plots, A, B, and C. She then created similar figures of each of the 3 plots. Identify the 3 sets of rectangular plots that create similar figures in the blueprint below.

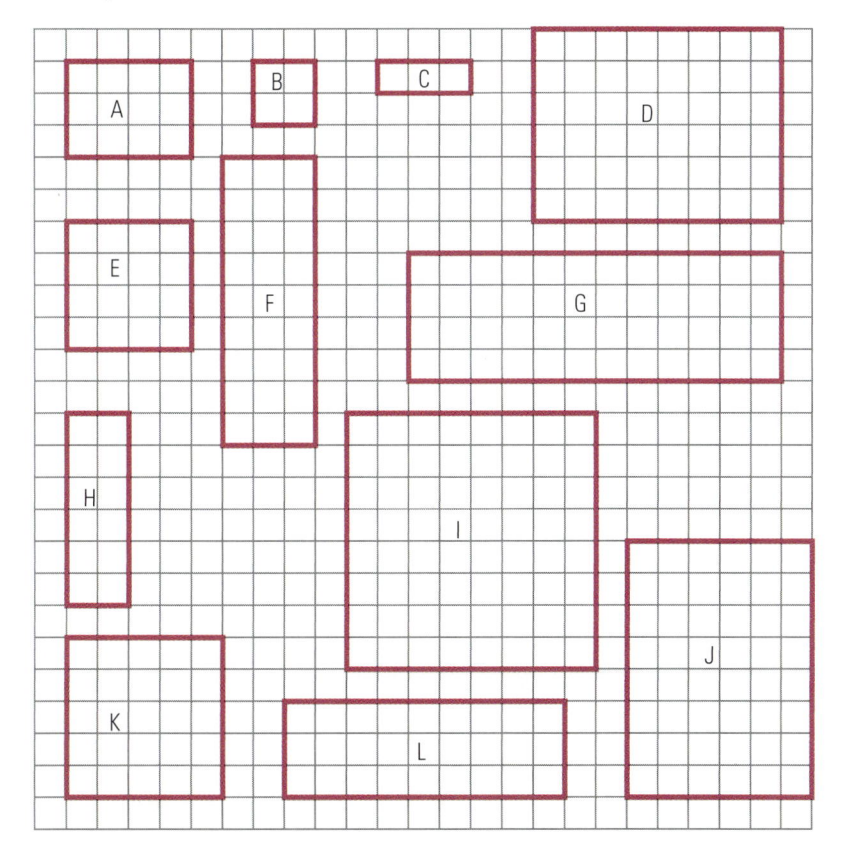

Building simple raised beds allows gardeners to care for different plants in different ways. For example, carrots grow better in sandy soil than celery.

Chapter 6 Similarity of Figures 233

5. Aaliyah works in a custom framing shop. She is given two paintings to frame. The customer wants a 20-centimetre wide mat (a decorative cardboard border surrounding the painting inside the frame) around each painting. For each painting, compare the dimensions of that painting with the dimensions of the framed painting. Are the dimensions similar? Justify your response.

A.

B.

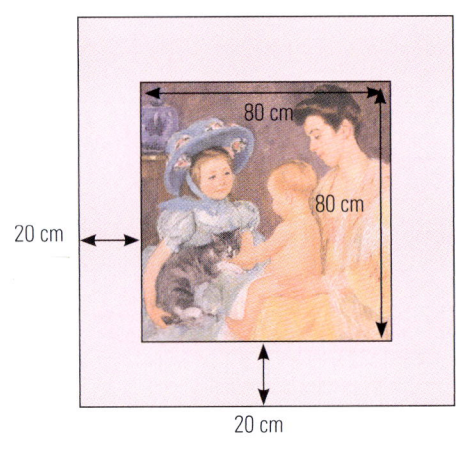

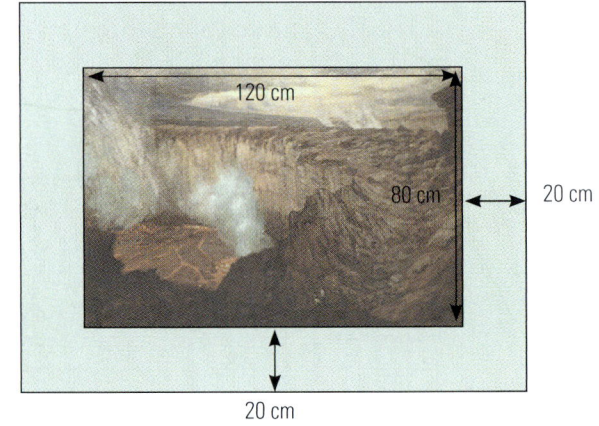

6. Renée is designing a pool for her client's backyard. She drew a sketch of the pool, which she labelled ABCD below. If the actual pool is represented by the similar figure RSTU, help Renée determine the corresponding angles and corresponding sides to make sure that she adds the right finishing details to each side.

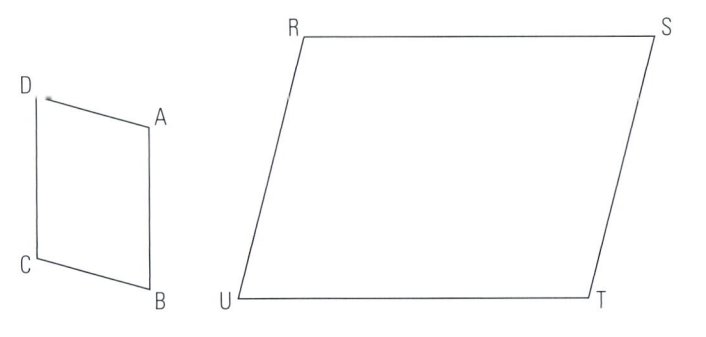

Swimming is a great way to strengthen muscles and improve stamina.

234 MathWorks 10

Extend your thinking

7. As a builder and contractor, George must determine and map out the placement of the buildings he will construct in relation to each other. He does this before he begins each new job.

   George has been hired to build a greenhouse and a retail building where the plants can be sold. George draws a rectangle on the grid below to represent the retail building. The greenhouse will be double the size of the retail space. He starts drawing the greenhouse so that point E corresponds with point A. If he plots point E at (-7, 2), what would be the other ordered pairs that represent the greenhouse (points F, G, and H)?

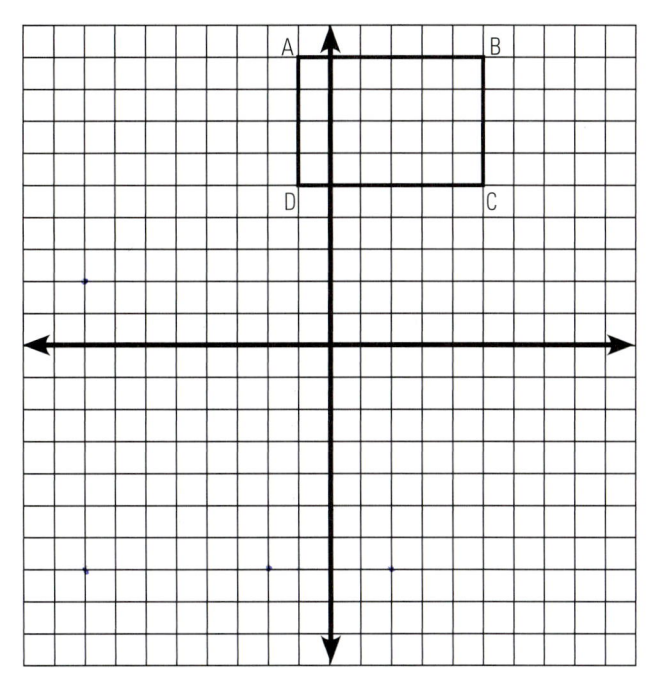

Chapter 6   Similarity of Figures   235

6.2 Determining if Two Polygons Are Similar

MATH *ON THE JOB*

Quinn Keast-Wiatrowski is a junior designer working for Relish Design Studio in Winnipeg, Manitoba.

Quinn is currently completing a graphic design diploma from Red River College. "I primarily use math for ratios and measurements," says Quinn. He cites the "golden section," a mathematical ratio that is often incorporated into design work like websites and print advertisements. Quinn also uses grids as a design tool. "By using a grid as a base structure to place content on, I'm able to create something that feels organized, balanced, and is easy to read and understand," he says.

As part of a branding strategy, Quinn designs a logo for an electronics store. He produces a diamond-shaped logo that will appear on the store's business cards, fliers, and website. When the logo appears on the business card, the two line segments composing the top of the diamond measure 21 mm and the line segments composing the bottom measure 26 mm. The logo must be made one third larger when it appears on the website and two thirds larger when it appears on fliers.

Quinn uses a computer to create his designs in any size he requires.

Quinn must calculate how big the logos will be, so that he can design the website page and flier in relation to it. Approximately what size will the logos on the website and the fliers be? Do your calculations to two decimal points and round your final answer up to a whole number.

EXPLORE THE MATH

A map is an example of a drawing that is a reduced image of the original. Most maps indicate a scale, which is the factor used to reduce the size of the original. Therefore, a correct map is an example of a perfect scale drawing.

A scale factor is written in this form:

>new measurement:old measurement.

This means that when you are asked to determine what scale factor was used to create a second figure, you need to compare a measurement from the new figure to the corresponding measurement in the old figure.

Like the scale on a map, a scale factor can be used to reduce or enlarge any figure. This is the number you multiply each side length by to create a similar figure.

236 MathWorks 10

DISCUSS THE IDEAS

SCALE FACTORS AND MAPS

The scale on the neighbourhood map on the next page shows that 1 cm on the map represents an actual distance of 2.5 km.

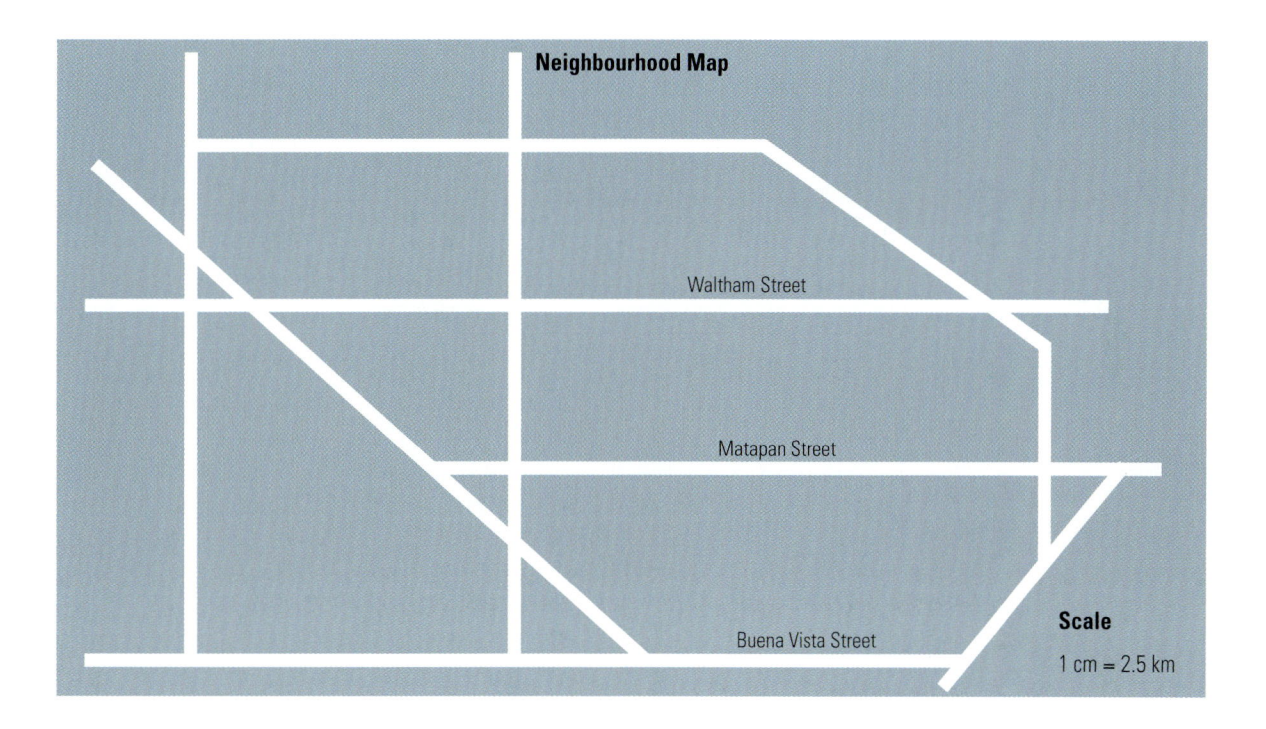

Neighbourhood Map

Waltham Street

Matapan Street

Buena Vista Street

Scale
1 cm = 2.5 km

1. On the map, Waltham Street has a length of 14 cm. Using the scale, what would be the length of the actual street?

2. Matapan Street has an actual length of 25 km. Show your work to find the right length of the street on the map. Use a ruler to see if your calculation is correct.

3. You have probably seen maps that are not proper scale drawings. What was the purpose of these maps? What advantages did the mapmakers get by distorting the scale?

DISCUSS THE IDEAS
SCALE FACTORS AND POSTERS

Ricardo was given the poster on the left and was asked by his employer to reduce the poster by a factor of $\frac{1}{2}$. Ricardo figured out the size of the new poster and drew the rectangle on the right.

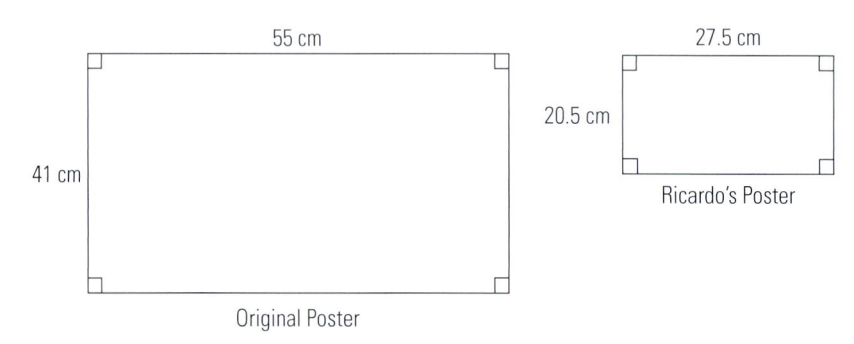

Original Poster: 55 cm × 41 cm

Ricardo's Poster: 27.5 cm × 20.5 cm

1. Do you think Ricardo correctly interpreted what his employer asked him to do?

2. What do you notice about the surface area with this reduction?

3. Do you think there could be more interpretations of what his employer asked? Draw a figure for each interpretation you can think of.

Example 1

This scale model shows the renovations of Edmonton's Cité Francophone. The building is a gathering place for those wishing to learn about and celebrate the francophone culture and language.

The Cité Francophone, Edmonton's francophone centre, is undergoing renovations. To display what the renovations will look like when completed, a scale model of the future centre was built.

a) If a building is reduced to 10% of its original size in order to build a scale model, what scale factor was used?

b) If a room measuring 16 feet by 12 feet in real life is reduced to 10% of its original size for its reproduction in the scale model, what would the room's new dimensions be?

c) If a rectangular hallway in the Cité Francophone were reduced in size by 60%, what would be the angle measurements of the new hallway?

SOLUTION

a) The percentage 10% can also be written as 0.10, so the scale factor used was 0.10.

238 MathWorks 10

b) The percentage 10% can also be written as 0.10 or $\frac{1}{10}$. You can multiply each side length by 0.10 or $\frac{1}{10}$ to get the new dimensions.

0.10 × 16 = 1.6 ft
0.10 × 12 = 1.2 ft

The new dimensions of the reduced room would be 1.6 ft by 1.2 ft.

c) Enlarging or reducing the size of a figure only affects the measures of the side lengths, not the angles. If the angles were changed, the shape would no longer be the same. So, the angle measurements of the new rectangle will still be 90°.

Example 2

Althea is designing cedar hats to sell at her shop at Skidegate on Haida Gwaii. She needs to make three sizes of the same hat. She sketches out the designs for each hat using their angle measurements.

a) How do you determine if the three sketches are the same shape?

b) Does this mean they are similar figures? Do you need to know the side length measurements? Explain your answer.

First Nations people on B.C.'s coast, such as the Haida, weave traditional hats from split spruce roots and cedar bark. The hats were used as trade items with other First Nations people. Hat weavers often incorporate images of animals such as frogs and ravens into their work.

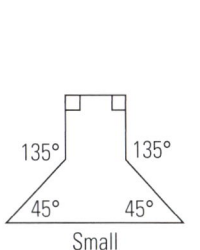

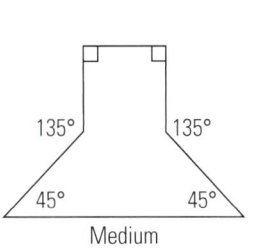

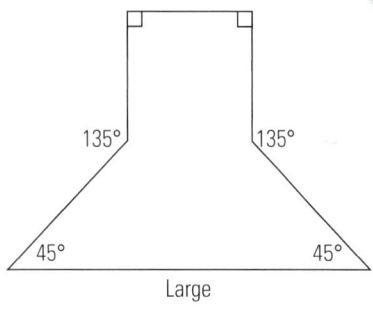

SOLUTION

a) Since the sketches all have the same corresponding angle measurements, each sketch is the same shape as the other two.

b) It is impossible to determine if the shapes represent similar figures without knowing the side lengths. It is possible that the enlargements are relatively wider or narrower than the original.

DISCUSS THE IDEAS
SCALE FACTORS IN SIMILAR FIGURES

Drew is a building contractor who sketched a window, labelled ABCD for a house. He wants to install a smaller but similar window at his next job. He drew the similar figure EFGH to represent the new window.

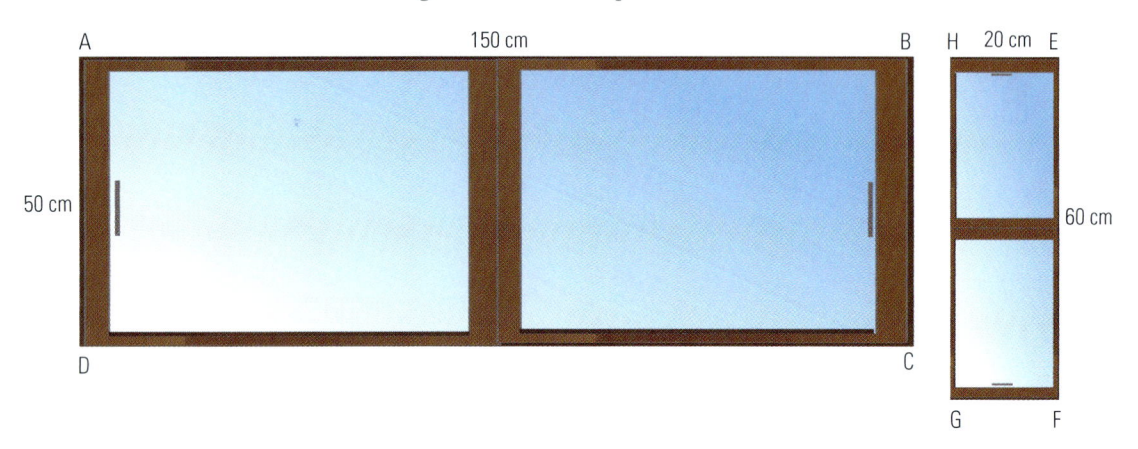

If you are not told which angles are corresponding, you should follow the letters alphabetically. That means that A corresponds to E, B corresponds to F, C corresponds to G, and D corresponds to H. That also means that the corresponding sides are AB corresponds to EF, BC corresponds to FG, CD corresponds to GH, and AD corresponds to EH.

What is the scale factor Drew used to draw the smaller figure? In a group, discuss how to solve this question.

Mental Math and Estimation

Determine the value of x in each proportion without the use of a calculator.

a) $\dfrac{x}{10} = \dfrac{30}{100}$ b) $\dfrac{50}{x} = \dfrac{45}{9}$ c) $\dfrac{72}{x} = \dfrac{108}{12}$

Example 3

Kirsten is a boat builder in Comox, BC. Figure MNOP is the pattern for the transom, or back end, of a simple plywood rowboat that she makes. To make a model of the rowboat as a gift for her brother, Kirsten sketches pattern QRST.

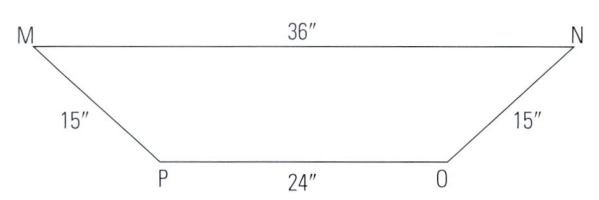

240 MathWorks 10

```
        Q ──────6"──────R
         \              /
      2.5" \          / 2.5"
           T ──4"── S
```

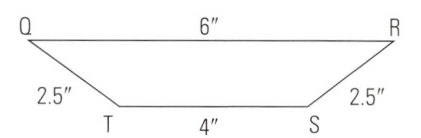

Is the model similar to the full-sized boat? If so, what scale factor is used to build the model?

SOLUTION

To determine if the figures are similar, the ratios of the corresponding side lengths of the two figures should be equal to each other. Determine the corresponding ratios of the side lengths.

$$\frac{MN}{QR} = \frac{36}{6}$$
$$\frac{MN}{QR} = 6$$

$$\frac{NO}{RS} = \frac{15}{2.5}$$
$$\frac{NO}{RS} = 6$$

$$\frac{OP}{ST} = \frac{24}{4}$$
$$\frac{OP}{ST} = 6$$

$$\frac{MP}{QT} = \frac{15}{2.5}$$
$$\frac{MP}{QT} = 6$$

A boat, such as these punt boats, can be built with basic tools such as a jigsaw, hand plane, and hammer.

Since the ratios of the corresponding sides are all equal to 6, the figure is similar.

The scale factor for the model is

$$\frac{\text{New measurement}}{\text{Old measurement}} = \frac{\text{model}}{\text{full-size}}$$

Since the figures are similar, pick any pair of corresponding sides, for example MN and QR.

$$\text{scale factor} = \frac{QR}{MN}$$
$$\text{scale factor} = \frac{6}{36}$$
$$\text{scale factor} = \frac{1}{6}$$

Chapter 6 Similarity of Figures **241**

ACTIVITY 6.2
SCALING MÉTIS SASHES

Métis sashes vary in colour and length. Different colours on the sash represent different information. Green can represent prosperity, while blue and white represent the Métis flag. Colours can also represent different information about the individual wearing the sash and his or her family. Métis sashes are about 3 metres long, but men's sashes tend to be longer, sometimes as long as 12 feet, and wider than women's sashes.

In pairs or groups, discuss how to solve the following questions.

1. A man's sash measures 3.5 m long and a woman's sash measures 2.8 m long. In comparison to the man's sash, by what scale factor has the woman's sash been reduced?

2. Métis sashes are made using a technique called finger weaving. Elizabeth starts weaving a man's sash that is 10 cm wide. She realizes that the sash is too narrow and starts again, this time weaving the sash so that it is 16 cm wide. By what scale factor did she enlarge the width of the sash?

Métis people use the sash as a symbol of cultural identity. It is also a practical item that can be used as a bag strap or rope.

ACTIVITY 6.3
APPLYING RATIOS TO DISTANCES

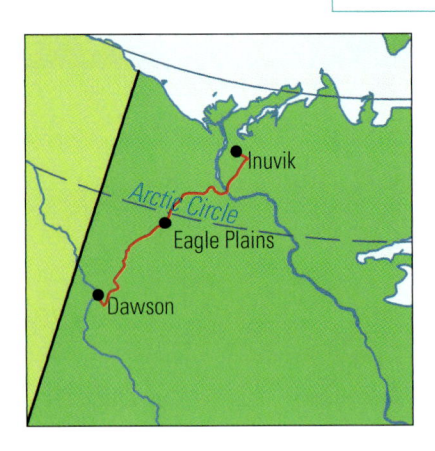

Shania lives in Inuvik, NT and wants to travel to Dawson, YT. She had been planning a picnic break at the Arctic Circle, but her brother Roland says they should stop in Eagle Plains, YT, which is closer to the halfway point of the trip.

Shania looks at a roadmap and determines the distance from Inuvik to Eagle Plains, and the distance from Eagle Plains to Dawson. She calculates that the ratio of these is 0.88.

Then she calculates the ratio of distance from Inuvik to the Arctic Circle over distance from the Arctic Circle to Dawson, and the ratio is 0.74.

1. Roland asks, "What are your units? Does 0.74 represent 0.74 centimetres, 0.74 inches, or something else?"

    Discuss how you think Shania should respond to Roland.

2. After Roland understands her explanation to his last question, he says the ratio proves that Eagle Plains is closer to the midpoint of the trip than the Arctic Circle. Do you agree? Why?

242 MathWorks 10

BUILD YOUR SKILLS

1. Mary is scaling down a pattern for a skating outfit to make a smaller size for her niece. One piece of the pattern is a rectangle, and the original and new piece that she cut are shown below.

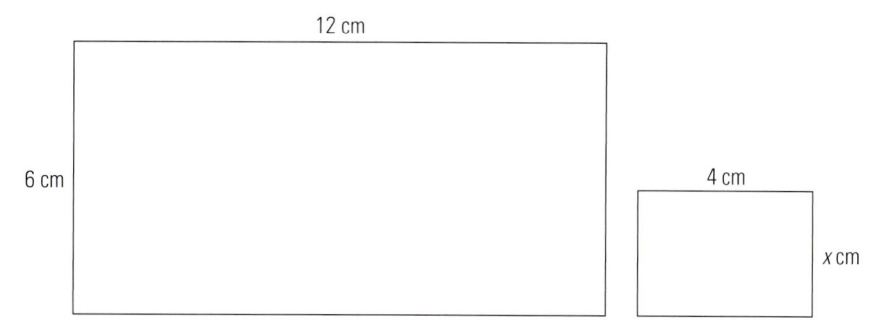

   a) What scale factor did Mary use on her pattern to create the pattern for her niece's outfit?

   b) What is the value of x?

2. Rhoniel is an interior decorator who is creating a wall pattern with similar parallelogram stencils. She created the three similar parallelograms shown. She wants to make the corresponding sides of each stencil have the same four colours: brown, yellow, blue, and orange.

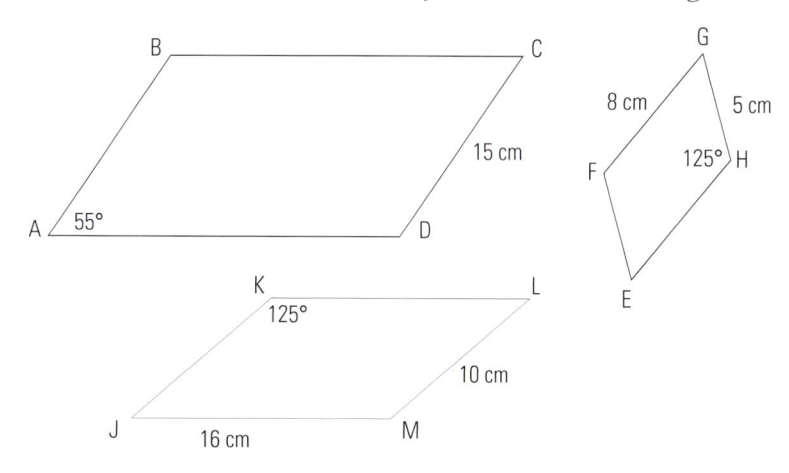

   a) Help Rhoniel list the pairs of corresponding sides to figure out her paint colours.

   b) What scale factor was used on ABCD to create EFGH?

   c) What is the measure of side BC?

   d) What is the measure of angle D?

   e) What is the angle measure of L? How do you know? Explain your answer.

Chapter 6 Similarity of Figures   243

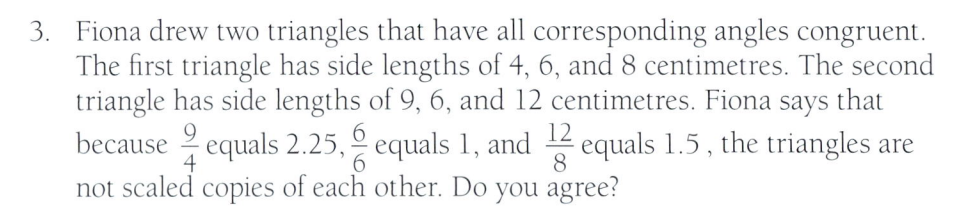

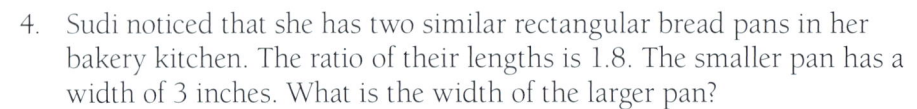

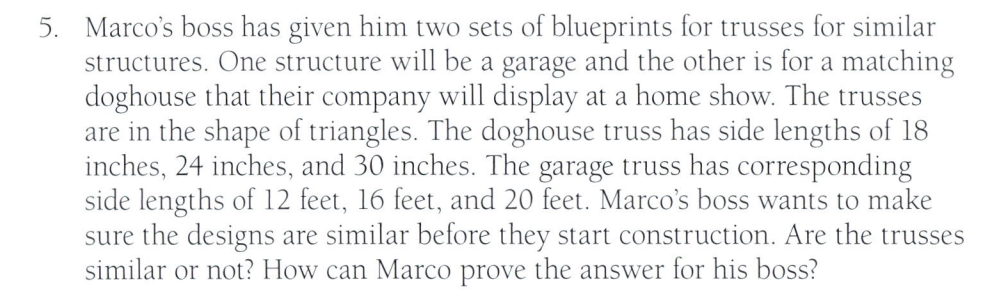

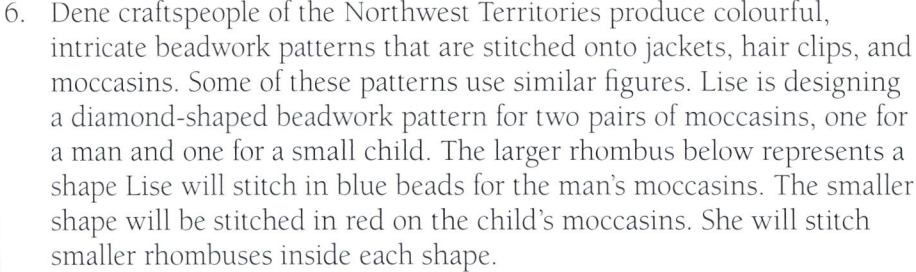

3. Fiona drew two triangles that have all corresponding angles congruent. The first triangle has side lengths of 4, 6, and 8 centimetres. The second triangle has side lengths of 9, 6, and 12 centimetres. Fiona says that because $\frac{9}{4}$ equals 2.25, $\frac{6}{6}$ equals 1, and $\frac{12}{8}$ equals 1.5, the triangles are not scaled copies of each other. Do you agree?

4. Sudi noticed that she has two similar rectangular bread pans in her bakery kitchen. The ratio of their lengths is 1.8. The smaller pan has a width of 3 inches. What is the width of the larger pan?

5. Marco's boss has given him two sets of blueprints for trusses for similar structures. One structure will be a garage and the other is for a matching doghouse that their company will display at a home show. The trusses are in the shape of triangles. The doghouse truss has side lengths of 18 inches, 24 inches, and 30 inches. The garage truss has corresponding side lengths of 12 feet, 16 feet, and 20 feet. Marco's boss wants to make sure the designs are similar before they start construction. Are the trusses similar or not? How can Marco prove the answer for his boss?

6. Dene craftspeople of the Northwest Territories produce colourful, intricate beadwork patterns that are stitched onto jackets, hair clips, and moccasins. Some of these patterns use similar figures. Lise is designing a diamond-shaped beadwork pattern for two pairs of moccasins, one for a man and one for a small child. The larger rhombus below represents a shape Lise will stitch in blue beads for the man's moccasins. The smaller shape will be stitched in red on the child's moccasins. She will stitch smaller rhombuses inside each shape.

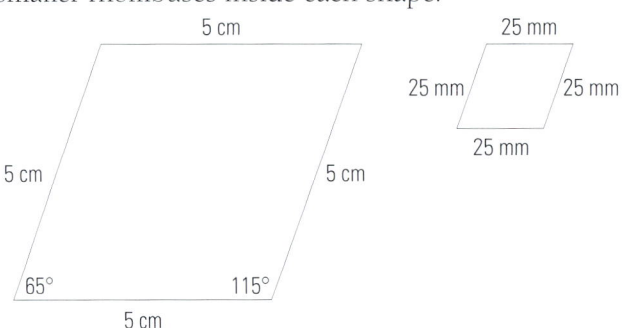

a) Are the two shapes similar? How do you know?

b) If they are similar, what scale factor should Lise apply to the rhombus in order to scale it from the larger moccasin to the smaller moccasin?

c) If Lise started by stitching the smaller rhombus and had to scale it up to the larger moccasin, what scale factor would she use?

7. Lance and Max are working together on a project about similarity. Lance writes, "All squares are similar." He states that since a square always has

four 90-degree angles, every square is similar to every other square. As a result, Max writes, "All rectangles are similar." He thinks that since every rectangle also has four 90-degree angles, all rectangles are also similar to each other.

a) Is Lance correct? Explain.

b) Is Max correct? Explain.

8. A chef creates three casseroles. He makes them so that the shape of casserole A is similar to the shape of casserole B. Casserole B is also similar in shape to the third casserole, casserole C. Can you conclude that casserole A is similar to casserole C? Explain your thinking.

Extend your thinking

9. Jonas drives a forklift in a warehouse. He uses a forklift pallet size of 48 inches wide by 40 inches long, a common size in North America.

   To make the best use of storage space in the warehouse, the product boxes should fit exactly onto the pallet, so the company uses two box sizes.

   Box 1: 24" long × 20" wide
   Box 2: 20" long × 16" wide

   a) Draw two diagrams showing how the two box sizes make the best use of warehouse space.

   b) Are either of the two box shapes similar to the shape of the pallet? Which one?

   c) How does the area of the similar box compare to the area of the pallet? How does the ratio of the areas compare to the ratio of edge dimensions? Why do you think this is?

Forklift drivers are expected to have good driving skills and know about vehicle maintenance. They are often required to use data entry and computer skills.

THE ROOTS OF MATH

EUCLIDEAN GEOMETRY

One of the greatest mathematicians of ancient Greece was Euclid, who lived around 300 BCE. His scholarly work in mathematics influenced the growth of many branches of science, including mechanics, astronomy, and reasoning.

Euclid lived in Greece, but was sometimes known as Euclid of Alexandria. Alexandria had the best library in the ancient world and many great scholars gathered there to study and share ideas.

Euclid contributed a great deal to our understanding of geometry. One theorem he developed describes the relationship between the sides in similar triangles ABC and A'B'C'.

Euclid was the first person to put many of the axioms and theorems that were known at the time into a book called *Elements*. His 13 volumes contain hundreds of definitions, propositions, common notations, and postulates. A postulate is something assumed without proof because it is self-evident or generally accepted. In Book 6, he uses similar polygons to build one of his propositions: He states:

"Similar polygons are divided into similar triangles, and into triangles equal in multitude and in the same ratio as the wholes, and the first polygon has to the second polygon the same ratio as the corresponding sides."

This proposition states that any two similar polygons can be divided into similar triangles. In the diagrams below, ABCDE is similar to RSTUV. This means BC corresponds to ST. This also means that CD corresponds to TU and has the same ratio to TU as BC does to ST.

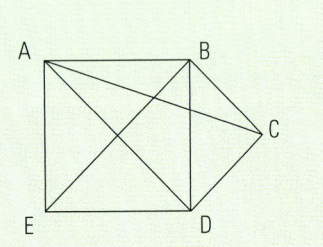

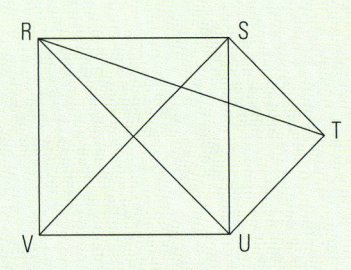

In the diagrams shown, can you prove that △BCD will always be similar to △STU?

246 MathWorks 10

Drawing Similar Polygons

6.3

MATH *ON THE JOB*

Ryan is a gas serviceperson trainee with Manitoba Hydro in Winnipeg, Manitoba. Before training with Manitoba Hydro, he completed courses at Red River College. Ryan's gas fitter training will take him four years to complete. To become a gas fitter at Manitoba Hydro, you need to have completed high school courses in mathematics and physics.

When at work, Ryan can be expected to install gas lines to appliances such as a natural gas burning fireplace. Before beginning this job, Ryan might read blueprints to familiarize himself with the layout of his work area. After assembling the materials needed to do the job, Ryan could be expected to cut openings in the walls to put gas pipes through, bend the pipes so that they will link the gas meter to the fireplace, and install valves, flues, vents, or burners.

Scale models can include many detailed features for which all the dimensions must be calculated.

Ryan is assembling the materials needed to help install two gas burning fireplaces. One fireplace is a small domestic model and the other is a large model for a hotel lobby. The face of the vent for the small fireplace is rectangular and measures 11 inches by 8 inches. Ryan's supervisor tells him the vent for the large fireplace is two-and-a-half times bigger and asks him to retrieve it from the warehouse where parts are stored. What is the scale used here? What are the measurements of the large vent?

EXPLORE THE MATH

Some museums have displays that are recreations of important times in history or displays of animals that may be extinct. When creating these displays, the museum may not have enough space to create each model using the full-size measurements. The museum needs to use the original measurements and apply a scale factor to each measurement to build a model that is similar to the original.

When creating a similar figure, there are two important characteristics to remember. The measures of their corresponding angles are equal, or congruent, and the measures of their corresponding sides are proportional because they have been increased or decreased by the same factor.

Mental Math and Estimation

A museum is building a dinosaur exhibit and wants to include a Tyrannosaurus Rex model. The original dinosaur was 13 metres long. The museum decides to use a scale factor of one-third to create the model. What would be the approximate length of the model?

ACTIVITY 6.4
ENLARGING A TRAPEZOID

Rochelle is an illustrator for a children's book. She drew the figure below, called a trapezoid, as the first step for drawing a cartoon mouse's house.

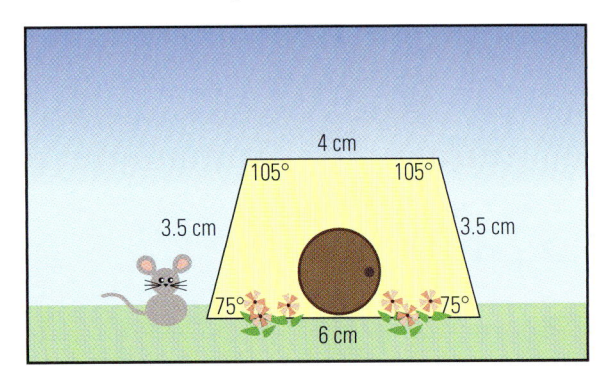

Rochelle decided she liked the shape, so she wanted to make a larger version for the story's cartoon raccoon. If Rochelle enlarges the trapezoid by a scale factor of 1.5, what would be the dimensions of the new trapezoid? Include the side lengths and angle measurements she would need to use.

Example 1

Lauren illustrates "how-to" manuals that show customers how to assemble furniture. One of her co-workers went home sick, and she was given the following diagram of a triangular shelf and told to redesign it. The triangular face of the new shelf has one side length of 60 cm and is defined as a similar triangle.

Now Lauren has to figure out the dimensions of the rest of the triangle. She needs to figure out what scale factor her co-worker used. Is there more than one triangle possible?

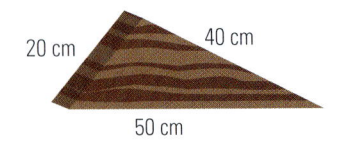

SOLUTION

Since each of the three sides can be multiplied by a number to result in a length of 60 cm, there could be three possible triangles.

Triangle 1: The 20 cm side can be made into a 60 cm side using a scale factor of 3.

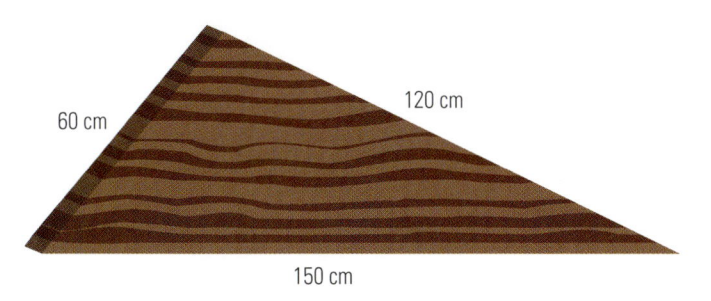

60 cm
120 cm
150 cm

Triangle 2: The 40 cm side can be made into a 60 cm side using a scale factor of 1.5.

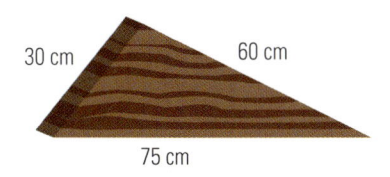

30 cm
60 cm
75 cm

Triangle 3: The 50 cm side can be made into a 60 cm side using a scale factor of 1.2.

24 cm
48 cm
60 cm

Example 2

An artist needs two similar slabs of cedar for a sculpture. They must have the same shape, as sketched by the artist, but two different sizes.

Determine what scale factor was used to create the larger piece and use the scale factor to calculate the missing side lengths.

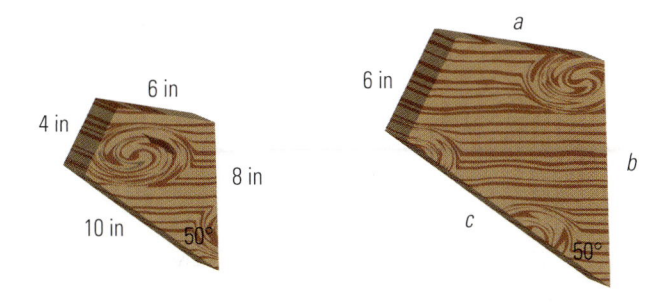

4 in
6 in
8 in
10 in
50°

a
6 in
b
c
50°

Chapter 6   Similarity of Figures   **249**

SOLUTION

The side that measures 4 inches in the first figure corresponds with the side that measures 6 inches in the second figure.

scale factor = $\frac{6}{4}$
scale factor = 1.5

You can apply the scale factor to each side length in the first figure to determine the lengths of *a*, *b*, and *c*.

a = 6 inches × 1.5
a = 9 inches

b = 8 inches × 1.5
b = 12 inches

c = 10 inches × 1.5
c = 15 inches

ACTIVITY 6.5
THE RATIO METHOD

You can create a reduction of many shapes by using the method below. Artists who create paintings and drawings that are true to life may use this method to make perspective drawings.

One method for reducing a figure to create a similar figure is called the ratio method.

1. Choose a point that is external to the shape. This point will become your centre of reduction. Draw lines connecting that point to each vertex of the shape.

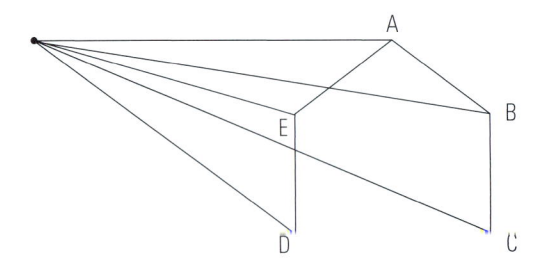

2. Choose a scale factor to reduce the image. For this image, we will scale the image by $\frac{1}{2}$. As a result, find the midpoint for each line segment you just created and connect the five points to create a shape that is half the size.

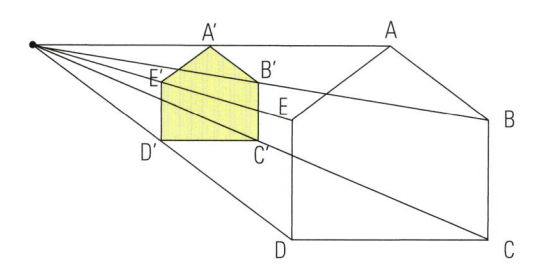

3. Draw an irregular pentagon in your notebook and use the ratio method above to create a similar pentagon that is half the size.

4. How do you think this method would change if you wanted to reduce a shape by a scale factor of $\frac{1}{3}$?

ACTIVITY 6.6
THE PARALLEL METHOD

The ratio method described above works when you want to reduce the size of a figure. There is another similar method you can use to enlarge a figure. This method is called the parallel method. Designers may find this method useful when designing logos and patterns that have concentric objects.

1. Choose a point that is inside the shape that you want to enlarge. This point does not need to be in the centre of the shape. This point will become your centre of enlargement. Draw rays connecting that point to each vertex of the shape and extend the lines. Use this method to enlarge the shape by a scale factor of 2.

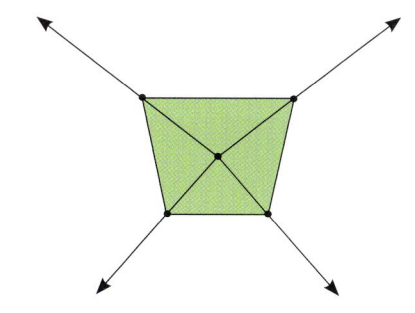

2. Measure the distance from the centre of enlargement to each vertex. To double the size of the shape, double that length and measure that length from the centre of enlargement along the ray. This will become a vertex of the new shape. Connect the new points to create your enlarged shape.

Chapter 6 Similarity of Figures

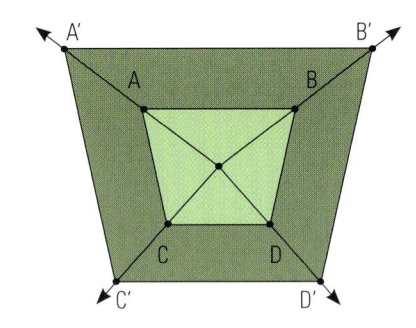

If you've used the method correctly, each side of your new shape will be parallel to the corresponding side in your old shape.

3. Draw an irregular quadrilateral in your notebook and use the parallel method above to create a similar quadrilateral twice the size.

4. How do you think this method would change if you wanted to enlarge a shape by a scale factor of 3?

BUILD YOUR SKILLS

1. The grid below shows a map of two rectangular holes that will be dug to start building a house, labelled R, and a garage, labelled M. The architect drew the two buildings so that their shapes would be similar.

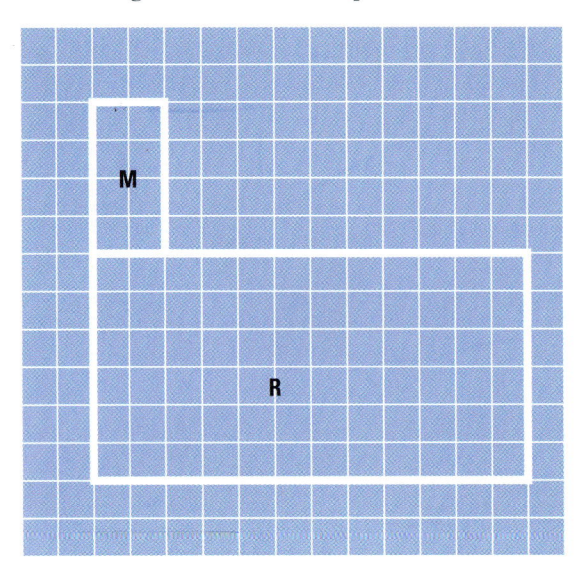

    a) Francis and Nipin take a look at the grid and agree that the two rectangles are similar. However, Nipin thinks the scale factor is 2 and Francis thinks the scale factor is $\frac{1}{2}$. Is either of them correct, or both of them? Explain your answer.

b) On graph paper, draw another rectangle that is similar to M and R. Determine the scale factor someone would use to create your rectangle from rectangle M and from rectangle R.

2. Kawa is planning on redesigning her room. She drew rectangle A below on a grid to represent the size of her room.

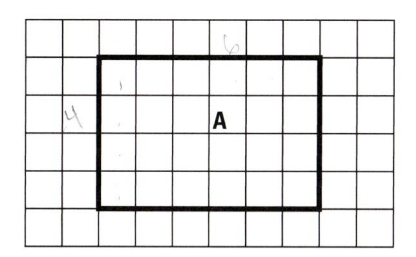

Kawa's brother's room is larger than her room. It is similar in shape, but not identical, to Kawa's room.

a) Suggest two possible dimensions for Kawa's brother's room.

b) Using graph paper, draw one possible rectangle that could represent Kawa's brother's room.

3. Marek is designing a garden in his backyard. He draws a rectangle on grid paper to represent the size of his garden.

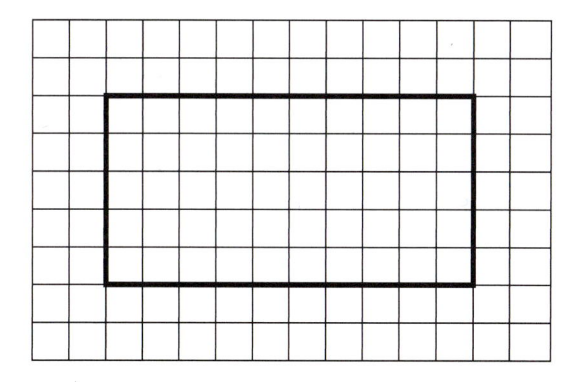

Marek wants to plant 25 different vegetables and herbs in his garden. He decides to divide the garden into 25 plots that are similar to the shape of the garden and are of equal size. On graph paper, trace the figure above and show what could be Marek's plan.

regular pentagon: a five-sided polygon where all sides have the same length and all angles have the same measure

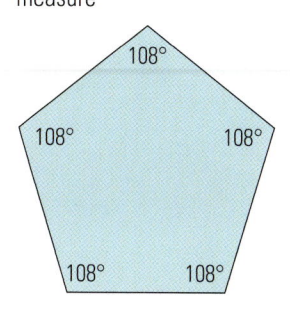

4. Shoshanna designs soccer balls. Each soccer ball is covered with several regular pentagons with a side length of 4 cm. She also creates smaller versions of her soccer balls that use pentagons with a side length of 2 cm.

What would be the perimeter of a pentagon on the smaller soccer ball? How does this value relate to the perimeter of a pentagon on the larger soccer ball?

Chapter 6 Similarity of Figures 253

5. Julia drafted two similar logos for a company, one for letterhead and a similar size for envelopes. Unfortunately, she forgot to mark the measurements on the smaller one. Find the missing measurements for her, and write an e-mail to Julia explaining how you solved the problem.

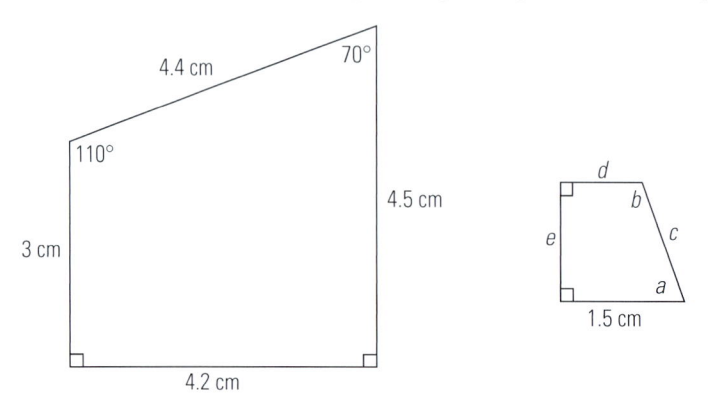

6. A bedroom has dimensions of 9 feet by 12 feet. The living room in the same house is built to be similar in shape to the bedroom, but is larger. The scale factor from the bedroom to the living room is 2.5. What are the dimensions of the living room?

Extend your thinking

7. Carrie designs charms for necklaces and bracelets. She designs a horoscope charm for a necklace in the shape of a trapezoid, and a smaller, but similar, bracelet charm. Determine the side lengths of the smaller charm. Show all the steps as if you were teaching someone how to solve this problem.

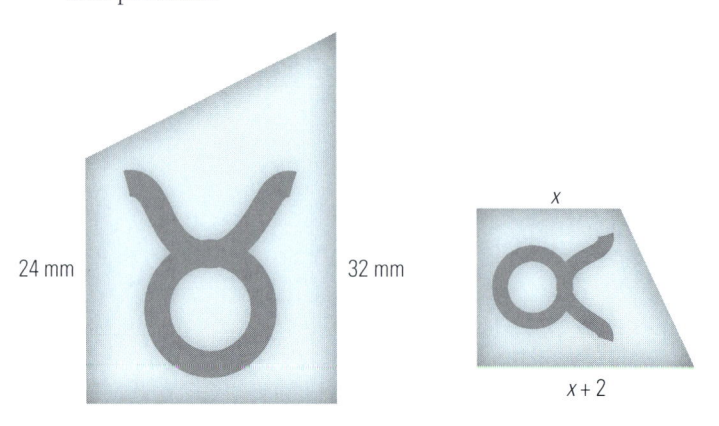

PUZZLE IT OUT

RATIONING CHOCOLATE BARS

Many chocolate bars come in the shape of a rectangle and are made up of smaller squares, like the chocolate bars shown below. Determine the minimum number of breaks you need to make to break each of the chocolate bars below into all of its smaller squares. How can you determine how many breaks it will take to break any chocolate bar made up of n squares?

PROJECT – DESIGN A COMMUNITY GAMES ROOM

DETERMINING DIMENSIONS

At the beginning of this chapter, you were given the role of an interior designer and were asked to design a layout for a rectangular community games room with an area of 70–80 square metres. Your design must have at least four pieces of community game equipment. To create a unique design, include other elements to furnish the room.

On a piece of graph paper, draw top-view sketches of the pieces of equipment and furniture with the dimensions you will use. Once you've determined the dimensions of each piece, use a scale ratio to determine the size of each of the pieces in your drawing. Your drawing must be 50 times smaller than the actual room.

Use a table similar to the one below, which your teacher will provide. Fill in your choice of community game equipment and other pieces of furniture you will be adding to the room, along with your calculations.

A pool table might be one of the features in a community games room.

SCALING DESIGN ELEMENTS

Type of Equipment	Length in Room	Length in Drawing	Width in Room	Width in Drawing

SAMPLE

Once you have completed the chart, start drawing a sketch of the room and think about how you will place each piece in the room. Where are the doors and windows in your room? Make sure there is enough room for someone to walk easily between the games.

Similar Triangles

6.4

MATH ON THE JOB

Maurice Yingst is a housing manager for the Wesley Band of the Stoney Nation in Morley, Alberta. He is in charge of housing inspections and renovations. When he lays out the location of new houses to be built, it is helpful to be able to calculate information about triangles with the same angles. He also uses knowledge of triangles in calculations about stairways, trusses, and other structures.

Maurice earned his journeyman carpenter's ticket from the Saskatchewan Institute of Applied Science and Technology in Moose Jaw, Saskatchewan, in 1963. He has been known as a hard worker all his life, and his willingness and ability to perform accurate math calculations have often inspired his bosses to promote him.

Maurice Yingst uses knowledge of similar triangles in carpentry and construction work.

Maurice needs to extend a staircase along the same angle as the existing staircase. The original staircase rises 8 feet over a horizontal distance of 10 feet. What horizontal distance will he need to extend the staircase to make it 6 feet higher?

EXPLORE THE MATH

Section 6.2 defined that two figures are similar if their corresponding sides are proportional to each other and their corresponding angles are congruent. The same rules apply to triangles, but you can determine if they are similar by using even less information.

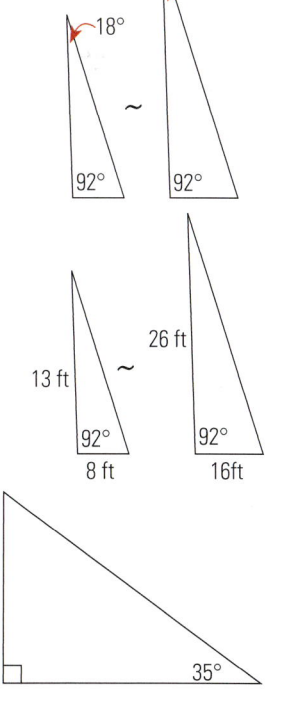

Two triangles are similar if one of the two following requirements is true.
- Any two of the three corresponding angles are congruent.
- One pair of corresponding angles is congruent and the corresponding sides adjacent to these angles are proportional.

Determining whether right triangles are similar is even more straightforward. A right triangle always has one known angle, the 90° angle or right angle. Because the two remaining angles add up to 90°, they are both always less than 90°, or acute angles.

Two right triangles are similar if the following requirement is true.
- One pair of corresponding acute angles is congruent.

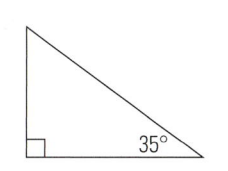

Chapter 6 Similarity of Figures 257

Mental Math and Estimation

Are any of the three triangular boat sails pictured here similar? How do you know?

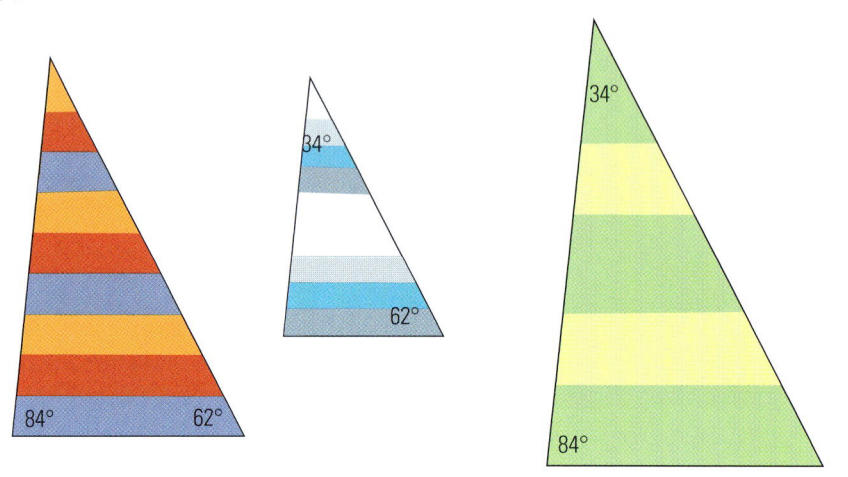

DISCUSS THE IDEAS
COMPARING TRIANGLES

Work in pairs to discuss the following questions.

1. Does the size of two or more triangles influence whether or not they are similar? Explain your reasoning.

2. Look at the three triangles shown here. Are they similar? Explain why or why not.

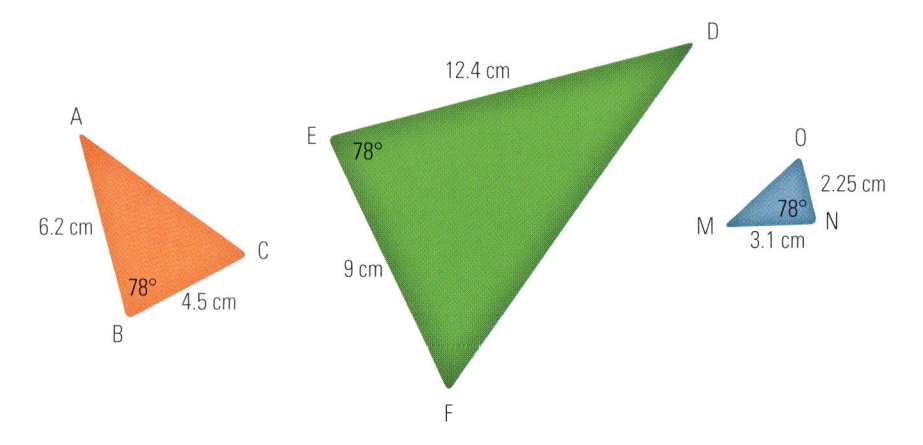

3. In triangle ABC, the side length of AC is 7 cm. What is the length of DF and MO?

258 MathWorks 10

Example 1

Adsila is designing a T-shirt and wants to use several triangles in her design. She drew triangle ABC below to represent the triangular shape she wants to use in her design. The side lengths of the triangle are as follows.

AB = 4

BC = 5

AC = 6

DC = 2.5, and

EC = 3

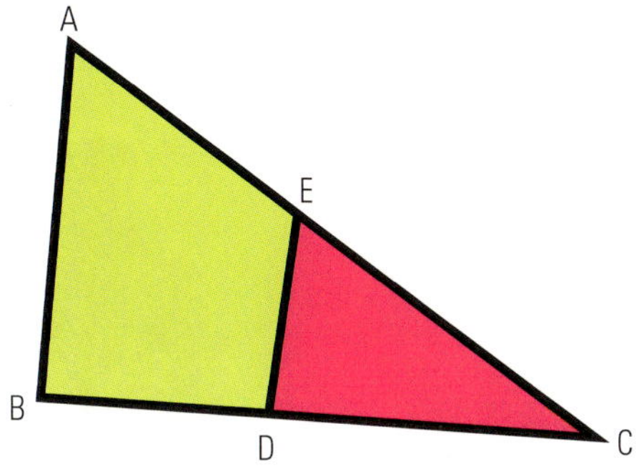

Adsila thinks that if she draws line ED so that it is parallel to side AB, then triangle ABC will be similar to triangle EDC. Prove that she is right and determine the length of ED.

SOLUTION

The triangles are similar because ABC and EDC share a common angle and the ratio of CD to CB is equal to the ratio of CE to CA. The sides that form that angle are proportional, meaning that the triangles have a congruent angle and two sides and are similar.

The scale factor used to create triangle EDC from triangle ABC is $\frac{1}{2}$. Since AB equals 4, the length of ED must be 2.

Example 2

Roberto and Marcos tie wires to either side of an artificial tree as part of the set-up of a concert stage. They decide to attach the wires so that they both make a 35° angle within a right triangle.

Are the right triangles created by the wires similar triangles?

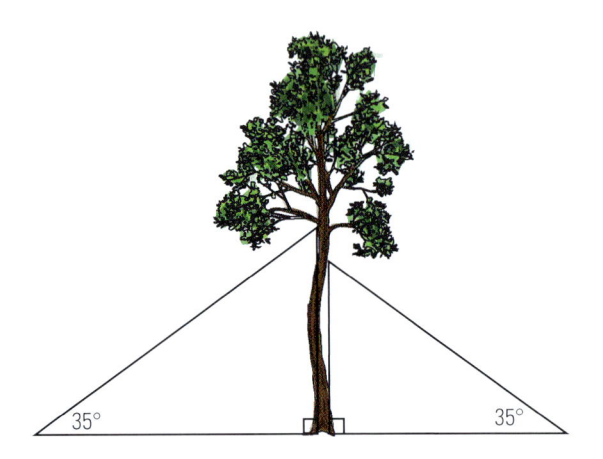

SOLUTION

Since two pairs of corresponding angles are given, the triangles are similar. The third angle would equal 55°, making all three pairs of corresponding angles congruent. Therefore the triangles are similar.

ACTIVITY 6.7
PROVING SIMILARITY OF TRIANGLES

Three students are working in a group to build model houses for a woodworking class. Each of them is designing the front view of the roof of their house in the shape of a triangle. As they sketch, they decide to make their roofs similar in shape to each other. They each come up with a plan for how they will build their roofs so that they are all similar triangles.

Student 1: "Let's build triangles that have their corresponding angles equal."

Student 2: "All the roofs should be isosceles triangles."

Student 3: "The roofs should have corresponding sides that are proportional."

Work in groups of three. Each person chooses one statement and tries to prove whether it will lead to the creation of similar triangles. Use diagrams to test whether the rule works. After you've shown whether your statement will or will not result in similar triangles, try to prove or disprove the other two statements. As a group, you will need to come to an agreement about which of the statements are true and which are false.

ACTIVITY 6.8
REDUCING TRIANGLES

A farmer in Manitoba keeps cows on an irregularly-shaped pasture resulting from the highway right-of-way across a corner of his property. As part of his pasture management plan he wants to keep the cows off a portion of the pasture, and puts a fence across from D to E parallel to pasture edge BC.

Show that the two triangles ABC and ADE are similar. What is the length of BC?

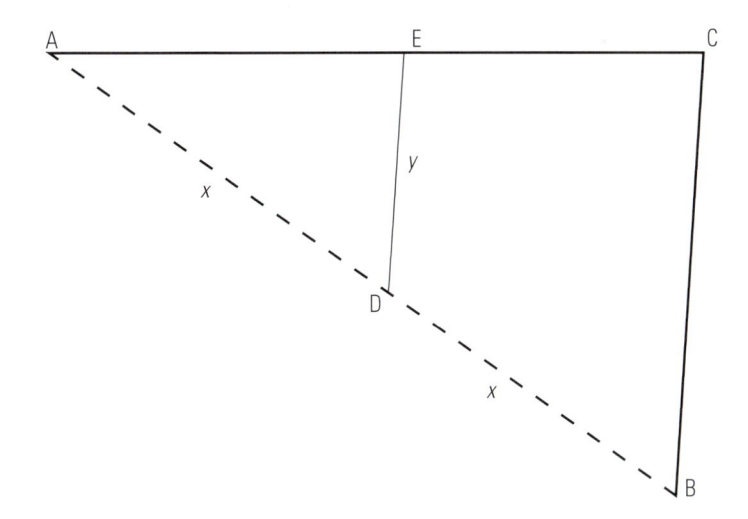

Some farmers build temporary fences to divide their land. For example, cattle can be allowed to graze on different fenced-off sections of land throughout the year.

BUILD YOUR SKILLS

1. Hillary and Kuruk have designs for building sets of nesting triangular tables. To ensure that the tables in a set match each other, the triangles must be similar in shape. Hillary cuts two sets of table tops with the angles shown below. Determine if the tops are similar.

   Set 1: Table 1: 90°, 45°
           Table 2: 45°, 45°

   Set 2: Table 1: 133°, 11°
           Table 2: 35°, 11°

Chapter 6   Similarity of Figures

2. Kaia baked a holiday cake in the shape of a tree. When it was done baking, she realized it was too big for her platter. She decided to cut off the stem, and trim the cake along line DE, and replace the stem.

   These are some of the cake's measurements.

   AD = 9″
   BC = 10″
   DE = 8″

   Given these measurements, what is the length of side AB?

3. Referring to the diagram in question 2, if

   AF = 8″
   FG = 2″
   AE = 9.5″

   What is the length of EC?

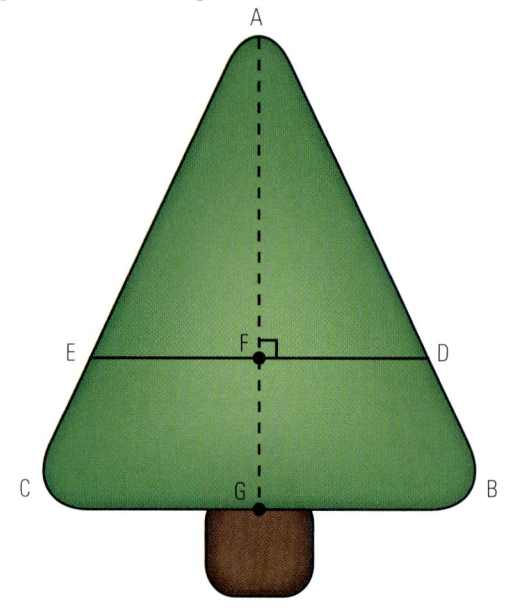

4. Tryna is hiking near Seebe, Alberta. She sees the top of Mount Yamnuska (Yamnuska means "cliff" in the Stoney language) in line with the peak of a tree, whose height she estimates to be 10 ft above her eye level. If the distances correspond as shown in the diagram, how tall is the face of the mountain above where Tryna is hiking?

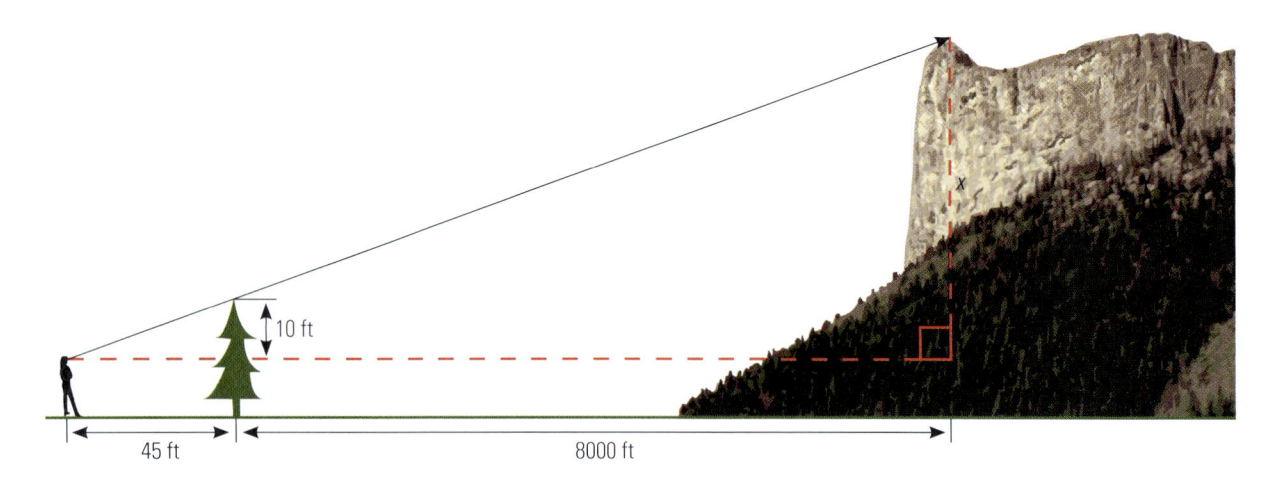

5. Mukako and Maya are constructing a quilt piece for their high school Fashion Studies class. They have some of the measurements they need, but they need to know the length of *x* below to ensure that the larger and smaller triangles are similar in their measurements. What should be the length of *x*?

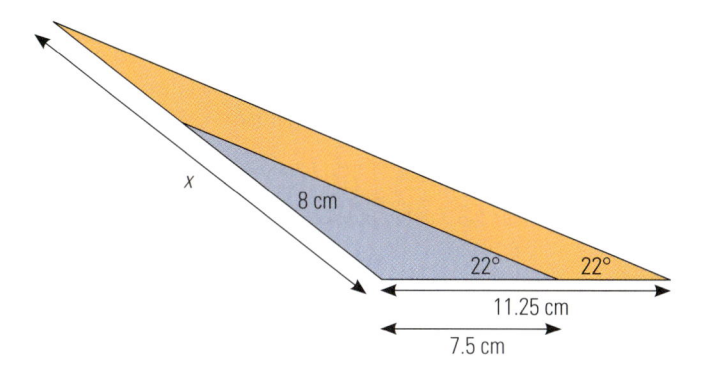

Extend your thinking

6. A company designs a slide for a children's playground near Kinngait, Nunavut. They make a sketch of the slide as a triangle. They place a beam parallel to the ground, labelled DE in the diagram below, to support the slide. Find the lengths of CE and EB in the diagram.

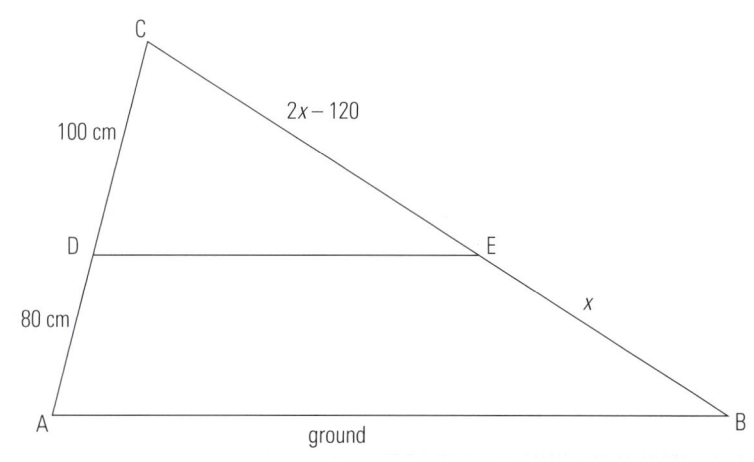

Playground equipment, such as a slide, is designed to meet safety standards.

Chapter 6 Similarity of Figures 263

PROJECT – DESIGN A COMMUNITY GAMES ROOM

PRESENT YOUR DESIGN

You are now ready to present your design for the community games room to the deciding committee at the meeting.

Decide how to present the project. Will you use computer sketching software, build a three-dimensional scale model, or use sketches on paper? What are the selling points of your design? What does your plan have that other designing committees may not offer?

Remember that your project must include:

- A sketch, computer sketch-up, or 3-D model of your room with all of the required elements in your design.
- A separate sheet of paper or spreadsheet with your calculations.

Be prepared to explain how you determined the measurements of each piece of furniture and community game equipment in your scale drawing.

When designing a community games room, make sure there is enough room for people to move around.

REFLECT ON YOUR LEARNING
SIMILARITY OF FIGURES

Now that you have finished this chapter, you should be able to

- ❒ determine if polygons are similar by their corresponding angle measures;
- ❒ determine if polygons are similar by their corresponding side lengths;
- ❒ explain why two polygons are not similar;
- ❒ find the scale factor between the corresponding sides of similar polygons;
- ❒ draw a polygon that is similar to another polygon; and
- ❒ explain why right triangles with one shared acute angle are similar.

You will also have finished a chapter project that allowed you to apply these skills in a practical way to a real-world task.

264 MathWorks 10

PRACTISE YOUR NEW SKILLS

1. Rayne is an industrial designer who designs food storage containers. He has designed a container with a width of 24 cm and a length of 36 cm. He now wants to design a nesting set of containers proportional to the first one. If he uses each of the scale factors below, what will be the new dimensions of each container?

   a) $\frac{2}{3}$

   b) 1.25

   c) 25%

   d) $\frac{5}{6}$

2. Chenna scaled a polygon by a factor of $\frac{3}{4}$.

   a) What is the ratio of any two corresponding sides?

   b) What is the ratio of the measures of any two corresponding angles?

3. Bill is ordering molding stock for carpentry work. He uses similar cross-section shapes for crown moldings and for chair rail moldings and trim.

   a) Determine what scale factor was used to create the smaller shape from the larger one.

   b) Use the scale factor to calculate lengths a, b, and c.

   c) Does Bill need to know length *e* to make the smaller shape?

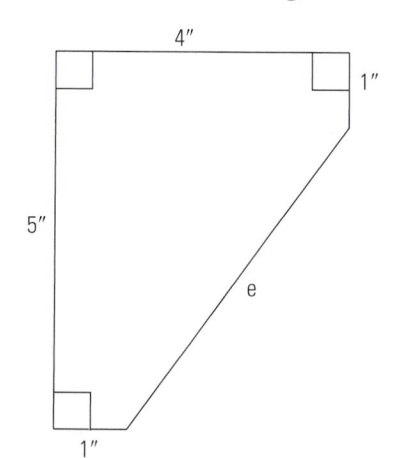

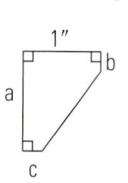

Stacking plastic containers are used in many workplaces. They might be used by chefs storing food, movers transporting goods, or hotel housekeepers organizing cleaning supplies.

Chapter 6 Similarity of Figures

4. Sherelle is designing a dresser with three sizes of drawers. She decides the largest drawer will be 80 cm wide by 32 cm high.

   a) For the middle size drawer she reduces the big drawer by a factor of $\frac{1}{2}$. What are the dimensions of the middle-size drawer?

   b) For the smallest drawer she reduces the middle drawer by 50%. What are the dimensions of the smallest drawer?

   c) What scale factor is used on the biggest drawer for the smallest drawer?

   d) If the drawers are arranged as shown in the diagram, what will be the height of the dresser if the feet are 10 cm high?

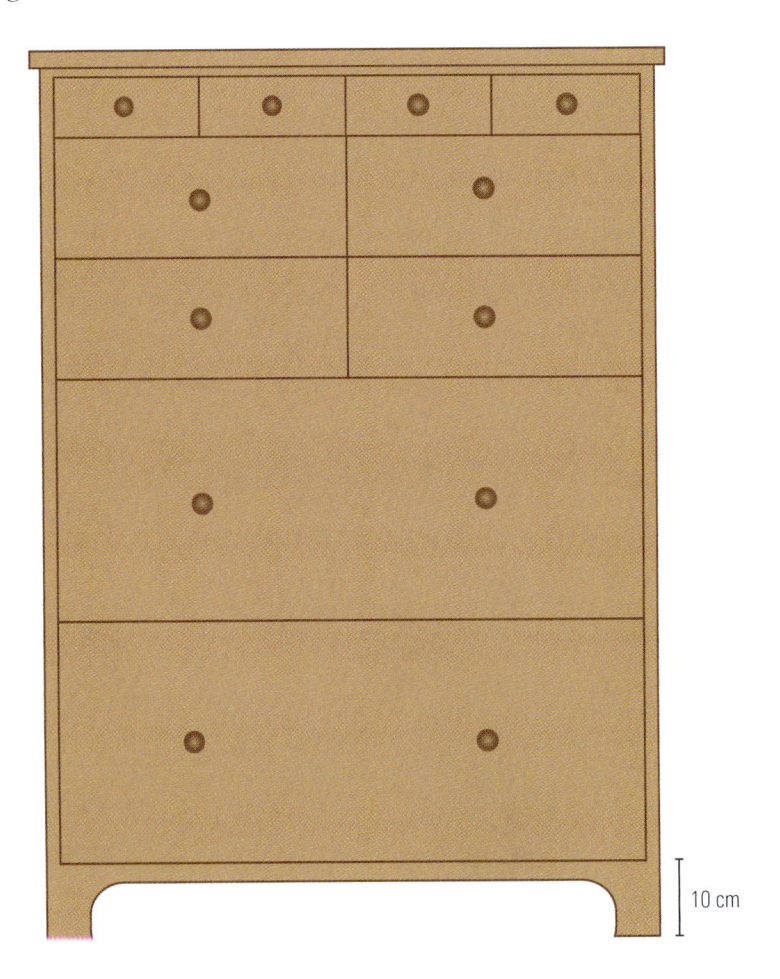

5. Tim is a park designer in Carrot River, Saskatchewan and is planning two fields outside a community building. He wants each field to be similar in shape, but one field needs to be larger than the other field, while each makes the best use of the available space. He creates the two diagrams below to represent the two fields.

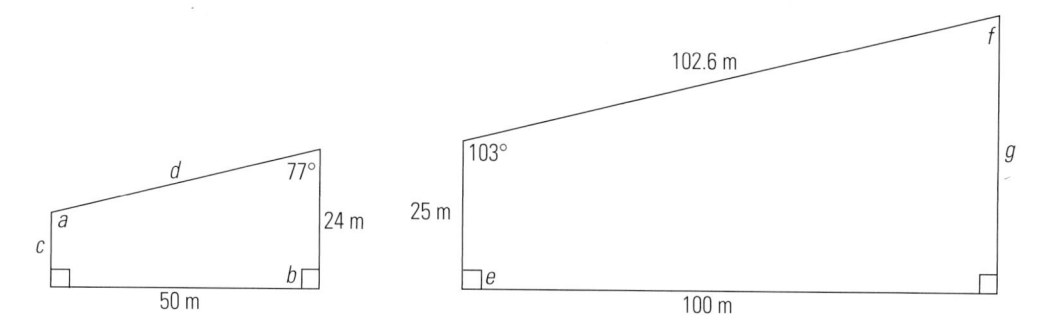

a) What scale factor did he use on the dimensions of the first field to create the dimensions of the second field?

b) If the two fields are to be similar in shape, what should be the angle measurements at *a* and *b*? What should be the missing side lengths, *c* and *d*?

c) In the larger field, what should be the measurements of the angles *e* and *f*? What should be the length of side *g*?

6. Elise works at a museum gift shop. A customer has asked for a poster that reduces the size of their favourite painting (measuring 57" wide by 76" long) by no more than a scale factor of $\frac{5}{8}$. Elise finds a poster that is 36" wide by 48" long. Will this satisfy the customer? Justify your response.

7. Ryan and Cyndi's parents have offered to supply materials for them to build a playhouse if they create a reasonable design. Ryan drew the rectangle below on 1 centimetre grid paper to use as the outline of the walls.

   Cyndi drew another rectangle on 1 centimetre grid paper. She says that she used a scale factor of 0.5 on Ryan's plan to create the new plan. Her playhouse plan has an area of 24 cm². Could the rectangles be similar? Justify your answer.

8. Jeremy is building a coffee table that separates into two triangles. He makes the first triangle using angle measures of 85° and 32°. He plans to make the second piece using angle measures of 63° and 32°. Will the two triangular pieces have a similar shape? Explain your response.

9. A tangram puzzle contains plastic triangular pieces for combining into different pictures. A company produces two pieces with the measurements shown below. Are the two pieces similar in shape? Explain your answer.

The tangram puzzle pieces combine to make a figure of a person running.

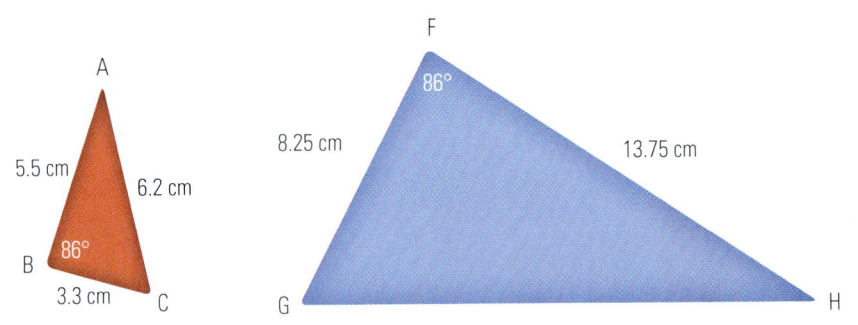

Triangle ABC: AB = 5.5 cm, BC = 3.3 cm, AC = 6.2 cm, angle B = 86°

Triangle FGH: FG = 8.25 cm, FH = 13.75 cm, angle F = 86°

268 MathWorks 10

10. Petra is building an obstacle course for her daughter in their backyard. She designs a sketch of the course so that it is in the shape of a triangle. She labels the triangle ABC and uses side lengths so that AB equals 10 ft, AC equals 20 ft, and BC equals 25 ft. When she goes to build the obstacles, she finds that she has fewer materials than she thought she had. She decides to make a new sketch using triangle FGH so that $\frac{AB}{FG}$ equals 2.5. What is the measure of FH?

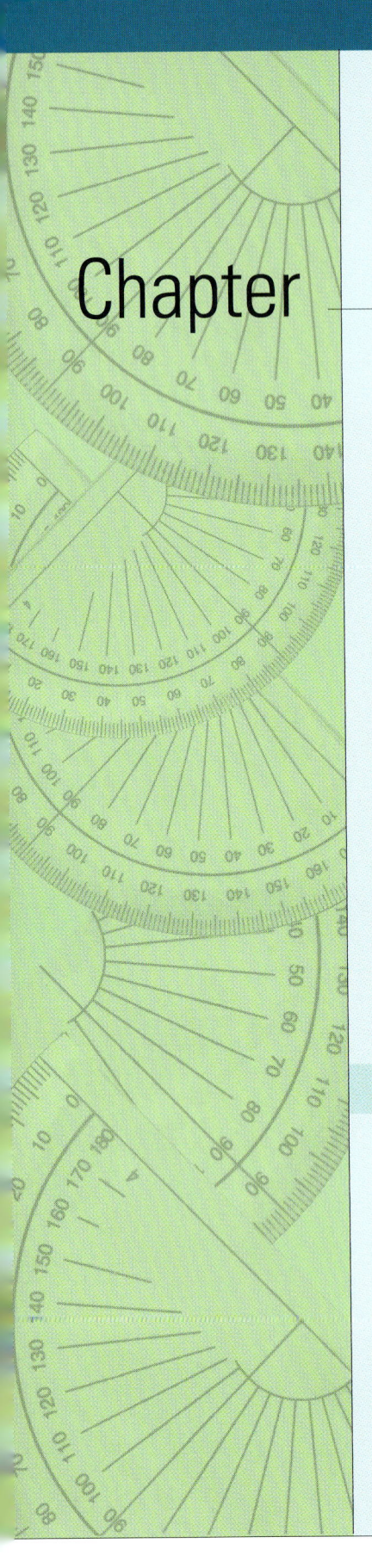

Chapter 7

Trigonometry of Right Triangles

GOALS

In this final chapter, you will be looking at trigonometric ratios. You will be actively involved in creating tables of values that will help you understand what the different ratios stand for and how to apply them.

Trigonometric ratios are used in many different professions and trades. Carpenters, pipefitters, and even seamstresses use them on a regular basis. In this chapter, you will be applying prior knowledge about triangles and similar figures to

- determine the trigonometric ratios;
- determine lengths of sides of right triangles using the ratios;
- determine the sizes of angles if you know the ratios.

KEY TERMS

- angle of depression
- angle of elevation
- cosine
- hypotenuse
- leg
- Pythagorean theorem
- sine
- tangent

PROJECT—DESIGN A STAIRCASE FOR A HOME

START TO PLAN

PROJECT OVERVIEW

There are many different structures in a community that enhance the visual appeal of its surroundings. One type of structure is a staircase, a necessary feature in architecture that adds beauty to an entranceway. For this chapter project, you will design a staircase to connect the main floor of a house to the second floor. The distance between the two floors is 9 feet 10 inches and the maximum floor area available for the staircase is 11 feet by 11 feet. You can design a straight staircase, one with a turn or landing in it, or a spiral staircase. You will need to consider the height, depth, and width of each stair and design your staircase so that it fits into the designated area.

GET STARTED

Most of you will have one or two staircases in your home. Take a look at them. Usually, each step is the same size, but sometimes there is a wider one, or a landing where the direction changes. Do you have a spiral staircase in your home? How do the steps on it differ from the ones on a straight staircase? Do you have a staircase on the outside of your house leading to a porch or sundeck? How is it different from the staircases inside your house?

To begin your project, look on the internet or talk to your woodworking teacher or a carpenter to learn about staircase design. Make a list of all the things you will need to consider. For example:

- What are the building code regulations for stairs? What are the allowable range of heights and depth of stairs?
- What types of lumber do you want to use?
- What types and thicknesses of finishing wood are available?
- What terms are used in stair construction?

Use your information to determine the number of stairs you will need and if you will have a turn or landing in your staircase. Begin by drawing top-down and side views of your ideas. Consider more than one possibility.

This set of stairs is in an ice castle built for Yellowknife's annual Snowking Winter Festival.

FINAL PRESENTATION CHECKLIST

You will present your final drawings and measurements as a poster or a scale model, along with instructions for a carpenter to build the stairs. The final presentation must include:

- a scale drawing of your staircase;
- accurate measurements of each part of the staircase;
- steps for the work involved, including tools and instruments that will be needed;
- at least one pair of similar figures in your diagram;
- the measurements calculated in imperial units; and
- a discussion as to why you designed your staircase as you did.

7.1 The Pythagorean Theorem

MATH ON THE JOB

Jim Jenner is a drywaller from Surrey, British Columbia. His passion is woodworking and he loves creating boxes with cedar, maple, and beech.

Jim often creates geometric designs to inlay on a box. These have to be cut perfectly. Why do you think this is? Also, the sides of a box are usually set at right angles to the base. Why do think this is important? What tools could Jim use to make sure that the bottom and sides are perpendicular?

Jim is designing a toybox for his grandson, Zack. He wants to decorate the top of it with large squares inlaid with smaller squares that are slightly rotated, as shown in the illustration.

Jim wants the inner squares to be rotated according to the measurements shown in the illustration. What is the length of the sides of the inlaid squares?

Should Jim then cut the inner squares to exactly those lengths? Why or why not?

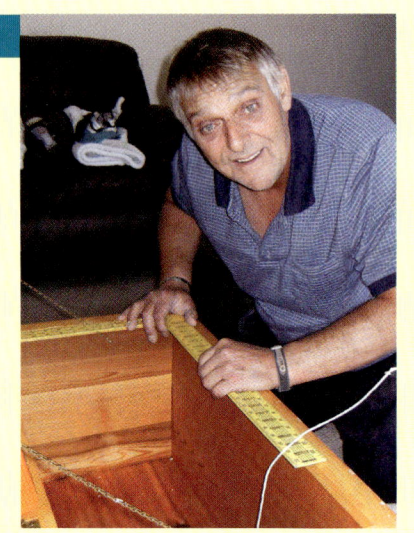

Building a toy box is a hobby for Jim, who loves working with specialty wood

12 in

9 in

EXPLORE THE MATH

right triangle: a triangle with one right angle

Pythagorean theorem: in a right triangle, the sum of the squares of the lengths of the legs is equal to the square of the length of the hypotenuse

In the example above, Jim used the **Pythagorean theorem**, often referred to as the Pythagorean relation, in order to determine the lengths of the sides of the **right triangles**. On a daily basis, carpenters, surveyors, bricklayers, and many other professionals use the formula below, which is based on the Pythagorean theorem. In the past you, too, have worked with this formula.

$$a^2 + b^2 = c^2$$

The longest side of a right triangle is always represented by the letter c. The two shorter sides are always represented by the letters a and b.

272 MathWorks 10

When a ladder is placed against a wall so that a painter can paint the house, the ladder, the wall, and the ground form a right triangle.

In this example, the wall and the ground form the right angle of the right triangle, and the ladder forms the **hypotenuse**. The ground and the wall are the **legs** (sometimes called the arms or sides).

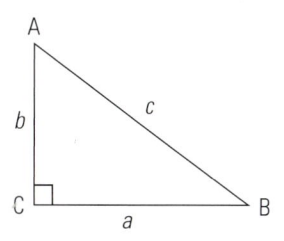

hypotenuse: the longest side of a right triangle, opposite the 90° angle

leg: in a right triangle, the two sides that intersect to form a right angle

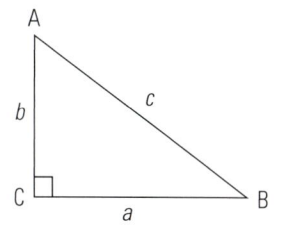

Triangle ABC represents the house and ladder. Leg BC of the triangle is said to be adjacent to angle B and opposite angle A. In general, a leg of a right triangle is adjacent to the angle if it, along with the hypotenuse, forms the acute angle. The other leg is said to be opposite that acute angle. In triangle ABC, leg AC is opposite angle B.

Leg AC, or b, is adjacent to angle A and opposite angle B

Leg BC, or a, is adjacent to angle B and opposite angle A

A lower case letter is used to label the side opposite an angle identified with a capital letter.

Mental Math and Estimation

In the diagram shown, if AB is 30 ft, and AC is 25 ft, approximately how far from the building is the back of the truck?

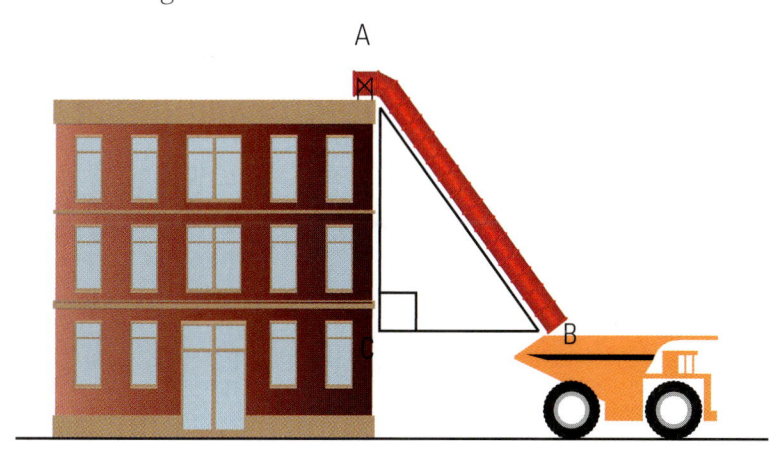

Chapter 7 Trigonometry of Right Triangles

Example 1

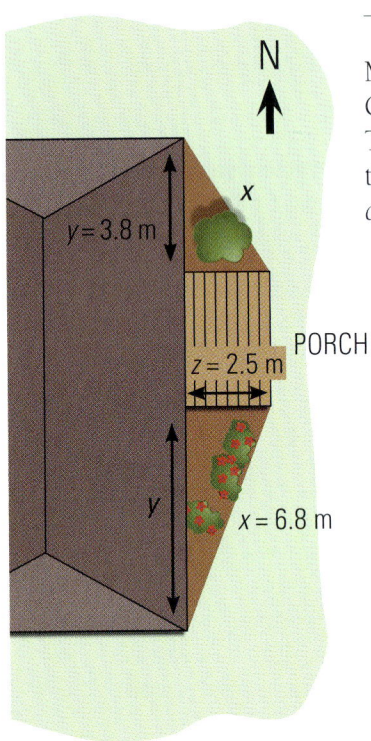

Mary has submitted a plan to plant a herb garden in front of the proposed Centre Communitaire Beaumont Community Centre in Beaumont, Alberta. The garden will be made of two triangular pieces of earth on either side of the centre's porch. It will be used to grow traditional French herbs such as *cerfeuil* (chervil), *sarriette* (savory), *thym* (thyme), and *romarin* (rosemary).

a) Given the dimensions of the legs of the triangle as shown in the diagram, what will be the length of the hypotenuse of the plot to the north of the porch?

b) How far along the front of the house will the garden in the plot to the south of the porch reach?

SOLUTION

Use the Pythagorean theorem.

$$x^2 = y^2 + z^2$$

a) x represents the hypotenuse.

$x^2 = (3.8)^2 + (2.5)^2$ Substitute known values into the Pythagorean theorem.

$x^2 = 14.44 + 6.25$

$x^2 = 20.69$

$x = \sqrt{20.69}$

$x \approx 4.5$

The hypotenuse will be about 4.5 m long.

b) The hypotenuse is 6.8 m.

$6.8^2 = (2.5)^2 + y^2$ Substitute known values into the Pythagorean theorem.

$46.24 = 6.25 + y^2$

$y^2 = 46.24 - 6.25$

$y^2 = 39.99$

$y = \sqrt{39.99}$

$y \approx 6.3$

The garden will extend approximately 6.3 m along the house.

DISCUSS THE IDEAS

PYTHAGOREAN TRIPLES

The theorem you have been using is named after Pythagoras, who was born about 570 BCE. But ancient Egyptians were putting the theory into practice as early as 2500 BCE.

After the Nile flooded its banks, the ancient Egyptians had to lay out the boundaries of their fields again. They had to make sure the fields were laid out at right angles. To do this, they marked off 12 even lengths in a cord (by tying 11 knots in it, evenly spaced from the two ends of the cord).

1. Using a felt marker and a piece of string, make 11 equally-spaced marks that separate the string into 12 equal lengths. How do you think the ancient Egyptians would have used this string to ensure that they had a right angle?

2. What would have been the lengths of the sides of the triangles the Egyptians used? Check with your classmates to see if you arrived at the same answers.

The numbers you have found are consistent with the Pythagorean theorem. They are referred to as a **Pythagorean triple**.

3. Using your understanding of similar triangles from chapter 6, if you doubled the lengths of the sides of your triangle, would it still be a right triangle? What if you tripled them?

4. Excluding multiples of the Pythagorean triple that the ancient Egyptians used, find at least 3 other sets of Pythagorean triples that are distinct, meaning not multiples of each other.

Pythagorean triple: any set of three natural numbers that satisfy the Pythagorean theorem

Mental Math and Estimation

In a right triangle, if the hypotenuse is 20 in and one leg is 12 in, how long is the other leg?

Example 2

Marc is going to paint the exterior of his house. He has a 40-foot ladder and knows that for safety reasons the base of the ladder must be between 9 and 12 feet from the base of the wall. What are the maximum and the minimum heights the ladder will reach up the wall?

SOLUTION

The ladder will form the hypotenuse of the right triangle whose legs will be the ground and the height up the wall.

If the ladder is 9 feet from the base, calculate its height.

$$g^2 + h^2 = l^2$$
$$9^2 + h^2 = 40^2$$
$$81 + h^2 = 1600$$
$$h^2 = 1600 - 81$$
$$h^2 = 1519$$
$$h = \sqrt{1519}$$
$$h \approx 39$$

The ladder will reach approximately 39 feet up the wall.

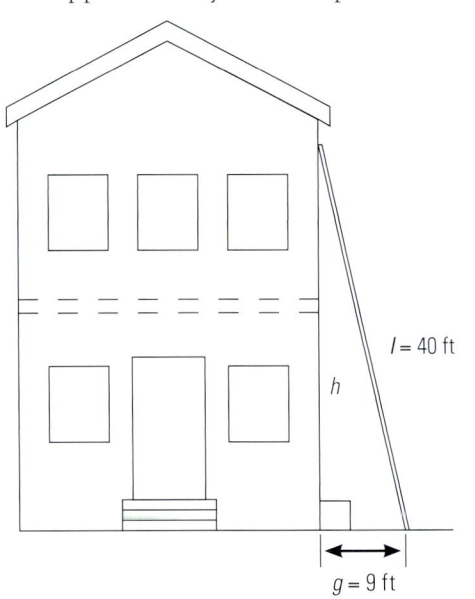

HINT

Choose letters that remind you of what they stand for. For example, use *l* for ladder, *g* for ground, *h* for height.

l = 40 ft

h

g = 9 ft

If the ladder is 12 feet from the base, how far up the wall will it reach?

$$g^2 + h^2 = l^2$$
$$12^2 + h^2 = 40^2$$
$$144 + h^2 = 1600$$
$$h^2 = 1600 - 144$$
$$h^2 = 1456$$
$$h = \sqrt{1456}$$
$$h \approx 38.2$$

The ladder will reach approximately 38.2 feet above the ground.

Therefore the ladder, when placed safely, will reach between 38.2 feet and 39 feet above the ground.

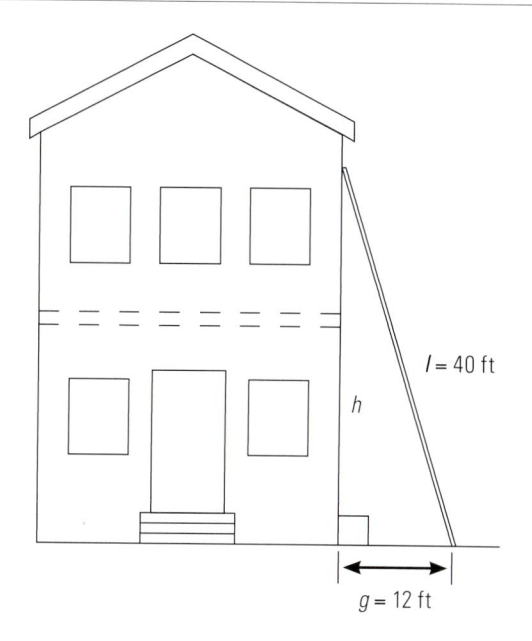

ACTIVITY 7.1
INDIRECT MEASUREMENT

Cam is a surveyor working in Nunavut. He needs to estimate the length of a small pond between the Iqaluit Airport and Sylvia Grinnell Territorial Park. He decides to use a right triangle, as shown in the diagram, as an indirect method of measurement.

1. Why might a surveyor use an indirect method of measurement in the example above?

2. What is the length of the pond?

3. With a partner, find two objects in your neighbourhood for which you cannot take direct measurements and use right triangles to find their lengths or widths.

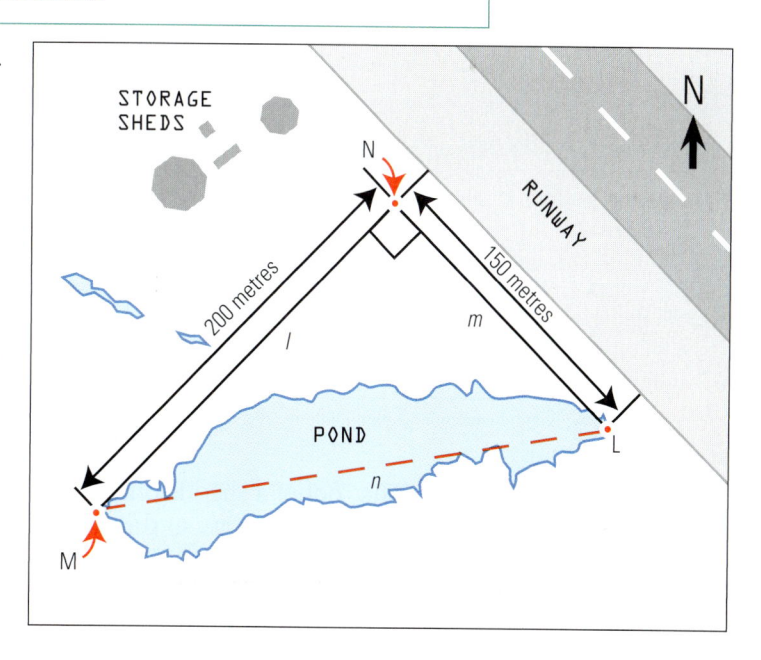

Chapter 7   Trigonometry of Right Triangles   **277**

ACTIVITY 7.2
GENERALIZATIONS OF THE PYTHAGOREAN THEOREM

Euclid (born circa 300 BCE) is called the Father of Modern Geometry. In his famous book *The Elements*, he generalized the Pythagorean theorem by stating that if one erects similar figures on the sides of a right triangle, then the sum of the areas of the two smaller figures will equal the area of the larger figure.

Work with a partner. Use grid paper and a 6-8-10 right triangle.

1. Draw a diagram to illustrate Euclid's statement for squares. Use your knowledge about areas to prove that the statement is true for this situation.

2. Draw a right triangle. Then, draw 3 isosceles triangles, with each one having a side of the right triangle as its base. Make the height of each isosceles triangle equal the length of its base. Find the area of each of these triangles. Does Euclid's statement hold?

BUILD YOUR SKILLS

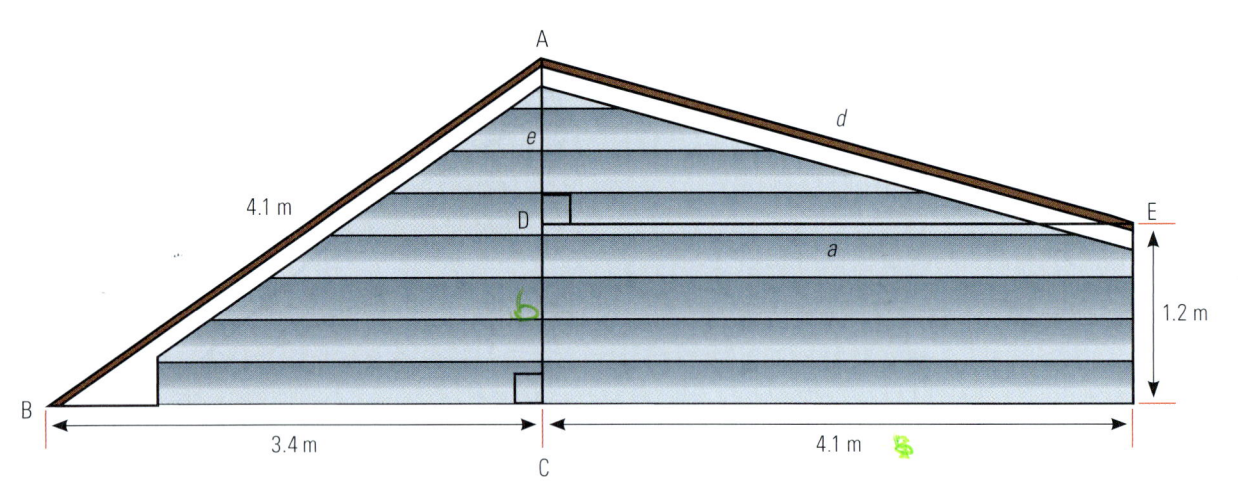

1. The roof of a shed is offset as in the diagram shown. Ben must determine its measurements so that he can order materials to repair it.

    a) How high is the peak (AC)?

    b) What is the length of the right-hand side (AE)?

2. Al has been contracted to build a garage in Prince Albert, Saskatchewan. The garage will be 7.5 m wide and the roof will have a 0.6 m overhang.

   a) If the peak of the garage is 1.2 m higher than the walls, how long does the rafter on each side have to be?

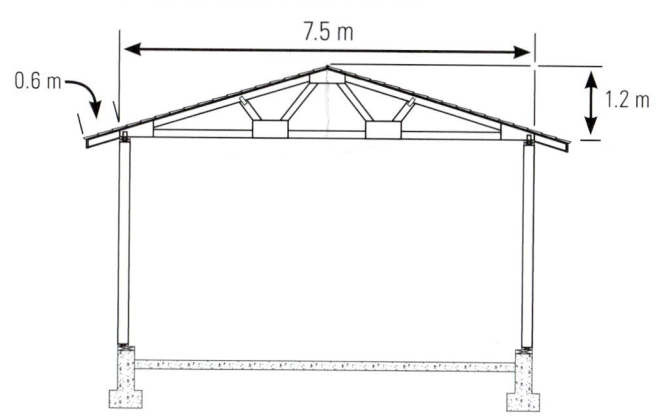

   b) The owner changes his mind and wants the peak to be off-centre. If it is 3 m from one side, how long will Al have to make each of the rafters? Note: There will still be a 0.6 m overhang.

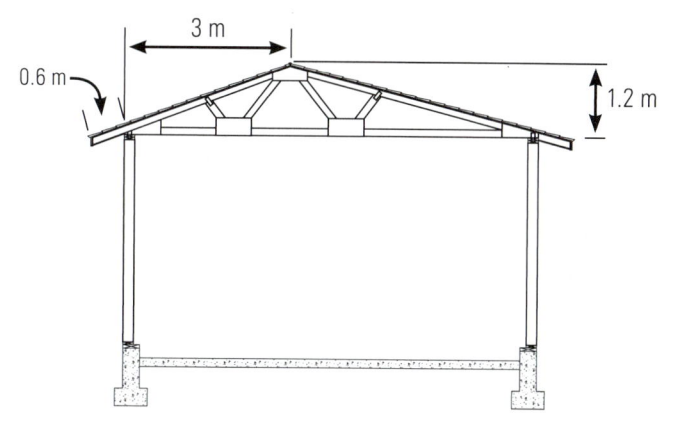

3. Suzanne is designing a rectangular storage box. The box will be built of solid oak. The lid of the storage box will extend above the sides by 10 cm. Each face except the bottom will have an embedded **X** made of thick copper wire as shown in the diagram. How much copper wire must Suzanne buy if the storage box is 90 cm long, 70 cm deep, and 70 cm high? Do you think she should buy any extra wire? Why or why not?

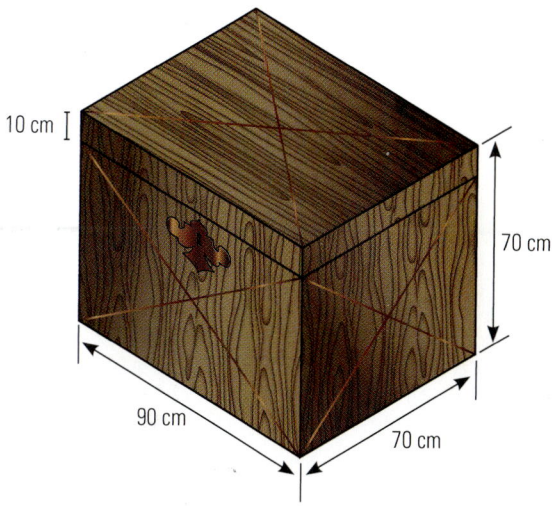

Chapter 7   Trigonometry of Right Triangles   **279**

4. Brigitte and René are installing a new flagpole at a community centre in Portage la Prairie, Manitoba. The height of the flagpole is 12 m. Two guy wires must be attached 10 m above the ground and secured 6 m from the base.

   a) Allowing 153 cm total for fastening both guy wires, how much guy wire will they need? Answer to the nearest centimetre.

   b) Why are guy wires necessary?

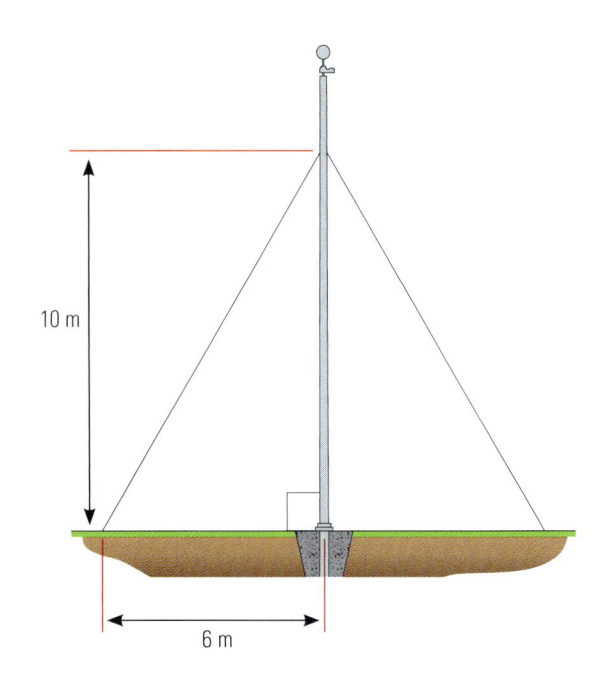

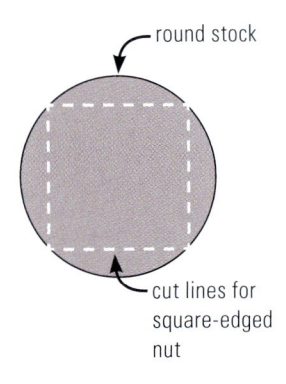

5. Bupinder must cut a square-edged nut from a piece of round stock in his machine technology class in Dawson City, Yukon.

   a) If metric round stock comes in diameters that are multiples of 5, what is the smallest diameter of stock needed if the nut must have a side of 30 mm?

   b) If imperial unit round stock comes in diameters that are multiples of $\frac{1}{4}"$, what is the smallest diameter of stock needed if the nut must have a side of $\frac{3}{4}"$?

6. Mining is a major industry in Saskatchewan, and safety is a primary concern. An air shaft must be drilled from a mine tunnel to the surface of a hill at 75 m intervals, measured horizontally along the tunnel.

   How long, to the nearest metre, is the shaft if it emerges 94 m up the slope of the hill as indicated in the diagram?

7. Suki is building an A-frame doghouse in her backyard. There will be a 90° angle at the vertex, and the base of the front will be 1.6 m wide. Answer to the nearest tenth of a metre.

   a) What will the lengths of the sloping roof pieces be?

   b) How high will the doghouse be at its peak? (Hint: H = height.)

   c) At 0.4 m in from the base, how high will the doghouse be?

   d) Would this be a suitable doghouse for a large dog? Why or why not?

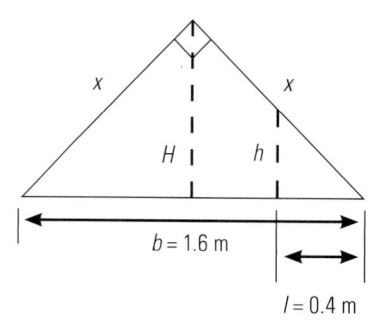

Extend your thinking

8. Marc works for a trucking company that makes regular trips between a stone quarry and a construction site. He usually follows a route that runs from the quarry north for one mile and then east for 2 miles to the construction site. He's now found a new route along a road that runs straight from the quarry to the site. How much shorter is the new route?

9. Sara is taking a course on quilt design so that she can make and sell her quilts at craft fairs. Her first quilt design has 100 rectangles on it, with a ribbon running across each rectangle in a single diagonal line, as in the diagram shown. Sara is trying to figure out how much ribbon to buy. She calculates:

   $$h^2 = a^2 + b^2$$
   $$h^2 = 81 \text{ cm} + 144 \text{ cm}$$
   $$h = 9 \text{ cm} + 12 \text{ cm}$$
   $$h = 21 \text{ cm}$$

   21 cm × 100 rectangles = 2100 cm

   Sara buys 2100 cm of ribbon.

   a) Sara has ribbon left over when she is finished the quilt. Why?

   b) How much ribbon should Sara have bought?

10. In the Math on the Job at the beginning of this unit, Jim could have built a box in which the sides were not perpendicular to the base, as shown in the image here. If so, what would Jim have had to consider?

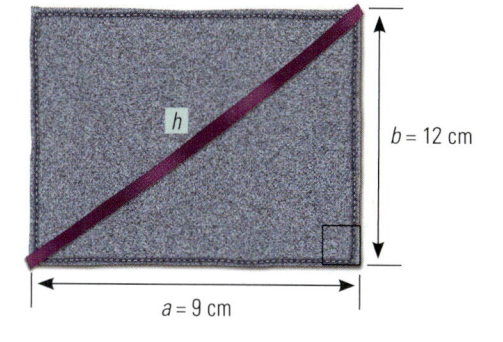

Sea chests were traditionally used by sailors to store their belongings in. They were commonly made of pine, with rope handles, and brass detailing.

11. Harpreet is designing a triangular garden plot in Saskatoon, Saskatchewan and will surround it by paving blocks that are 30 cm long. If the legs of the plot are 4.5 m and 3.6 m respectively, how many paving blocks will he need? (Ignore the corner overlap.)

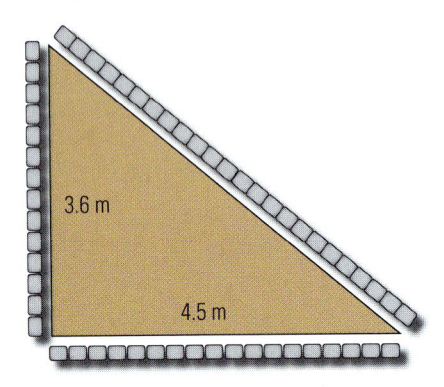

12. John is a surveyor who is asked to measure the height of a hill in Hinton, Alberta. He is unable to do so directly, so reverts to measuring the slant distance and the horizontal distance of shorter segments as he climbs up.

    a) How high is the hill?

    b) Why would John measure the hill in this manner?

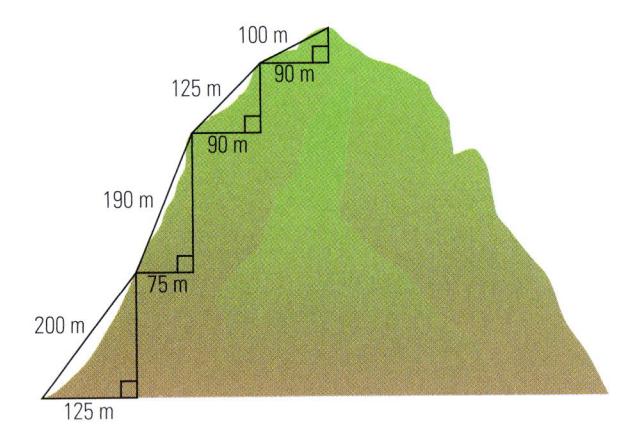

13. Can you find any other value of n so that

    $a^n + b^n = c^n$

    where *a*, *b*, and *c* are positive integers? Explain your reasoning.

The Sine Ratio 7.2

MATH *ON THE JOB*

Alexia is a plumber/pipefitter who works in the Northwest Territories installing and repairing pipes. Often the pipes have to be fitted around obstructions, and Alexia must take careful measurements, then cut and attach the pipes using elbows of different angles. An elbow is a curved fitting that is used to form a corner joining two pieces of straight pipe. Three terms Alexia uses in her work are *offset*, which is the vertical displacement between the centres of the pipes; *run*, which is the horizontal displacement between the end of one pipe and the beginning of the next; and *travel*, the diagonal distance between the centres of the two pipes.

In construction projects, professionals often simplify a 3-D object by drawing a 2-D sketch, as shown. Also, their professional installation manuals often provide them with a formula that helps them determine what they need to know. When Alexia consults her manual, it gives her a formula that indicates that, in joining a lower horizontal pipe to a travel pipe with a 60° elbow, she must use the following formula.

$$\frac{\text{offset}}{\text{travel}} = 0.866$$

If the offset in a particular project is 75 inches, what must the length of the travel pipe be?

A pipefitter must know how to cut, install, maintain, and repair pipes.

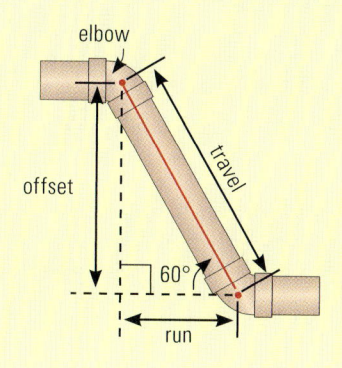

EXPLORE THE MATH

Many trades use terms for particular situations. In Math on the Job, above, Alexia was working with a right triangle whose "travel" was the hypotenuse. The side opposite the base was the "offset." Alexia uses a formula that mathematicians refer to as the **sine** ratio. In this section we will explore what is meant by sine ratio by considering the ratio of sides *within* triangles.

sine: in a right triangle, the ratio of the length of the side opposite a given angle to the length of the hypotenuse (abbreviated as sin)

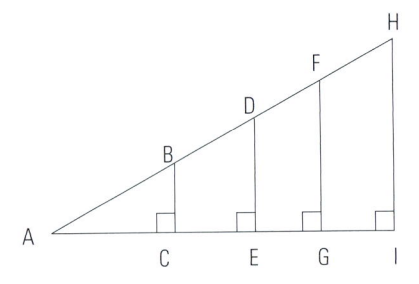

In the diagram above, you will notice that you have four similar right triangles, △ABC, △ADE, △AFG and △AHI. Explain how you know the four triangles are similar.

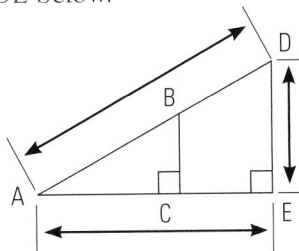

Consider △ABC and △ADE below.

1. Because the triangles are similar, you know that $\frac{BC}{DE} = \frac{AB}{AD}$. Use your understanding of equations to rearrange the letters in this equation so that each side represents a ratio of sides from the same triangle.

2. How would you describe sides BC and DE with respect to ∠A?

3. What is the name given to sides AD and AB in their respective triangles?

4. Write the ratios from question 1 in words relating to the sides of the triangles.

5. Consider △AFG and △AHI. What would the corresponding ratios be?

DISCUSS THE IDEAS
THE SINE RATIO

In the previous section, you looked at the ratios of sides within given right triangles. You discovered that when the triangles are similar (have the same acute angle measures), the ratio of the length of the side opposite a given angle to the length of the hypotenuse of the triangle remains the same, regardless of the overall size of the triangle. This ratio is the sine ratio that Alexia was given to use in the Math on the Job. She was told that, anytime she had a 60° angle, the ratio of the opposite side (offset) to the hypotenuse (travel) will be approximately 0.866.

$$\text{sine } A = \frac{\text{length of side opposite } \angle A}{\text{length of hypotenuse}}$$

284 MathWorks 10

or, simply, $\sin A = \dfrac{\text{opposite}}{\text{hypotenuse}}$

or, $\sin A = \dfrac{\text{opp}}{\text{hyp}}$

In the diagram shown here, look at angle Y.

$\sin Y = \dfrac{y}{z}$

or, $\sin Y = \dfrac{y}{z}$

Angle X is also an acute angle.

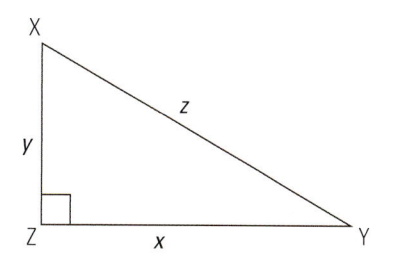

$\sin X = \dfrac{x}{z}$

ACTIVITY 7.3
THE SINE OF AN ANGLE

In the preceding Discuss the Ideas, you learned that the sine of an acute angle of a right triangle is calculated by finding the ratio of the side opposite the angle and the hypotenuse. Because of similarity, in a right triangle, the ratio of the opposite side to the hypotenuse will be the same if the angle is the same. You therefore need to calculate this ratio only once. In this activity, you will develop a table of values for the sine ratio. You will then use it to draw a graph and solve related problems.

Part A: Taking Measurements

1. Work with a partner. Your teacher will provide you with a set of three similar right triangles with a specified acute angle. Your assigned angles will be labelled as $\angle A_1$.

2. Carefully measure, to the nearest millimetre, the length of the side opposite each $\angle A$ and the hypotenuse of each triangle. Record the results on the table provided by the teacher.

THE SINE OF ANGLES

size of ∠A	length (o) of side opposite ∠A$_i$			length (h) of hypotenuse			ratio $\left(\frac{o}{h}\right)$: opposite hypotenuse			sine ratio [average of ratio $\left(\frac{o}{h}\right)$]	sin A values
	Δ$_1$	Δ$_2$	Δ$_3$	Δ$_1$	Δ$_2$	Δ$_3$	Δ$_1$	Δ$_2$	Δ$_3$		
10°											

SAMPLE

3. Calculate the ratio of the opposite side to the hypotenuse for each of your triangles to the nearest hundredth.

4. If your ratios are not all the same, find the average of the three ratios and record this in the column labelled sine ratio.

5. Record your sine ratio on an overhead chart provided by your teacher. The last column will remain empty for now.

Part B: Discussion

1. When the class has filled in the overhead chart, compare the sine ratios. What do you notice about the values of sin ∠A as A increases from 10° to 80°?

2. Do the data appear to form a linear relationship between an angle and its sine? Discuss why or why not.

3. Between what two values do you think sin 45° would fall?

4. Approximately what do you think sin 5° would be?

5. About what value do you think sin 85° would be?

6. What is the smallest value the sine of an acute angle of a right triangle can have? How about the largest? Use diagrams of right triangles with very small acute angles and acute angles that are near 90° to discuss and explain your reasoning.

Part C: Drawing a Graph

1. Using the table supplied by your teacher, fill in the data from the table that was generated by the class. Leave the last column empty for now.
2. Using the data from your table, sketch a graph of y equals sin ∠A.
3. Extrapolate to extend the graph to values of A near 0° and 90°.
4. Do the values correspond to your predicted values above?

DISCUSS THE IDEAS
REPAIRING A TRUSS BRIDGE

Benson is a structural engineer working in Sainte-Anne, Manitoba. He is repairing a truss bridge on which the angle of one of the beams is 60° compared to the horizontal. He knows that the height of the bridge is 2.8 m. Using the sine table you developed in Activity 7.3, determine approximately how long the beam that he must replace will be.

In designing and construction, accuracy is important. Engineers cannot rely on approximated values such as we determined for the sine above because slight errors can lead to serious flaws in a design. Thus, they generally rely on a calculator to determine the values.

T Using your scientific calculator, find sin 60.

1. Once you have the answer of approximately 0.8660, what does this tell you?
2. How does this compare with the value you found in Activity 7.3 for the sine of a 60° angle?
3. Use your calculator to find the values of sin A for the values in your table. Put these values in the last column of the table and compare them to your measurement values. Were your measurements accurate? Discuss possible sources of error.

Many mathematical operations, including finding the sine, cosine, or tangent of an angle, can be performed on a scientific calculator.

HINT

Make sure your calculator is in degree mode.

Example 1

In this and the next example, we will use the terms angle of elevation and angle of depression. Based on your understanding of the terms "elevation" and "depression," what do you think is meant by these expressions?

Hélène is building a garage on her farm near Stavely, Alberta. She knows that the angle of elevation of the roof must be 23° for the peak of the roof to be 3.2 metres above the ends of the rafters, as shown in the diagram. How long is each rafter?

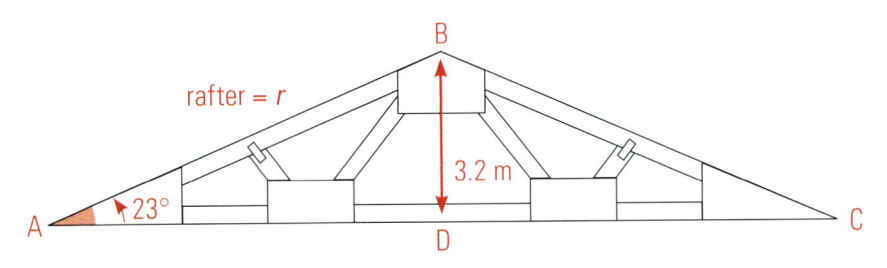

SOLUTION

In the diagram, BD is opposite the 23° angle, and the length of the rafter is the hypotenuse of the right triangle ABD.

$$\sin A = \frac{BD}{AB}$$

$$\sin 23° = \frac{3.2}{r}$$

$$\frac{r \sin 23°}{\sin 23°} = \frac{3.2}{\sin 23°}$$

$$r = \frac{3.2}{\sin 23°}$$

$$r \approx 8.2$$

Each rafter is 8.2 m long.

Example 2

angle of depression: the angle formed between the horizontal and the line of sight while looking downwards

From the top of a cliff by the ocean, Cedric sights a boat at an **angle of depression** of 48°. If the top of the cliff is 73 m above the surface of the water, and Cedric is 2 m tall, how far is Cedric from the boat?

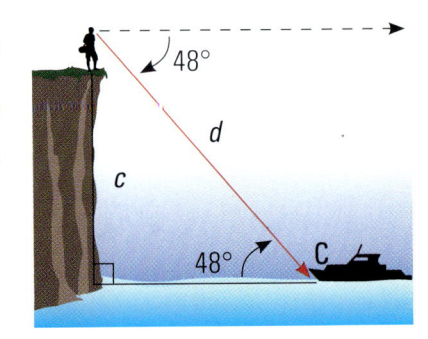

288 MathWorks 10

SOLUTION

Sketch the scene described.

Since the angle of depression from Cedric to the boat is 48° and the angle of depression is measured from the horizontal, the **angle of elevation** from the boat to him is also 48°. Thus, using the definition, we solve the distance as follows.

$$\sin C = \frac{c}{d}$$

$\sin 48° = \dfrac{75}{d}$ Substitute the known values.

$d \sin 48° = 75$ Multiply both sides by d.

$d = \dfrac{75}{\sin 48°}$ Divide both sides by $\sin 48°$.

$d \approx 101$

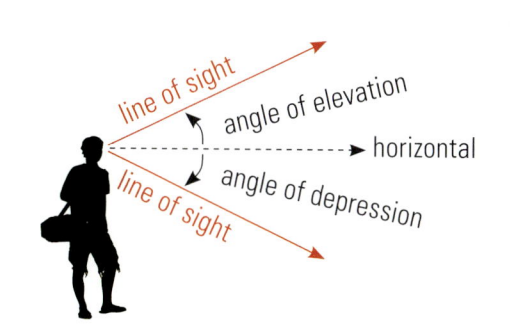

Cedric is approximately 101 m from the boat.

angle of elevation: the angle formed between the horizontal and the line of sight while looking upwards; sometimes referred to as the angle of inclination

BUILD YOUR SKILLS

1. Use your calculator to find sin 16°, sin 28°, sin 51°, and sin 83°, to four decimal places.

2. Joanne is designing a children's slide for a playground in the community of Carcross, Yukon. She has submitted three scaled designs, as shown here.

   a) For each design, determine the sine ratio of angle X.

   b) Find the length of each slide if the actual height is to be 2.6 m.

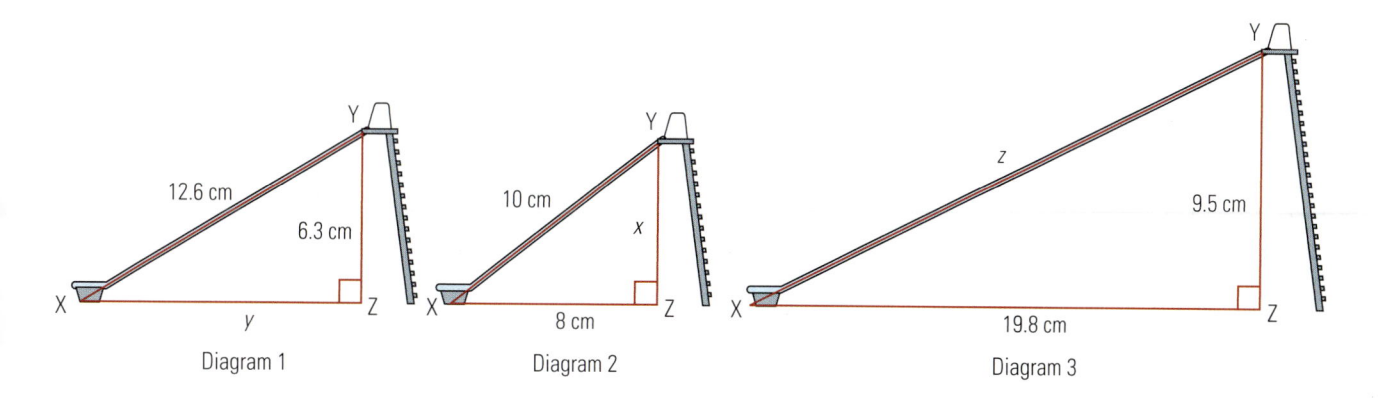

Diagram 1: 12.6 cm (XY), 6.3 cm (YZ), y (XZ)

Diagram 2: 10 cm (XY), x (YZ), 8 cm (XZ)

Diagram 3: 9.5 cm (YZ), z (XY), 19.8 cm (XZ)

Chapter 7 Trigonometry of Right Triangles **289**

3. Downstream from the confluence of the North and South Saskatchewan Rivers, archaeologists are excavating the site of a former Cree settlement. They find a stone circle that represents where a tipi once stood. (Stones were used to weigh down the hides that covered the tipi poles.) The average tipi had about 17 poles, which ranged from 10 to 24 feet long. An archaeologist determines that the tipi was 15 feet high at its peak and 12 feet wide. What would the length of the tipi poles be?

4. Laiwan, who lives in Grand Forks, BC, must have a wheelchair ramp built to her front porch. The porch is 1.9 m above ground level and the steepest angle of elevation allowed by the building code is 6°.

   a) What is the shortest ramp that Laiwan can have installed?

   b) About how many metres (to one decimal) from the base of the porch must the ramp start?

   c) Why do you think regulations state that the ramp cannot be any steeper?

5. Johan's barn is 12.3 m long. He is constructing a lean-to against the side of it. The angle of elevation of the roof of the lean-to is 21° and it meets the side of the barn at a point 4.8 m above the ground. How much roofing will he need to cover the roof of the lean-to? Give your answers in square metres, to one decimal.

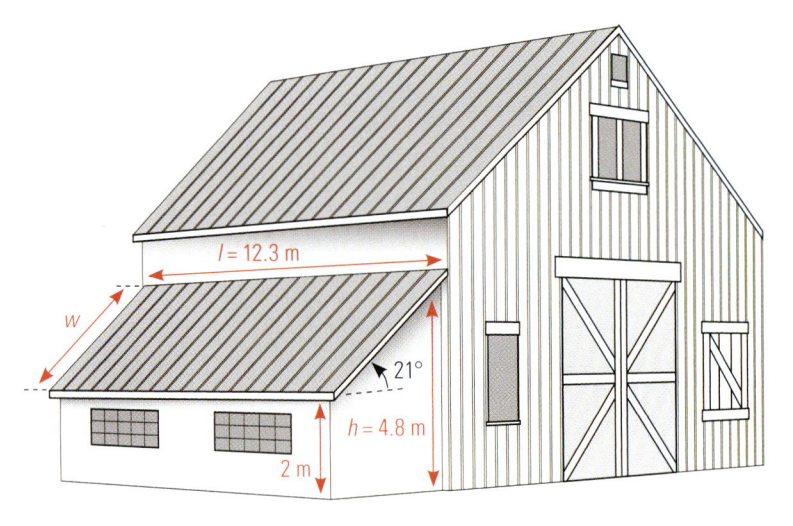

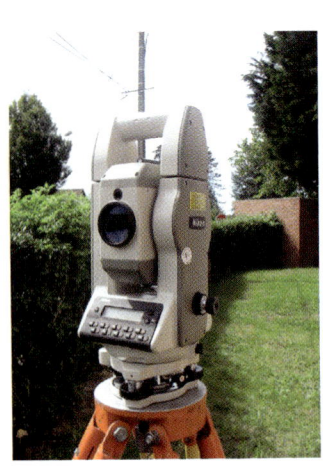

Theodolites are small mounted telescopes that can be moved horizontally and vertically. Navigators and surveyors use them to measure angles and bearings.

6. Darren works on a road construction crew in Wha Ti, Northwest Territories. He is able to measure the angle of elevation using an instrument called a theodolite. The angle of elevation from one point to another is 9°. The slope distance between the two points is 250 m.

   a) How much does the road rise over that distance?

   b) Do you think this would be considered a steep road? Explain your thinking.

290 MathWorks 10

7. Sally is flying a kite in Cochrane, Alberta. She has let out 210 m of string. Ignore Sally's height for the following calculations.

   a) If the angle of elevation is 50°, how high above the ground is the kite to the nearest metre?

   b) If an updraft catches the kite so that the angle of elevation changes to 65°, how high is the kite now?

8. The Leaning Tower of Pisa leans at an angle of approximately 84.5° to the ground. If the guardrail at the top of the tower is 55.86 m on the lowest side and 56.70 m on the highest side, determine the length of the two sides.

The Leaning Tower of Pisa in Italy was built over a span of 177 years. It began to sink, and lean, while its third floor was being built.

Extend your thinking

9. Refer to Example 1 on p. 288. Hélène wants her roof to be steeper but keep the width the same. How will this affect the length of the rafter? What happens to the distance between the peak and the line of the ends of the rafters? Explain and create a scenario with a diagram and actual measurements to illustrate your answer.

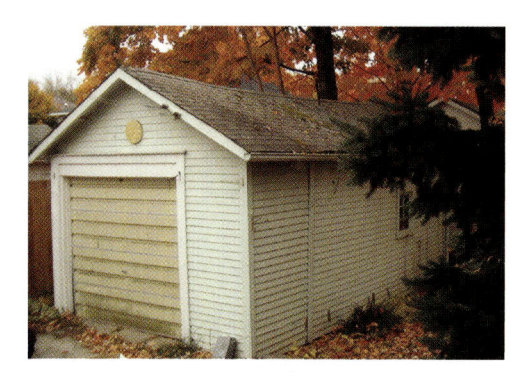

The roof of a garage gains strength and stability from its triangular form. By supporting a roof with triangular trusses, the roof is made even stronger.

10. Bridge builders use trigonometry to complete their work. They must be familiar with the sine ratio and its values, since right triangles are frequently used to construct bridges. Imagine you are a bridge builder using trigonometry at work. Given any right triangle, between what two values must the sine of an acute angle fall? That is, what are the maximum and minimum values for sin x when x is greater than 0° and less than 90°? Explain.

THE ROOTS OF MATH

TRIGONOMETRY IN HISTORY

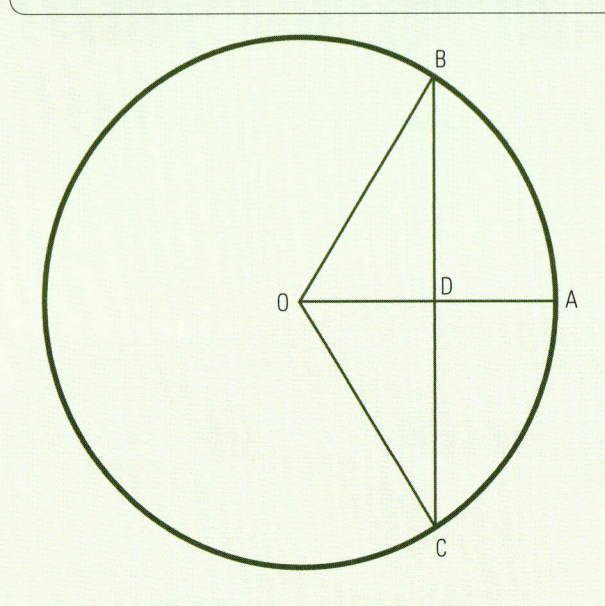

The term trigonometry is derived from the Greek words trigon (triangle) and metria (measure). It was first used in 1595 by Bartholomaeus Pitiscus, in his influential work *Trigonometria: sive de solutione triangulorum tractatus brevis et perspicuus*. When this book was translated into English and French in 1614 and 1619 respectively, the term *trigonometry* became used in these languages.

However, the development of the mathematics of triangles began long before that in many cultures. Ancient cultures dating back to as early as 4500 BCE in Britain may have used some Pythagorean triples. Old Sanskrit texts from India dating back to about 3100 BCE discuss the concepts of angles and measurement. The Rhind Papyrus, copied from an older document in about 1650 BCE by the Egyptian scribe Ahmes, displays some use of what we now call trigonometry in discussions about building pyramids. Much later (about 150 BCE), Hypsicles of Alexandria used chord functions of angles in a circle to make triangular computations.

In about 140 BCE, a Greek astronomer named Hipparchus is believed to have been the first to make systematic use of trigonometry. He computed a table of chords roughly equivalent to trigonometrical sines. However, it was not until the fifth century CE that trigonometry was introduced in its present form.

BC is a chord, a straight line segment joining any two points on a circle. If the radius (OA) of the circle is 1 unit, then the sine of the angle AOB is the half-chord DB.

For thousands of years, people used tables of calculated trigonometric values, like the one you calculated for sine. These tables were replaced by calculators only in the latter part of the twentieth century.

1. Using your understanding of circles, the sine function, and the image provided, explain how ancient scholars could have used this information to create a table of half-chords to represent the sine function.

2. Conduct research on the internet to find ways to determine the sine function other than by taking measurements of the sides of triangles.

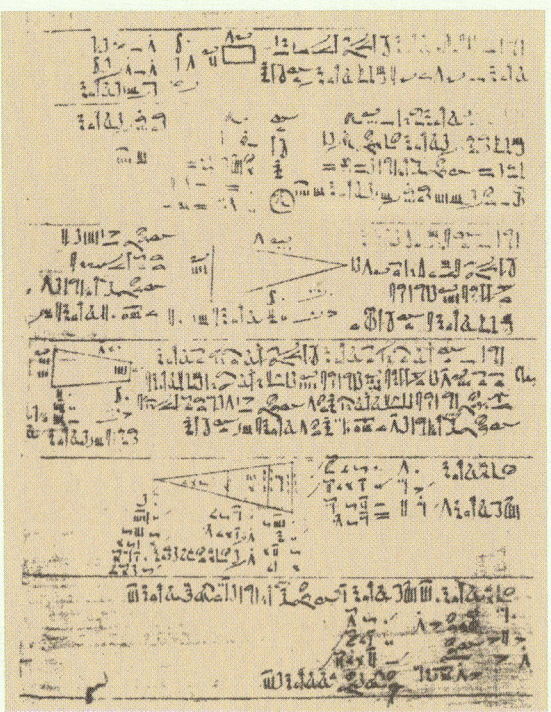

The Rhind papyrus, kept in the British Museum, contains problems and tables that show how ancient Egyptians used mathematics.

The Cosine Ratio 7.3

MATH ON THE JOB

Richard McCaffrey works at an auto parts warehouse in Burnaby, BC. His work involves keeping inventory of what parts are in stock, ordering new parts when stock is low, and delivering parts to various dealers in the Lower Mainland. Often stock arrives and is stored on one level, but is then transported to a different level for loading into a truck for delivery. Since the parts are often too heavy to lift, a conveyor belt is used to move them.

The conveyor belt needs replacing, and Richard must determine approximately what length of belt to order. He knows that the angle of depression from the upper floor along the conveyor belt is 38°. The belt reaches the lower level at a point 6.1 m further along the floor. How can Richard use similar triangles with a scale diagram to determine the length of belt he must order? Remember that a conveyor belt is a continuous loop with the belt returning on the underside of the conveyor. Drawing a scale diagram of the situation can help you understand it.

Richard uses a conveyer belt in his warehouse job.

EXPLORE THE MATH

Using similar triangles is one way that Richard could determine the length of the conveyor belt. However, he could also use a second trigonometric ratio, the **cosine** ratio, to find the length. While the sine ratio considers the ratio between the side opposite an acute angle in a right triangle to the hypotenuse, the cosine ratio considers the ratio of the side adjacent the acute angle to the hypotenuse.

cosine: in a right triangle, the ratio of the length of the side adjacent to a given angle to the length of the hypotenuse (abbreviated as cos)

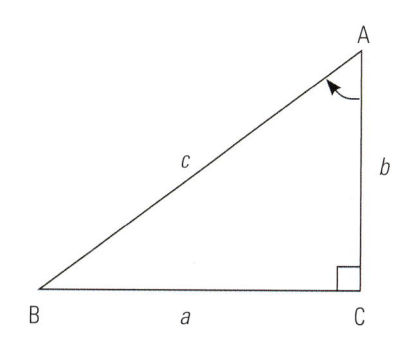

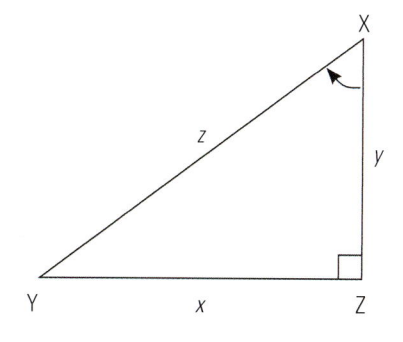

Begin by comparing the two similar triangles, $\triangle ABC \sim \triangle XYZ$.

1. Because the triangles are similar, you know that $\frac{x}{a} = \frac{z}{c}$. Use your understanding of equations to rearrange the letters in this equation so that each side represents a ratio of sides from the same triangle.

2. How would you describe side a with respect to angle B? How would you describe side x with respect to angle Y?

3. What is the name given to sides c and z in their respective triangles?

4. Write the ratio a/c with respect to angle B in words. Write the ratio x/z with respect to angle Y in words.

The ratio of the adjacent side and the hypotenuse is equivalent in both triangles. It is defined as follows

$$\text{cosine } X = \frac{\text{length of the side adjacent to } \angle X}{\text{length of the hypotenuse}}$$

$$\cos X = \frac{\text{adjacent}}{\text{hypotenuse}}$$

$$\cos X = \frac{\text{adj}}{\text{hyp}}$$

Example 1

Now that you know how to use the cosine function, use it to determine the length of conveyor belt that Richard needs to order in the Math on the Job on p. 293.

SOLUTION

Consider $\triangle PQR$. The distance from P to Q represents the distance from the loading edge to the place where the conveyor belt meets the floor.

Therefore:

$$\cos P = \frac{r}{q}$$

$$\cos 38° = \frac{6.1}{q}$$

$q \cos 38° = 6.1$ Multiply both sides by q.

$q = \frac{6.1}{\cos 38°}$ Divide both sides by $\cos 38°$.

$q \approx 7.74$

The distance along the conveyor belt is approximately 7.74 m. Richard therefore has to order at least twice this amount, at least 15.5 m.

Example 2

Given, △PQR where ∠Q equals 90°, q equals 4.3 cm, and ∠R equals 51°, solve the triangle.

SOLUTION

First, draw a diagram.

Since the sum of the two acute angles of a right triangle is 90°, you can find the third angle.

∠P = 90° − 51°

∠P = 39°

Find r.

$$\sin R = \frac{r}{q}$$

$$\sin 51° = \frac{r}{4.3}$$

$$4.3 \sin 51° = r$$

$$r \approx 3.3$$

Therefore r is approximately 3.3 cm.

Find p.

$$\cos R = \frac{p}{q}$$

$$\cos 51° = \frac{p}{4.3}$$

$$4.3 \cos 51° = p$$

$$p \approx 2.7$$

Therefore p is approximately 2.7 cm.

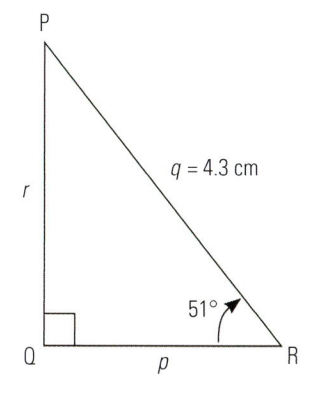

ACTIVITY 7.4
MOVEMENT OF A FERRIS WHEEL

You and your friends are on a Ferris wheel at the local summer fair. As your chair moves, you will always be the same distance from the centre as this is the radius of the wheel, but you will be closer or further away from the vertical diameter and the horizontal diameter depending on the movement. Consider the angle formed by the horizontal diameter, the axis to your chair (the radius of the Ferris wheel) and the vertical line from your chair to the horizontal axis. If you let the radius of the Ferris wheel be represented by 1 unit, the cosine of the angle formed will be the length of the horizontal leg of this triangle. Using angle measurements that are multiples of 10°, find the lengths of these horizontal segments by filling in a chart like the one below. You may use your calculator to find the values. Use this information to sketch the graph of $y = \cos A$.

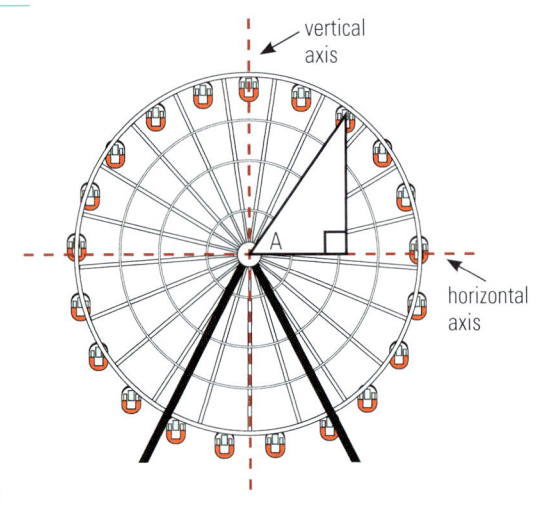

Ferris wheels are constructed using many right angle triangles.

COSINE RATIOS

A	10°	20°	30°	40°	50°	60°	70°	80°
$y = \cos A$								

1. What do you notice about the value of y as A increases from 10° to 80°?

2. Does this appear to be a linear graph? Explain how you know.

3. How does this graph compare to the graph of $y = \sin A$ from the previous section? Explain.

4. Extend your graph to values of A = 0° and A = 90°.

5. As the value of A approaches 0° (gets very small), what happens to the value of cos A? Using diagrams of right triangles, discuss why this is so.

6. What happens to the value of cos A as A gets close to 90°? Explain using diagrams.

7. What does this graph tell you about the horizontal distance of the chair from a vertical line through the centre of the Ferris wheel?

Example 3

In construction, Marie knows that a force acting at an angle can be broken up into a vertical force and a horizontal force. If a force of 365 Newtons is exerted diagonally downward at an angle of 30° to the horizontal, what force will be applied horizontally?

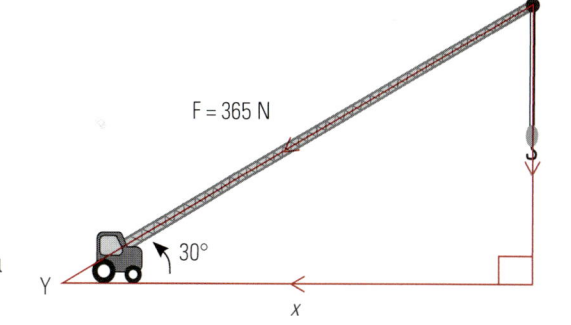

SOLUTION

The horizontal force x is adjacent to the 30° angle, so you use the cosine function.

$$\cos Y = \frac{x}{F}$$

$$\cos 30° = \frac{x}{365}$$

$$365 \cos 30° = \frac{x}{365} \times 365 \quad \text{Multiply both sides by 365.}$$

$$316 \approx x$$

The horizontal force will be about 316 N.

BUILD YOUR SKILLS

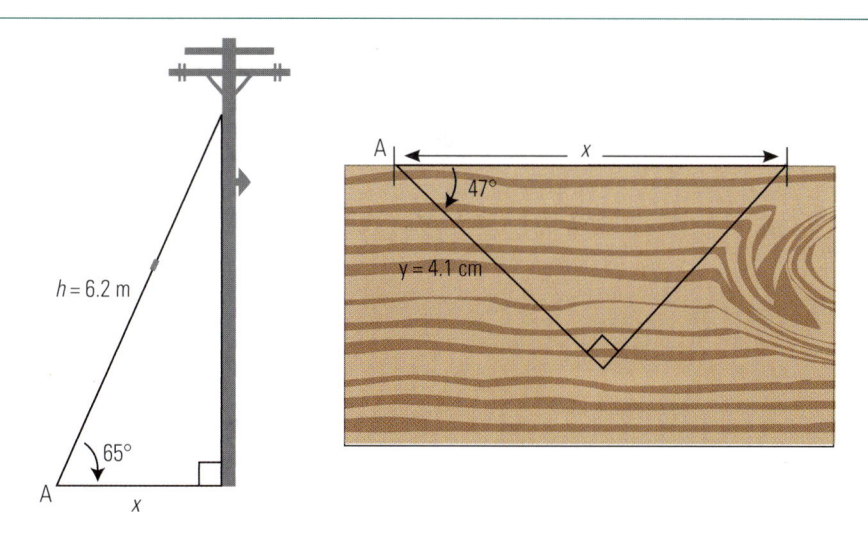

Guy wires add stability to poles carrying electrical lines.

1. Refer to the diagrams above.

   a) How far from the base of a pole must a 6.2 m long guy wire be attached if the angle of elevation is 65°?

   b) A notch is cut from a block of wood as indicated. What is the width of the opening of the cut-out portion?

2. The angle of elevation between a grain auger and the grainery to which it is to be connected is 30°. If the run is 72 m, how long must the travel pipe be?

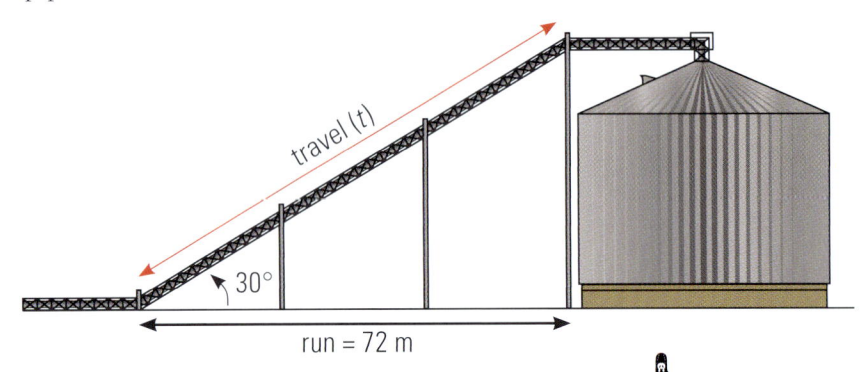

3. Totem poles are almost always erected by being pulled upright with ropes into a wooden scaffold support until they are stable. Suppose that two of the ropes attached to a pole are at angles of elevation of 47° and 57° respectively. If the base of the ropes is approximately 26 m from the base of the totem pole, how long is each rope?

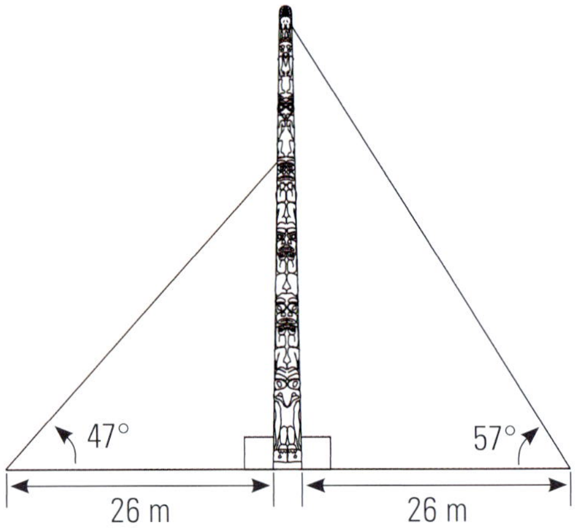

This freestanding totem pole is in Victoria, BC's Beacon Hill Park. Standing 38.9 m tall, it was carved by Henry Hunt, David Martin, and Mungo Martin.

4. A surveyor standing at the edge of one building notes that the angle of elevation to the top of another building is 23°. If the buildings are 200 m apart at the base, how far is the surveyor from the top of the second building?

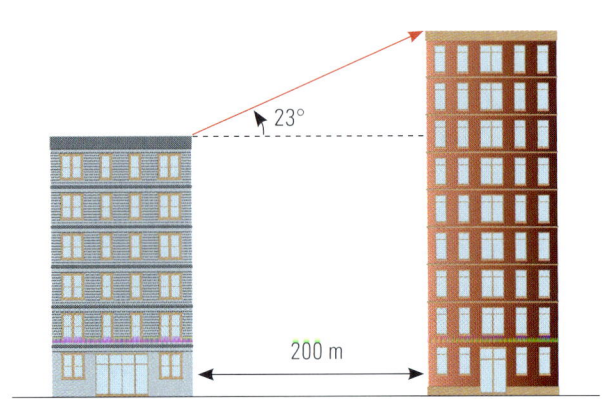

5. A telephone pole is diagonally braced by a piece of timber 6.8 feet long. The angle between the pole and the timber is 34°. How high up the pole does the timber reach?

298   MathWorks 10

6. Roger is a craftsperson and boat builder who lives and works in Iqaluit, Nunavut. One of Roger's skills is building kayaks. While traditional kayaks are covered in sealskin and use sinew as fastenings, Roger's boats are covered in canvas and use epoxy as a fastening. Roger must know the length of the tapered part at the front of the kayak to ensure he builds a boat with enough leg room. Each tapered side that forms the kayak's nose is 3 ft long. The kayak is 2 ft wide. What is the length (l) of the tapered section of the kayak?

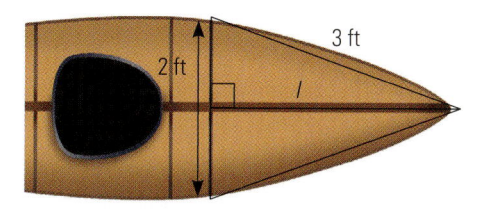

The kayak was originally used by Inuit people for hunting and transportation. The frame was made of driftwood or whalebone and the kayak's surface was made waterproof with whale fat. Today, kayaks can be made of fiberglass or molded plastic.

Extend your thinking

7. Laurie has been hired to design ski chalets in Jasper, Alberta. In her blueprint, she draws a right triangle with acute angle x, for which $\sin x = \cos x$, to represent the roof of the building. Draw the same figure Laurie drew. What type of triangle is it?

8. Frank uses a truck with a long arm called a "cherry picker" in his job repairing telephone lines. The arm has a maximum length of 9.8 m. If the angle of elevation from the mount to the top of the telephone pole is 48°, how far from the pole is the mount?

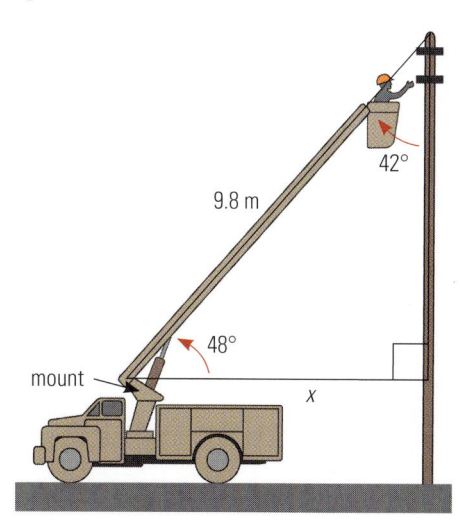

9. Two parallel chords of a circle are 4 cm apart and subtend angles of 120° and 90° at the centre. Find the radius of the circle and the length of each chord.

Chapter 7 Trigonometry of Right Triangles **299**

PROJECT—DESIGN A STAIRCASE FOR A HOME

MAKING A SCALE DIAGRAM OR A SCALE MODEL

Now that you have decided what type of staircase you will build, you can draw a scale diagram using similar triangles. Remember:

- the stringer is a timber that supports the treads and risers in a staircase
- the riser is the vertical distance between two stairs
- the run is the distance from the front to the back of each stair
- the tread is a separate piece of wood that covers a stair.

Determine the length and width of the stringer and the amount of wood needed for the risers and treads.

Be sure to keep track of all your calculations, because you will need them for the final presentation. Because many measurements in the construction trade are given in imperial, you may want to work in those units.

Discuss how tools such as dividers, stair gauges, and set squares will be used in helping you construct your stairs. How will the application of the tread boards affect the height of the steps?

A scale model of a staircase can help you to ensure that all the proportions are accurate.

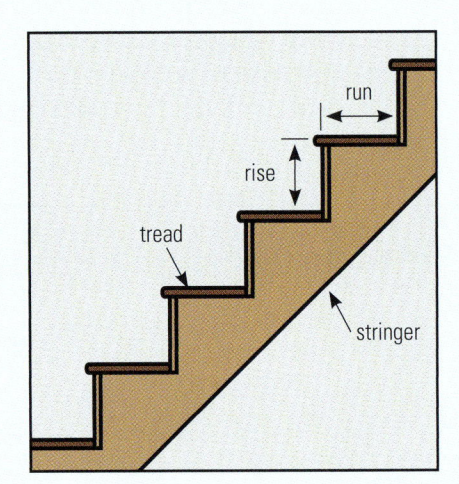

The Tangent Ratio

7.4

MATH *ON THE JOB*

When Chris Haika, of Calgary, Alberta, was in elementary school, he knew he wanted to fly airplanes. He got his pilot's licence in his last semester of high school and went on to Mount Royal College to get his aviation diploma. He worked part time washing airplanes, which helped him make contacts in the airline industry.

After getting his diploma, Chris worked as a customer agent for an airline in Grande Prairie, Alberta. After seven months, he was promoted to pilot.

Chris later moved back to Calgary. He's now a pilot in a small airline company that does charter flights as well as regular routes in Alberta and British Columbia.

When flying into Calgary, Chris has been at an elevation of 28 000 ft. His descent to the airport is at an angle of depression of 3°. At what horizontal distance from the airport must he begin his descent?

Chris Haika applies mathematical skills on the job as an airline pilot.

EXPLORE THE MATH

In previous sections, you worked with the sine and the cosine ratios, and in the example above you used them to determine the horizontal distance from the airport at which Chris must begin his descent. However, there is a more direct method for doing this calculation. You can use the **tangent** function. In the diagram shown, the tangent of angle A is $\frac{a}{b}$.

tangent: the ratio of the sides opposite and adjacent to an angle in a right triangle; abbreviated as tan

tangent ∠A = tan A

$$\tan A = \frac{\text{opposite}}{\text{adjacent}}$$

$$\tan A = \frac{\text{opp}}{\text{adj}}$$

1. Use this definition to calculate the distance from the airport where Chris must begin his airplane's descent.

2. Did you arrive at the same answer as before? Explain any discrepancy.

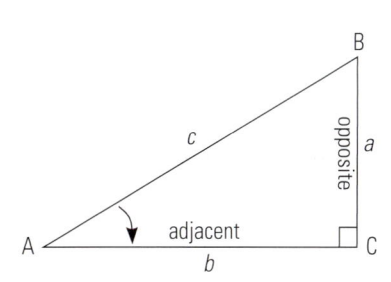

Chapter 7 Trigonometry of Right Triangles

ACTIVITY 7.5
DRAWING A TANGENT GRAPH

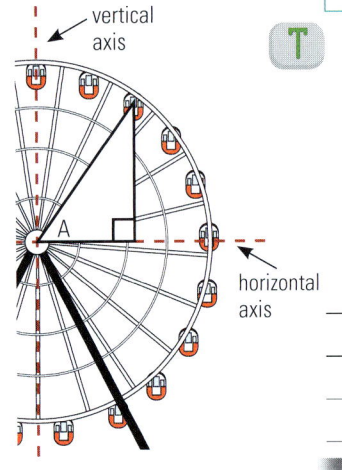

In Activity 7.4 you were asked to consider the horizontal distance of your Ferris wheel chair from a vertical line through the centre as you moved up the circle. Consider, now, the ratio of the vertical distance to the horizontal distance. This ratio would be the tangent of the angle. Using a table like the one provided, and determining the values using your calculator, fill in the values for y equals tan A for values of A that are multiples of 10° as before. Use these values to sketch the graph.

SOLVING TANGENTS

A	10°	20°	30°	40°	50°	60°	70°	80°
y = tan A								

1. You will notice that tan A can be greater than one, whereas sine and cosine cannot be greater than one. Explain why this is so.

2. What do you notice about the value of y or tan A as A increases from 10° to 80°?

3. Does this appear to be a linear graph? Explain how you know.

4. What do you think will happen to the value of tan A as A approaches zero (becomes very small)? Explain.

5. What do you think will happen to the value of tan A as A gets close to 90°. Explain.

6. Extend the graph to verify your prediction.

Example 1

Gull Harbour Lighthouse is located on Manitoba's Lake Winnipeg. Assume the lighthouse is 14.6 m tall and stands 7 m above the surface of the lake. If the angle of depression to a boat on Lake Winnipeg is measured at 27°, approximately how far away from the base of the lighthouse is the boat?

The Gull Harbour lighthouse is located on Lake Winnipeg in Hecla Provincial Park. It was built in 1898.

SOLUTION

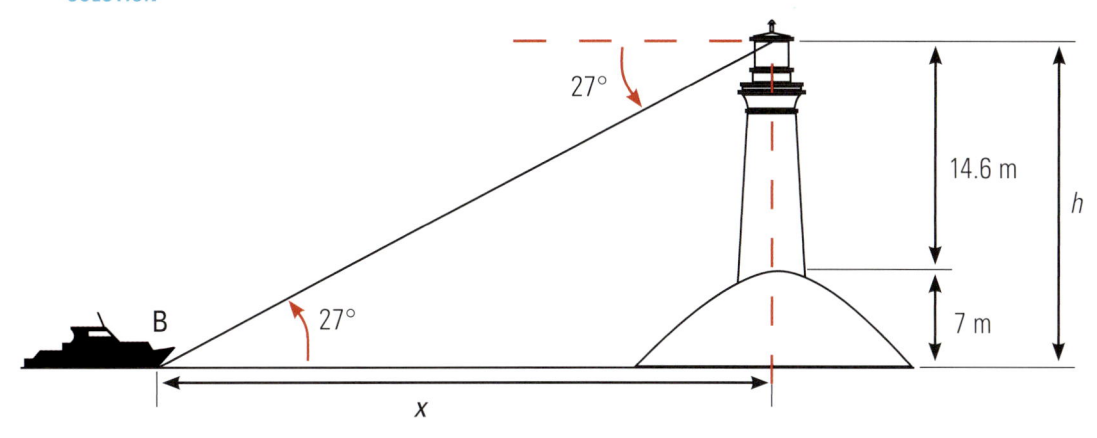

$\tan B = \dfrac{h}{x}$

$\tan 27° = \dfrac{h}{x}$

$\tan 27° = \dfrac{21.6}{x}$ Substitute known values into tan formula.

$x \tan 27° = 21.6$ Multiply both sides by x.

$x = \dfrac{21.6}{\tan 27°}$ Divide both sides by tan 27°.

$x = 42.4$ m

The boat is approximately 42.4 m from the island.

ACTIVITY 7.6
MAKING AND USING A CLINOMETER

To measure the angle of elevation or depression, several different instruments can be used. A clinometer can be improvised using a protractor, a straw, a string with a weight attached, and some tape for attaching them together.

1. Working with a partner, refer to the image shown here and use the necessary materials to help you construct a clinometer.

2. Explain how you will use your clinometer to find the angle of elevation.

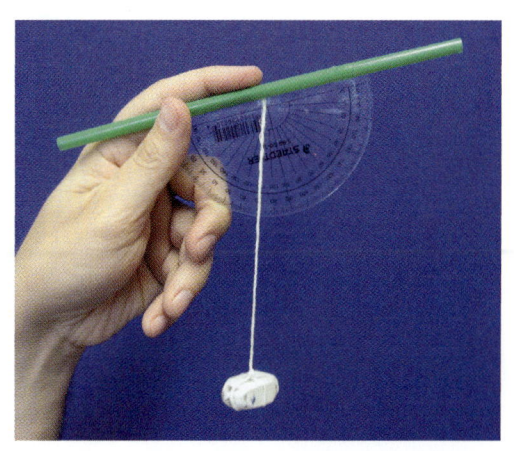

You can assemble a basic clinometer using a few common objects.

Chapter 7 Trigonometry of Right Triangles **303**

3. Using your clinometer, with a partner, determine the angle of elevation to the top of at least five buildings in or around your school or other objects whose height you cannot measure directly. Record the angle as well as your distance from the base on a chart similar to the one shown. Use this information to determine the height of each object.

DETERMINING HEIGHTS

object	angle of elevation	tangent of angle	distance from base	height of object

SAMPLE

Example 2

A dockworker pulls a light crate (measuring 2 m × 2 m × 2 m) up to the dock using a pulley system. The angle of elevation of the rope is 50°. The man is 2 m from the edge of the pier and the bundle clears the pier by 0.5 m. How close are the pulleys to each other when the bottom pulley is at hand level?

SOLUTION

Draw a simplified diagram.

$$\tan M = \frac{h}{d}$$

$$\tan 50° = \frac{h}{3.5}$$

$3.5 \tan 50° = h$ multiply both sides by 3.5

$4.2 \approx h$

The distance between the pulleys is approximately 4.2 m.

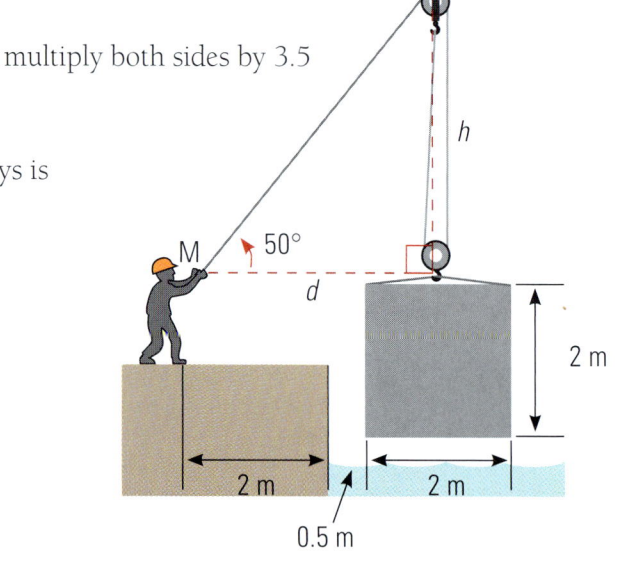

Mental Math and Estimation

The angle of depression from the top of a cliff to a boat in the water is 52°. What is the angle between the cliff and the line of sight?

BUILD YOUR SKILLS

1. The Lethbridge Viaduct, often referred to as the High Level Bridge, is the longest railway structure in Canada, at a length of 1624 m. It was built in 1908–09, at a cost of $1.3 million. The horizontal distance between the two sides of the coulees is 1620 m. An observer standing at one end notes that the angle of depression to the opposite side of the coulee over which it passes is 4°. What is the difference in elevation between the two sides of the coulee?

   Napi, whose name means "old man," is a mythical being in the Siksika Nation's culture. Napi is a respected figure who sometimes personifies the sun. He is also portrayed as a powerful trickster. Alberta's Oldman River, over which the High Level Bridge (pictured here) passes, is named after Napi.

2. Near Estevan, Saskatchewan, Mary and James like to lie on their backs in an open field to watch planes landing. One day as they watch, a helicopter approaches and hovers over a building 1 km away from them. If the angle of elevation is 25°, how high above the ground is the helicopter?

3. Una observed a boat from the top of a 70 m cliff near Atlin, BC. She noted that the angle of depression to the boat was 25°.

   a) The height of the cliff is what fraction of the distance to the boat?

   b) How far is the boat from the base of the cliff?

4. Mike and Lianne are lighting technicians who work for a special events company. Their current job is to set up the spotlights for an outdoor music festival. The performers want to suspend a banner with the name of their troupe directly above the stage, as high as possible, with a spotlight shining on it. Mike and Lianne have only one spotlight left. It is 50 m away from the stage and mounted on a stand 1.9 m high. It has a maximum angle of elevation of 41°. How high will the performers be able to suspend the banner?

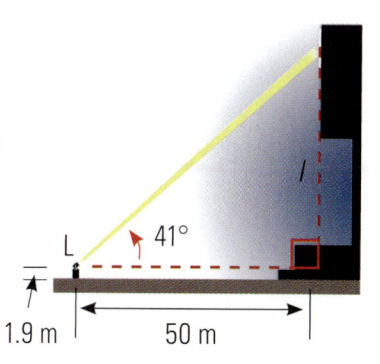

5. Johnny is in a hot air balloon 400 m above the ground. He observes his house at an angle of depression of 30°, his school at an angle of depression of 45°, and the soccer field house at an angle of depression of 60°.

   a) Which building is farthest away from Johnny?

   b) How far is the farthest building from a point on the ground directly under Johnny?

   c) How far is the closest building to the point on the ground directly under Johnny?

   A hot air balloon can float above the ground because the hot air contained within its fabric is less dense than the cold air outside it. This makes the balloon buoyant.

6. A crime scene investigator (CSI) is investigating a bullet hole in the side of a building. The hole is 2.4 m above the floor and entered the wall at an angle of 83°.

   a) In order to determine how far from the wall the gun was fired, what other information does the CSI need to know?

   b) If the suspect was lying on the ground when he took the shot, about how far from the wall was he?

   c) If his target was 1.7 m tall and 4 m from the wall, would he have been hit?

7. If the angle of elevation to the top of a tree is 30° from a point 12 m from its base, how tall is the tree to the nearest metre?

Extend your thinking

8. For more than 25 years, Whitehorse's *Association franco-yukonnaise* (AFY) has served as a cultural association for the 3550 francophones living in Yukon Territory. Manjula finds that the angle of elevation to the top of the *Centre de la francophonie*, the AFY's meeting place, is 55°. She walks back 100 feet in a straight line from her initial observation point and finds that the angle of elevation is now 42°. Find the height of the centre, to two decimals.

Finding Angles and Solving Right Triangles

7.5

MATH *ON THE JOB*

Betsy is a highway engineer who works in Saskatchewan. A highway engineer is a civil engineer who specializes in the design and constructions of roads. Training for this job involves a great deal of higher mathematics, but at times it is the simple mathematics that proves most useful. For example, when designing a road, Betsy must consider the steepness or grade. Cars and trucks will have to brake excessively while going down a hill that is too steep, or they will slow down too much trying to drive up a hill that is too sleep. There are several different ways in which one can talk about the steepness or grade of a road.

Betsy has been told that the grade of a particular road is 6.6%. This means that the road rises 6.6 vertical units for every 100 horizontal units. For calculation purposes, however, Betsy finds it more convenient to use the angle of elevation.

When highway engineers design and build highways, they must know the grade, or slope of the road.

Using the table of tangents you developed in Activity 7.5, determine the approximate angle of elevation of this road.

EXPLORE THE MATH

In the previous sections, you determined the length of the sides of right triangles when you knew the size of an acute angle. However, many times in industry, it is the size of the angle that needs to be determined. Fortunately you can usually do this using your calculator. You will notice that above each of the trigonometric functions the same word appears with what looks like an exponent of negative 1. It is not really an exponent, but indicates something referred to as "the inverse" of the function. This means it "undoes" the function, or that it will give you the angle if you know the value of that particular trigonometric function. To do this, you will need to use the "second function" or "shift" button on your calculator.

Make a table similar to the one shown and use your calculator to fill in the second row, accurate to 4 decimal places.

To fill in the last row, press the 2nd function or shift button on your calculator then the same trig function as in the first row. Enter the value from the second row. Put this answer in the third row.

HINT

Make sure your calculator is in degree mode.

TRIGONOMETRIC RATIOS

trig function	sin 20°	cos 43°	tan 71°	sin 47°	cos 82°	tan 47°	sin 35°	cos 75°	tan 12°
value									
inverse trig function									

SAMPLE

T 1. What do you notice about the first and third rows?

2. Can you think of any other times when you "undid" an operation?

Now that you can find an angle given the trigonometric ratio, you can "solve" right triangles. This simply means that you can find all unknown parts of the triangle given two sides or one side and one acute angle of the triangle.

Example 1

Determine the angle indicated in each of the following.

a) A guy wire 8.5 m long is attached 5.7 m from the base of a pole.

b) The angle of depression from a point 10.1 m down a hill if the horizontal distance is 6.9 m.

c) The angle between the side of a house and the glass roof of a small bay window, if the bay window is 75 inches deep and the vertical displacement of the roof is 42 inches.

SOLUTION

a) $\cos B = \dfrac{adj}{hyp}$

$\cos B = \dfrac{a}{c}$

$\cos B = \dfrac{5.7}{8.5}$

$\cos B = 0.6706$

$\cos B = \cos^{-1}(0.6706)$

$\cos B = 48°$

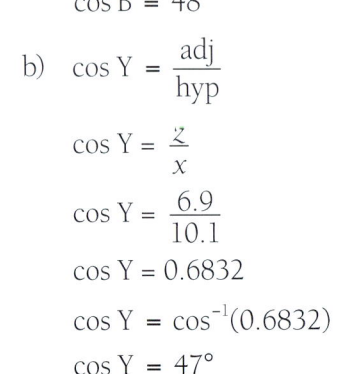

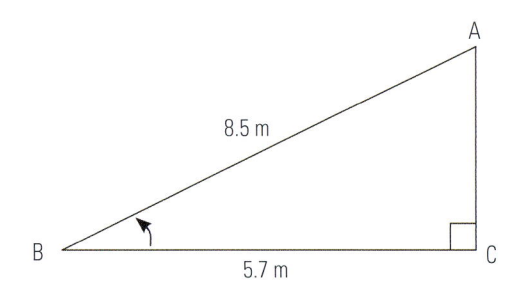

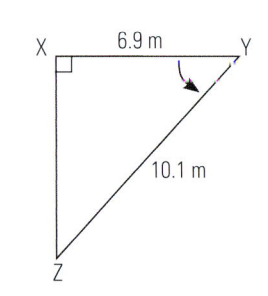

b) $\cos Y = \dfrac{adj}{hyp}$

$\cos Y = \dfrac{z}{x}$

$\cos Y = \dfrac{6.9}{10.1}$

$\cos Y = 0.6832$

$\cos Y = \cos^{-1}(0.6832)$

$\cos Y = 47°$

c) Find the hypotenuse using the Pythagorean theorem.

$n^2 = m^2 + l^2$

$n^2 = (42)^2 + (75)^2$

$n^2 = 1764 + 5625$

$n^2 = 7389$

$n = \sqrt{7389}$

$n \approx 85.96''$

Next, find the cosine of L.

$\cos L = \dfrac{\text{adj}}{\text{hyp}}$

$\cos L = \dfrac{m}{n}$

$\cos L = \dfrac{42}{85.96}$

$\cos L = 0.4886$

$\cos L = \cos^{-1}(0.4886)$

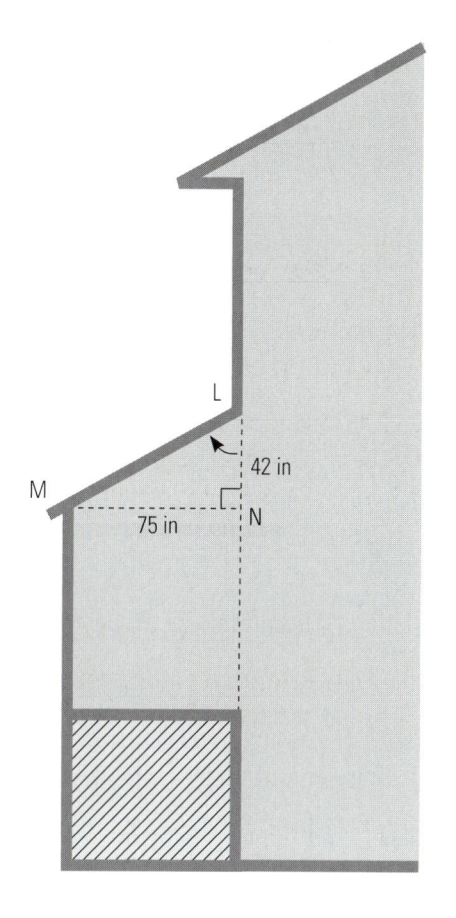

$\cos L = 61°$

DISCUSS THE IDEAS
ALTERNATIVE APPROACHES

In Example 1a, b could be determined using the Pythagorean theorem, or by using trigonometric ratios and angles. Calculate b using both methods. Which method would be more accurate in this case? Why?

Example 2

The Pulaarvik Kablu Friendship Centre in Rankin Inlet, Nunavut, is a place where elders share their skills and knowledge with young people. Tagak is one of the maintenance people who cares for the centre. Her current job is to replace the centre's front steps. She knows that the distance between the ground and the landing is 0.86 m and that the stairs end at a point 1.2 m from the edge of the landing.

a) What will be the angle of elevation from the bottom to the landing?

b) What is the distance between the bottom of the stairs and the landing?

A staircase that is easy to use has wide steps and a gentle grade.

Chapter 7 Trigonometry of Right Triangles **309**

SOLUTION

a) First, find the tangent ratio. Remember that it is standard to keep four decimals in a trigonometric ratio.

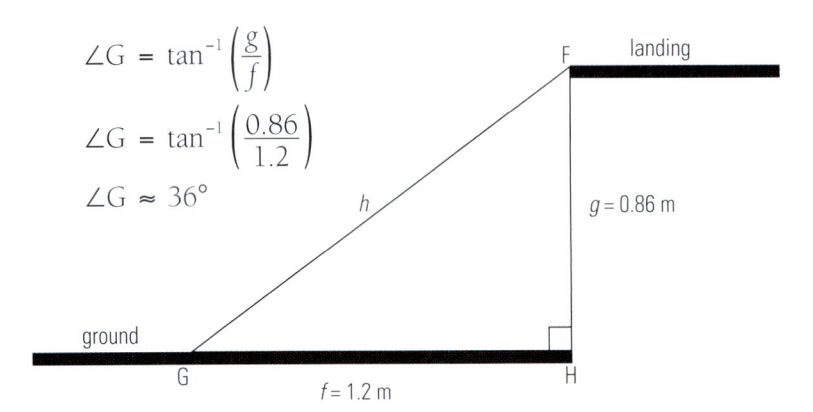

$$\angle G = \tan^{-1}\left(\frac{g}{f}\right)$$

$$\angle G = \tan^{-1}\left(\frac{0.86}{1.2}\right)$$

$$\angle G \approx 36°$$

Therefore, the angle of elevation is approximately 36°.

b) Distance h is the hypotenuse of the right triangle. Use the Pythagorean theorem.

$$f^2 + g^2 = h^2$$
$$(1.2)^2 + (0.86)^2 = h^2$$
$$h^2 = 1.44 + 0.7396$$
$$h^2 = 2.1796$$
$$h = \sqrt{2.1796}$$
$$h \approx 1.5 \text{m}$$

Therefore the distance from the bottom of the stairs to the landing is approximately 1.5 m.

ALTERNATIVE SOLUTION

$$\angle G = 36°$$

$$\sin G = \frac{0.86}{h}$$

$$\sin 36° = \frac{0.86}{h}$$

$h \sin 36° = 0.86$ Multiply both sides by h.

$h = \dfrac{0.86}{\sin 36°}$ Divide both sides by $\sin 36°$.

$h \approx 1.5$ m

ACTIVITY 7.7
ROCK BAND LIGHTING

You and your partner are working as lighting technicians for a rock band, L & N. The band has asked that you position lights off the floor 10 m from the lead singer. The red, blue, and green lights are to be placed at heights of 10 m, 9 m, and 7 m respectively.

Determine the angle of elevation at which to set each light so it lights up the lead singer.

Lighting technicians find work on television and film sets, or in theatres.

HINT

Draw a diagram to help you visualize the lighting arrangement.

Mental Math and Estimation

What is the tangent of a 45° angle?

BUILD YOUR SKILLS

1. Emile is cutting pieces of stained glass to replace a window in his local church. He's been given rough diagrams of the pieces he needs to cut, but some of the measurements are missing. Provide the missing measurements for a) and b).

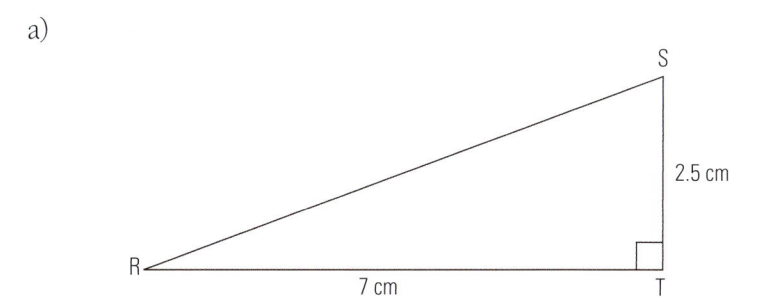

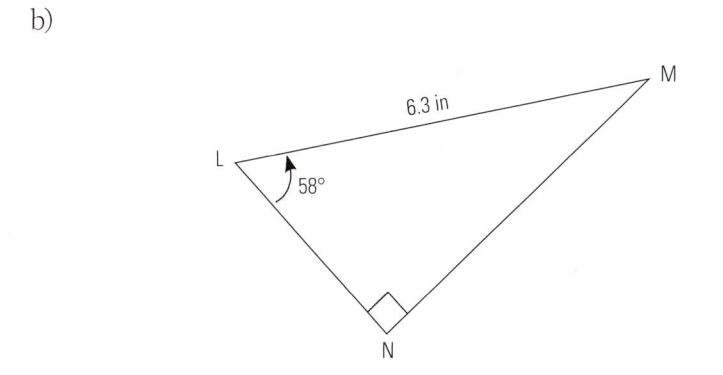

   a)

   b)

2. Heather is working on a brochure about hiking trails in Prince Albert National Park. One of the hills on a trail has an angle of elevation of 15°, with a viewpoint 100 m from its base. Imagine that you walk along the trail from the base to the viewpoint.

   a) How much altitude would you gain?

   b) What horizontal distance would you cover?

   c) What is the grade of the trail, written as a percent?

3. David is a carpenter who is planning to renovate his own house. He is now working on the specification for the roof.

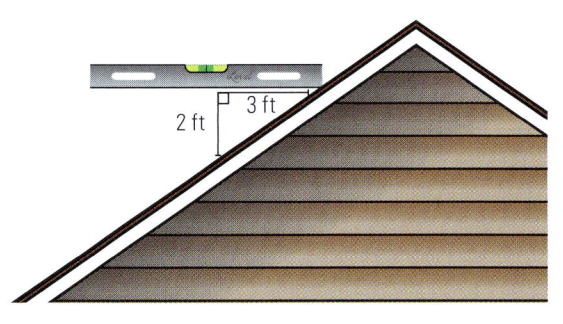

   a) The roof rises 2 feet for every 3 horizontal feet. What should David write in the specification as its angle of elevation?

   b) The roof is going to be 20 feet long and rise 12 feet. David wants to cover it with shingles. What should he write in the specification as the roof's total area?

4. The Commodity Exchange Building in Winnipeg is 117 m tall. Pia is a telescopic crane operator who has been hired to do some repairs to the building's exterior. The base of her crane is 2 m tall and her crane is positioned 8 m away from the building. Pia extends the extension cylinder, or arm, of the crane until its tip is positioned 15 m up the side of the building.

   a) How long must the extension cylinder be to reach the side of the building?

   b) What is the angle of elevation of the crane's extension cylinder?

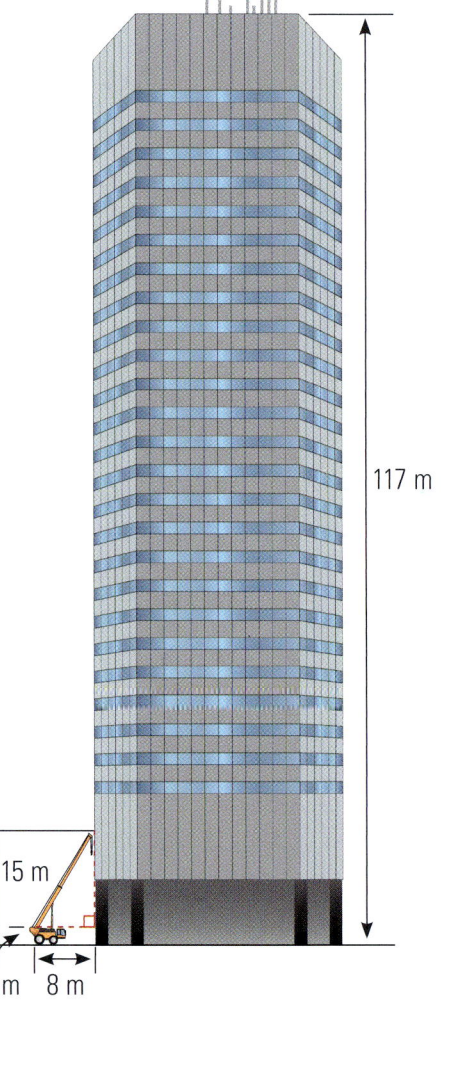

Hiking is a great activity to do with friends.

Wheat, barley and canola are some of the commodities that are traded at Winnipeg's Commodity Exchange Tower. The tower opened in 1979.

312 MathWorks 10

5. A 15 m ladder is placed against the side of an apartment and reaches a windowsill that is 12 m above the ground.

   a) What is the angle of elevation of the ladder?

   b) How far from the base of the apartment is the ladder?

6. Georges is a surveyor working near North Battleford, Saskatchewan. He looks through his theodolite, which is 1.8 m high, and sights the top of a small rock bluff from 15.9 m away. Georges determines that the bluff is 7.2 m tall.

   What is the angle of depression from the top of the bluff to George's theodolite?

7. A traffic helicopter is hovering over the evening rush hour in Vancouver, BC. The traffic reporter observes a traffic accident at an intersection. Using her GPS she determines that the horizontal distance from the helicopter to the intersection is 400 m. She also estimates that the angle of depression from the helicopter to the intersection is 20°. The helicopter begins to rise vertically, and 3 minutes later the reporter estimates that the angle of depression to the intersection is 45°.

   Electric streetcars, which run along tram tracks, came to Lisbon, Portugal in 1901. These bright yellow cars connect Lisbon's many neighbourhoods.

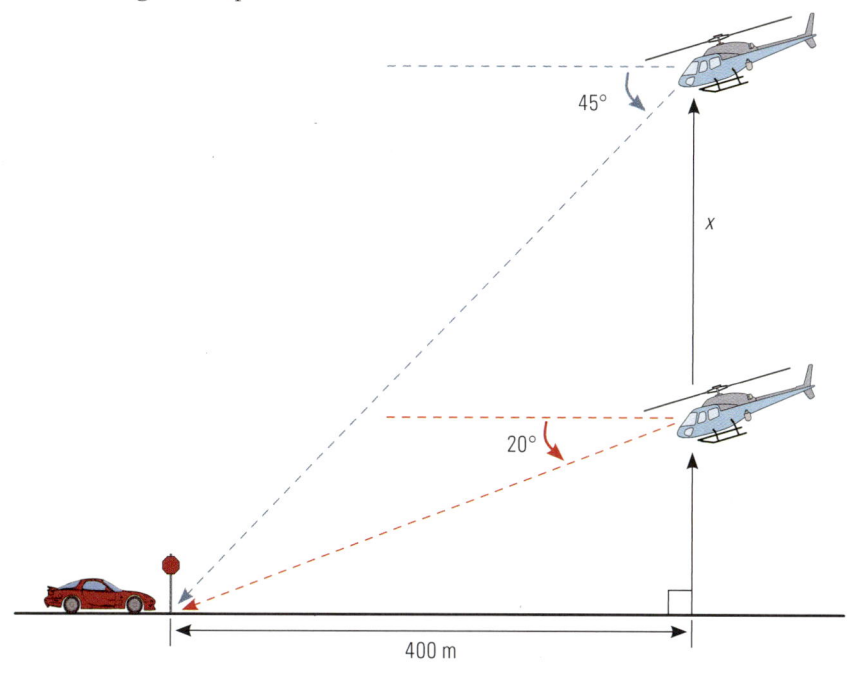

   a) How far did the helicopter rise in 3 minutes?

   b) At what speed did the helicopter rise, assuming constant speed?

8. Railway engineers must consider the steepness or grade of the terrain when constructing tracks. Early train tracks in England had very gentle gradients such as 0.05% because locomotive engines were weak. Now, locomotives are much more powerful. One of the steepest non-track railway lines is the Lisbon tram in Portugal. It has a grade of 13.5%. What is the angle of elevation of this track?

Extend your thinking

9. A pipe fitter must install pipes around an obstruction as in the diagram. He uses a 60° elbow at the left top, and a 45° elbow at the right top. The offset in each case is 1.8 m and the horizontal pipe is 2.6 m.

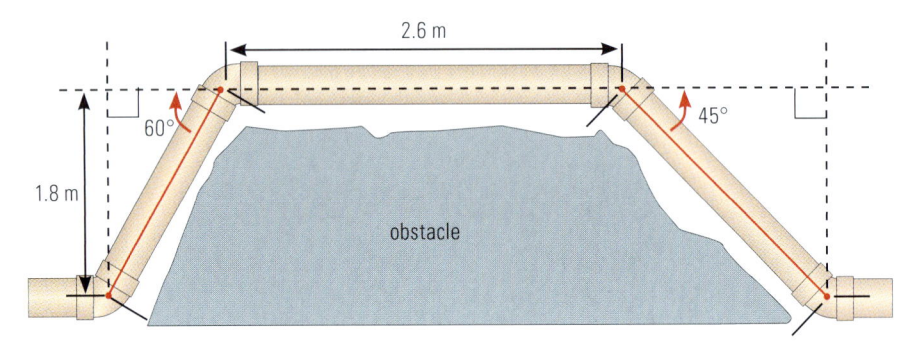

   a) How far is it from the end of one lower pipe to the other? (Round to the nearest tenth.)

   b) How much pipe will he need in total to get around the obstruction? (Round to the nearest tenth.)

   c) Do you think the pipe fitter would have to be more accurate than the nearest tenth of a metre in his measurements? Why or why not?

PUZZLE IT OUT

16 SQUARES

In this game, you will work with the Pythagorean theorem and trigonometric functions.

You will be given 16 squares with either an expression that needs solving or a solution on each side.

To play the game, calculate the value of a question on one side of a square and find the corresponding answer or an equivalent expression on the side of another square.

Match corresponding sides. The aim is to have all the pieces form a 4 by 4 square, with all the sides corresponding.

HINT

Some answers match more than one place and some do not match any side at all.

PROJECT—DESIGN A STAIRCASE FOR A HOME

COMPILING YOUR WORK AND PREPARING YOUR PRESENTATION

You now have a package that you could present to a carpenter so that she or he could easily build the staircase that you designed. Your package includes:

- a staircase design drawn to scale, with all measurements shown;
- a list of all materials needed for construction (in imperial units) and the steps involved;
- a written discussion of how you would use the various tools to help you construct your staircase; and
- an organized set of calculations used in designing your staircase.

Good tradespeople often ask questions to clarify the requirements of a job. Your teacher and classmates may also ask you some questions about your staircase design. Be prepared to answer questions about your work, including:

- What is the angle of elevation of your staircase?
- Where are there pairs of similar triangles?
- Where did you use the Pythagorean theorem and the sine, cosine, or tangent functions in your calculations?
- Why did you select this design?

Determining the angle of elevation of a staircase is an important step in its design and construction.

REFLECT ON YOUR LEARNING
TRIGONOMETRY OF RIGHT TRIANGLES

Now that you have finished this chapter, you should be able to

☐ use the Pythagorean theorem to find the missing side of a right triangle;

☐ determine which of the three basic trigonometric functions applies to a given situation;

☐ apply the three basic trigonometric functions to find a missing side or angle of a right triangle;

☐ determine workplace applications of trigonometry.

You will also have finished a chapter project that allowed you to apply these skills in a practical way to a real-world task.

PRACTISE YOUR NEW SKILLS

1. Are the triangles with the following lengths of sides right triangles? Show how you know.

    a) 6 cm, 12 cm, 18 cm

    b) 4 ft, 5 ft, 9 ft

    c) 16 cm, 30 cm, 34 cm

    d) 25", 60", 65"

    e) 0.5 m, 0.12 m, 0.13 cm

2. Renée is on a canoe trip on Tramping Lake, Manitoba. She chose to visit the area so that she could see the pictographs of snakes, birds, and other animals that First Nations people drew on the lake's cliffs. They are estimated to be between 1500 and 3000 years old. Renée is in her canoe, 5 m away from the base of the cliff on which some pictographs are drawn. The distance from the tip of her canoe to the pictographs measures 10 m. How high up the cliff are the pictographs?

3. Sarbjit can walk to his school in Prince Rupert, BC, on the road or he can cut diagonally across the field. The field is 150 m by 90 m.

    a) How much distance does he save if he takes the shortcut?

    b) Why do you think he might not want to take the shortcut?

4. The grade of a road averages 5° to the horizontal.

    a) If you move 2 km along the road, what is your change in altitude?

    b) If the grade were decreased, would the change in altitude be more or less? Explain your answer.

5. Marcy, who is 1.5 m tall, looks up towards a tree directly in her line of vision. Beyond the tree she sees the top of another tree. If the first tree is 2 m taller than Marcy and 5 m away from her and the second tree is 7 m beyond the first, how tall is the second tree?

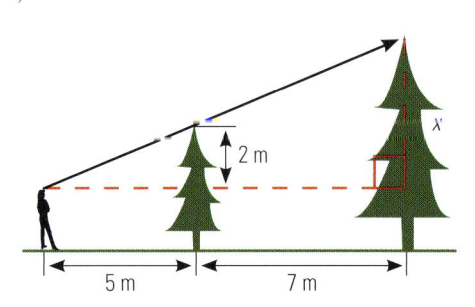

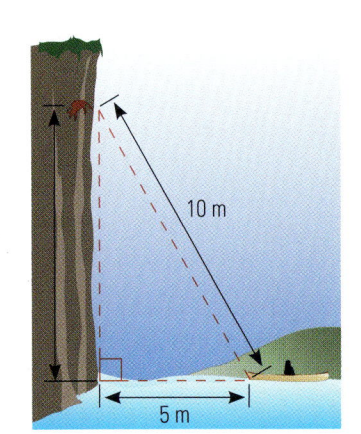

A road's steepness is measured by grade. For example, from Skagway to White Pass, the grade of the South Klondike Highway is 11%

316 MathWorks 10

6. Wei Lee is trying to determine the length of the lake in the diagram shown. How long is it?

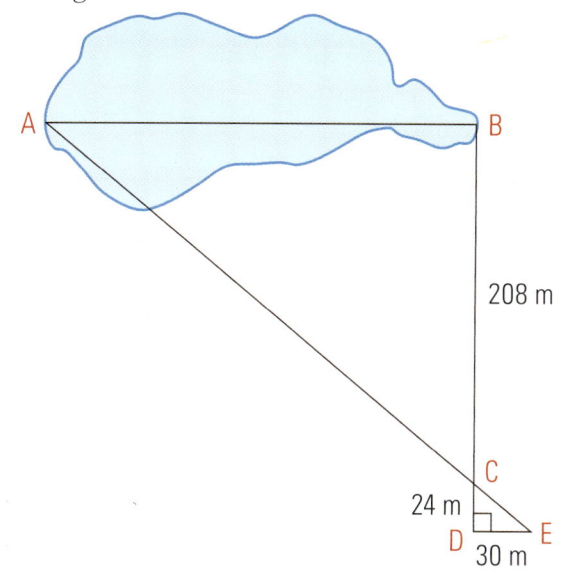

This view of Bennett Lake shows a bridge in Carcross, Yukon. Bennett Lake is well-known by boaters as a lake that can quickly become wavy and difficult to navigate when winds are strong.

7. The angle of elevation of a rafter is 32°. The width of the structure is 8 m.

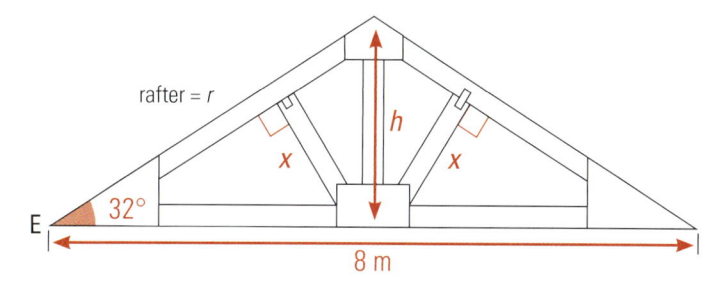

   a) Find the vertical height (h).

   b) How long are the support pieces (x)?

   c) What is the length of the rafter (r)?

8. To determine how much gravel has been removed from a gravel pit, a surveyor must determine the depth of the pit. Using a theodolite and electronic distance measurement equipment (EDM), he determines that the distance down the slope to the bottom of the pit is 300 m and the angle of depression of the slope is 46°.

   a) How deep is the gravel pit?

   b) How would knowing the depth help the surveyor determine the amount of gravel removed? What else would he have to know?

Saskatchewan has several active gravel pits. The extracted gravel is used for road construction and maintenance.

Chapter 7 Trigonometry of Right Triangles **317**

9. Nicolas is working as a lighting technician at the Paralympic Games. One of his jobs is to position spotlights on a podium during the medals ceremony for wheelchair racing. The lights are fixed on a backdrop that is 6 m tall. They must shine on the spot where the medalists are located, 2.5 m from the base of the backdrop. By how many degrees must the light directly behind the medalists be depressed?

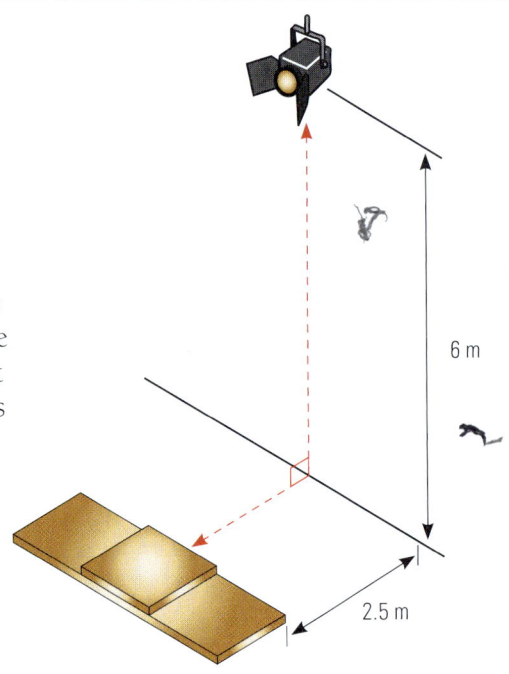

At the Paralympic Games, the fastest athletes in wheelchair racing have reached speeds of more than 30 kilometres an hour.

Extend your thinking

10. The cylindrical part of a grain storage bin is 9.8 m high and 7.3 m in diameter. The grain must enter through a hole on the centre of the top.

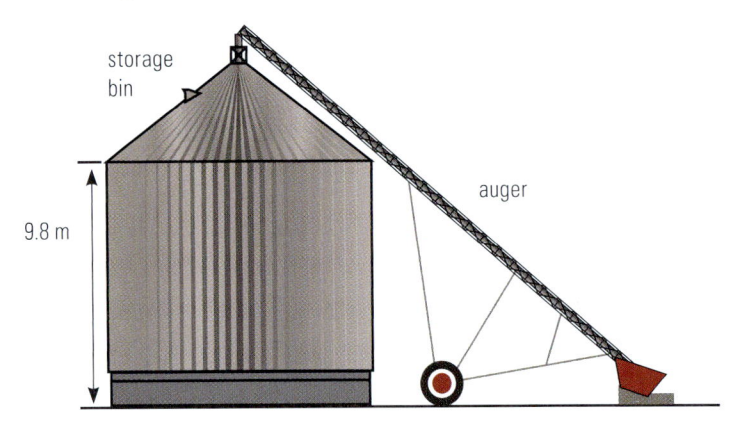

    a) Sketch the storage bin and the auger and label the dimensions and the angle of elevation.

    b) What is the shortest auger that can be used to fill the bin if the angle of elevation must be no more than 40°?

11. What is the grade of a flat road (one that does not have a hill)?

12. The world's tallest building, the Burj Dubai, was scheduled for completion in 2009. From a point 2 km above the ground, the angle of depression to the top of the Burj is approximately 17°. The angle of elevation from a point on the ground directly below this and to the top of the building is approximately 12°.

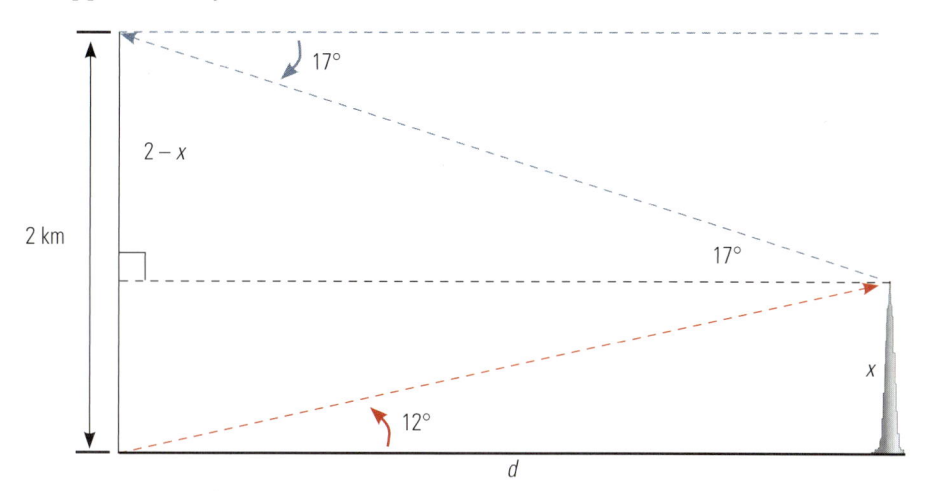

Determine the approximate height of the Burj.

13. Katarina says she does not need a calculator or table of trigonometric functions to solve right triangles that have acute angles of 45° or 60°. Explain (using diagrams) how she might do this.

The world's tallest building, the Burj Dubai, also contains the world's tallest service elevator. It has the capacity to carry 5500 kg.

Glossary

alternate exterior angles: angles in opposite positions outside two lines intersected by a transversal

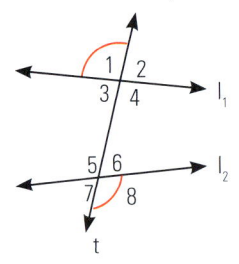

alternate interior angles: angles in opposite positions between two lines intersected by a transversal and also on alternate sides of the same transversal

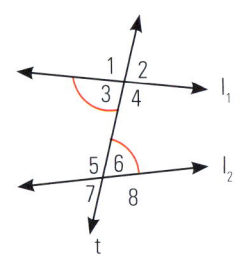

angle bisector: a segment, ray, or line that separates two halves of a bisected angle

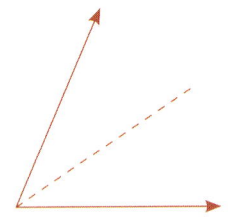

angle measure: the gap between the two rays, expressed in degrees

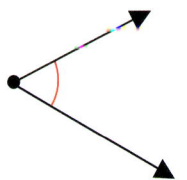

angle of depression: the angle formed between the horizontal and the line of sight while looking downwards

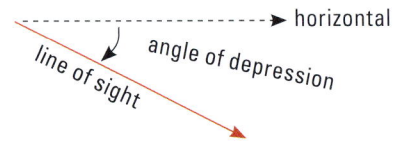

angle of elevation: the angle formed between the horizontal and the line of sight when looking upwards; sometimes referred to as the angle of inclination

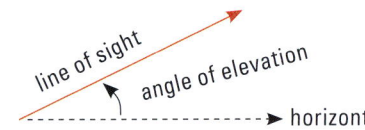

angle referent: a common standard of angle measure, for example, 0°, 45°, 90°, 180°, and 360°. They are used to estimate angles.

angles: two rays or line segments that meet at a point, called the vertex

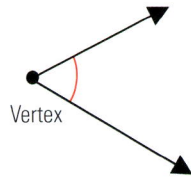

base unit: a unit of measurement on which other units are based

benefits: a range of programs that benefit employees; these vary from employer to employer

biweekly: every two weeks

bonus: extra pay earned when certain conditions of employment have been met or exceeded

buying rate: the rate at which a currency exchange buys money from customers

capacity: the maximum amount that a container can hold

commission: an amount, usually a percentage, paid to someone for a business transaction

complementary angles: two angles that have measures that add up to 90°

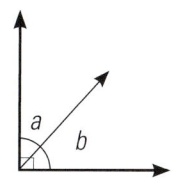

congruent: the same shape and size

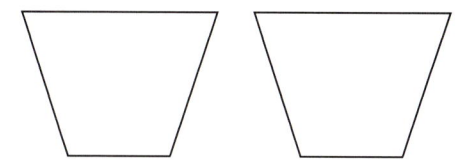

contract: a legal agreement that outlines terms, conditions, and payments for work to be done

conversion factor: a number by which a quantity expressed in one unit must be multiplied to convert it

convex polygon: a two-dimensional shape that has three or more sides that intersect at vertices that point outwards

corresponding angles: two angles that are congruent and occupy the same relative position in similar figures or at two different intersections

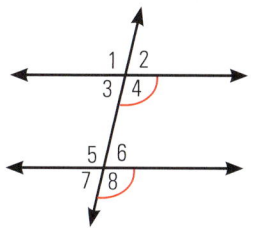

corresponding sides (in similar figures): two sides that occupy the same relative position in similar figures

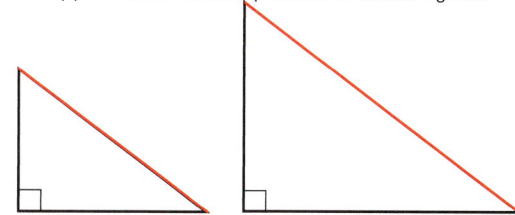

cosine: in a right triangle, the ratio of the length of the side adjacent to a given angle to the length of the hypotenuse (abbreviated as cos)

currency: the system of money a country uses

exchange rate: the price of one country's currency in terms of another nation's currency

framing square: a metal tool used to lay out right angles

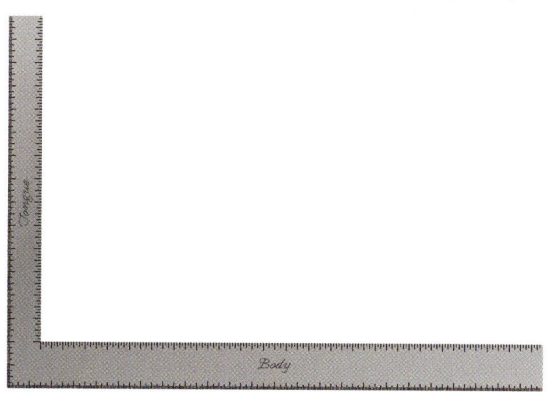

geometric net: a two-dimensional pattern used to construct three-dimensional shapes

gross pay: the total amount of money earned; also called gross earnings

hypotenuse: the longest side of a triangle, opposite the 90° angle

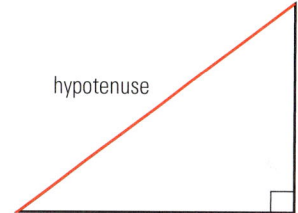

kilogram: the mass of one litre of water at 4°C

leg: in a right triangle, the two sides that intersect to form a right angle

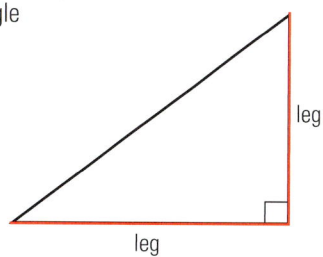

markup: the difference between the amount a dealer sells a product for and the amount he or she paid for it

mass: a measure of the quantity of matter in an object

minimum wage: the minimum amount a worker must be paid an hour; this rate varies, depending on which province or territory you live in

Glossary

net pay: also known as take-home pay; refers to the money paid to an employee after deductions have been made

pay statement: a form an employer gives an employee that shows earnings and deductions from earnings for a defined pay period

percent: percent means "out of 100"; a percentage is a ratio in which the denominator is 100

piecework: when someone is paid a set rate for an amount produced

promotion: an activity that increases awareness of a product or attracts customers

proportion: a fractional statement of equality between two ratios and rates

Pythagorean theorem: in a right triangle, the sum of the squares of the lengths of the legs is equal to the square of the length of the hypotenuse

Pythagorean triple: any set of three natural numbers that satisfy the Pythagorean theorem

rate: a comparison between two numbers with different units

ratio: a comparison between two numbers with the same units

regular pentagon: a five-sided polygon where all sides have the same length and all angles have the same measure

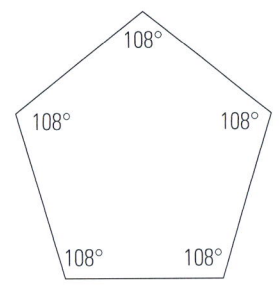

right triangle: a triangle with one right angle

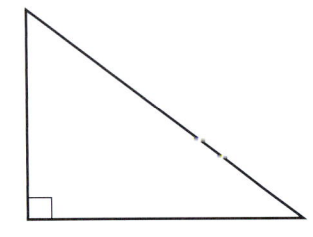

scale factor: the ratio of the lengths of corresponding sides of two polygons

self-employed: a person who works for him- or herself rather than for an employer

selling rate: the rate at which a currency exchange sells money to its customers

semi-monthly: twice a month

shift premium: extra payment for non-standard work hours

similar figures: figures that have the same shape

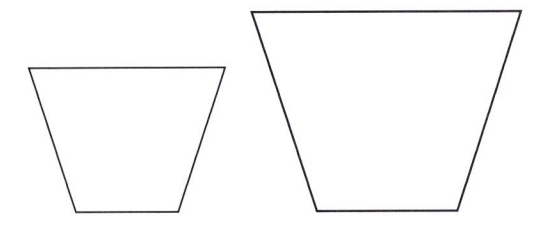

sine: in a right triangle, the ratio of the length of the side opposite a given angle to the length of the hypotenuse (abbreviated as sin)

supplementary angles: two angles that have measures that add up to 180°

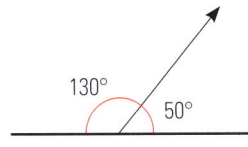

surface area: the total area of the surface of a three-dimensional object

tangent: the ratio of the sides opposite and adjacent in a right triangle (abbreviated as tan)

taxable income: income on which federal and provincial/territorial tax is paid

tonne: a metric ton; 1000 kilograms

transversal: a line that intersects two or more lines

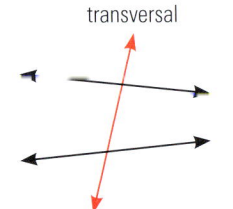

true bearing: the angle measured clockwise between true north and an intended path or direction, expressed in degrees

unit price: the cost of one unit; a rate expressed as a fraction in which the denominator is 1

unit rate: the rate or cost for one item or unit

vertically opposite angles: angles created by intersecting lines that share only a vertex

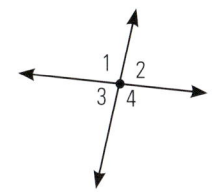

volume: the amount of space a solid occupies

weight: a measure of the force of gravity on an object

Answer Key

CHAPTER 1
UNIT PRICING AND CURRENCY EXCHANGE
1.1 PROPORTIONAL REASONING

PRACTISE YOUR NEW SKILLS, PAGE 21

1. 4 to 1; 4:1; $\frac{4}{1}$

2. 36 minutes, rounded to the nearest minute.

3. 5 trucks: 75 minutes; 2 tires: 7.5 minutes

4. 13 cars were sold on each day; the proportion of cars sold on Saturday is 13:36.

5. 121 cm tall, to the nearest centimetre.

6. 50 DVDs: $637.50; 900 DVDs: $11 475.00

7. The restaurant could buy 25 kg of olives for $75.00; it would cost $60.00 to buy 20 kg of olives.

8. red mahogany: 6.86 L; Spanish oak: 5.14 L

Extend your thinking

9. Yuki is closer to being right (5.57 days). However, both Keiko and Yuki underestimated how fast the Shinkasen can go.

1.2 UNIT PRICE

BUILD YOUR SKILLS, PAGE 26

1. $87.75

2. The third package (21 kg for $50.99) has the lowest unit cost of $2.43/kg.

3. The first supplier has the lower cost per lock; Answers may vary. Example: You should consider the quality of the locks, since you want them to be secure.

4. a) package of two: $7.75/shirt; package of three: $7.66/shirt

   b) The best combination is to buy one package of 3 shirts and two packages of 2 shirts for $53.97.

5. The second price is the best at $12.50/kg; the customer should buy 1 kg at the second price and 1.5 kg at the third.

6. The last package of meat, $29.50 for 2 kg, has the lowest unit price; the store from question 5 has two unit prices that are lower than this, so it would be better to buy your meat at the other store.

Extend your thinking

7. The least expensive combination is 3 large kits and 1 medium kit at a price of $269.75.

1.3 SETTING A PRICE

BUILD YOUR SKILLS, PAGE 32

1. $36.40/shirt

2. $325.34; the GST is $15.49.

3. $217.68

4. $1099.76

5. a) $1373.25

   b) Parminder receives $150.00 more if she sells directly from her farm; answers may vary. Example: Parminder might receive larger orders by selling to wholesalers.

6. a) $2.88

   b) $38.00

   c) Answers may vary. Example: Julie could source less expensive ingredients and supplies.

7. Answers may vary. Example: 50% discount is common for out-of-season items. Marie's profits will be lower, but some revenue is better than no revenue. Marie might reason that it would be best to recover some of her costs.

Extend your thinking

8. At cost, 250 g is $4.38.

   a) Answers may vary. Example: Pricing factors include overhead costs such as the rent and utilities.

   b) $6.13

   c) $5.21

d) Yes, you would still be making a gross profit because your product has still been marked up by 25%.

1.4 ON SALE!

BUILD YOUR SKILLS, PAGE 37

1. a) $8.84

   b) Marylyn saves 25% because she has saved $2.94, which is about 25% of $11.78.

2. a) Ross's store: $52.45; Al's store: $49.94

   b) Yes, Al is right. With the sale, the racquet at his store is less expensive.

3. a) Morning appointments will get you the lowest price.

   b) Answers may vary. Example: The coupon will appeal more because you know how much you are saving without having to do any calculations.

4. $1831.50; $28.80

5. a) store 1: $3132.15; store 2: $3129.00

   b) The second wholesaler offers a better buy.

6. a) shirts: 38%; shorts: 32%; jacket: 50%

   b) $45.00 total savings. The customer would save the most money on the jacket ($25.00).

Extend your thinking

7. a) regular price: $1601.60; discount price: $1521.52; savings: $80.08

   b) $7.28

1.5 CURRENCY EXCHANGE RATES

BUILD YOUR SKILLS, PAGE 47

1. a) 1.644 814
   b) 0.133 451
   c) 0.019 360

2. a) 0.009 295
   b) 0.950 964
   c) 1.004 350

3. a) $375.49 CAD
   b) $3211.28 CAD
   c) $3477.79 CAD
   d) $17 057.07 CAD

4. €729.57

5. a) 395.18 euros
   b) 639.13 francs
   c) 3702.48 kronor
   d) $612.98 CAD; Opal receives a lower amount back because bank buy and sell rates are different—the banks build in a profit margin for exchanging money.

6. Pebble Beach: $5193.25 CAD
   St. Andrew's: $17 511.24 CAD
   Spring City Golf & Lake Resort: $4325.16 CAD
   SAFRA Resort & Country Club: $11 434.20 CAD
   Leopoldsdorf: $6579.26 CAD

Extend your thinking

7. a) Answers will vary because conversions change daily. Example: US$8.73 (rate: 1 CAD = 0.975229 USD); AU$9.39 (rate: 1 CAD = 1.04905 AUD)
   b) US price: US$9.91; Australian price: AUD$11.51

PRACTISE YOUR NEW SKILLS, PAGE 50

1. a) 40 km; 200 km
   b) $15.90 CAD

2. 300 loaves

3. a) 7.5 m/second
   b) $0.23/egg

4. No, you can't use a photocopier to enlarge a 4 × 6 photo to another standard photo size because the sizes are not proportional to each other; you can make any proportion that is equivalent to 8:10. For example, 4:5 or 2.5:3.125.

5. a) unit price of 5 lb bag: $0.38/lb; unit price of 20 lb bag: $0.30/lb; the 20-lb bag is the better buy.
   b) Answers may vary. Example: You will want to consider the quality of the potatoes and the quantity that you can use.
   c) This is the best buy at a unit price of $0.20/lb. However, you may have reasons other than price to consider. Example: You may not be able to use 75 lbs of potatoes.

6. Too Good To Be True offers the best deal ($955.49 instead of $999.99).

7. a) 5 cups of flour

   b) flour: $1\frac{2}{3}$ cups; sugar: $\frac{1}{3}$ cup

8. a) $795.00 CAD

   b) $798.98 CAD

9. $1284.05 CAD

10. a) $9.50/h

    b)

CALCULATING EARNINGS	
Hours	Dollars earned
0	0
1	$9.50
2	$19.00
3	$28.50
4	$38.00
5	$47.50

    c)

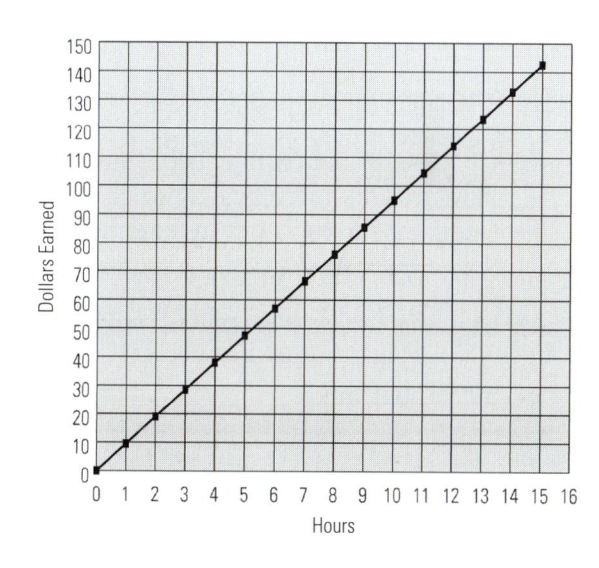

    d) 3.5 hours of work: $33.25; 12.5 hours of work: $118.75

CHAPTER 2
EARNING AN INCOME
2.1 WAGES AND SALARIES

BUILD YOUR SKILLS, PAGE 60

1. a) $947.20/week

   b) $49 254.40/year

2. Biweekly payments occur every second week; semi-monthly payments occur twice a month.

3. Calculate how many hours Luc works in a month (4.33 weeks). Then, divide Luc's monthly pay by his monthly hours (52 h/month). Luc earns about $9.56/h.

4. Factors to consider: how many lawns you can cut in an hour; whether you are a particularly fast worker; whether the job would take longer under some conditions (such as wet grass).

5. Her monthly wage is $496.74. Her earnings would increase by $152.76 a month.

6. $30.00/h

7. a) $30 539.19

   b) $32 398.91

8. **Nov. 15**

   a) 3 h 2 min

   b) 3.03 h, rounded

   Nov. 16

   a) 5 h 4 min

   b) 5.07 h, rounded

Nov. 17

a) 3 h 2 min

b) 3.03 h, rounded

Nov. 18

a) 5 h 31 min

b) 5.52 h

Nov. 19

a) 3 h 28 min

b) 3.47 h

c) $192.00

d) It is preferable to start and end at the specified times because you don't get paid more for starting a few minutes early or leaving a few minutes late.

9. a) Errors on Franco's pay statement: End date is earlier than the begin date; end date year is 2100 instead of 2010; total hours should be 32.5; gross earnings should be $290.88.

b) Errors on Christine's pay statement: Two different pay rates are listed; her gross earnings should be $224.19.

c) Inform your supervisor or payroll clerk of the error.

Extend your thinking

10. a) Some factors to consider include pay, length of time the jobs last, cost and time involved in commuting, additional perks or benefits each job provides, and how interested you are in each kind of work.

b) How many hours a week you would be working at the community centre job and the cost of transportation for the painting job.

c) The house-painting job may require some overtime if a particular job has a deadline that must be met because of weather.

d) Overtime might be appealing to earn extra money; you might not want to work overtime if you have other commitments.

2.2 ALTERNATIVE WAYS TO EARN MONEY

BUILD YOUR SKILLS, PAGE 69

1. Benefits of self-employment include being your own boss and being able to set your own hours. Disadvantages include that you don't get paid holidays or benefits and you have to promote your business yourself. Answers to the last question will vary.

2. a) The profit is $75.00.

b) The profit is 15%.

c) He could not adjust the price because he signed a contract to deliver the product for a fixed price.

3. a) $14.87/h

b) To raise his hourly rate, Leo would have to work more quickly so he could complete the contracts in fewer hours, or lower his material costs.

4. If she is a fast worker, piecework might be the better option because she could earn $0.50 an hour more.

5. a) $2200.00

b) An average of 4 h at $50.00/h. She would not want to spend more than 5 or 6 h.

c) $15 200.00

6. $66 666.67

7. a) $360.00

   b) Piecework is beneficial if the worker is efficient and can earn more than he or she would on an hourly basis. Working piecework allows the worker to decide how much work to take on.

   c) For an employer, paying by piecework means not paying benefits such as holiday pay or sick time. A disadvantage would be that a worker may not always be available.

Extend your thinking

8. a) Measure the length, width, and height of each wall and the dimensions of the fireplace and patio door, along with other open space such as a hallway.

   b) Other calculations include the price of primer, paint, edging tools, plastic, brushes and rollers, and so on. You would need to estimate the time involved, having determined how many coats of paint are needed.

   c) Let x = cost of supplies

   Let y = cost of labour

   Total cost = $x + y$

   Profit equals total costs subtracted from contract amount.

   Let P = profit

   Let C = costs

   Let A = amount of contract

   $P = A - C$

   Percentage profit equals amount of profit divided by amount of contract.

   Let Z = percentage profit

   $Z = P \div A$

2.3 ADDITIONAL EARNINGS

BUILD YOUR SKILLS, PAGE 76

1. a) $74 050.00
   b) $6170.83

2. $7.60

3. Tristan will earn about $2240.00 in 4 weeks.

4. a) Let x = number of hours worked

   Let y = number of workers per shift

   Let z = amount of tips

   $x (\$8.00/h) + \frac{z}{y}$

   b) No, Layla is incorrect. She earned $65.87, not $68.21.

5. $48 300.00

6. $225.73

7. a) 6 h
   b) $150.88
   c) 75%
   d) 25%

Extend your thinking

8. a) $196.81

   b) This mileage allowance is probably fair, although if there is too much wear and tear on a personal vehicle, it might be too low. Consider the costs of fuel, insurance, and repair and maintenance.

2.4 DEDUCTIONS AND NET PAY

BUILD YOUR SKILLS, PAGE 87

1. Gross income is the total income earned in a pay period. Taxable income is gross income minus before-tax deductions such as union dues, pension contributions, dental coverage, and so on.

2. a) Friend 2 has a higher salary.

   b) The person who gets paid twice a month would have higher deductions per pay period.

3. Look up the EI premium rate for the year and multiply the gross pay by this rate.

4. a) $3026.54 semi-monthly

   b) Taxable income is higher than net pay because income tax, CPP, and EI are deducted from the taxable income to calculate the net pay.

5. Amber's net pay is $811.12.

6. a) Prince Rupert job: $109.31.

   Skeena River job: $109.31

   b) $86.50

   c) Prince Rupert job: $305.50

   Skeena River job: $304.00

   d) $4086.88

7. a) Yes, Pierre was paid the correct amount. After his pay deductions, he received $1379.58.

   $1730.77 − $172.98 − $69.82 − $78.45 − $29.94 = $1379.58

   b) No, he was not paid the correct amount. After his pay deductions, he should have received $1317.08.

   $1730.77 − $172.98 − $69.82 − $78.45 − $29.94 − $62.50 = $1317.08

Extend your thinking

8. a) $5770.00

   b) $4012.50

PRACTISE YOUR NEW SKILLS, PAGE 89

1. $8.40

2. The waiters will earn slightly more on Thursday than on Friday.

   Steps:

   1. Divide the total amount of tips from each day by the number of waiters working that day.

   2. Calculate the wages earned on each night.

   3. Add each waiter's tips to the wages and compare the amounts for the two nights.

3. a) $252.00

   b) $84.00

4. a) $2075.00

   b) 23%

   c) A business with 23% of total income as earnings is healthy, but there are probably other expenses, such as the cost of renting space or marketing activities.

5. $500.00

6. Info required: earnings; pay period; claim code; EI premium rate; CPP basic exemption and contribution rate; benefits and other deductions.

   Equipment needed: calculator, computer with internet access, tax tables or online payroll calculator.

7. a) Federal: $130.15

   b) Provincial: $63.50

   c) You would need the provincial tax tables for BC.

8. a) $1423.08

   b) CPP: $63.78; EI: $24.62; federal tax: $132.40; AB tax: $66.50

   c) $1135.78.

9. Answers will vary. A straight commission job may provide more freedom, for example, the opportunity to work from home or to only work when you want to. Also, your compensation is directly tied to your performance. However, you wouldn't have the regular paycheque and employment benefits that come with a salaried job. The advantages of a salary-plus-commission job include the security of a regular paycheque and benefits; however, having to work full time and report to a supervisor could be seen as a disadvantage.

CHAPTER 3
LENGTH, AREA, AND VOLUME
3.1 SYSTEMS OF MEASUREMENT

BUILD YOUR SKILLS, PAGE 102

1. a) 2 miles

   b) $120 \frac{3}{16}$ inches

   c) $26 \frac{1}{4}$ ft

2. 360 bouquets

3. No, her suitcase is 3″ too big.

4. a) You will need 25 sheets of plywood.

   b) The plywood will cost $353.75.

5. It will cost $39.96 to put edging around the garden.

6. The fitter will need 14 rails.

7. a) Noah must buy 8 yards of fabric.

   b) The drapes will cost $120.00.

8. If baseboards are installed around the vanity, the job will cost $254.53. If baseboards are not installed around the vanity, the job will cost $213.41. Assume that the carpenter will not put baseboards in front of the tub or in the door opening.

Extend your thinking

9. The insulator will need seven packages.

3.2. CONVERTING MEASUREMENTS

BUILD YOUR SKILLS, PAGE 111

1. The bridge is 2.286 m high. The truck will not fit under the bridge.

2. The altitude is 13 779.5 feet.

3. Valerie is 172.72 cm tall.

4. The total cost is $728.00.

5. Company A will charge $3827.08 and Company B will charge $4000.00, so Company A should get the job.

6. Hardwood will cost $2126.67 and carpet will cost $2206.05, so hardwood costs less.

7. a) Irina can plant 658 seedlings.
   b) The seedlings will cost $429.00.

8. The total estimate is $872.50.

Extend your thinking

9. The total cost will be $983.30.

3.3 SURFACE AREA

BUILD YOUR SKILLS, PAGE 121

1. a) He can make 4 pond liners from one roll.
   b) It costs $37.25 to line one pond.

2. Can A requires 45.16 in² of aluminum to manufacture and Can B requires 42.41 in² of aluminum to manufacture, so Can A requires more aluminum to manufacture.

3. Jashandeep needs enough paint to cover 48 ft², so she needs one quart of paint, which costs $14.99. She needs enough stain to cover 4.46 m², so she needs one litre of stain, which costs $12.99. The stain is the cheaper option.

4. To build the hopper will require 81.70 yd² of sheet metal.

5. a) Francine should buy 155 bricks.
   b) The bricks will cost $124.00.

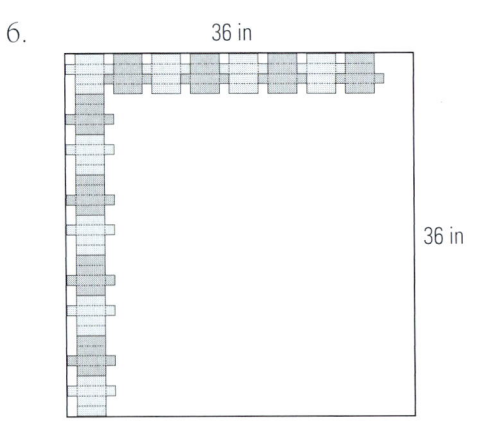

6.

36 in
36 in

Extend your thinking

7. It will cost $151.20 to carpet the scratching post.

3.4 VOLUME

BUILD YOUR SKILLS, PAGE 132

1. He will need 750 mL of milk.

2. 12 US fl oz = 355 mL

   16 US fl oz = 474 mL

   28 US fl oz = 829 mL

   40 US fl oz = 1184 mL

3. The box measures 30.48 cm × 15.24 cm × 20.32 cm, so the game will fit in the box.

4. It will cost him $55.00 to fill his tank.

5. J & L Concrete charges $931.48 and M & W Concrete charges $823.35, so Everett should buy from M & W concrete.

6. Elann should order 2.5 yd³ of concrete.

Extend your thinking

7. The car uses 5.22 L per 100 km, so the car is more fuel efficient than the minivan.

PRACTISE YOUR NEW SKILLS, PAGE 134

1. It will cost $7800.00 to install the benches.

2. It will cost $270.25 to replace the mouldings.

3. The painter will charge $3342.95 to do this job.

4. The total cost of the metal primer will be $141.39.

5. The cone is made from 4.78 ft² of aluminum.

6. It is 141.06 miles to the next service station. She has enough gas to drive another 252 miles, so she doesn't need to stop for gas now.

7. If the farmer buys the 1 yd³ bales, he will need 10 bales, which will cost $390.00. If he buys the 3.8 ft³ bales, he will need 71 bales, which will cost $886.79. The 1 yd³ bale would give the farmer the best total price.

8. Dawai needs 1.665 yd³ of soil. At Dirt for Less, 1.665 yd³ of soil would cost $26.62 and 2 yd³ would cost $31.98. If he converts the volume to metres, he needs 1.27 m³ of soil. At Rocks and Soils, 1.27 m³ of soil would cost $24.11 and 2 m³ would cost $37.98.

   a) If Dawai can buy fractions of a cubic yard or metre, he should buy from Rocks and Soils.

   b) If he must buy whole cubic yards or metres, he should buy from Dirt for Less.

9. a) The total volume of concrete needed to build the wall is 4.57 yd³.

   i) Steve will need 0.65 yd³ of cement.

   ii) Steve will need 1.31 yd³ of sand.

   iii) Steve will need 2.61 yd³ of gravel.

   b) The job will cost $1589.29.

CHAPTER 4
MASS, TEMPERATURE, AND VOLUME
4.1 TEMPERATURE CONVERSIONS

BUILD YOUR SKILLS, PAGE 143

1. ground meats: 71°C; beef (medium rare): 63°C; beef (well-done): 77°C; chicken (whole): 74°C

2. Mandy will have to modify the asphalt paving mixture if the temperature falls below 70°F. Temperature would affect it because asphalt becomes more fluid as it is heated.

3. Chan will not have to work if the temperature is above 41°C or below −26°C.

4. The surface temperature of the crimper is (446 ± 18)°F. The temperature of the crimper is between 428°F and 464°F.

5. a) Answers will vary.
   b) Answers will vary.
   c) Bev likes to keep her house between 64°F and 72°F.

Extend your thinking

6. −40°C = −40°F

4.2 MASS IN THE IMPERIAL SYSTEM

BUILD YOUR SKILLS, PAGE 151

1. a) i. a pat of butter
   b) ii. a small basket of raspberries
   c) iii. blue whale

2. a) pounds
   b) pounds
   c) ounces or for a larger box, pounds
   d) tons
   e) pounds or pounds and ounces
   f) pounds
   g) tons

3. a) Newborn babies are small and a few ounces is a relatively large portion of their size.
   b) 121 oz
   c) It is easier to visualize between 7 and 8 pounds than it is to visualize 115 ounces.
   d) 8 lb 1 oz
   e) Johan weighed approximately $\frac{8}{121} \approx 0.07$ more at 5 weeks than at birth.
   f) If he had weighed less at birth, the amount lost during the first week would have been less, and his weight gain would have been proportionately more, but if he weighed more at birth it would have the opposite effect.

4. $3504\frac{1}{6}$ lb or 3504.2 lb

5. a) Petroleum products are the most highly traded commodity.
   b) The farmer received $1181.25 and Hon received $12 116.25. Hon received $10 395.00 more for his coffee than the farmer received. This is almost 10 times more than the farmer received.

Extend your thinking

6. a) Although it doesn't sound like much, this would be a fair price for coffee beans given the cost of living for farmers in the countries that grow beans.

    b) Hon would have paid considerably more for the beans than $1.35/lb because of the distributors involved, the cost of transportation, and so on.

7. Sam forgot to consider the maximum weight that Pete's truck can carry. Pete will have to make 9 trips.

4.3 MASS IN THE SYSTÈME INTERNATIONAL

BUILD YOUR SKILLS, PAGE 158

1. a) ii. a penny
   b) i. this textbook
   c) i. a thumbtack
   d) i. a bull

2. a) No. Even a small truck would weigh more than a tonne.
   b) No. A newborn baby weighs 3000 or 4000 grams.
   c) No. A hockey puck weighs considerably less—about 150 to 170 g.
   d) Yes
   e) Yes
   f) Yes
   g) No. One tonne is 1000 kg, which is about 2200 lb.
   h) No. A pound is less than half a kilogram.

3. a) You will have to take 2 pills at a time.
   b) 7500 mg
   c) 0.0075 kg

4. nitrogen: 30 kg; phosphorus: 35 kg; potassium: 25 kg

5. The air in the tank weighs 44 956.5 g or approximately 45 kg.

6. You would buy 398 g, 124 g, and 97 g of cheese.

7. 625 kg

Extend your thinking

8. a) Jupiter
   b) Mercury

4.4 MAKING CONVERSIONS

BUILD YOUR SKILLS, PAGE 165

1. Each ball weighs approximately 142 g.

2. Raj will need to order 36 bags.

3. a) 146.73 kilograms per square metre
   b) i. 30 770 pounds
      ii. 13 986.36 kg

4. a) 102.24 kg
   b) 225 lb

5. a) 520 lb
   b) 236.4 kg

6. There are approximately 1062 bushels of wheat in the pile.

Answer Key   **335**

7. Jason should have an elevator with at least a 2000 pound capacity.

Extend your thinking

8. a) $180.98

   b) $4.77/kg

   c) ground beef: 21.8 kg; chuck roast: 3.4 kg; sirloin roast: 3.1 kg; grilling steak: 4.5 kg; T-bone: 3.3 kg; stewing meat: 1.8 kg

   d) When you check the prices of the meat in the grocery store, especially if the meat was on sale, you will probably find that Arduk did not save much, if any money.

   e) Answers will vary. Example: Fruits and vegetables can often be purchased directly from the producer.

   f) Answers will vary. Example: The food would often be fresher.

PRACTISE YOUR NEW SKILLS, PAGE 169

1. 113°F is equivalent to 45°C; −55°F is approximately equivalent to −48°C

2. The coldest recorded temperature would have been approximately −81°F.

3. a) A 5-US gallon pail of water weighs approximately 19 kilograms.

   b) 1000 kg

4. a) 13 565 g or 13.565 kg

   b) 200 g

   c) 5

5. 150 lb

6. 1334.28 kg; 2935.42 lb

7. 47.6 tonnes

8. You could create a type of balance using a sawhorse or some other device as the fulcrum and a solid piece of wood or a 2 × 4 as the arms. Place the rock on one end of the 2 × 4. Place the cement bags, one at a time, on the other end. When the cement balances the rock, count the number of bags and multiply by 20.

9. a) 378 787.88 kg

   b) 421.6 ft^3

   c) 660 lb

Extend your thinking

10. pork: $8\frac{2}{3}$ oz; beef: 4 oz; potatoes: $4\frac{2}{3}$ oz

CHAPTER 5
ANGLES AND PARALLEL LINES
5.1 MEASURING AND ESTIMATING ANGLES

BUILD YOUR SKILLS, PAGE 184

1. a) 26.5° (A good estimation would be either 25° or 30°.)

   b) 243° (A good estimation would be either 240° or 245°.)

2.

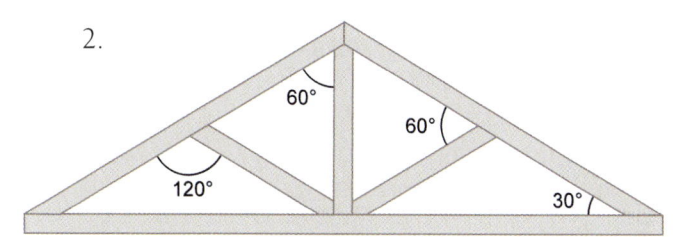

3. Only a 40° angle will add up to 90° with a 50° angle. So, the bottom ends of the side pieces of the frame must be cut so that the angles measure 40°.

4. The measures of the angles of the cuts should be 30° to 40° (from the horizontal) and 50° to 60° (from the vertical.) The exact measurements are 33.7° from the horizontal and 56.3° from the vertical.

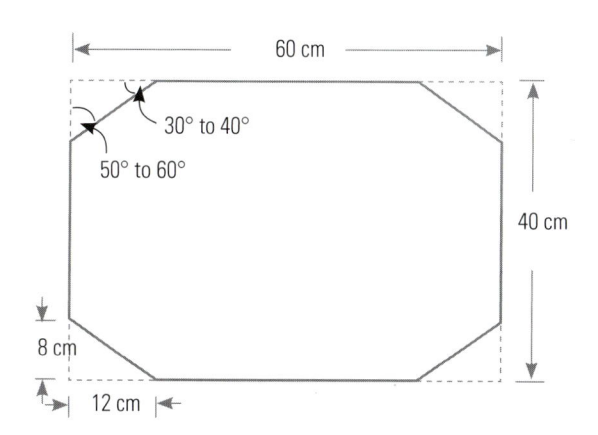

5.

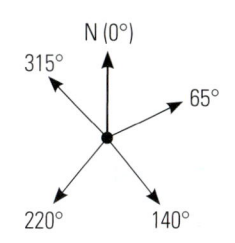

6.

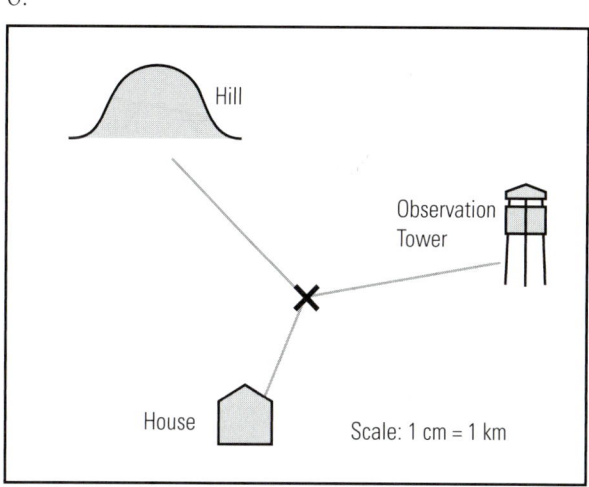

Extend your thinking

7. a) Subtract 6° from the azimuths to get the compass degrees.

   b) The compass reading for the first leg is 48°.

   The compass reading for the second leg is 189°.

   The compass reading for the third leg is 101°.

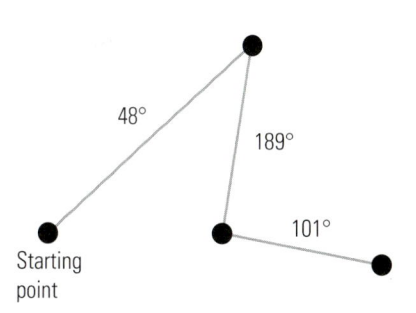

5.2 ANGLE BISECTORS AND PERPENDICULAR LINES

BUILD YOUR SKILLS, PAGE 192

1. a) The angle measures 27°. The bisected angle measures 13.5°.

   b) The angle measures 84°. The bisected angle measures 42°.

   c) The angle measures 90°. The bisected angle measures 45°.

   d) The angle measures 262°. The bisected angle measures 131°.

2. a) Angle made by strips 1 and 2: 50°
      Angle made by strips 2 and 3: 100°
      Angle made by strips 1 and 3: 30°

   b) Bisector for strips 1 and 2:

      50° ÷ 2 = 25°

      Bisector for strips 2 and 3:

      100° ÷ 2 = 50°

      Bisector for strips 1 and 3:

      30° ÷ 2 = 15°

   c) The ends of strips 1 and 2 must be cut at 25° angles where they meet.
      The ends of strips 2 and 3 must be cut at 50° angles where they meet.
      The ends of strips 1 and 3 must be cut at 15° where they meet.

3. Regular octagons have internal angles with measures that equal 135°. The reflex angle to each of these will have measures equalling 360° − 135° = 225°. The mitre joints will bisect these angles so that the measures of the angles between each piece's ends and the straight sides equal 112.5°.

4. ∠A measures 150°. The bisected angle measures 75°.

   ∠B measures 140°. The bisected angle measures 70°.

   ∠C measures 130°. The bisected angle measures 65°.

   ∠D measures 130°. The bisected angle measures 65°.

5. The total angle between the left pair of light rays equals 76°. The angle of reflection and the angle of incidence equal 38°.

   The total angle between the middle pair of light rays equals 100°. The angle of reflection and the angle of incidence equal 50°.

   The total angle between the right pair of light rays equals 124°. The angle of reflection and the angle of incidence equal 62°.

6. The piece of wood must be cut at a 140° angle. If one angle of a bisected straight line is 40°, the supplementary angle must equal 140°.

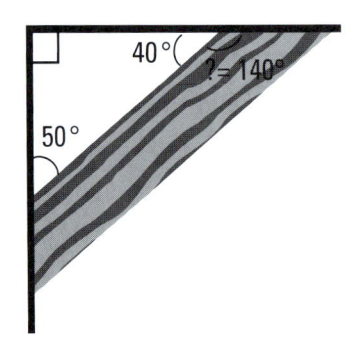

7. Diagrams should look approximately like this.

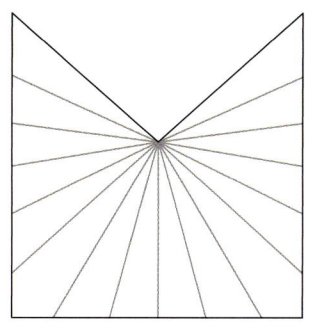

Extend your thinking

8. The reflector must be rotated 6° counter-clockwise.

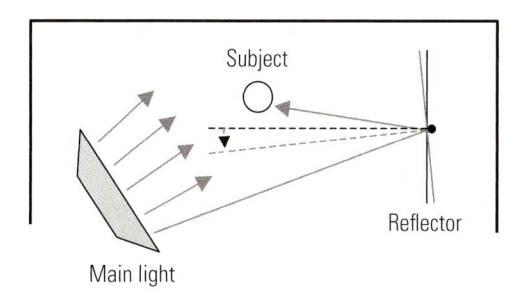

5.3 NON-PARALLEL LINES AND TRANSVERSALS

BUILD YOUR SKILLS, PAGE 204

1. a) Angle 6 is vertically opposite to angle 1. Both have a measure of 81°.

   b) Angle 5 is the alternate exterior angle to angle 4. No, their measures are not equal.

   c) Angle 8 is the corresponding angle to angle 6. No, their measures are not equal.

   d) Angle 3 is the other interior angle on the same side of the transversal in the pair formed with angle 2. No, these angles are not supplementary.

2. a) The king post is the transversal, because it intersects with both the left and right rafter.

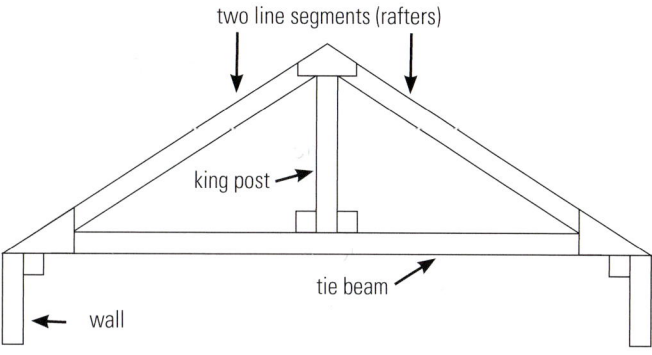

   b) Angles 3 and 5 are supplementary angles. They are two right angles that equal 180° when combined.

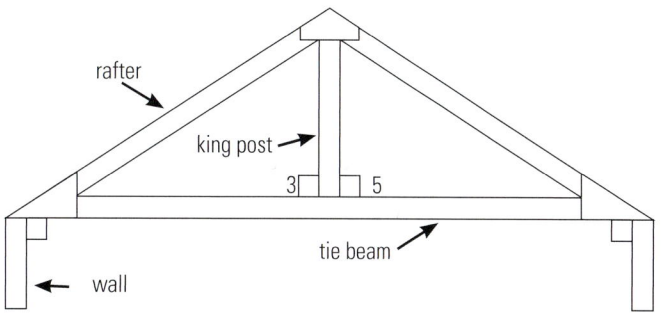

   c) Angles 7 and 8 are interior angles on the same side of a transversal. The sum of their measures equals 180°.

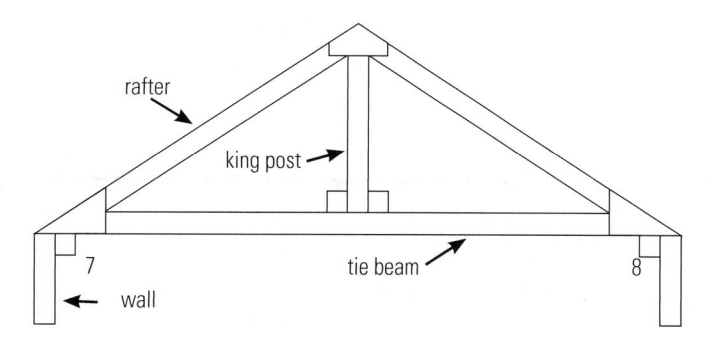

Answer Key 339

d) If angles 1, and 2 and 4 combined are interior angles on the same side of a transversal, then the two main line segments would be the right rafter and the tie beam, and the transversal would be the left rafter.

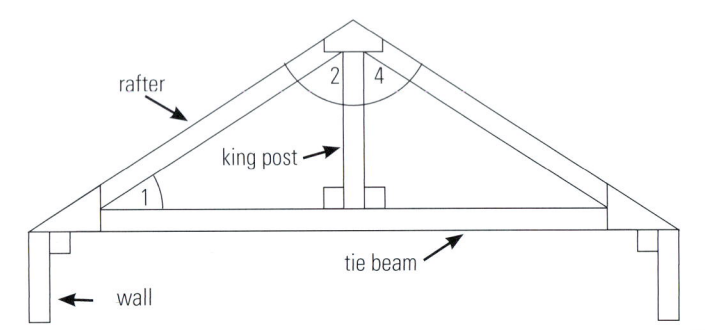

3. a) The seat and the runner are the main line segments. The transversal is the main support and back.

   b) Angles 1 and 2 are alternate interior angles.

   c) $\angle 1 = 78°$

   $\angle 2 = 85°$

Extend your thinking

4. a) i) $\angle 1 = 90°$

   $\angle 2 = 90°$

   $\angle 3 = 45°$

   Angle 1 is greater than angle 3.

   ii) Angles 2 and 3 are not supplementary angles because they do not equal 180°.

   b) i) $\angle 1 = 45°$

   $\angle 2 = 135°$

   $\angle 3 = 45°$

   Angle 1 equals angle 3.

   ii) Angles 2 and 3 are supplementary angles because they equal 180°.

   c) i) Corresponding angles for parallel lines have equal measures, whereas corresponding angles for non-parallel line segments do not.

   ii) Interior angles on the same side of the transversal for parallel lines are supplementary angles. Interior angles on the same side of the transversal for non-parallel lines are not supplementary angles.

5.4 PARALLEL LINES AND TRANSVERSALS

BUILD YOUR SKILLS, PAGE 214

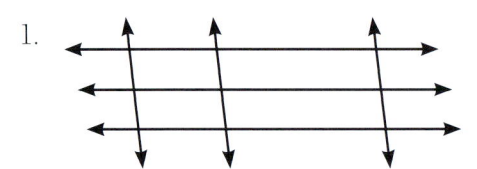

1.

2. Answers will vary. One way is to ensure that the tracks are an equal distance apart. Another way is to ensure that the rail ties always form supplementary interior angles on the same side of the transversal formed by the rails.

3. The first diagram contains parallel lines, but the second diagram does not.

   a) Use a ruler to confirm that the distance between the lines is the same throughout, or measure angles by drawing a transversal and determining that alternate interior or corresponding angles are equal.

   b) Use a ruler to confirm that the distance between lines is not constant.

340   MathWorks 10

4. *x* = 75° because it is an interior angle on the same side of the transversal with the 105° angle and together they must equal 180°.

5. The top and bottom faces are parallel.

   The front and back faces are not parallel.

6. The boat operator must adjust her boat's heading 8° to starboard.

7. Line segments 1 and 3 are parallel. Using 2 as the transversal, there are two equal alternate interior angles that both measure 85°.

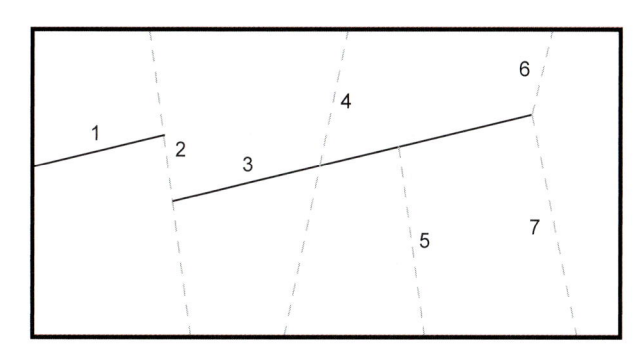

Line segments 2 and 5 are parallel. Using 3 as the transversal, there are two angles on the same side of the transversal that are supplementary (95° + 85° = 180°).

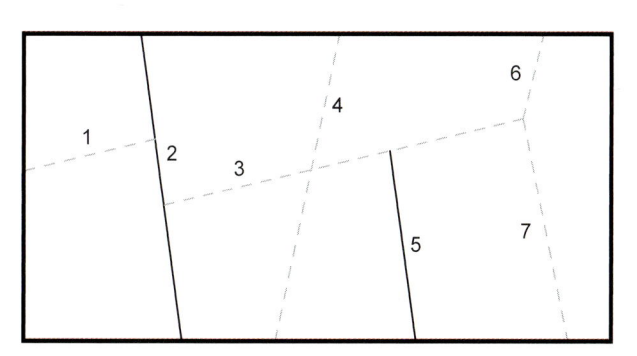

Line segments 4 and 6 are also parallel. Using 3 as the transversal they have two corresponding angles that both measure 115°.

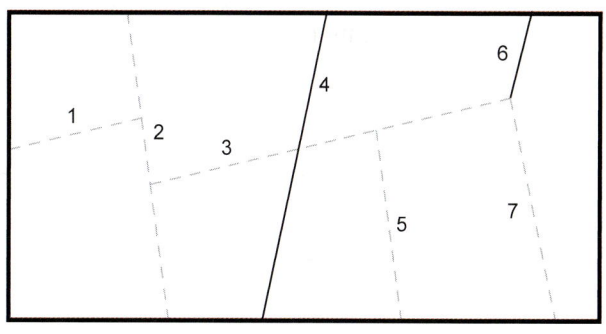

Extend your thinking

8. a) Answers will vary. Mirrors can be attached to plywood sheets that are joined so that they are perpendicular. L-shaped metal braces could be attached to the backs.

   b) If the angle measure is less than 90°, the reflected ray will intersect the incident ray. Reflections could be distorted, or unseen by the viewer.

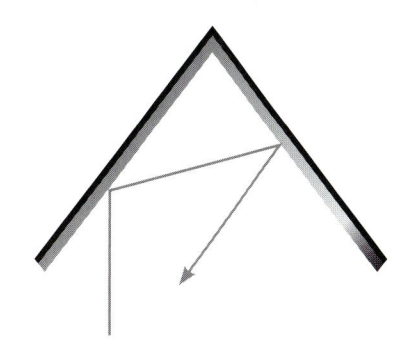

c) If the angle measure is greater than 90°, the reflected ray will diverge from the incident ray. Reflections could be distorted, or be unseen by the viewer.

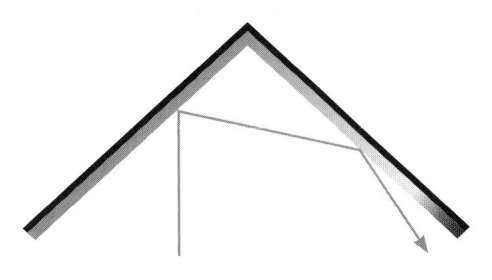

PRACTISE YOUR NEW SKILLS, PAGE 220

1.

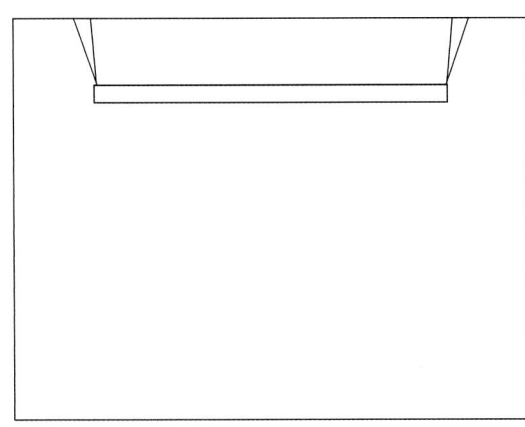

2. The diagrams should look like those below.

3. Leg 1 is approximately 30° (the sailboat's current position to the first buoy).

   Leg 2 is approximately 83° (first buoy to the second).

   Leg 3 is approximately 250° (second buoy to other boat).

4. The fifth wall is approximately 4 feet long. It makes a 153° angle with the top wall and a 117° with the right wall.

5. The west-facing and south-facing sides will get the most wind, so they should be the ones to get the 3-pane windows.

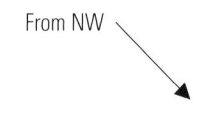

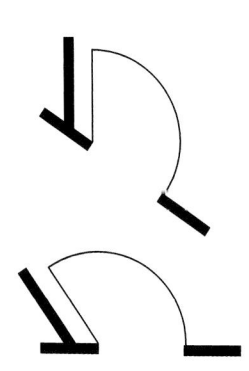

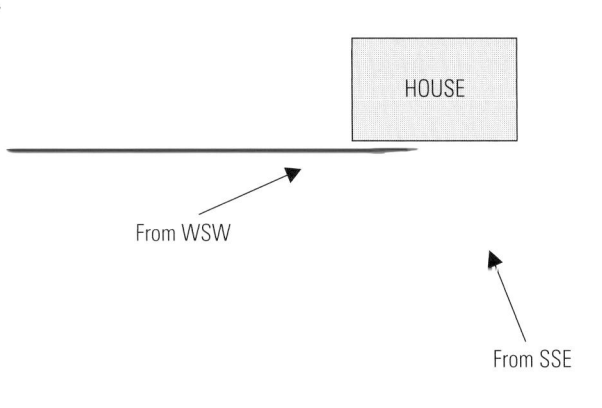

6. a) The measures of the top angles in each window frame are 35°. The measure of each bottom angle is 55°.

   b) The measures of the angles at each end of the window frame section are 17.5° (at the top), 45° (at the right-angle vertex), and 27.5° at the remaining vertex.

7. Students should have created a template of a similar shape to the gusset shown in the diagram, with 120° angles in the centre.

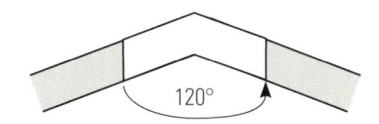

8. a) Studs 2 and 3 are perpendicular to the wall plates. (Studs 1 and 4 are not.)

   b) Studs 2 and 3 are parallel to the left end of the wall. Let the bottom wall plate be the transversal of the studs. The interior angles on the same side of the transversal between the left end of the wall and studs 2 and 3 are supplementary, making them parallel to the left end. The interior angles on the same side of the transversal between the left end of the wall and studs 1 and 4 are not supplementary, so studs 1 and 4 are not parallel to the left end of the wall.

9. a) The aircraft travelling west will travel 60 km, while the one travelling south will travel 50 km.

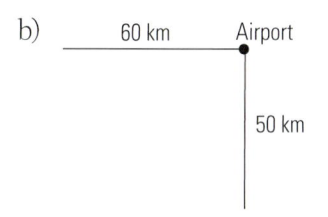

   b)

   The bearing of the southbound aircraft relative to the westbound aircraft is 220°.

CHAPTER 6
SIMILARITY OF FIGURES
6.1 SIMILAR POLYGONS

BUILD YOUR SKILLS, PAGE 232

1. a) The side lengths will be doubled and the angle measurements will stay the same.

   b) The side lengths will be tripled and the angle measurements will stay the same.

   c) The side lengths will be halved and the angle measurements will stay the same.

2. Statement c is correct.

3. The two figures are not similar because they do not have the same shape. Their angles measures are not the same.

4. Plots similar to Plot A: Plots D and J

   Plots similar to Plot B: Plots E, I, and K

   Plots similar to Plot C: Plots F, G, H, L

5. Painting A is similar. Painting B is not similar.

   Calculate the ratios of the lengths and widths of the paintings and the frames to determine if they are similar.

   Painting A

   $$\frac{\text{frame length}}{\text{painting length}} = \frac{120}{80}$$
   $$\frac{\text{frame length}}{\text{painting length}} = 1.5$$

   $$\frac{\text{frame width}}{\text{painting width}} = \frac{120}{80}$$
   $$\frac{\text{frame width}}{\text{painting width}} = 1.5$$

Painting B

$$\frac{\text{frame length}}{\text{painting length}} = \frac{160}{120}$$

$$\frac{\text{frame length}}{\text{painting length}} = 1.3$$

$$\frac{\text{frame width}}{\text{painting width}} = \frac{120}{180}$$

$$\frac{\text{frame width}}{\text{painting width}} = 1.5$$

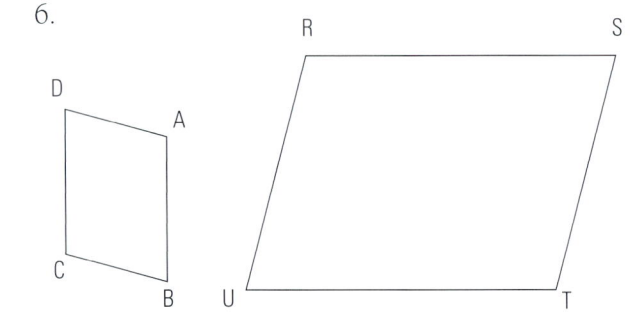

6.

Corresponding angles: A and R, B and S, C and T, and D and U.

Corresponding sides: AB and RS, BC and ST, CD and TU, and AD and RU.

Extend your thinking

7. Point F: (−7, −6)

   Point G: (5, −6)

   Point H: (5, 2)

6.2. DETERMINING IF TWO POLYGONS ARE SIMILAR

BUILD YOUR SKILLS, PAGE 243

1. a) The scale factor used was $\frac{1}{3}$.

   b) $x = 2$ cm

2. a) Side AB corresponds to EF

      Side BC corresponds to FG

      Side CD corresponds to GH

      Side AD corresponds to EH

   b) The scale factor used was $\frac{1}{3}$.

   c) BC has a length of 24 cm.

   d) Angle D measures 125°.

   e) Angle L measures 55°. Angle L corresponds to angle C. The measure of angle C is equal to the measure of A. That means that angle L and angle A also have the same measure.

3. Fiona might not be right, because she may not have compared the corresponding sides. If the corresponding sides were 6:4, 9:6, and 12:8, the second triangle would be 1.5 times the size of the first triangle and could be a scaled copy.

4. The width of the larger rectangle is 5.4 inches.

5. The two triangles are similar figures.

   Marco can prove his answer to his boss by comparing the lengths of the corresponding sides and determining that they are proportional.

6. a) Yes, they are similar. The side lengths are proportional and the angles are congruent.

344 MathWorks 10

b) Lise can use a scale factor of $\frac{25}{50}$ or 0.5.

c) Lise can write the scale factor as $\frac{50}{25}$ or 2.

7. a) Lance's statement is correct. Squares have 4 equal sides. So when one side is resized using a scale factor, all sides must be increased by the same number to keep the shape a square.

   b) Max's statement is incorrect because rectangles will have two pairs of sides with equal side lengths, but the two pairs do not need to be resized by the same number to keep the shape of a rectangle.

8. Yes, casserole A is similar to casserole C.

   If casserole A is similar to casserole B, then each side was multiplied by the same factor. If casserole B is similar to casserole C, then each side was multiplied by the same factor. That means that each side of casserole A could be multiplied by some number that would result in the length of casserole C.

Extend your thinking

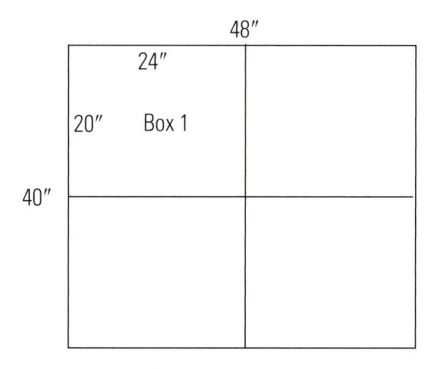

9. a) [diagram of Box 1: 48" × 40", with Box 1 shown as 24" × 20"]

   [diagram of Box 2: 48" × 40", with Box 2 shown as 16" × 20"]

b) Box 1 is similar to the pallet shape with a scale factor of one-half. Compare the dimensions of Box 1.

$$\frac{24}{48} = \frac{1}{2}$$
$$\frac{20}{40} = \frac{1}{2}$$

Box 2 is not similar to the pallet shape. Compare the dimensions of Box 2.

$$\frac{20}{48} = 0.417$$
$$\frac{16}{40} = 0.40$$

c) The ratio of areas is 0.25.

The area of the pallet is 1920 in^2.

The area of the similar box is 480 in^2.

$$\frac{480}{1920} = 0.25 \text{ or } \frac{1}{4}$$

The ratio of areas equals the square of the ratio of sides, that is,

$$\frac{1}{4} = \frac{1}{2} \times \frac{1}{2}$$

Area = length × width
Area factor = length factor × width factor

For similar shapes,

length factor = width factor = scale factor
scale factor = length factor × width factor
area factor = scale factor × scale factor.

6.3 DRAWING SIMILAR POLYGONS

BUILD YOUR SKILLS, PAGE 252

1. a) Both Nipin and Francis are correct. Nipin has found the scale factor used on M to create R. Francis has found the scale factor used on R to create M.

   b) Answers will vary. To fully answer this question, students will need to draw a rectangle on graph paper where the length and width have a ratio of $\frac{1}{2}$. Students will then need to determine the scale factor used to create their new rectangle.

2. a) Answers will vary.

   b) To fully answer this question, students will need to draw a rectangle where the length and width do not have a ratio of $\frac{2}{3}$.

3. Each rectangle will have dimensions of 1 unit by 2 units.

4. The perimeter of the smaller pentagon is 10 cm. The perimeter of the larger pentagon is 20 cm. The new pentagon's perimeter is $\frac{1}{2}$ of the larger pentagon's perimeter.

5. The scale factor used was $\frac{1}{3}$. Angle measurements will be the same.

   $a = 70°$

   $b = 110°$

   $c = 4.4 \text{ cm} \times \frac{1}{3}$

   $c = 1.5 \text{ cm}$

   $d = 3 \text{ cm} \times \frac{1}{3}$

   $d = 1 \text{ cm}$

   $e = 4.2 \text{ cm} \times \frac{1}{3}$

   $e = 1.4 \text{ cm}$

6. The living room has dimensions of 22.5 feet by 30 feet.

Extend your thinking

7. The value of x plus 2 must be 2 units longer than x. The side lengths of 6 and 8 give a difference of 2, so the value of x is 6 and the value of x plus 2 is 8.

6.4 SIMILAR TRIANGLES

BUILD YOUR SKILLS, PAGE 261

1. Set 1:
   Yes, they are similar.

   Table 1: 90°, 45°, 45°

   Table 2: 45°, 45°, 90°

   Set 2:
   No, they are not similar.

   Table 1: 133°, 11°, 36°

   Table 2: 35°, 11°, 134°

2. Side AB measures 11.25 inches.

3. Side EC measures approximately 2.38 inches.

4. The height of the mountain is 1788 ft above Tryna's position.

5. Side x equals 12.

346 MathWorks 10

Extend your thinking

6. $x = 160$

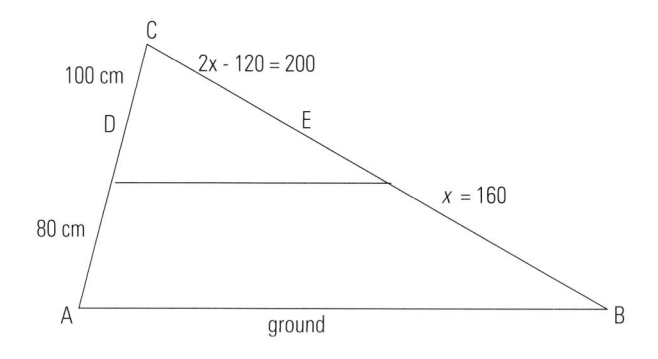

   BC = 360 cm

   [Diagram: Triangle with vertex C at top, A at bottom left, B at bottom right. D on AC with CD = 100 cm and DA = 80 cm. E on CB with CE labeled $2x - 120 = 200$ and EB labeled $x = 160$. DE is parallel to AB (ground).]

PRACTISE YOUR NEW SKILLS, PAGE 265

1. a) new width = 16 cm
      new length = 24 cm
   b) new width = 30 cm
      new length = 45 cm
   c) new width = 6 cm
      new length = 9
   d) new width = 20 cm
      new length = 30 cm

2. a) The ratio of any corresponding sides will be $\frac{3}{4}$.
   b) The ratio is 1.

3. a) The scale factor is $\frac{1}{4}$.
   b) $a = 1.25$
      $b = 0.25$
      $c = 0.25$
   c) Bill does not need to know length e because the given angles and dimensions define the shape.

4. a) Reduce the large drawer's dimensions by one half to find the answer.

      middle drawer width = 40 cm

      middle drawer height = 16 cm

   b) Reduce the middle drawer by 50% to find the answer.

      small drawer width = 20 cm

      small drawer height = 8 cm

   c) The scale factor of the smallest drawer from the biggest drawer is 0.25 or $\frac{1}{4}$.

      scale factor = $\dfrac{\text{small drawer height}}{\text{large drawer height}}$

      scale factor = $\dfrac{8 \text{ cm}}{32 \text{ cm}}$

      scale factor = $\dfrac{1}{4}$

   d) The dresser height is 114 cm.

      Dresser height = (2 × large height) + (2 × middle height) + small height + feet

      Dresser height = (2 × 32) + (2 × 16) + 8 + 10

      Dresser height = 114 cm

5. a) A scale factor of two was used.
   b) $a = 103°$, $b = 90°$, $c = 12.5$ m, $d = 51.3$ m
   c) $e = 90°$, $f = 77°$, $g = 48$ m

6. The poster is approximately 36 inches wide and 48 inches long, so these dimensions will satisfy the customer.

   57 inches reduces to 35.625 inches.

   76 inches reduces to 47.5 inches.

7. No. Her rectangle would have to have dimensions of 4 times 3, which would give an area of 12 cm², not 24 cm².

8. Yes, the triangles are similar because they each have angle measures of 85°, 32°, and 63°.

9. The two triangles are similar.

   Two triangles are similar if one angle is congruent and the two sides adjacent to the congruent angle are in the same proportion.

   Angle B ~ Angle F

   AB ~ ED
   $\frac{AB}{FH} = \frac{5.5}{13.75}$
   $\frac{AB}{FH} = 0.4$

   BC ~ FG
   $\frac{BC}{FG} = \frac{3.3}{8.25}$
   $\frac{BC}{FG} = 0.4$

   The ratio of $\frac{AB}{FH}$ and $\frac{BC}{FG}$ are both 0.4. Therefore the triangles are similar.

10. Side FH is 8 feet long.

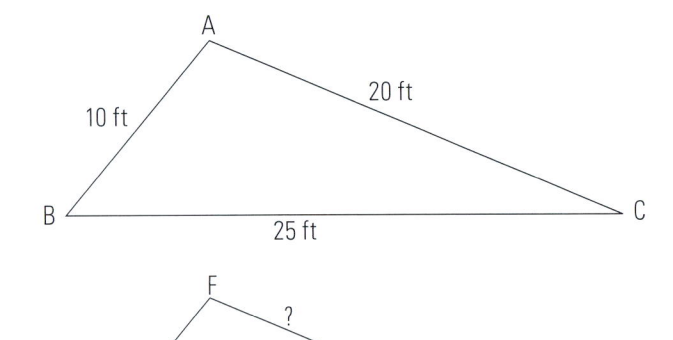

    The triangles are similar.

    $\frac{AB}{FG} = 2.5$

    Therefore,
    $\frac{AC}{FH} = 2.5$
    $\frac{20}{FH} = 2.5$
    $20 = 2.5 \times FH$
    $\frac{20}{2.5} = FH$
    $8 \text{ ft} = FH$

CHAPTER 7
TRIGONOMETRY OF RIGHT TRIANGLES
7.1 THE PYTHAGOREAN THEOREM

BUILD YOUR SKILLS, PAGE 278

1. a) AC is 2.3 m high.

   b) AE is 4.2 m long.

2. a) Each rafter is 4.5 m long.

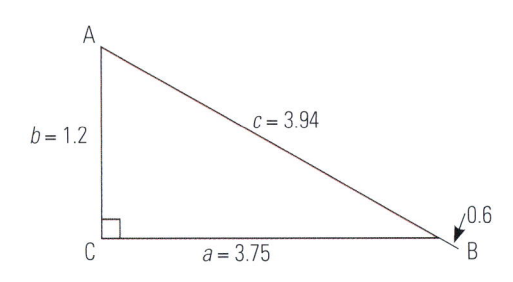

   b) The rafters will be 3.83 m and 5.26 m long.

   The shorter rafter is 3.83 m long (3.23 + 0.6).

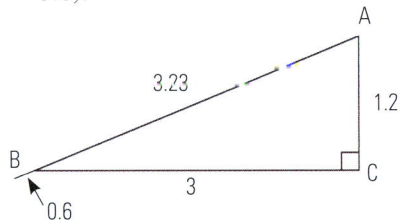

348   MathWorks 10

The longer rafter is 5.26 m long (4.66 + 0.6).

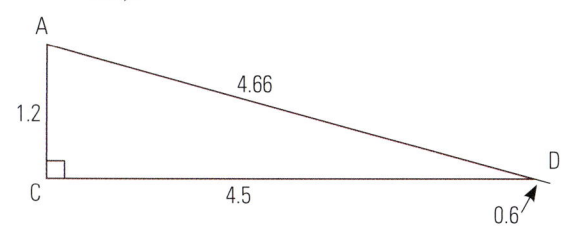

```
        A
       /|
      / | 1.2
 4.66/  |
    /   |_____D
   C      4.5         0.6↘
```

3. Suzanne will need 1028 cm or 10.28 m of wire. She should buy a little extra wire because some numbers in the calculation were rounded down.

4. a) They need 2485 cm or 24.85 m of wire.

   b) Guy wires increase a structure's stability.

5. a) The diameter must be 45 mm because the answer must be a multiple of five.

   b) The diameter must be 1.25″.

6. a) 57 m

   b) Air shafts are legislated so that fresh air comes into the mines for the safety of the workers.

7. a) Each sloping roof piece will be 1.13 m long.

   b) The height of the doghouse will be 0.8 m long.

   c) The doghouse will be 0.4 m high.

   d) No, this doghouse would not be suitable for a large dog because there would not be enough room for it to move around.

Extend your thinking

8 The new route is 0.76 miles shorter.

The new route is 2.24 miles and the old route is three miles because 3 minus 2.24 equals 0.76.

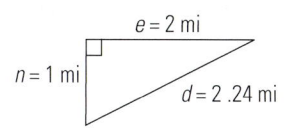

```
         e = 2 mi
    ┌──────────────
n = 1 mi\         │
         \   d = 2.24 mi
          \      │
```

9. a) Sara is wrong because she took the square root of each figure in the Pythagorean theorem. To calculate correctly, she must take the square root of each side.

   b) Sara should have bought 15 m of ribbon.

10. Yes, Jim could have built a box whose sides were not perpendicular to the base. If they angled outward, he would have to be sure that they had enough support and wouldn't fall outward. If they angled inward, he would have the same type of problem —they couldn't angle inward too much in case of falling inward. He would also have to ensure that the opening was big enough so that the toys would fit in.

11. Harpreet will need 47 paving blocks.

12. a) The hill is approximately 462 m high.

    b) John would not likely be able to measure the horizontal distance in one measurement so he would have to break the hill up into parts.

    Also, he would get a different result if he measured along the hill because the hill is steeper at different sections. However, if he were able to measure the straight distance (see diagram) from the bottom to the top, along with the horizontal distance, he would get the same result.

13. No. Fermat's Last Theorem states that there are no such numbers. He initially stated this in 1637, but it remained unproven, albeit there were many tries to do so, until 1995.

Answer Key   349

7.2 THE SINE RATIO

BUILD YOUR SKILLS, PAGE 289

1. $\sin 16° = 0.2756$

   $\sin 28° = 0.4695$

   $\sin 51° = 0.7771$

   $\sin 83° = 0.9925$

2. a) Diagram 1: $\sin X = 0.5$

   Diagram 2: $\sin X = 0.6$

   Diagram 3: $\sin X = 0.4$

   b) Diagram 1 slide is 5.2 m long.

   Diagram 2 slide is 4.3 m long.

   Diagram 3 slide is 6 m long.

3. a) Each tipi pole is approximately 16 ft long.

4. a) The ramp must be 18.2 m long.

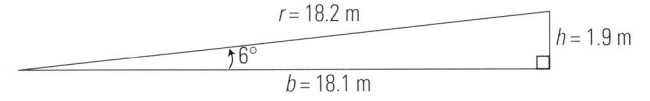

   $r = 18.2$ m, $6°$, $h = 1.9$ m, $b = 18.1$ m, H

   b) The ramp will start about 18.1 m from the base of the porch.

   c) If the ramp were too steep, the person in the wheelchair might not have control.

5. He will need about 95.9 m² of roofing.

6. a) The road rises about 39 m.

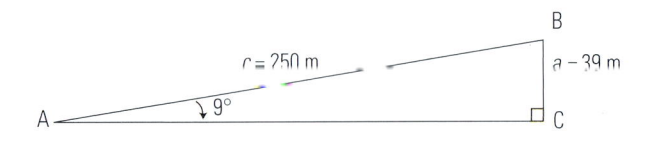

   $c = 250$ m, $9°$, $a = 39$ m, A, B, C

   b) In road construction, this is considered a steep road.

7. a) 161 m

   b) 190 m

8. a) length of low side = 56.1 m

   b) length of high side = 57 m

Extend your thinking

9. Both the length of the rafter and the vertical distance will increase. Suppose the angle is increased and the width stays the same, the height must be greater, and then the angular distance must also be increased.

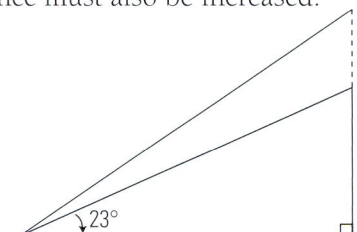

   $23°$

10. Zero is less than sin x which is less than 1. That is, since the sine is defined as the ratio of the side opposite an acute angle to the hypotenuse, if the angle is very small, the opposite side is very small, and the ratio is close to zero, but if the angle is close to 90°, the opposite side is close in length to the hypotenuse and the ratio would be close to 1.

7.3 THE COSINE RATIO

BUILD YOUR SKILLS, PAGE 297

1. a) $x = 2.6$ m

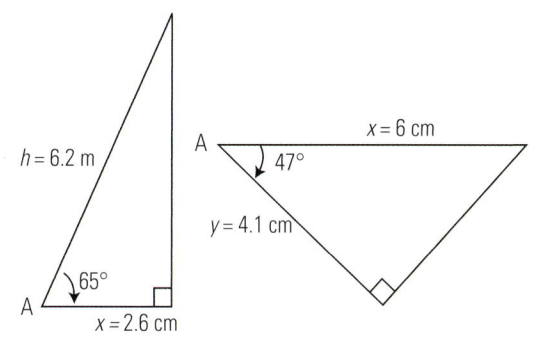

   b) $x = 6$ cm

2. The travel pipe must be 83.1 m long.

3. The wires are 38.1 m and 47.7 m long.

4. The surveyor is 217.3 m from the top of the second building.

5. The timber reaches 5.6 ft up the pole.

6. The length of the tapered section of the kayak is 2.8 ft.

Extend your thinking

7. If the opposite and the adjacent sides of a triangle are equal, the triangle must be isosceles and so the angles must be 45°. In this case, sin x equals cos x.

8. The mount is approximately 6.6 m from the post.

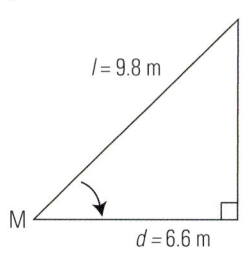

9. The radius measures 3.4 cm.

   The measure of x is 1.7 cm. Therefore, 1 chord equals 1.7 cm and the other equals 2.3 cm.

7.4 THE TANGENT RATIO

BUILD YOUR SKILLS, PAGE 305

1. The difference in elevation is 113.3 m.

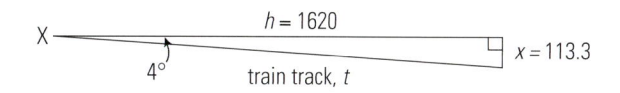

2. The helicopter was 466 m above ground.

3. a) The height of the cliff is 0.466 of the distance to the boat.

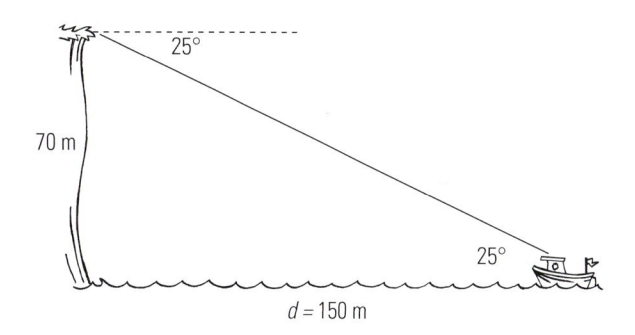

   b) The boat is 150 m from the cliff.

4. The maximum banner height is 45.4 m.

5. a) His house is farthest away.

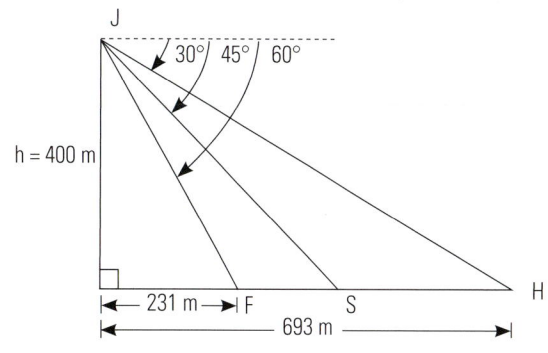

Answer Key   351

b) The farthest building is 693 m away.

c) The closest object is the field house, which is 231 m away.

6. a) The CSI needs to know at what height from the ground the bullet was shot.

   b) He was about 19.5 m from the wall.

   c) No.

7. The tree is about 7 m tall.

Extend your thinking

8. The centre is 243.6 ft tall.

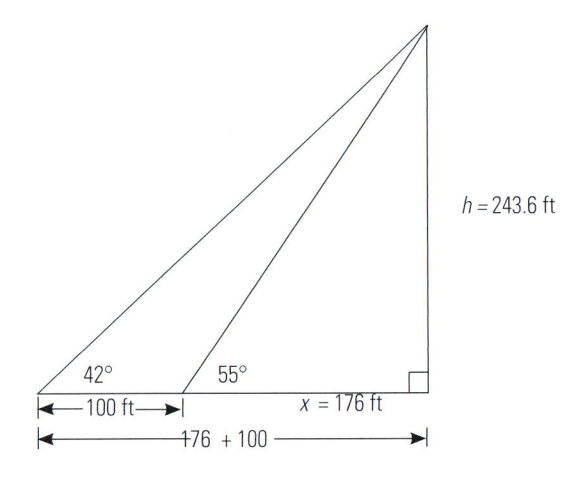

   (triangle diagram: 42°, 55°, 100 ft, x = 176 ft, 176 + 100, h = 243.6 ft)

7.5 FINDING ANGLES AND SOLVING RIGHT TRIANGLES

BUILD YOUR SKILLS, PAGE 311

1. a) $t = 7.43$ cm

   $\angle R = 20°$

   $\angle S = 70°$

   b) $\angle M = 32°$

   $l = 5.3$ in

   $m = 3.3$ in

2. a) You would gain 25.9 m.

   b) You would cover 96.6 m.

   c) The grade is 26.8%.

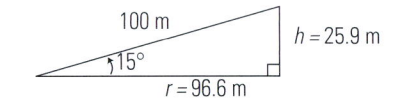

   (triangle diagram: 100 m, 15°, h = 25.9 m, r = 96.6 m)

3. a) The angle of elevation is 34°.

   b) The total shingled area is 864 ft².

4. a) The crane's arm must be 15.3 m long.

   b) The angle of elevation is 58°.

5. a) The angle of elevation is 53°.

   b) The ladder is 9 m from the base of the apartment.

6. a) The angle of depression is 19°.

7. a) The helicopter rose approximately 254.4 m in 3 minutes.

   b) The helicopter's speed was 84.8 m/min, or 1.4 m/sec.

8. The angle of elevation is 8°.

Extend your thinking

9. a) The total distance between the pipes is 5.4 m.

   b) The pipe fitter will need 7.2 m of pipe to get around the obstruction.

   c) The pipe fitter would have to be more accurate. He could round to the nearest centimetre.

PRACTISE YOUR NEW SKILLS, PAGE 316

1. a) No.
   b) No.
   c) Yes.
   d) Yes.
   e) No.

2. The pictographs are 8.7 m up the cliff.

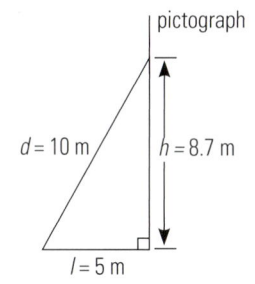

3. a) Sarbjit will save 65 m if he takes the shortcut.

   Add the length plus the width of the field to get 240 m.

   To calculate the amount of distance Sarbjit will save, subtract the shortcut distance from the figure above.

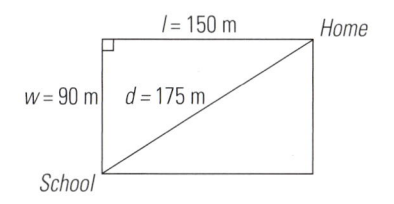

   240 − 175 = 65

   b) Answers will vary.

4. a) You gain approximately 174 m in altitude.

   b) The change in altitude would be less because the rise would have to decrease as the angle decreased for the same distance along the road.

5. To calculate the height of the second tree, add 4.8 m to Mary's height.

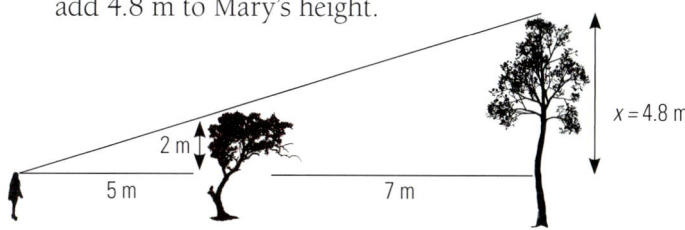

   The second tree is 6.3 m tall.

6. The lake is 260 m long.

7. a) The vertical height is 2.5 m.
   b) The support pieces are approximately 2.1 m long.
   c) The rafter is approximately 4.7 m long.

8. a) The pit is 215.8 m deep.
   b) The surveyor would need to know the shape of the pit, how long the pit was, or if it were circular or oval. Then he could find the volume of the pit to determine the amount of gravel removed.

9. The angle of depression is 67°.

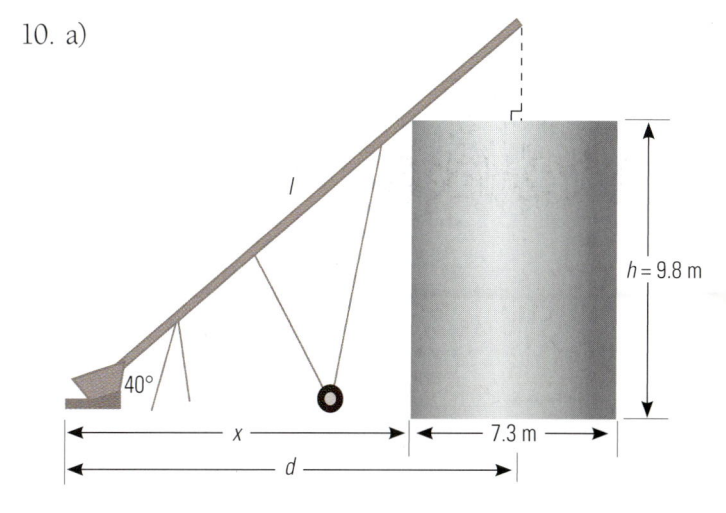

10. a)

Answer Key   353

b) The auger is 20.1 m long.

11. The grade would be zero.

12. The Burj Dubai is approximately 820 m tall.

13. These are "special triangles." If one angle of a right triangle is 60°, then the other is 30°. Using the Pythagorean theorem, Katarina could solve any right triangle with a 60° angle.

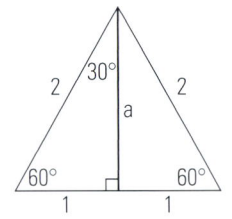

Similarly, for a right triangle with a 45° angle, she could use the following diagram.

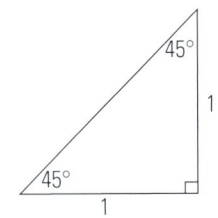

The two legs of the triangle will be equal and she can solve any right triangle with a 45° angle using the Pythagorean theorem.

Index

A

Activities
- 1.1 Visualize a proportion, 15–16
- 1.2 Fruit drink taste tester, 16–17
- 1.3 Which price is right?, 25–26
- 1.4 Taking advantage of sales promotions, 36–37
- 1.5 What's your ride? Survey, 42–43
- 1.6 Calculate foreign exchange, 46
- 2.1 Interpreting pay statements, 55
- 2.2 Mind mapping for trades, 60
- 2.3 Piecework versus hourly rates, 65
- 2.4 A babysitting service, 73
- 2.5 Pros and cons of deductions, 81
- 2.6 Comparing deductions, 84
- 3.1 Exploring imperial measurement, 96–97
- 3.2 Visualizing a measurement, 101
- 3.3 Designing a tin can layout, 101–102
- 3.4 Converting between SI and imperial units, 107
- 3.5 Designing a CFL field logo, 110
- 3.6 Designing a tool box, 116
- 3.7 Surface area formulas, 117
- 3.8 A redecorating project, 120
- 3.9 Converting a recipe, 126–127
- 3.10 Driveway construction, 130–131
- 4.1 Prepare a temperature graph, 139
- 4.2 Develop a conversion formula, 139–140
- 4.3 Cooking at higher altitudes, 143
- 4.4 Choosing imperial units, 149
- 4.5 Using SI prefixes, 154
- 4.6 Equivalent masses, 155
- 4.7 Protein vs fat content, 156–157
- 4.8 Estimating mass, 157
- 4.9 Using conversion factors, 163
- 4.10 How much can a forklift lift?, 165
- 5.1 Five angles, 179
- 5.2 Create a referents diagram, 181
- 5.3 Using angles in weather reporting, 182
- 5.4 Draw a kitchen countertop plan, 190–191
- 5.5 Cross-bracing and cross-stitching, 191
- 5.6 Mapping an airport runway, 201–202
- 5.7 Designing a French pattern tile floor, 212
- 6.1 Enlarging blueprints, 231
- 6.2 Scaling Métis sashes, 242
- 6.3 Applying ratios to distances, 242–243
- 6.4 Enlarging a trapezoid, 248
- 6.5 The ratio method, 250–251
- 6.6 The parallel method, 251–252
- 6.7 Proving similarity of triangles, 260
- 6.8 Reducing triangles, 261
- 7.1 Indirect measurement, 277
- 7.2 Generalizations of the Pythagorean theorem, 278
- 7.3 The sine of an angle, 285
- 7.4 Movement of a Ferris wheel, 296
- 7.5 Drawing a tangent graph, 302
- 7.6 Making and using a clinometer, 303–304
- 7.7 Rock band lighting, 311

alternate exterior angles, 199–200, 202, 204, 210
alternate interior angles, 199, 200–201, 202–204, 207, 210, 213
altitude, 111, 143, 312, 316
angle bisector, 187–195
angle measure, 175–185, 192
angle referent, 175, 178, 179–180, 181, 184, 185
angles, 172–223
  alternate exterior, 199–200, 202, 204, 210
  alternate interior, 199, 200–201, 202–204, 207, 210, 213
  bisection, 187–195
  complementary, 181, 184, 191, 194
  corresponding, 199, 200–201, 202–204, 206–207, 210, 213
  definition, 174

Index 355

of depression, 288, 302, 303–304, 305, 306, 308, 312–313, 317–318
drawing, 175–178, 189–190
of elevation, 289, 303–304, 305, 306, 309–310, 311, 312, 313, 316–318
estimation, 175, 178, 179–180, 181, 184, 185
exterior (on same side), 202, 203–204, 210
of incidence, 194, 195
interior (on same side), 199–200, 202–203, 204, 205, 206–207, 210, 213
kinds, 179
measurement, 174–175, 178, 179, 183, 184, 192
of reflection, 194, 195
replicating, 177–178
right, 175–176, 187–188
supplementary, 181, 191, 201, 202, 204, 206–207, 213
true bearing, 174, 182–183, 185, 220
vertically opposite, 198, 202, 204
area
of a circle, 101–102, 109, 110
of a rectangle, 101–102, 108, 110, 130–131, 245
of an irregular shape, 111, 113
surface area (of three-dimensional objects), 115–122, 134

B

base salary, 67–68
base unit, 94
benefits, 78, 80, 88
biweekly pay period, 56, 57, 60
bonus, 72, 74–75, 77
Build Your Skills
  1.2 Unit Price, 26–27
  1.3 Setting a Price, 32–33, 37–38
  1.4 On Sale!, 37–38
  1.5 Currency Exchange Rates, 47–48
  2.1 Wages and Salaries, 60–62
  2.2 Alternative Ways to Earn Money, 69–70
  2.3 Additional Earnings, 76–77
  2.4 Deductions and Net Pay, 87–88
  3.1 Systems of Measurement, 102–103
  3.2 Converting Measurements, 111–113
  3.3 Surface Area, 121–122

  3.4 Volume, 132
  4.1 Temperature Conversions, 143–144
  4.2 Mass in the Imperial System, 151–153
  4.3 Mass in the Système International, 158–160
  4.4 Making Conversions, 165–167
  5.1 Measuring and Estimating Angles, 184–185
  5.2 Angle Bisectors and Perpendicular Lines, 192–195
  5.3 Non-Parallel Lines and Transversals, 204–207
  5.4 Parallel Lines and Transversals, 214–217
  6.1 Similar Polygons, 232–235
  6.2 Determining if Two Polygons Are Similar, 243–245
  6.3 Drawing Similar Polygons, 252–254
  6.4 Similar Triangles, 261–263
  7.1 The Pythagorean Theorem, 278–282
  7.2 The Sine Ratio, 289–291
  7.3 The Cosine Ratio, 297–299
  7.4 The Tangent Ratio, 305–306
  7.5 Finding Angles and Solving Right Triangles, 311–313
bushel, 162
buying rate, 41

C

Canada Pension Plan, 81–82
capacity, 124
cardinal directions, 182
Celsius scale, 138
  conversions, 139–140, 141–142, 164, 169
  history of, 145
circle
  area, 101–102, 109, 110
  circumference, 100–101, 102, 118
  trigonometric ratios and, 292, 299, 302
circumference, 100–101, 102, 118
commission, 64, 67–68, 70, 90, 91
common denominator, 15, 19, 20
compass rose, 182, 185
complementary angles, 181, 184, 191, 194
cone, 117, 119, 121, 134
congruent angles, 227
contract, 64–65, 68–70, 90
conversion factor, 95, 96–97

use of, 127, 162–163, 169
conversions
   of foreign prices, 42–43, 46, 47–48, 51
   between imperial and SI units, 106–113, 125–130, 132, 157–159, 163–164, 169
   temperature, 139–142, 144, 169
   from volume to weight, 148, 149–153, 159, 161–163, 169
   from weight to volume, 170
   within imperial system, 97–103, 132, 169
corresponding angles, 199, 200–201, 202–204, 206–207, 210, 213
   similar figures and, 227, 228–229
corresponding sides, 227, 228–229, 230–231, 240–242
cosine, 293–299
cost of materials and labour, 28, 38, 68–69, 70, 90, 97–98, 103, 111, 112, 114, 131, 134, 135
cube, 120
cubic centimetre, 159
cubic yard, 124, 148
currency
   definition, 41
   exchange rates, 41–48, 50, 51
   history of, 40
custom work, 66
cylinder, 101–102, 117, 118, 121, 122, 134

D

danger pay, 72, 76
decimal places, rounding to, 19, 20
decimals, changing fractions or percents to, 30
deductions, 79–91
degrees (angle), 174
degrees (temperature), 138–145, 164, 169
denominator
   common, 15, 19, 20
   of conversion factor, 97
directions (compass), 182, 185, 221
discounts, 33, 34–38
   on contract, 65
   on custom work, 66
   on large purchases, 66–67
Discuss the Ideas

Adapting a recipe, 13
Agricultural conversion factors, 163
Alternative approaches (to determining cosine), 309
Cindy Klassen, speed skater, 18
Comparing triangles, 258
Concert promoter, 29
Custom work, 66
DART (Disaster Assistance Response Team), 95–96
Drawing parallel line segments, 211
Earning tips, 74
Estimation or measurement?, 178
Gross Vehicle Weight Rating (GVWR), 156
Home renovation contracts, 65
Installing a chandelier, 107
Lake Winnipeg, 111
Lifestyle benefits, 80
Lines and transversals, 200–201
Mass/weight conversions between imperial and SI, 157–158
Packaging (soft drinks), 125–126
Pythagorean triples, 275
Repairing a truss bridge, 287
Scale factor (cardboard boxes), 116
Scale factors and maps, 237
Scale factors and posters, 238
Scale factors in similar figures, 240
Seasons and holidays, 31
Separation of crude oil, 140
Similar figures, 227
The sine ratio, 284
The weight of waste, 148
Types of earnings, 55
Ways to bisect angles, 188
distance, 95–97, 102, 107, 111, 242–243
double time, 58

E

earnings *see* income
EI (Employment Insurance), 82, 83, 87
equations with fractions, 14, 15, 18–20
Euclid, 246, 278
exchange rate, 41–48, 50, 51

Index **357**

expenses, reimbursement of, 73, 77
exterior angles
   alternate, 199–200, 202, 204, 210
   on same side, 202, 203–204, 210

F

Fahrenheit scale, 138
   conversions, 139–140, 141–142, 164, 169
   history of, 145
federal income tax, 80, 82–83, 84–85, 90–91
fluid ounce, 124
   conversions, 125–126, 132
foot, 95–96, 104
   linear foot, 97–98, 134
foreign exchange, 41–48, 50, 51
foreign prices, 42–43, 46, 47–48, 51
fractions
   changing to decimals, 30
   conversion factors as, 95, 97
   equations with, 14, 15, 18–20
framing squares, 187–188

G

gallon, 124
   conversions, 106, 127, 128, 169
geometric net, 115, 123
goods and services tax (GST), 29, 30–31, 32, 37, 38, 39
gram, 158–159
gross pay, 54, 60, 87
GST (goods and services tax), 29, 30–31, 32, 37, 38, 39

H

holiday earnings, 57–58, 89
horizon lines, 197
hourly rate of pay, 38, 57–58, 61, 63, 65, 69–70, 77, 78, 89
hours *see* time (worked)
hypotenuse, 273

I

imperial system
   conversion between SI and, 106–113, 125–130, 132, 157–159, 163–164, 169
   conversions within, 97–103, 132, 169
   length, 94–95, 96–103
   mass or weight, 146–153, 165–167
   volume, 124–125, 134–135
inch, 94–95, 104
   conversions, 98–100
income, 52–85
   additional earnings, 72–78
   alternative ways to earn money, 60, 64–70
   deductions, 79–91
   gross, 54, 60, 87
   taxable, 84–85, 87
   wages and salaries, 54–63
income tax, 80, 82–83, 84–85, 90–91
intercardinal directions, 182
interior angles
   alternate, 199, 200–201, 202–204, 207, 210, 213
   on same side, 199–200, 202–203, 204, 205, 206–207, 210, 213
irregular shapes, area of, 111, 113
isolation allowance, 77

K

kilogram, 154, 158–159
   conversions, 147, 163, 164

L

leg (of right triangle), 273
length, 94–101, 102, 104
   conversion between imperial and SI, 107–108
   in imperial system, 94–95, 96–103
linear foot, 97–98, 134
lines
   horizon, 197
   non-parallel, 201, 204–207, 212–213
   parallel, 197, 198, 206–207, 209–218, 223
   perpendicular, 187–188, 190–191, 223
litre, 94, 124
   conversions, 106, 124, 127, 159, 169
lowest common denominator, 19

M

markup, 28–33
   and discounts, 66–67, 90
mass

in imperial system, 146–153, 165–167
  relation to weight, 146–147, 154, 160
  in Système international, 154–159, 165–167
materials and labour, cost of, 28, 38, 68–69, 70, 90, 97–98, 103, 111, 112, 114, 131, 134, 135
measurement, 94–132, 138–165
  angles, 174–175, 178, 179, 183, 184, 192
  of area, 101–102, 108–110, 130–131
  history of, 104, 145
  indirect, 277
  of length, 94–101, 102, 104
  of mass, 146–159, 165–167
  of surface area, 115–122, 134
  systems of, 94–97
  of temperature, 138–145, 169
  of volume, 94, 124–132, 134–135
  see also conversions
Mental Math and Estimation
  angle of depression, 305
  angles, 179
  cost of hotel in Paris, 42
  cost of pipe straps, 21
  discounted bike helmets, 31
  distance from building, 273
  distance in miles, 111
  earnings for 10 hours, 60
  earnings for 35-hour week, 69
  enlarging a poster, 229
  face and side of a cube, 120
  hours in a work week, 56
  leg of a right triangle, 275
  length of field goal, 102
  net pay, 84
  proportions, 240
  sale price of barbecue, 36
  scale model, 247
  similarity of triangular sails, 258
  tangent, 311
  temperature in degrees Celsius, 140
  weight conversions, 158
  weight of salmon in pounds, 151
mile, 95
  conversions, 97, 102, 111

millilitre, 125–127, 132
minimum wage, 54, 63, 78

N

net pay, 79–80, 82–83, 84, 86, 87, 89
non-parallel lines, 201, 204–207, 212–213
numerator of conversion factor, 97

O

ounce, fluid, 124, 125–126, 132
ounce (weight), 147, 151–152
overtime, 54, 57–59, 61, 62, 75–76, 78, 89

P

parallel lines, 197, 198, 206–207, 209–218, 223
parallel method, 251–252
pay
  alternative ways to set amount of, 60, 64–70
  gross, 54, 60, 87
  holiday earnings, 57–58, 89
  hourly rate of, 38, 57–58, 61, 63, 65, 69–70, 77, 78, 89
  net, 79–80, 82–83, 84, 86, 87, 89
  overtime, 54, 57–59, 61, 62, 75–76, 78, 89
  see also income
pay period, 55, 56, 57, 60
pay statement, 55–56, 61–62
  with deductions, 79–91
payment schedules, 65, 66
pension contributions, 80
percent, 28, 30
perimeter, 97, 102, 103, 113
perpendicular lines, 187–188, 190–191, 223
perspective, 173, 186, 196, 218, 219
  history of, 197
perspective diagram, 186, 196
piecework, 64, 65, 69
pint, 124
polygons *see* similarity of figures
pound, 151–152
  conversions, 147, 163, 164
Practise Your New Skills
  Angles and Parallel Lines, 220–223
  Earning an Income, 89–91

Index **359**

Length, Area, and Volume, 134–135
  Mass, Temperature, and Volume, 169–171
  Proportional Reasoning, 21–22
  Similarity of Figures, 265–269
  Trigonometry of Right Triangles, 316–318
  Unit Pricing and Currency Exchange, 50–51
price
  foreign, 42–43, 46, 47–48, 51
  sale, 34–38
  setting of, 28–33
  unit, 23–27, 32–33, 39, 50
prism
  geometric net, 123
  surface area, 116–117, 122
  volume, 128–130, 134–135, 150
Projects
  1. The party planner, 11, 39, 49
  2. A payroll plan for a summer business, 53, 78, 86, 88
  3. Design an ice-fishing shelter, 93, 105, 114, 123, 133
  4. Culinary competition, 137, 161, 168
  5. Create a perspective drawing, 173, 186, 196, 219
  6. Design a community games room, 225, 256, 264
  7. Design a staircase for a home, 271, 300, 315
promotion, 34–38
proportion, 12–17, 21–22, 50, 170–171
  exchange rates and, 44
  rates and, 18
  similarity of figures and, 226–228, 231–232
protractors, 174, 182–183, 188–189
provincial income tax, 80, 82–83, 84–85, 90–91
provincial sales tax (PST), 29, 30–31, 32, 38, 39
Puzzle It Out
  The counterfeit coin, 160
  The decanting puzzle, 131
  The impossible staircase, 218
  Magic proportions, 22
  Rationing chocolate bars, 255
  16 Squares, 314
  A weird will, 71
Pythagorean theorem, 272–282, 309, 316
Pythagorean triple, 275

Q
quart, 128

R
rate, 17–22
  exchange rates, 41–48, 50, 51
  hourly, 38, 57–58, 61, 63, 65, 69–70, 77, 78, 89
  unit, 23
ratio, 12–18, 21, 50
  applied to distance, 242–243
  similarity of figures and, 226–228
  see also trigonometry
ratio method, 250–251
rectangles
  area, 101–102, 108, 110, 130–131, 245
  similarity of, 245
rectangular prism
  geometric net, 123
  surface area, 116–117, 122
  volume, 128–130, 134–135, 150
referents, 96–97, 155, 157
  angle, 175, 181
referents diagram, 181
right angle, 187–188
  drawing, 175–176
right triangle, 15–16
  definition, 272
  see also trigonometry
The Roots of Math
  Canadian currency, 40
  Euclidean geometry, 246
  Geometric perspective in art, 197
  Measuring temperature, 145
  The minimum wage in Canada, 63
  Origins of standard measurement, 104
  Trigonometry in history, 292
rounding
  amounts of money, 19, 20
  amounts of time, 61
ruler and compass, to draw angles, 175–178, 189–190

360 MathWorks 10

S

salary, 54, 55, 56–57, 61
  with bonus, 72, 77
  with commission, 67–68, 70, 91
  with danger pay, 76
  with isolation allowance, 77
sale prices, 34–38
sales tax, 29, 30–31, 32, 38, 39
scale diagram, 101, 110, 122, 185, 190–191, 220, 221, 256, 300
scale factor, 116, 123, 229, 236–245, 247–254, 256, 265–268
scale model, 123, 133, 300
seasonal prices, 31, 33
self-employment, 64, 65, 66–67, 69
selling rate, 41
semi-monthly pay period, 56, 57, 60
shift premium, 72–73, 75–76, 77
SI *see* Système internationale d'unités (SI)
similarity of figures, 224–269
  definition, 227
  determining if two polygons are similar, 236–246, 268
  drawing similar polygons, 247–254, 265–267
  history of, 246
  similar polygons, 224–269
  triangles, 246, 257–263, 268–269
sine, 283–292
slug, 147
speed, 18, 22, 50
straight angle, 187
supplementary angles, 181, 191, 201, 202, 204, 206–207, 213
surface area (of three-dimensional objects), 115–122, 134
Système internationale d'unités (SI), 94–97, 154
  conversion between imperial system and, 106–111, 125–130, 132, 157–159, 163–164, 169
  length, 94, 107–108
  mass, 154–159, 165–167
  volume, 124–127

T

take-home pay, 79, 88
tangent, 301–306, 311
taxable income, 84–85, 87
taxes
  goods and services tax (GST), 29, 30–31, 32, 37, 38, 39
  income, 80, 82–83, 84–85, 90–91
  sales, 29, 30–31, 32, 38, 39
temperature, 138–145
  altitude and boiling point of water, 143
  conversions, 139–142, 144, 169
  history of measurement, 145
tetrahedron, 117
thermometers, 145
three-dimensional objects, measurement of, 115–120
time and a half, 57, 89
time (worked)
  overtime, 54, 57–59, 61, 62, 75–76, 78, 89
  rounding, 61
tips, 72, 74, 76–77, 89
ton
  metric, 155
  short, 147, 151–152
tonne, 155, 158–159, 162
transversals, 199–207, 209–217
triangles
  right, 15–16
  similar, 246, 257–263, 268–269
  see also trigonometry
triangular prisms, 116–117
triangular pyramids, 117
trigonometry, 270–318
  cosine ratio, 293–299
  finding angles and solving right triangles, 307–314, 317–318
  history of, 292
  inverse functions, 307–308
  Pythagorean theorem, 272–282, 309, 316
  sine ratio, 283–292
  tangent ratio, 301–306, 311
true bearing, 174, 182–183, 185, 220

U

union dues, 80
unit price, 23–27, 32–33, 39, 50
unit rate, 23

V

vanishing points, 173, 186, 196, 197
vertex, 174, 198
vertically opposite angles, 198, 202, 204
volume, 94, 124–132
   conversion from weight, 170
   conversion to weight, 148, 149–153, 159, 161–163, 169
   in imperial system, 124–125, 134–135

W

wages, 54, 60–62, 69
   with benefits, 78, 80
   with bonus, 72, 74–75
   with holiday pay, 57–58, 89
   minimum wage, 54, 63, 78
   with overtime, 57–59, 61, 62, 75–76, 78, 89
   and pay statements, 55–56, 61–62, 79–91
   with shift premium, 72–73, 75–76, 77
weight, 146
   choice of units, 149
   conversion from volume, 148, 149–153, 159, 161–163, 169
   conversion to volume, 170
   conversions between imperial and SI, 157–159, 163–164
   in imperial system, 146–153
   relation to mass, 146–147, 154, 160

Y

yard, 95, 104
   conversions, 97, 98–100, 102, 107, 128–129

Credits

Images in the text for which no page numbers are listed are copyright Pacific Educational Press.

Cover
Colin Pickell

Contents page
Colin Pickell

Chapter 1
p. v Colin Pickell; p.vi United States Navy, ID 081202-N-6764G-093, Wikimedia Commons; p.vii PEP; p.10 PEP; p.11 Sharlene Eugenio; p.12 Sandra Tuccaro; p.14 David Bourne; p.17 Courtesy Government of Alberta; p.18 Wikimedia Commons; p.21 MacKinnon Media; p.22 Adam Page/scx.hu; p.23 Linda Fogarty; p.24 Shawna Larence; p.26 Barbara Kuhne; p.28 Sharlene Eugenio; p.29 Joe Perez/www.xone5photo.com; p.31 Sharlene Eugenio; p.32 Pierre Geumez; p.33 Courtesy Vancouver Community College, photo Laughlin McKenzie; p.34 PEP; p.35 Frank Dawson; p.36 MacKinnon Media; p.37 Courtesy Vancouver Community College, photo Laughlin McKenzie; p.38 Stockxpert; p.39 J.R. Goleno/sxc.hu; p.40 UBC/MOA, photo B. McLennan; p.41 Courtesy Potato Growers of Alberta, photo Jeff Bronsch; p.42 Courtesy CarAdvice.com.au; p.45 Euros courtesy Steve Woods; Australian dollars courtesy Adrian van Leen; Yen and US dollars courtesy PEP; p.46 Gary Cowles/sxc.hu; p.47 Barbara Kuhne; p.49 Melodi T/sxc.hu.; p.50 Courtesy Le Marché St. Norbert Farmers' Market, photo Tommy Allen; p.51 Troy Hunter.

Chapter 2
p.52 Deb Hutton; p.53 candicelo/sxc.hu; p.54 Catherine Edwards; p.57 Nick Saltmarsh; p. 59 Stockxpert; p.60 Stefanie Leuker/sxc.hu; p.63 Wikimedia Commons, National Archives of Canada/PA-163001; p.64 Catherine Edwards; p.65 Courtesy Government of Alberta; p.66 Courtesy Métis Nation of Ontario; p.69 Walter Siegmund, Wikimedia Commons; p.70 PEP; p.71 Sangman Grant; p.72 Catherine Edwards; p.74 Courtesy Government of Alberta; p.75 Jelmer Rozendal/stock.xchng; p.77 Courtesy Government of Alberta; p.78 hardhat courtesy Davide Guglielmo; tools courtesy Cris DeRaud; p.79 Holzi Holzer; p.80 Catherine Edwards; p.84 Natalie Kwee; p.87 Herry Lawford; p.88 Stockxpert; p.90 Reproduced with permission of the Canada Revenue Agency and the Minister of Public Works and Government Services Canada, 2009; p.91 Reproduced with permission of the Canada Revenue Agency and the Minister of Public Works and Government Services Canada, 2009.

Chapter 3
p.92 PEP; p.93 scol22/sxc.hu; p.94 Stéphanie Klassen; p.100 David Lat; p.104 Ricardo Liberato;

p.105 James Wheare; p.106 Manuel Marques; p.108 Daniel Hendricks; p. 109 Brandon Blinkenberg; p.110 John Griffiths; p.111 Courtesy Manitoba Conservation, Product Distribution, Canadamapsales.com; p.114 James Wheare; p.115 David Kattegatsiak; p.119 PEP; p.112 Tom Arthur; p.123 James Wheare; p.124 Marcin Wichary; p.127 Stephen Mitchell; p.128 J. Godsey; p.129 Marc Smith; p.132 Josh Calder; p.133 Stockxpert; p.134 Anthony B./sxc.hu; p.135 audreyjm529/www.flickr.com.

Chapter 4

p.136 Wikimedia Commons; p.137 Miguel de Unamunoc; p.138 Katharine Borgen; p.141 PEP; p.143 Laszlo S. Ilyes; p.144 Glenn Pebley/sxc.hu; p.145 Galileo thermometer courtesy Peter Gervai, Wikimedia Commons; Fahrenheit's burial marker courtesy Donar Reiskoffer, Wikimedia Commons; p.146 Laraine Coates; p.147 Steve Woods/sxc.hu; p.148 T.A. Peck; p.149 Jessica Zuidema/sxc.hu; p.150 Brad Pende; p.151 Stockxpert; p.152 Tracey Johnson/sxc.hu; p.153 Courtesy CuppaJoe Coffee; p.154 Katharine Borgen; p.155 Barbara Kuhne; p.158 bull courtesy Brian Forbes, Kinross; chair, tack, iPod courtesy Deb Hutton; p.160 astronaut courtesy NASA Kennedy Space Centre(NASA-KSC); balance courtesy Stockxpert; p.161 Deb Hutton; p.162 Louise Niwa; p.163 Dan McKay; p.164 Robert Owen-Wahl; p.165 Courtesy Government of Alberta; p.167 Joanna Poe; p.168 Alpha Lau; p.170 Courtesy Saskatchewan Ministry of Agriculture; p.171 George Showman.

Chapter 5

p.172 PEP; p.173 Warren Clark; p.174 Werner Aschbacher; © Google. Map data © 2009 Tele Atlas, Google; p.175 © Google. Map data © 2009 Tele Atlas, Google; Daren Lewis; p.176 PEP; p.178 Wonderlane; p.180 Leah Giesbrecht; p.185 Ahmed Al-Shukaili/sxc.hu; p.187 pizza courtesy Randy Robertson; p.188 mitre saw courtesy Ewen Roberts; mitre joint and protractor courtesy PEP; framing square courtesy Ruslan Moldashev/sxc.hu; p.190 PEP; p.191 Craig Yuill; p.197 The School of Athens, public domain; p.198 Michelle Diaz; p.201 Google Maps©Google Imagery © 2009 DigitalGlobe, GeoEye Google Maps; p.203 Gavin Schaefer; p.206 Leah Giesbrecht; p.207 Michael Scheltgen; p.209 Stockxpert; p.210 Joshin Yamada; p.211 Chris Lott www.flickr.com/photos/fncll/; p. 212 tile courtesy Chrstphre Campbell; Esplanade Riel courtesy Jason Smith; p.219 Warren Clark; p.221 Della McCreary; p.222 cliff1066™/www.flickr.com.

Chapter 6

p.224 Stockxpert; p.225 Stockxpert; p.226 Paul Messier courtesy Christa Bedwin; toolboxes courtesy Leah Giesbrecht; p.227 Jean-Pierre Lavoie; p.229 Casper Moller; p.232 Wikimedia Commons; p.233 Courtesy Sown Together, photo Gabriel Kamener; p.234 Children Playing, Mary Cassatt, Wikimedia Commons; Kilauea Caldera, Ernst William Christmas, Wikimedia Commons; swimming pool courtesy Scott Snyde/stock.xchng; p.236 Quinn Keast-Wiatrowski; p.238 Monique Raymond; p.239 Jason Hall; p.241 Donna Rutherford; p.242 Sharlene Eugenio; p.244 doghouse courtesy Stockxpert; moccasins courtesy Leah Giesbrecht; p.245 United States Navy, ID 070406-N-3659B-086, Wikimedia Commons; p.247 Ryan Kraemer; p.256 Stockxpert; p.257 Christa Bedwin; p.261 Simon Cohen; p.263 Robert

Alberola; p.264 Sharlene Eugenio; p.265 Frank Hebbert; p.268 PEP.

Chapter 7

p.270 PEP; p.271 Cody Peterson; p.272 Donna Jenner; p.281 Michael Darch at Island Cutter Inc.; p.283 Les Chatfield; p.287 Vera Bernard; p.290 Wikimedia Commons; p.291 Leaning Tower of Pisa courtesy Andy Hay; garage courtesy Jessica Short; p.292 Wikimedia Commons; p.293 Richard McCaffrey; p.296 Basheer Tome; p.297 PEP; p.298 public domain; p.299 Michael L. Baird flickr.bairdphotos.com; p.300 Scott Suess; p.301 Chris Haika; p.302 Ted Sali; p.303 PEP; p.305 Dave Reichart; p.306 Anne Reid; p.307 Bruno Marie; p.309 Leah Giesbrecht; p.311 Derek McClintock; p.312 hiking trail courtesy Leah Giesbrecht; downtown Winnipeg courtesy Michael Lamirande; p.313 Miguel Saavedra; p.315 Leah Giesbrecht; p. 316 Jeremy Price; p.317 Bennett Lake courtesy Richard Martin; gravel pit courtesy Josh Wallaert; p.318 Wikimedia Commons; p.319 Burj Dubai courtesy Joi Ito.